296
D263y

cop.2

Davis.

The Yom Kippur war.

THE YOM KIPPUR WAR

Israel and the Jewish People

THE YOM KIPPUR WAR

Israel and the Jewish People

Edited by
MOSHE DAVIS

ARNO PRESS
A New York Times Company

Arno Press
A New York Times Company

Manufactured in the United States of America

Library of Congress Catalogue Card Number: 74–10466
ISBN: 0–405–06192–7

מַהֵר וְהָבֵא עָלֵינוּ בְּרָכָה וְשָׁלוֹם
מְהֵרָה מֵאַרְבַּע כַּנְפוֹת כָּל הָאָרֶץ

*Hasten, bring swiftly upon us blessing and peace
from the four corners of the earth*

from the Daily Prayers

*Dedicated
to those who fought,
the fallen and the living*

Foreword

Professor Ephraim Katzir

In convoking the Seminar on World Jewry and the Yom Kippur War which was held in Jerusalem at the end of 1973 and serves as the basis for this volume, I felt that the surging reaction among Jews throughout the world demanded concentrated attention and analysis. For myself, after many years in the seclusion of laboratories, the meetings I had with visiting Jewish groups after the war taught me how closely linked millions of Jews throughout the world are to Israel and with what trepidation they view possible defeat for the State as not only unthinkable in itself but as mortally endangering the survival of the Jewish people. Thus the Yom Kippur War is their war, as Israel's peace is their peace.

The Seminar discussions taught us many things and all of us felt that we had learnt much from each other. Perhaps I might summarize our experience by pointing out how helpful it was to raise the most important questions affecting Israel and the Jewish world, although we certainly did not find conclusive answers for each and every one of them. I am reminded of a charming and, I think, very meaningful story once told me by I.I. Rabi, the famous physicist. I asked him if his development as a scientist had been influenced by his mother, and he replied that this had clearly been the case: "As a small child studying Hebrew in the *heder*, I used to be greeted by my mother when I came home; invariably she asked me not what I had learnt from the Rebbe that day but whether I had asked the Rebbe any good questions!"

The volume, I think, will testify that we really asked good questions, and that the mixture of scholars and men of action in the group proved most helpful. The circumstances in which we met were far from normal: in the very midst of the Israeli Government's discussions of the political stand to be taken at Geneva, and with the resumption of hostilities never out of the question. Yet precisely under such circumstances it was no less than vital to explore basic issues which may well determine the future of Israel and of Jews throughout the world.

Asking questions, voicing uncertainty, groping for answers—all these do not indicate weakness. They are rather clear proof of new vitality in Jewish and Zionist thinking. For years I have been disturbed by a certain dogmatism in the younger generation and have found myself remembering and admiring the spiritual struggles which enriched and fortified the lives of Israel's founding fathers. Ideas both conventional and unconventional were expressed at the Seminar, but throughout all that we heard from our lecturers, as well as in our discussions, one central theme was ever present: the common destiny of Jews everywhere.

At the same time, as we live in the war's aftermath, a fundamental change seems to be coming about in the thinking of Israelis, soldiers and civilians alike. They now have a far more serious regard for Diaspora Jewry, and like its thoughtful youth, are concerned with the basic questions of Jewish existence: the centrality of Israel, the mutual relations between it and the Diaspora, Israel's future adjustment to its neighbors, the retention and activation of the ethical and intellectual values of the Jewish tradition.

It is precisely those ethical and intellectual values, deeply rooted in Jewish history, which we must see as the sources of all our life and activity. Indeed as one long involved in the problems of Israel's security and particularly its scientific aspects, I have no hesitation in saying that without the sustaining strength of our moral and cultural legacy our physical power would be very limited.

I sometimes think that for a small and weak people like the Jews great ideals served as the source of strength. Jewish revival in our time is inconceivable in any other framework, and here Israel has a central role to play—in spiritual and social terms alike. If the State meets the test of realizing our ideals, it will become not only the center but the magnet for Jews everywhere and provide the humane answer of a small, free state to some of the overwhelming and frightening problems of our time.

The joint thinking of those participating in seminar and book leads, it seems clear, to emphasis on a new, worldwide effort in Jewish education and culture, whereby Israel and Jews abroad would achieve a far greater measure of true partnership than before. Perhaps the Yom Kippur War and what we will have learned to see as its effects may bring us to a new plateau of Jewish cooperation—culturally, economically, scientifically—to new and stronger links and to new opportunities for the State of Israel to develop the spiritual strength and fulfill the central role in our vision of the Jewish future.

Introduction

The project which President Katzir describes in the Foreword was originally planned within the framework of the President's Study Circle on World Jewry. During the grim days following the hostilities, delegations from the countries of the free Diaspora presented themselves at the President's Residence to express solidarity with the *Yishuv* and to reinforce a mutual faith in the future of Israel. Responding to their mood and with the aim of gaining deeper insight into world Jewish interaction beyond the crisis, the President enlarged the Seminar's scope to include scholars and representative personalities from abroad. The cooperation of all departments of the World Zionist Organization was enlisted with the wholehearted support of Acting Chairman Arye Dulzin.

To collect and analyze pertinent materials, a special documentation unit was created at the Shazar Library of the Institute of Contemporary Jewry. Two research teams were assembled. One, under the direction of Paul Glikson, gathered reports from the general and the Jewish press, communications from organizations, placards, posters, photographs, and films. A second team, working within the Institute's Oral History Division directed by Geoffrey Wigoder, recorded interviews with key figures in Israel and abroad as well as with immigrants and volunteers who came to Israel during and following the cease-fire. This body of data was organized according to major geographical areas of Jewish settlement and to such themes as political implications, economic response, impact on local communities, Jewish-Christian relations, and so forth. The Shazar Documentation Unit, in itself a remarkable example of the spontaneity and simultaneity of Jewish reaction, now serves the scholarly community as a research and pedagogic resource.

The Seminar dealt with three major aspects: a global survey of Jewish community response, reactions in Jewish and

XI

non-Jewish intellectual circles, and evaluations of and reorientation to the world Jewish condition. In this volume, the thematic preoccupations and substantive reports of the participants are intertwined. As observers and analysts, the contributors reveal a variety of sensitive interpretations in terms of personal philosophies and particular ideological orientations. There are also practical suggestions: for example, applying the "Winnipeg experience" as a model for community relations programs; creating the concept of total community action in the European setting; building an *aliyah* movement by means of a "Judaized Diaspora"; and establishing university research institutes on contemporary Israel in different countries.

The four panels of the Seminar which followed the survey and evaluation sessions were conducted with a view toward eliciting specific recommendations to relate the current condition to future considerations and developments in Israel and the Diaspora. Because of the obvious need for continuing discussion beyond the Seminar, the record of the panels' deliberations is not included in the present volume. The themes, however, reflect the long-range concerns of an interdependent Diaspora and Israel in a world Jewish community:

Changing Jewish identity and its significance for Jewish policy (Simon Herman, chairman);

One People: implications for Israel education (Seymour Fox, chairman);

Israel and the Diaspora: ideology and relationships (Yehuda Bauer and Israel Kolatt, co-chairmen);

The sense of peoplehood through literature and communications (Shulamit Nardi, chairman).

Another dimension of the volume is the section on personal experiences selected from the Institute's oral history program. These selections attempt to capture feelings and recollections as to "how it was," and to provide insights into the highly charged and varied emotions of the period. Interviews record statements of Israeli and Zionist leaders who were sent out on special missions during the first crucial weeks of the war, voices and opinions of Jews in the Diaspora, and reactions of volunteers and new immigrants.

XII

Editing a volume of this kind is akin to orchestrating a composition of many voices that must be heard as one. My task was considerably eased by the ready consent of authors to permit deletion of duplications. Not all repetitions were removed, however, since the same events are mirrored differently in the many countries in which Jews live; these need to be recorded. One fundamental principle was scrupulously guarded. Although the official auspices and sponsorship of the Seminar are clearly identified, this volume is in no way an authorized version; it is an author's version.

The entire project has been a labor of dedication for many. What was involved was the literal bringing together in thought and program the working minds of people from several continents, whose common task only began at their first meeting.

Foremost of those who made this work possible is Assistant to the President Shulamit Nardi, an inspiring colleague, whose insight and wisdom are a blessing.

Members of the Seminar Planning Committee in Israel included Yehuda Bauer, Zvi Gastwirt, Simon Herman, Menahem Kaufman, Moshe Rivlin, Nathan Rotenstreich, Avraham Schenker and Zvi Yaron.

In the United States, the facilities of the World Zionist Organization-American Section were made available for editorial work. We gratefully acknowledge the cooperation of Executive Director Itzchak Hamlin and his staff. I thank Seymour Fishman, Executive Vice-President of the American Friends of the Hebrew University, for his cordial assistance during my stay in New York. Considerable help was given by Harold Manson, Director of the Office of Academic Affairs of the American Friends of the Hebrew University, and his departmental assistant, Rebecca Winograd; and by Lucy Manoff, Contemporary Jewry Institute Project Coordinator in the United States. We wish also to thank Yvonne Glikson for adapting several of the essays from the original Hebrew version; and both Esther Goldman and Rachel Goldberg for preparing the list of Jewish organizations and typing the various versions of the manuscript under great pressure.

It was the collective will of all who participated in the Seminar that the volume appear before the coming High Holy

Days as a document of Jewish life in 5734, 1973–74. If this will is realized, it is due to the people whose names and associations attest but in part to the constant support they offered: Daniel G. Ross, Chairman of the Institute's International Committee; Philip M. Klutznick, Founding Chairman of the International Committee; Arnold Zohn, President, Arno Press; Marie Syrkin, Editor, Herzl Press; Sam Bloch, Director of Publications, World Zionist Organization-American Section; David Zucker, Unitron Graphics.

Above all others, Lottie, who saw in this work a *mitzvah* appropriate to the hour.

On behalf of the authors we present this volume one year after—in consecration.

Moshe Davis

May 15, 1974
Anniversary of Israel's Independence

Contents

Contributors

MORDECHAI ALTSHULER. Director, Division of Jews in the Soviet Union and Eastern Europe, Institute of Contemporary Jewry, Hebrew University of Jerusalem

HAIM AVNI. Director, Division of Latin American Jewry, Institute of Contemporary Jewry, Hebrew University of Jerusalem

ISAIAH BERLIN. Master of Wolfson College, Oxford University

HAYYIM J. COHEN. Director, Division of Jews in Africa and Asia, Institute of Contemporary Jewry, Hebrew University of Jerusalem

IRWIN COTLER. Professor of Law, McGill University, Canada

MOSHE DAVIS. Head, Institute of Contemporary Jewry (on leave 1973–75); Stephen S. Wise Professor of American Jewish History and Institutions, Hebrew University of Jerusalem

ARYE L. DULZIN. Acting Chairman, Executive of the Jewish Agency for Israel and the World Zionist Organization

DANIEL J. ELAZAR. Professor of Political Science, Bar Ilan University, Ramat Gan, and Temple University, Pennsylvania

EMIL L. FACKENHEIM. Professor of Philosophy, University of Toronto

MAURICE FREEDMAN. Professor of Social Anthropology, Oxford University; Editor, *Jewish Journal of Sociology*

ALFRED GOTTSCHALK. President, Hebrew Union College-Jewish Institute of Religion; Professor of Bible and Jewish Thought

AVRAHAM HARMAN. President, Hebrew University, Jerusalem

THE YOM KIPPUR WAR

Israel and the Jewish People

United States of America: Overview

Daniel J. Elazar

When the Arabs attacked at 2:00 P.M. Middle East Time on October 6 most of the Jews of Israel were completing the *Musaf* service of Yom Kippur. Six thousand miles to the west (and six hours earlier), the morning services were just beginning for the great centers of American Jewry from the Atlantic coast to the Great Lakes and the dawn had not yet broken on the Pacific coast. Thus American Jews confronted the Yom Kippur War at the beginning of their sojourn in the synagogues of the land. In the course of that day, few Jews who identified themselves as such were to be out of touch with their fellows. As a consequence, the mobilization of the Jewish community for this latest crisis in Jewish history was to take on a unique dimension in the United States, as in the rest of the Jewish world.

The response of American Jewry to the crisis took on four aspects:[1] (1) *political action,* namely those activities

The author acknowledges with gratitude the assistance of Alex Grobman, whose diligent efforts made it possible for this project to be completed in a very short time, and the help of the staff of the Institute of Contemporary Jewry in the preparation of the manuscript in its various transmutations.

1. The data collection for this study was undertaken in the two months from the outbreak of the war to mid-December 1973. Consequently, the study is necessarily based upon fragmentary materials. Heavy reliance was placed on documentary evidence from the daily news dispatches of the Jewish Telegraphic Agency, including clippings from the Anglo-Jewish press and press releases, memoranda and information bulletins from several of the major Jewish organizations. Most important of all, a number of the leading figures of American Jewry—the men who played a central role in organizing the community's efforts during the war, as they have before and since—were interviewed immediately after the war. They were able to put the documentary evidence into perspective and supplement it with valuable first-hand accounts of events. The documentary material and the interviews are now on deposit in the Shazar Documentation Unit of the Hebrew University's Institute of Contemporary Jewry.

involving direct efforts to influence American policy toward
Israel and the war; (2) *fund raising,* including the United
Jewish Appeal (UJA), Israel Bonds, and other miscellaneous
fund-raising efforts; (3) *volunteering,* including volunteering
for service in Israel, voluntary efforts to mobilize the
community in the United States, especially in connection
with fund raising; and (4) *public identification,* including
those activities designed to enable people, primarily as
individuals, to identify with Israel and Jewry at the time of
crisis, with or without a direct political motivation or purpose
(e.g., advertisements in newspapers, rallies, demonstrations
and the like).

In general, responses were channeled through the
organized Jewish community which either mobilized those
eager to take action or directed spontaneous efforts toward
productive ends. To some extent, other organized bodies,
while prodominantly or heavily Jewish, not in themselves
part of the organized Jewish community, also became vehicles
for action. There were a variety of individual responses that
did not begin as organized efforts.

Overall, there is strong evidence of an overwhelming
response on the part of American Jewry as a whole.
Tens—even hundreds—of thousands of Jews came forward in
one way or another to do something for Israel either through
organized channels or spontaneously. In a very real sense,
they represent the American Jewish community and it is in
light of their actions that we can speak of "American Jewry" in
the following pages. At the same time, there is evidence that a
not inconsiderable segment of the Jewish population in the
United States did not respond in any visible way. While many
of these "Jews of silence" did identify with the struggle of
their people in their hearts and minds, others simply did not
care, and at least some supported the other side. The present
state of our knowledge makes it difficult to assess either the
amount of weak or negative responses or to determine the
reasons for such behavior, because we simply do not know
who or how many absented themselves from the community.

Organized Jewry sprang into action on all four fronts as
soon as Yom Kippur ended. On the night of October 6, the
leaders of the United Jewish Appeal, the Council of Jewish

Federations and Welfare Funds (CJFWF) and member federations, the Conference of Presidents of Major American Jewish Organizations and their various constituent organizations, and myriad Jewish organizations across the length and breadth of the country gathered together or contacted one another via conference calls to begin turning the wheels for total mobilization of their resources.

Political Action

In the intervening years between 1967 and 1973, the organization of American Jewry for political action had moved toward greater coordination. The Conference of Presidents of Major Jewish Organizations, formed some years ago in an effort to coordinate the "external relations" of the American Jewish community, has acquired a certain institutionalized character and general recognition as the channel for Jewish representations to American authorities. In part, this is because the American community as a whole has moved toward greater internal order; in part, it is because the Conference of Presidents serves as a central medium of communication between the Israel government and American Jewry on matters affecting Israel. This is not to say that the Conference of Presidents has become an independent entity with operating powers of its own. It is not the umbrella organization of the American Jewish community—even in its limited sphere—but a coordinating body, able to pull together the various groupings in American Jewish society on many, if not most, foreign issues.

If anything, the 1973 war confirmed the position of the Conference of Presidents as the coordinating body in its sphere and strengthened its role. The policy committee of the Conference met on the night of October 6 and moved immediately to call together on October 7 the leadership of American Jewry to indicate American Jewry's support for Israel, communicate with the Israeli government, and begin to mobilize for political action. At the meeting no specific requests for action were made and the Conference proceeded on the assumption that the first task was to support efforts to gain the return of the "armistice regime" and to restore the post-1967 borders. The single most important outcome of the meeting was a strong endorsement of the fund-raising efforts of the American Jewish community. At the same time the Conference's policy committee decided to call a national leadership convocation in Washington for Tuesday, October 9, to which would be invited ten delegates from each of its affiliated organizations, plus other Jewish leaders, in order to give public expression to solidarity with Israel in the capital of the United States. It was assumed that by that time Jewish leaders would determine what kind of political action was required.

The convocation was a great public success with 1,000 people in attendance from all parts of the country. By the time it was held it had become apparent that the fighting was going to continue for longer than had initially been expected. Moreover, American Jewry had witnessed the incredible spectacle of a United Nations Security Council which refused to label the Arabs aggressors, much less to bring about a cease-fire because of the adamant position of a majority of its members, particularly the Soviet Union, in support of the Arab states. American Jews were deeply shocked and impressed by the pictures broadcast on American television of Ambassador Yosef Tekoah sitting alone, isolated from his colleagues and being subjected to verbal attacks. This was one of the greatest shocks of the war.

In light of reported Arab successes and the U.N. stalemate, the mood of the Conference was one of great anxiety and eagerness to act, but Israeli authorities discouraged premature action. The highest priority item on the agenda was no longer a cease-fire but American replenishment of the Israeli arsenal. The key demand of the emergency convocation was that the American government undertake to supply Israel immediately with military equipment. Beyond that, the meeting generally reaffirmed the Israeli position regarding peace in the Middle East: the Arabs were termed aggressors and the nations of the world were criticized for their indifference to Arab terrorism, an indifference which actually encouraged further terrorist attacks. Reliance on the U.N. as a peacekeeping mechanism was rejected and a call was made for direct negotiations among the parties concerned.

A major field of action for the Presidents Conference was in connection with the Arab pressure on Japan to change its Middle East policy and to break off diplomatic relations with Israel. The Presidents Conference requested local Jewish communities to make their views known to the Japanese authorities and met with the Japanese ambassador to convey formally the sentiments of American Jewry. Beyond this, informal steps were taken to make clear that American Jewry was willing to consider appropriate counter-measures to any unfavorable Japanese actions. It seemed that the Presidents Conference had at least the tacit support of the American government which made public its own highly critical views of Japan's actions. This may indeed have had some effect on the Japanese refusal to break off relations with Israel, even though it announced a shift in its policy from neutrality to a pro-Arab stance.

In addition to the Presidents Conference, every constituent organization undertook to mobilize its membership on behalf of Israel, generally but not entirely within the limits passed on to them by that body. One of the salient characteristics of the American Jewish community is the lack of centralized control over the actions of individual groups and organizations. Another is American Jewry's knowledge of the techniques of political influence. Together, these two characteristics create a spontaneous combustion of their own on the political front. Most organizations asked their members to make their views known to the President, his Secretary of State, and the Congress as soon as the war broke out.

The Jewish community took steps to mobilize support for President Nixon's request for a Congressional appropriation of $2.2 billion to support Israel's purchase of American war materiel. Jewish organizations contacted their local affiliates and provided names of the relevant senators and congressmen to be contacted.[2]

2. In terms of this kind of intra-American foreign policy effort, the National Jewish Community Relations Advisory (NJCRAC) also played an important role. It moved to mobilize the local Community Relations Advisory Councils, all of which were standing by of their own accord, and served primarily to provide them with up-to-date information on the situation in the Middle East and on the activities of the Presidents Conference and other American bodies. They, too, sent telegrams to the appropriate political figures and sought to mobilize their local affiliates to secure

There was one area of overt conflict within the Jewish community during the crisis. The supporters of the struggle to secure emigration rights for Soviet Jewry insisted upon continuing their work even during the war. The Presidents Conference and other major American Jewish organizations wanted to concentrate on the immediate problem of the war. This conflict was not resolved. To the extent that it surfaced publicly it did so in connection with the proposed Jackson-Vanik amendment to the Administration-backed trade bill, which would forbid granting "most favored nation" status to Russia as long as the Soviets interfered with Jewish emigration. As things developed, the Administration itself withdrew its request for "most favored nation" status for Russia, at least temporarily. If this was in any respect a "victory" for American Jewish political action, it was really a greater victory for the senators and congressmen who remained steadfast in support of the bill.

Support of Non-Jewish Groups

American Jewish agencies concerned with intergroup relations took the lead in appealing to their friends in the Christian community for support. There is every reason to believe that American Jewish leadership looked upon the Christian community's response to the present crisis as a test of Christian-Jewish dialogues following the Six Day War, at which time the place of Israel in Jewish religious and historical experience was clearly not understood by most Christians.

Between 1967 and 1973 Christian-Jewish relations underwent a change. Jews, recognizing that they live in a predominantly Christian world, felt that it was necessary to talk profoundly with their Christian counterparts about Israel, the State and the People, even though they could not expect "instant brotherhood" to evolve from such talks. This was a

---

statements of support from local political, labor and religious leaders. One of the major functions of the NJCRAC was to distribute information on responses obtained in different communities so as to encourage other communities to move in the same direction. Several of the local community relations councils and various other organizations established "hot lines" for people to call for news about the war.

major retreat from a pre-1967 optimism but reflected a realistic assessment of Jewish-Christian relations.

Viewed from the perspective of the Yom Kippur War, even that assessment may have been too optimistic. The Christian response was stronger than in 1967 but was still quite limited. The few recognized Christian leaders who have consistently demonstrated their philo-Semitic feelings or their interest in maintaining a close alliance with the Jewish people did speak out, although most of them did so after an appeal by Jewish friends.[3]

Strong support for Israel came from Fundamentalist Christians. Much of it was probably unsolicited, indicating once again that Christian belief is far more important a determinant in shaping Christian response than Jewish contacts. The Fundamentalists, who continue to believe in the validity of Biblical prophecy, see in Israel a fulfillment, or a step toward the fulfillment, of that prophecy. The essentially liberal mainstream Christian denominations, whose leaders treat Biblical prophecy as a metaphor, start from a far more neutral stance toward Israel and thus their position is subject to considerations of interest that frequently work against Israel. Finally, there are those Christians whose doctrine is to some degree anti-Jewish and whose representatives, no matter how liberal in practice, still find it difficult to overcome that doctrinal base.

A new element on the scene this time was a response from the ethnic groups. Here, the American Jewish Committee (AJC) played a prominent role. Some years ago, the AJC launched a program to reach out to white ethnic Americans on the grounds that they had been a substantially neglected element in the American population and that their legitimate interests deserved more attention, both for reasons of justice and in the light of Jewish interests. This resulted in some public support for Israel in 1973, although, in the main, it, too, was limited to individuals who had personally become

---

3. Two American bodies that worked hard to generate Christian support were the National Conference of Christians and Jews and, most especially, Christians Concerned for Israel, an exceptional group of Christian leaders who have sought to arouse the conscience of Christianity on matters pertaining to Jews and Israel.

involved in the AJC effort, or to groups that had a political stake in Israel's anti-Soviet stance. Thus, the bulk of the response came from American groups representing ethnics from Eastern European countries now under Soviet domination, and the anti-Soviet element in their statements of support was clear. Much less support was forthcoming from Italian or Greek groups, for example, who clearly had no stake in the issue except that of friendship for Jews. Where such ties of friendship existed, some public expression of identification with Israel was forthcoming.

The response from the Black community was confined to those Black leaders who had a record of commitment to Jewish causes and were seeking to preserve the old Black-Jewish alliance. A. Philip Randolph, Bayard Rustin, and Percy Sutton (president of the Borough of Manhattan) were the principal national leaders heard from. A statement was obtained from the National Association for the Advancement of Colored People (NAACP); James H. Jones, the president of the Negro Trade Unions Leadership Council of Philadelphia, spoke at the solidarity rally held in that city; and the Chicago Jewish community obtained a strong statement from the Chicago *Defender.* Nothing was forthcoming from the younger and more militant Black leadership.

As in the past, the Jews' greatest support came from the leadership of organized labor. George Meany was the most prominent non-political American officeholder to speak up on behalf of Israel. He stated that Israel is the nation that "bears the union label." He was joined by the highest bodies of the AFL-CIO and individual international union leaders also issued strong statements. The first issue of the *AFL-CIO News* to appear after the war began carried a number of pro-Israel items. The movement's executive council established a Labor War Relief Fund for Israel with a $50,000 contribution from the AFL-CIO treasury and a call for shop collections throughout union ranks. In general, labor remained friendly to Israel in the manner of twenty-five years ago.

Similarly, the Jewish War Veterans worked among the general veterans organizations in the United States and obtained their support for Israel. By and large, they also received a sympathetic ear because of a convergence of interests. The American veterans organizations tend to be highly suspicious of the Soviet Union and the détente, and strongly supportive of those forces in the world that oppose Soviet expansionism. Moreover, Pentagon opinion seems to be strongly behind Israel, and this carries great weight with veterans groups, who maintain strong connections with the Defense Department.

Despite many disappointments nationally with regard to obtaining support from non-Jews, as is invariably the case in the United States, there was a great diversity in local reactions. In some communities a broad spectrum of non-Jewish leaders spoke out strongly for Israel; in others, there was relatively little to no response. In almost every case the crucial factor was the relationship between the local Jewish leadership and their non-Jewish counterparts.

In Illinois the Jewish community, led by the Jewish United Fund (Federation) Public Affairs Committee and the local American Jewish Committee chapter, prevailed upon Governor Daniel Walker (who was elected with strong Jewish support but who was previously not known to be pro-Israel) to proclaim October 19 *(Simchat Torah)* as "Full Support for Israel Day." In his proclamation, he made reference to the *Simchat Torah* holiday and its meaning, and he declared the State of Illinois to be in support of Israel's survival with defensible boundaries. Chicago Jewry was additionally active in getting statements of support from the Hellenic Council of Education, the Midwest District Council of the Japanese-American Citizens League, and the presidents of the Polish-American Congress and the Polish-American Alliance.

The Jews of Omaha secured widespread support from among the church leaders in Nebraska for a public statement on behalf of Israel. The New Jersey Council of Churches offered a somewhat moderate resolution, affirming support, in carefully tempered wording. The Church Council of Greater Seattle, on the other hand, provided a strong statement. In Union Township, New Jersey, Jews and Christians came together in a public demonstration called "Union Township Rallies for Israel." All the foregoing were produced by solicitation on the part of the Jewish community; they were not spontaneous outpourings of good will. Responses came primarily from those with whom the Jews had already forged close and friendly contacts. Those who had resisted such contacts in the past remained immune to Jewish requests.

The influence of the American Jewish community on the press and media responses is much less apparent. By and large, no group in the United States can directly solicit editorial support from any American newspaper worth its salt, and certainly not from the television networks. At best, a group can obtain a right of reply to a local radio or television statement if they so choose, or write letters to the newspapers and negotiate for their publication as an informal means of gaining the right of reply in print. Jewish influence on the American press, to the extent that it exists, comes from slow and patient educational efforts over many years to make the men who determine the editorial position of newspapers, radio, or television stations aware of the justice of the Israeli cause. In fact, this work has been undertaken by a variety of Jewish groups over the years, with editors and editorial writers being invited to visit Israel, and being provided with relevant information, and the like. At least partly as a result of this, the overwhelming majority of the American press that took a stand were favorable toward Israel, and only a few papers, of which only the *Christian Science Monitor* has a respectable professional reputation, took stands in opposition.

Fund Raising

As would have been predicted, the most obvious, complete, and overt means for American Jews to respond to the crisis was through fund raising. American Jews remain uneasy about the fact that donating money still represents their best channel for sharing in the Israeli experience. Indeed, many of the other forms of response attempted this time reflect that unease. Significantly, those American Jews who care at all wish to do more than simply give money, to give of themselves, as it were, in ways that are parallel to the way Israelis necessarily give of themselves by being on the spot.[4]

---

4. This phenomenon alone deserves further exploration for its specific meaning in the context of Jewish culture. There is abundant evidence that, while Jews consider money to be a good thing, and worth hard work, money itself is not that important when compared to other things, such as human life and the social experiences that

The outpouring of funds was far greater than any known by the American Jewish community before, paralleling the experience in the rest of the Jewish world, but even more significant, because the Jews in the United States started from a higher base. The major contributors were already habituated to giving large sums and to increasing generous gifts in times of crisis. The sense of crisis deepened as the first few days passed, creating an emotional need on the part of many Jews to demonstrate concretely their support of Israel. This need was expressed by the act of giving money, a traditional means of channeling feelings into material support.

In addition, the community was better organized than ever before to mobilize funds and to solicit large amounts from affluent donors. By nightfall of October 6 an experienced, multi-faceted organization went into operation. Built upon patterns established during the Six Day War and strengthened through several intervening emergencies, this organizational instrument took on new dimensions as part of the war-time experience. The fact that the news of the Yom Kippur War was heard by multitudes in synagogues led to wider mobilization of potential donors at the very beginning. This is especially true since American Jews have come to turn to their synagogues in times of crises, and synagogues have access to far more Jews on an immediate basis than any other body in the United States. Recognizing this, the Federations utilized the opportunity they provided for fund raising and, in the hour of crisis the rabbis and synagogue leadership responded. In the past, federations and synagogues have pursued their own agendas separately, and the gap between these two key institutions has been a matter of no little concern to those seeking a better integration of the American Jewish community. While no formal agreements were made at this time, it was reasonably clear that a new page had been turned in Federation-Synagogue relations.

"make life worth living." The myth of the Jews' love of money was probably strengthened—both among Jews and non-Jews—by the results of the fund-raising efforts in connection with this war but, in fact, a closer look at the Diaspora war effort shows how clearly Jews consider giving money a surrogate for other more important gifts and are disturbed by the fact that they cannot give the latter. As in most things, the attitudes of Jews toward money is far more complex than the stereotypes would indicate.

Fund raising fell into four categories. First and central was the United Jewish Appeal whose leadership pledged itself to raise $900 million, of which $750 million was to go to Israel as part of an emergency drive that would encompass the 1974 campaign. These funds were to be raised, as usual, through the local Jewish Welfare Federations and more than six hundred independent campaigns. The start of that effort was the commitment taken within the first twenty-four hours of the war, to raise $100 million in cash immediately. By the end of the first week, $107 million had been raised, an unprecedented figure.

Second was the drive to purchase Israel Bonds, which is coordinated with the general fund-raising apparatus in the United States for obvious reasons, even though the Bonds themselves represent an investment rather than a gift. The American Jewish leadership committed itself to raise $600 million for the purchase of Israeli bonds through 1974, utilizing the regular mechanisms of the Israel Bond organization in the United States.

Third was the imperative to concentrate on gathering extraordinary sums for the Israel Emergency Fund and the UJA. Other authorized campaigns for Israeli institutions, normally conducted during that time of the year, were voluntarily suspended for several months. Among such were campaigns for Histadruth, Hadassah, the universities, and the various Zionist and religious institutions.

In addition, organizations ranging from the Labor Zionist Alliance to the B'nai B'rith informed their members that fund raising for their special purposes would not go on as usual. Unlike the Six Day War, which came at the end of the campaign year and did not directly impinge upon ongoing efforts, the Yom Kippur War came at the height of many of the important special purpose drives held annually in the fall. This unprecedented act of unity through the Israel Emergency Fund was one of the most stunning developments in American Jewish community life. It led to the negotiation of an agreement which affirmed that a strong American Jewish community was essential in the Jewish world, and that the local communities' needs and expanding efforts on the Jewish educational front had to be met as part of the overall emergency effort.

Finally, there were the special crisis-oriented drives, e.g. for ambulances for American Red Magen David (the Israeli "Red Cross"). In this connection, many "instant" fund-raising efforts were initiated, mostly by people with the best of intentions. The organized Jewish community, however, viewed such activities as a potential distraction from the major needs of Israel and the American Jewish community and did not encourage them.

Barely twenty-four hours after first word of the Yom Kippur attack had been received, a meeting was held in the UJA national headquarters on October 7 in New York to determine campaign strategy. More than one hundred community and campaign leaders from around the country met and announced a $100 million cash drive for the first week of the war. A series of nationwide telephone appeals was begun as well as daily community telethons, assignment of community cash quotas and acceptance of a heavy load of cash solicitation assignments at the highest levels in the communities represented.[5]

When the historic 1974 campaign goal of $900 million—$750 million for UJA and $150 million for Federations—was announced at the second extraordinary meeting in New York on Sunday, October 14, the fund-raising machinery was in full motion. Flying through three nights to four major cities, UJA's ranking leaders, Paul Zuckerman (General Chairman), Edward Ginsberg (President), and Irving Bernstein (Executive Vice-Chairman), accompanied Minister Pinchas Sapir and Acting Chairman of the Jewish Agency, Leon Dulzin. They reached representatives of the Federations and elicited pledges totaling $60 million. At the same time, other senior UJA officers, in what amounted to a nationwide airlift, covered dozens of other major cities with similar success.

In December, three thousand community leaders attended the UJA annual National Conference which inau-

5. See Minutes of the Emergency Meeting of United Jewish Appeal officers, October 7, 1973.

gurated the second phase of the historic campaign. The theme
of the Conference was movingly expressed in Elie Wiesel's
address *Against Despair*, which was distributed in 250,000
copies to meet the demand.

These gatherings represented the more formal aspects
of the initial drive; informally there were continuous contacts
between communities and major contributors from Saturday
evening on. To obtain cash, people were requested to pay
outstanding pledges and make cash advances on future gifts.
Many donors chose to borrow funds to provide necessary
cash. Major banks in each community were contacted and
lines of credit were arranged so that money would be
available. The story of how $107 million was raised is really a
dramatic enactment of self-sacrifice, men borrowing money
despite high rates of interest, women selling jewels, people
mortgaging homes, and so on.

In the meantime, less affluent givers began to make
their contributions, either through their synagogues or by mail
to their local Federations. In some cases, congregations called
special meetings to pray for Israel's victory and to raise funds
to make that victory possible. Synagogues and rabbis offered
their manpower to the Federations as part of the mobilization
effort. By mid-November, the Conservative movement announced that it had raised $82 million through its congrega-
tions. The Orthodox Young Israel movement broke all
precedent by setting up bicycle brigades to collect pledges on
Saturdays. On Tuesday night, October 9, communities across
the country held open rallies to raise funds from their general
contributors. The rallies themselves had varying degrees of
success. In New York City, where mass meetings to raise
money were not feasible, WPIX-TV became the vehicle for an
Israel Emergency Fund Telethon on Sunday night, October 21,
and the many celebrities who appeared raised approximately
$3.5 million from tens of thousands of viewers.

People also began raising funds literally in the streets of
the major cities. In New York, Los Angeles, Detroit, Cleveland,
St. Louis, and Hartford, sound trucks were driven through
Jewish city neighborhoods and suburbs asking for contributions. In communities outside of New York City, means for
small givers to respond in at least a semi-spontaneous manner

were institutionalized once the regular campaign apparatus was mobilized. In some cities merchants in predominantly Jewish shopping districts staged sale days in which either the gross receipts or the profits from their sales were contributed to the local Federation drive for Israel.

In drawing conclusions from the fund-raising response, two important points stand out: first, the effect of education; second, the effect of organization on the overall effort. Regarding the first, the best response came from those people who had been informed about Israel's situation and her needs. The young men who mortgaged their homes to contribute additional funds to Israel were almost invariably those who in recent years had been through young leadership programs (specifically those of the UJA and CJF and its local affiliates), or who had been on an in-depth tour of Israel, or who had been educated through seminars and conferences in the United States, and whose general Jewish consciousness had been raised by serious efforts on the part of the UJA and the Federations. These people were receptive to the effects of the crisis and responded accordingly. Faculty members, who are notably not large contributors, gave more freely in cases where campaigns were conducted in combination with educational programs. College students came forward because concerted efforts had been made within their own ranks and by the organized Jewish community over the past several years to sensitize them to their Jewish heritage.

The educational effort itself would not have been accomplished without the availability of the organizational framework to stimulate and manage it. That organizational framework has become increasingly better articulated in recent years. By now there exists in the American Jewish community a reservoir of personnel who can be mobilized at time of emergency, a framework within which they can be activated, and a set of procedures for their mobilization which enables the work to be done on a mass basis with considerable dispatch.

There was another, hidden organizational dimension as well. Masses of people mailed in their checks spontaneously to their local Federations, so much so that as of a month later the Federation workers had not yet been able to open all of the envelopes.[6] This meant that the continued Federation campaigns have left their impact. An announcement of need in the synagogue or simply listening to the television was sufficient to trigger a response in an entirely voluntary manner. In sum, the combination of a desire to help with mechanisms through which to help made the difference.

Volunteering

The handling of volunteering also reflected certain organizational improvements over 1967. There was greater sophistication in the selection and screening of potential volunteers. The management of volunteers was the one major task which fell exclusively to organized Zionism in the United States. In matters of fund raising and political action, Zionists played a role as individuals or together with larger groupings, but volunteering, because of its connection with *aliyah*, is a task which falls within their purview. The organization of the bulk of the volunteer effort fell to the American Zionist Youth Foundation (AZYF), which managed its volunteer recruitment and screening program through its *Sherut La'am* (volunteer service program) division.

The entire effort reflected part of the Israeli ambivalence toward volunteers. On one hand, Israel wanted to stimulate *aliyah* but, on the other, it wanted to avoid a repetition of the 1967 experience when large unorganized numbers of volunteers descended upon Israel and created problems for the government. In 1973 there was a tremendous outpouring of volunteers. Some 30,000 to 40,000 people actually made their names known to the American Zionist Youth Foundation in the first month.

Volunteers fell into two categories: the skilled, especially doctors, and the unskilled, particularly young people who wanted to lend a hand in a general way. Insofar as the former are concerned, no precise figures are available at the

6. The preliminary figures from Philadelphia exemplify this. As of December 17, 1973, contributors to the regular 1973 campaign had been contacted for the 1974 drive. Of them, 11,877 had contributed and 96 had not. Furthermore, 2,354 new contributors had come forward.

moment of writing, but it is clear that many doctors were willing to leave their practices or university positions to come to Israel to offer their specialized skills for anywhere from the duration of the war to the duration of the need. In some cases, whole groups of doctors volunteered, and it was even reported that one doctor was able to volunteer with his entire staff. The principal characteristic of the 1973 volunteering effort was its relative sophistication. Volunteering was especially heavy among doctors who could sense or knew what was likely to be needed in Israel—orthopedists, plastic surgeons, and burn specialists, for example. Many doctors who had served in Vietnam came forward to share their expertise in dealing with the kinds of wounds created by modern weaponry.

To cope with the many problems, the American Zionist Youth Foundation established a fairly elaborate screening program in New York City and worked with its contacts in other major cities to do the same thing, except for medical personnel, which was processed by Hadassah. In at least some cases organizations which had been activated during the Six Day War and which had continued to exist in a tenuous way, perhaps as screeners for the *Sherut La'am* program, sprang into action again. Thus in Philadelphia, the Philadelphia Volunteers for Israel was able to reactivate itself on a full scale basis and to undertake screening tasks as they had before. In many cities the Jewish community centers, which had been involved with the AZYF through the Israeli *shaliah* program, served as the centers for screening volunteers.

Placement was a cardinal rule of the AZYF program. It was determined that no volunteer group would be sent unless there was some reasonable indication in advance that there was a need for the group in Israel. By the end of the first month, less than 2,000 prospective volunteers had actually been accepted in New York out of the tens of thousands who offered their services, even though most of those who came forward passed the screenings.[7] At that time, Israel had

7. Approximately one third of the volunteers accepted came from the greater New York area and another two thirds from the rest of the country, a ratio not disproportionate to the general distribution of Jewish population in the United States. It should be noted that the vast majority paid for their own passage to Israel.

offered 1,155 places for American volunteers and 812 volunteers had actually been sent, with another 293 being prepared. As a result, even of these accepted, relatively few had arrived in Israel in the first month following the war, although other groups were scheduled to come thereafter. At the same time, people who did come under organized auspices were not left to wander about aimlessly. '

In addition to the organized volunteers, a certain number of individuals managed to get to Israel on their own. Almost without exception, they were people who had been in Israel for extended periods before and knew how to deal with Israeli bureaucracy. Through friends and connections, they managed to wangle space on aircraft for Israel (a difficult problem even for the AZYF) and then found themselves assignments in the country. Some were very helpful filling a variety of tasks, even such menial work as garbage collecting, in order to keep Israel functioning. It is to the credit of the American Jewish community that quite a few young people, many of whom are candidates for advanced degrees in American universities, were so committed to Israel that they were willing to drop their studies and do manual labor, precisely because they understood what was required.

In retrospect, there was a substantial outpouring of prospective volunteers as a result of the war, and there would have been even more had Israel embarked on a major effort to encourage volunteering. Where efforts were made, people did come forward, but most of the efforts themselves were spontaneous and were not necessarily geared to the realities of the Israeli situation, or to Israeli needs. Overall, it must be concluded that, unlike fund raising, which was of great importance to Israel, the volunteering effort was primarily of importance to Diaspora Jews, as a means of giving them a chance to participate more actively in the war effort.

Public Identification

The line between political action and public identification is a thin one. Fifty or sixty thousand Jews gathered in a square in New York City in support of Israel is not an apolitical phenomenon. No sensible observer doubts that political figures take note of such a demonstration. And, regardless of who organized the demonstrations, the people who came to them did so to express personal solidarity with Israel in the most public kind of manner.

One of the most significant aspects of the 1973 war is that American Jews, like those in other countries, took to the streets to express their solidarity with Israel. For generations the most apt expression summarizing the character of Jewish survival in the post-emancipation world was Y. L. Gordon's famous "Be Everyman in the street and a Jew at home." The Yom Kippur War may very well have been a final step in the reversal of that dictum. Many Jews who are for all intents and purposes simply men and women in their homes, in the sense that they do little in a conscious way to set themselves apart as Jews from their fellows, wished to be Jews in the streets, where the differences would be markedly visible. The implications of this wish will be with us for a long time.

In some respects the public manifestations of Jewish solidarity in 1973 were extensions of a mood which had begun at the time of the Six Day War. In 1967 Jews did not go into the streets as readily. Only one mass rally, in Washington on the Thursday of that week, was of any public consequence; it was a product of the American experience of the 1960s, a period when Blacks and opponents of American governmental policy in Vietnam began to use the mass rally as a technique for political action. In 1973 the organized Jewish community was there, ready to call the rallies into being, to set up the sound amplification systems and the podia, to invite the appropriate public figures and Jewish leaders to attend, to organize a program, and to notify the media to arrange for proper coverage.

In New York the American Zionist Youth Foundation took the lead in organizing the largest of the American Jewish rallies, one that brought fifty to sixty thousand people together on October 7 in the United Nations Plaza at the same time as the first meeting of the Presidents Conference. In the various Jewish communities outside New York local community relations councils assumed responsibility for organizing rallies. The Jews who came were highly committed to Israel's cause and anxious to proclaim their commitment publicly.

Among the young, there were some willing to fight with any who came to oppose them. Thus, in the first few days scuffles broke out between Jewish demonstrators and Arab counter-demonstrators.

The meetings that were held after the cease-fire reflected an organized effort to apply pressure, nevertheless they were a continuing manifestation of the emotional response of American Jewry. Thus, on November 5 an assembly was held in New York's garment district on behalf of the Israeli prisoners of war. Officially sponsored by the Presidents Conference, it was scheduled for the day before the New York City elections and all the mayorality candidates, as well as other political leaders, attended it. Similarly, an emergency demonstration and prayer service, in which some Christian clergy participated, was held before the Syrian mission to the United Nations on behalf of the POWs held by Syria. A similar rally was held outside the Red Cross building in Washington.

Perhaps a more useful way of examining public identification is to scrutinize the responses of various groupings within the American Jewish community. First of all, it is clear that youth were the most visible when it came to demonstrations, a factor that is practically a sociological law. What is significant is that this time adult Jewish leaders also participated in the demonstrations, as marchers as well as on the platforms across the nation. Even a casual look at television screens would indicate that young people who participated were preponderantly those already highly involved in Jewish life—the number of *kipot* (skull caps) visible was evidence of this. More systematic inquiry reveals that youth groups and particularly Jewish schools were major sources of rally participants, since it was relatively easy to mobilize such young people on short notice.[8]

Furthermore, Jewish schools were natural centers for organized activity in identification with Israel. For most schools, the pattern of activity was the same: religious services, an emergency fund drive, perhaps a special

8. In addition to the general rallies, the New York Board of Jewish Education held a demonstration of Jewish school children on October 25, with a turnout of approximately 15,000 students.

fund-raising activity such as a cake sale, perhaps a letter-writing campaign to Israeli soldiers, or to congressmen, or to the President of the United States asking for American support for Israel, or to Holland thanking it for its stand. In some cases, children in the schools marked on the map of Israel the names and addresses of friends and relatives living there. After the casualty figures were announced, many schools held memorial services for the Israeli fallen. The fund-raising drives in the schools alone collected some one million dollars for Israel. In general, it seems that the Yom Kippur War continued the process, begun during the Six Day War, of making American Jewish schools more cognizant of Israel and making their curricula more related to Israeli issues.

Perhaps the sharpest change in reaction between 1967 and 1973 was that found among college students. Jewish college students were stirred in 1967, but then a whole host of issues impinged upon their response. There was still much anti-Vietnam war agitation on and off campuses, the New Left had turned its support to pro-Black militancy on campuses, and Jewish student activity in support of Israel was the exception rather than the rule.

In 1973 there was a much greater campus response than in 1967 because of three significant factors. First, was the existence of a separate Jewish student movement that had emerged and survived despite a decline in general student activism. In the late 1960s, a certain percentage of activist Jewish students of all persuasions discovered their unique Jewish interests and how those interests distinguished them from their non-Jewish peers (and even from those Jewish students committed to undiluted universalism); thus, a Jewish student's movement developed. In some cases, it was as radical in orientation as the general student New Left; in others, it was far more moderate. But in any case, it was Jewish. This is not to say that the Jewish student movement was a very large one, but it showed a real staying power not evident among most other movements. Today, it survives almost alone on campus after campus. As a result, there was a Jewish student press available when the 1973 war broke. The various campus newspapers were connected through a countrywide Jewish student news service. There were local unions of Jewish students or the equivalent in various cities around the country connected through the North American Jewish Student Network. A national campaign on college campuses raised one million dollars during the war through the University Programs Department of the UJA in cooperation with B'nai B'rith Hillel Foundations, Federations, and other Jewish student organizations.

Second, a sense of Jewish isolation from Third World politics had grown among sensitive Jewish students on the campus so that increasingly, as student radicals began to vocalize support for the Arab position, committed Jewish radicals felt a greater sense of political separation.

Third, the Jewish student movement had successfully rallied around the cause for Soviet Jewry and had kept its *esprit de corps* because it had a cause, while other movements were falling apart. Moreover, it was a "respectable cause" among radicals, an effort on behalf of an underdog, at a time when the central Jewish cause—Israel—was being defined as "imperialist aggression" by many leftists.

Finally, there were organized vehicles for Jewish student response. On the campuses, as every place else, organization seemed to be the key to effective response, to the channeling of spontaneous activity not only in useful directions, but in directions that made those activities count far more than sheer numbers would suggest. The campus situation, it should be noted, is a good test case by which to assess the differences between organized and unorganized response in times of crisis. In addition to the structures developed by the students themselves in cooperation with the overall Jewish community leadership, Jewish student unrest in the late 1960s had led to some drastic changes in the personnel and even the program of the B'nai B'rith Hillel Foundations, long the central Jewish address on the campus. Thus many Hillel Foundations found themselves in a better position to provide campus leadership, or at the very least, a base from which student campus leaders could function during the crisis.

All this is to emphasize that the campus response was impulsive. It was not that all the students were active in campus Jewish life prior to the war or simply waiting for the opportunity to express themselves—quite the contrary. Under normal circumstances, only a relatively small cadre of students is active. But when the otherwise uninvolved students spontaneously "turned on" to Israel, they had a place to go and people to guide them into demonstrations, fund raising, volunteering, or teach-ins. In that regard Network established student-run "hot-lines," students in various communities made concerted efforts to present Israel's position on talk shows, which, because of Arab protests, were more "balanced" than in 1967. Students raised funds to pay the fares of volunteers to go to Israel. On October 22 and 23, Network and the AZYF sponsored a series of teach-ins on campuses across the country.

It should be noted that the campus response, while very visible in one sense, was mixed to a certain degree, perhaps somewhat more so than in the general Jewish community. Although thousands of students came to rallies, given the total number of Jewish students it is hard to say how many actually showed any visible signs of support for Israel. It was on the campus that the first visible signs of polarization in the Jewish community became apparent, albeit in a modest way. There were Jews on campus who spoke out against Israel, although fewer and more quietly than a few years ago when the New Left was stronger. This marks the campus off to some extent from the general Jewish community, where even those Jews who were apathetic were not actually opposed to Israel.

The presence on most major campuses of large numbers of students who had been personally involved with Israel, made a real difference. Even if they were critical of aspects of their experiences in Israel (and many American Jewish students who spend time in Israel are critical of Israelis), they had a positive attitude toward the country as a whole, as well as connections with specific friends for whom they felt deep concern.

The war seems to have bridged whatever was left of the generation gap among committed Jews. Perhaps the best example of this was the reaction of the youth at the annual assembly of the Council of Jewish Federations and Welfare Funds. The General Assembly has become, in the view of many, the most important single public event of American

Jewry. It can be conceived as the American Jewish equivalent
of the Lublin Fair of centuries ago, where those who "count"
in American Jewish life make an appearance, to see one
another, display their "wares," and discuss their common
problems. One major aspect of the General Assembly has been
its role as a vehicle for stimulating involvement of college
youth and faculty in the affairs of the American Jewish
community. The initial plans made by youth for the annual
General Assembly were originally oriented toward issues of
confrontation, as they have been in the past several years. But
these were abandoned because of the war. Young people came
to the General Assembly to seek advice on how to mobilize
their efforts on behalf of Israel, rather than to seek a
confrontation. The community was knit together in a way that
it had not been in the past.

A further note about the General Assembly is in order.
One of the great gains made by Jewish college youth in past
confrontations with participants in the General Assembly was
the introduction of overt Jewish themes into the program,
ranging from public Jewish observances to a spirit of
conscious Jewish behavior previously lacking. Indeed, one of
the most important aspects of the General Assembly now is
the way in which it offers Jewish leaders the opportunity to
live in a Jewish environment for nearly a week. The 1973
General Assembly showed the results of the campus-induced
change. Some 2,500 people from 150 communities came
because they wanted to be with fellow Jews in a Jewish milieu.

If the reaction among Jewish college students seemed
on the whole to be on the plus side, the reaction among Jewish
faculty was somewhat more mixed. On the one hand, the
successful construction of organizational and institutional
links between faculties and communities in many different
localities since the Six Day War seems to have created more
campus activity, particularly in the fund-raising sphere, than
in the past. Concrete identification with Israel was made
possible in specific ways, rather than simply through signing
ads to appear in the *New York Times*.

On the other hand, polarization among Jewish faculty
may have been greater than in 1967. There was also a division
between the involved and the indifferent, with many of the

latter virtually apologizing for their apathy after the war reached its successful conclusion. In 1973 there were fewer indifferent faculty members, but there was a larger group which was either overtly or covertly hostile to Israel, having been persuaded that Israel was a territorial expansionist and colonialist oppressor of the Arabs.[9]

These negative points are made in order to give special emphasis to the positive ones. The fact that very few Jewish professors were willing to criticize Israel openly, and that many who disagreed with Israel's policies, for whatever reason (and it must be remembered that the American professoriat tends to be dovish in any case, particularly so in the aftermath of the Vietnam experience), were still willing to support Israel in her hour of need, is of great significance.

The key organization in the faculty effort continued to be the American Professors for Peace in the Middle East (APPME), a group born out of the Six Day War, kept alive in the intervening years through a number of academically-oriented programs designed to bring Israel and its problems to the campus in an intellectually respectable and honest way, and available as an instrumentality of action in time of crisis. While the organization's sympathies had always been clear, the Yom Kippur War produced a more forceful pro-Israel stance. APPME has become for certain members of the Jewish academic community their "shul"—the place where they can express their Jewish identity and commitment. Many of them have spent time in Israel since 1967 as visitors and on sabbaticals, and they are the faculty who can identify with the country in very personal ways, particularly with colleagues whom they have come to know and appreciate in Israel.

It is extremely hard to estimate the number of Jews who actually participated in public identification actions, but the

9. Even among those faculty who actively and publicly supported Israel in the war, there was a large percentage who thought that the policy of the Israeli government toward the Arabs and peace had been too rigid and not sufficiently flexible to encourage a peaceful settlement, and that the Israelis were now paying for their past intransigence. Many of these people would not express such sentiments openly because of their basic support for Israel, but not a few of them indicated privately that they would not be opposed to a settlement imposed upon both sides by the United States and the Soviet Union, even at the expense of Israel's territorial gains in 1967, because they believed that was the only way Israel would ever achieve peace.

figure is probably between five and ten per cent. Since that would involve some 300,000 to 600,000 people, the impression made is extremely vivid. Moreover, it is true that for every person who actually made himself visible in this way, there was an indeterminate number of others who identified with the action passively, for a whole host of legitimate reasons that do not reflect any lower level of identification with Israel. Still, it would be a mistake to assume that 300,000 or even 600,000 Jews identifying strongly, plus all those passively associated with that identification, means that the Jewish community is united, with a positive concern for Israel as a special ingredient in their lives. By the very nature of things, we do not know how many American Jews were apathetic in the real sense of not caring—how many had assimilated so far that the problem of Israel did not touch them deeply. There is some reason to believe that those who cared at all, cared even more than they did in 1967, while those who cared little, cared even less than six years earlier.

Sources of Response

The response to the Yom Kippur War is a classic example of how organization makes the whole greater than the sum of its parts. Five to ten per cent of American Jewry could make its weight felt so that it sent waves throughout American society (any doubt that this was so can be dispelled by the extent of coverage that *Time, Newsweek* and the general press gave to the American Jewish response to the war) because that response was organized. Take, for example, one community of 20,000 Jews in the Midwest. The first word of the war was spread through the community as individuals came to synagogues on Yom Kippur morning after having heard the radio reports. After a certain point, radios were set up in the synagogues themselves (a phenomenon occurring even in some very orthodox synagogues in the United States) and news bulletins were announced from the pulpit as the services proceeded. Following Yom Kippur, the leaders of the local Federation called a meeting of the influential citizens of the community to begin fund raising. As word was received from New York, they arranged mass meetings and fund-raising activities. On the campus, Jewish students flocked to the Hillel Foundation where they found the base for creating their own rallies and fund-raising campaigns.

As it turned out, the major link between the Jewish communities of America and Israel was provided by the UJA and the Council of Jewish Federations. As in 1967, the two groups set up a telex system linking eighty-five Jewish communities across the country. Bulletins were sent out twice a day over that network to Federation offices in those cities giving news of campaign progress and also UPI news bulletins, so that information could be provided without relying upon the general media.

A second institutionalized channel was that of the public and community relations organizations, such as the American Israel Public Affairs Committee, the American Jewish Committee, the American Jewish Congress and the Anti-Defamation League of B'nai B'rith, as well as the Conference of Presidents.

A third conduit was that of organized Zionism. The surge of Zionist organizational activity since the creation of the American Zionist Federation (one of the results of the Six Day War) is related to its responsibility for *aliyah* activities, particularly volunteer work. Organized Zionism plays its independent role in educational activities, providing technical assistance to educational agencies in the United States.

Finally, there were the synagogues. American Jews have shown that, at least for those among them who care, the synagogue is the first place Jews turn in times of trouble when they want to be with their fellows.[10] This phenomenon has clearly strengthened the synagogue in American Jewish societal structure, and it has also brought the synagogues into closer cooperation with communal agencies. The synagogues can serve as gathering places for large number of Jews, but by their very nature, they are not capable of mobilizing the Jewish community for a major national effort.

---

10. Curiously enough, one manifestation of this phenomenon came ten years earlier, at the time of John F. Kennedy's assassination. President Kennedy was murdered on Friday noon, and that Friday night, Jews from all over the United States flocked to their synagogues to find comfort with one another.

While not all the evidence is in, everything points to the fact that every Jewish organization in the United States wanted somehow to act in a positive way. Even the American Council for Judaism, now a shadow of its former self, issued a statement deploring the war and expressing special concern as a Jewish group for their "co-religionists" in Israel. For most Jewish organizations, action meant attempting to educate and mobilize their members to work through the major channels of the community. In some cases, where an organization offered specialized services (e.g., Hadassah, APPME), it was able to play a special role.

At least one relatively new organization received a certain impetus as a result of the war. The American Sephardi Federation, organized a year earlier to unite the Sephardic Jews of the United States, both in order to strengthen their own Jewish commitment and to assist their brethren in Israel, was able to mount its first major mass appeal as a result of the war. Since approximately half of the Sephardim in the United States are relative newcomers, refugees from Arab lands who have arrived in the United States since 1956, they are in some respects the least integrated group of American Jews, separated from their Ashkenazi fellows not only by two generations of immigration history, but also by different mother-tongue and culture. Even the half of the Sephardic population in the United States which has been in the country for several generations (for ten or twelve, in the case of the old-timers among them) has been at a loss to integrate with the overwhelmingly Ashkenazi American community. The war gave the Sephardic group a real opportunity to mobilize for the UJA and Bond drives in which $6 million was raised for the former and $12 million for the latter, from a population of between 100,000 and 150,000 people, many of whom were still struggling to establish themselves in this country.

Individual Response

There seems little question but that most of the response of American Jewry came from Jews who were already in the fold, whether fully or more tenuously, and whose ties were strengthened by the crisis. The war, at first sight, does not seem to have "converted" many unconcerned Jews by evoking in them a Jewish concern. The greater the original Jewish commitment, the stronger the reaction—that seems to be the general rule. This war was so stirring in that respect that even traditional opponents of the Jewish State from ultra-orthodox ranks came forward in support of Israel. The Satmarer Rebbe (a leader of the most extreme of the ultra-orthodox elements) made public statements to the effect that the war was to save the lives of Jews, and consequently of religious significance.

Perhaps the most important element in the spontaneous response of individual American Jews was that forged as a result of growing personal links with Israel. The Six Day War stimulated a far greater level of *aliyah* from the United States than ever before. While the numbers are still not very large, but considerable for a small country, there are now some thirty to forty thousand American Jews living in Israel on either a permanent or temporary basis. This means that, for the first time, many Jews in the United States have family or friendship ties with people living in Israel fully exposed to the dangers of war, and even many who are serving in the Israel armed forces.

The fact that the telephone lines between the United States and Israel were continuously jammed for the first week of the war, and calls were limited to five minutes, with long waiting periods before lines could even be obtained, was a reflection of this new situation. In the aftermath of the war, there was hardly a Jewish community of any size in the United States that had not lost a former member or suffered some casualties in the fighting. The New York Board of Rabbis, for example, set up a visitation committee to contact families in New York City whose sons were casualties on the fighting fronts. Even in smaller communities like Minneapolis, families suffered casualties. The sense of immediacy in all this was enhanced by the rapidity of communications. On October 16, the day the first casualties were revealed, the President of the Central Conference of American Rabbis informed his members of the loss of one of their colleagues in Israel. Thus,

American Jews followed the news of the war with a far more personal interest than in the past and contributed to the fight for Israel's survival on a very personal basis.

Conclusions

Given our closeness to the events, what can we tentatively conclude about the response of American Jewry to the Yom Kippur War? I suggest the following:

First, the American Jewish community, or at least those within it who act or support the actions of others, has become increasingly sophisticated about Israel and Jewish matters in general. Many more American Jews have had first hand contact with Israel and Israelis. Even those who have seen the country in the usual tourist manner have, as a result, a different sense of things, while young people and communal leaders of all ages, who have been in Israel for extended periods or on missions sponsored by the UJA and various Jewish organizations, have a far sharper impression of the Israeli situation and scene. In addition, the increased coverage of Israeli and Jewish news on the part of the general media has added something to the knowledge base of American Jews. Finally, Americans in general are more in touch with world affairs and political problems. This, too, has a certain carry-over within the Jewish community. Thus the response to Israel this time was a response made with open eyes, a fact most noticeable among the volunteers, most of whom have had far more contact with Israel than the average American.

Greater individual sophistication was paralleled by greater organizational efficiency as well, as we have already noted. Aside from that, what is noticeable is the war's impact on the continuing organizational integration of American Jewry, and the growing centralization of organized American Jewish life. In respect to the former, elsewhere this writer has suggested that the activities of American Jewry can be divided for analytical purposes into five spheres: religious-congregational; educational-cultural; community relations; communal welfare; Israel-overseas.[11]

11. See Daniel J. Elazar, "Decision Making in the American Jewish Community" in David Sidorsky, ed., *The Future of the American Jewish Community*, New York, 1973.

Hardly more than a generation ago, these five spheres functioned substantially separated from one another. In the 1950s, the first two developed integrating ties with one another and so did the last two. After the Six Day War, the community relations sphere began to be pulled into the communal-welfare/Israel-overseas orbit, and tentative links were forged between the latter and the educational-cultural sphere as well. The Yom Kippur War seems to have strengthened the links between all of them and even initiated, at least on a temporary basis, greater links between the religious-congregational and the communal-welfare spheres for the first time.

The Yom Kippur War, like the Six Day War before it, has led to increased centralization of power and authority within the American Jewish community. The process of centralization within the communal-welfare and Israel-overseas spheres has been going on for a long time. In addition to centralization at that level, the war has probably contributed to centralization on another level as well; the great need for funds to Israel caused independent institutions not connected with Israeli needs to suspend or abandon their own campaigns. It is likely that, even as those campaigns resume, the only American Jewish body to increase substantially its revenues in the current year will be the Federations and Welfare Funds. Thus there will be every incentive for other Jewish institutions and organizations to come to the Federations in search of more money.

This is a trend that is already very visible. As the Federations have taken on greater planning and programming responsibilities, they have sought to extend their funding to all the other spheres, except the religious-congregational one. In so doing, they have generally supported the upgrading of communal services, as well as the fostering of greater unity in the Jewish community. But even with their general commitment to self-restraint in imposing their policies on constituent and recipient agencies, their extension to funding privileges has been accompanied, quite properly, by a demand on their part for participation in the programs of those agencies. This process is not only likely to continue, but has probably been accelerated as a result of the war and the funding agreement that emerged from it. Synagogues are already beginning to turn to Federations for support for their schools. This trend is likely to be enhanced and it may even be that Federation funding will find its way into other activities of American Jewry.

One area in which there has been almost no evidence of increasing sophistication or organizational strength is that of the Anglo-Jewish press. Comparison of the reporting in the general press and the local Anglo-Jewish press in several communities during the war period shows that not only did American Jews have to rely upon the general press for more detailed and realistic information about the war, but even for information about the response of their own local communities to the war effort. While the mere fact that the general press provides such coverage takes some of the pressure off the Anglo-Jewish papers, it is also clear that the general press does not cover such issues with either the depth or the accuracy required for an informed Jewish community. The question can indeed be raised as to how long the Anglo-Jewish press can continue to avoid responding to the new needs of a younger and more enlightened reading public.

Yet another conclusion that can at least be tentatively advanced is that the war generated contradictory pulls within the circles that comprise American Jewry. Elsewhere, this writer has suggested that the American Jewish community, like all post-emancipation Diaspora communities, is essentially structured in a series of concentric circles, uneven in size and shape, surrounding a central magnet of Jewishness which pulls these circles toward it.[12] In the innermost circles are the most committed and involved Jews, those who live their Jewishness every day in every way. Beyond them, are the circles of those who are active in the community or simply affiliated with it. Finally, there are those peripheral groups of people who identify as Jews but do no more. They blend into a grey area where, given the manner of modern intermarriage and conversion, there exist people who do not really know whether they are Jewish or not.

It was also posited that, in times of crisis, the circles as a

12. *Ibid.*

whole are pulled closer to the magnet, while in times of normalcy, those further removed tend to drift away from its orbit. During the 1967 crisis, the people who seemingly came out from nowhere were actually already linked to the community in a tenuous way but were stimulated to move from their peripheral circle into one closer to the magnet. Only the rare exceptions moved from indifference to intensive Jewish living, although those who were merely affiliated might have become active, and the active ones, really intense Jews.

The initial evidence from the Yom Kippur War indicates that, with all the visible excitement of the response of large segments of the American Jewish community, this tendency for the circles to spread apart was sharpened. It may be that some people who had been in the outer circles were pulled across the gap into the inner ones, while many people in the outer circles were totally separated from the main body of the Jewish people. If that is indeed so, it means that American Jewry stands to lose a significant segment of its total population. At the same time, there seems to be almost no question that within the inner circles, the intensity of Jewish feeling grew as a result of the war, and the willingness of Jews to express themselves openly as Jews became even more apparent.

One aspect of these shifting relationships is that those people who are becoming more Jewish are becoming integrated into a worldwide Jewish community, and expect to be mobilized to meet Jewish crises wherever they may occur. The relatively large-scale interest in volunteering is perhaps the best example of that new spirit. What is missing is a way to develop it.

There is overwhelming evidence, even at this early date, that educational efforts represent part of the first line of defense of the Jewish people. The best responses to the war came from those who had been exposed to Jewish education. This does not necessarily mean a formal Jewish education, although it is becoming clear that formal Jewish education is highly correlated with continued interest in Jewish concerns. The educational programs associated with the fund-raising efforts of the past several decades in American Jewish life

have been directed to producing knowledgeable Jews. For the
most part, the people who were in these programs are the ones
who made real contributions during the Yom Kippur War.

Two lessons emerge: first, the redoubled efforts to
educate Jews to be Jews are of the utmost importance for the
very safety of Israel; and, second, education linked with
experience, is perhaps the best education of all. Again, the
American Jewish community has recognized both of these
things for some time, and has been moving in the direction of
acting in response to them. The war may well accelerate that
movement.

Another, and perhaps most important, lesson to be
derived from the Yom Kippur War is that the Zionist dream
that Israel would bring about the normalization of the Jewish
people has been proved fundamentally wrong. It is true that,
in the immediate sense, the social structure of Israeli Jewry
has become more nearly normal and the mentality of the
Israeli Jew has changed markedly from that of the *galut* Jew of
the past. But the war has shown once more that Jews, for one
reason or another, fail to arouse the sympathy of the world
when they are victims of aggression or even when they act as
the world would have them, waiting for the enemy to strike.
This is a hard truth, one that has struck the Israelis with great
ferocity.

It has struck the American Jews no less, though in a
slightly different way. They have traditionally looked upon
their experience in America as one of normalization, akin to
that of the Jews in Israel. The United States, a country bound
together by an implicit covenant among the immigrants who
have chosen to settle within its boundaries, in which all men
are equal citizens, no one having more "American status"
than any other, seemed to the Jews who came to its shores to
be an answer to the Jewish problem of normalization. Jews
could simply become Americans like others, without ever
having to feel that they were strangers, dependent upon the
bounty of their hosts. That, indeed, proved to be and
continues to be substantially true for those Jews for whom
serious Jewish ties or identity are no problem.

However, for those Jews who do not wish to assimilate,
the question of normalization has emerged into sharp focus as

a result of the Yom Kippur War. *Newsweek* referred to the "nervous American Jews." While that article was typical of the kind of impressionistic journalism characteristic of American news magazines, it still pointed to a certain fundamental truth, namely, that American Jews have to confront the fact that they have different interests from other sub-groups within American society, interests which transcend their American background.

Thus American Jews have also gone beyond the stage of normalization. The Yom Kippur War has brought that stage to an end whether American Jewry is prepared to recognize it or not. After the Six Day War, it was widely suggested that Jewry had entered into a post-emancipation age. The willingness of young Jews to express their Jewishness openly, precisely because they had grown up in an emancipated modern society, was the surest sign that this was a fact. The Yom Kippur War may have brought us to a post-Zionist age, in the sense that what will come to the fore now is a renewed sense of the Jewishness of the Jewish people—not in the ways of nineteenth century nationalism, or eighteenth century emancipation, but in a new version of Jewish living. That, indeed, may be the key lesson to be learned from the response of American, Israeli, and world Jewry to the Yom Kippur War.

United States of America: Perspectives

Alfred Gottschalk

In recent years the Jewish people seemed to have overleapt the bounds of their own limitations and shed their self-definitions to begin creating a oneness perhaps unparalleled in all of Jewish history. A profound sense began to prevail that the structural realities of modern Israel and world Jewry had changed. Somehow the seemingly vacuous debates on Israel and the *galut* disappeared in a ground-swell of Jewish out-reach, in Jewish striving for unity on a worldwide scale—a striving which defied the neat categories developed by cautious historians and theologians. Much has been said and written of the emergence of a greater Israel, not merely in geographic terms but also in terms of the newly emergent ethnic spirit which transcended or spurned ideologies and ideologues and heralded a new expression of Jewish globalism.

An ancient injunction on prayer, for example, took on a multi-dimensional significance. Religionists and secularists, even quasi-assimilationists, understood the instruction.

> Those who stand up to pray in countries outside the land of Israel, direct their hearts toward the land of Israel and pray, for it is said: "They shall pray unto the Lord toward the land which . . . thou hast chosen." Those who rise to pray within the land of Israel direct their hearts toward Jerusalem and pray, for it is said: "They shall pray toward this city." Those rising for prayer in Jerusalem direct their hearts toward the Temple and pray, for it is said: "And they shall pray toward this place." Hence, those standing north of Palestine face the south, those south face the north, those east face the west, and those standing in the west face the east. Thus all Israel prays toward one place" (*Tosefta B'rachot* 3:15; *Sifre Deut.* 28).

Within Israel, too, there occurred almost instantaneously an awakening to the fact that the much maligned *golah* also

36

contained its share—an abundant share—of courageous and profoundly concerned Jews.

Equally qualitative changes began to take place in world Jewish communities. In the free world sleeping giants of Jewish communities bestirred themselves. Many Jews who had never imagined that a grave danger to Israel could dominate their consciousness to the exclusion of virtually everything else found themselves linking their personal fate inextricably to the fate of their brethren in Israel. Jews who had undergone the assimilatory process in all its fullness found the redeeming spark of Jewish affinity becoming a high flame animating their very being. Surely, this was a phenomenon unexpected by those in Israel who had written the Diaspora off as *galut,* where the atrophy of Jewish consciousness in the absence of *aliyah* has long been predicted.

American Jews—whether religious or not, whether officially Zionist or not—responded not only with an outpouring of funds, but with an outpouring of anxious concern. Even those critical of Israel began living from news broadcast to news broadcast. The well-known American academician and intellectual, Irving Kristol, surely spoke for a respectable number of his fellow American Jews when he described in the *Wall Street Journal,* how he found himself "getting up at dawn to listen anxiously to the radio reports." Kristol went on to ask himself: "Why am I so deeply affected? I am not an Orthodox Jew, and only a barely observant one. I am not a Zionist and I did not find my two visits to Israel to have been particularly exhilarating . . . none of the Israeli ways of life . . . had any great appeal for me." Why, then, was he able to say: "I care desperately"? His answer was that he sensed, as he put it, "deep down, that what happens to Israel will be decisive for Jewish history, and for the kinds of lives my grandchildren and great-grandchildren will be leading."

Irving Kristol is no utopian or messianist. He does not hesitate to criticize "the dominant political tradition" of Israel which he labels "democratic-socialist," and he admits to being "a warmer admirer of the Old Testament than of modern social democracy" and to "preferring the patriarchs to the prophets." Most probably it would not be an egregious error to designate him a conservative in his political and social philosophy. Morris U. Schappes, editor of *Jewish Currents,* a periodical which refers to itself as "progressive," is not a man who could be expected to show much sympathy for Kristol's philosophy. Schappes, too, is an intellectual and an academician, but for him the prophets—and his canon includes Karl Marx and Vladimir Lenin—are much to be preferred to the patriarchs. Yet Schappes was no more able than Kristol to conceal his concern for Israel's fate. The spectacle of American Jews "straining," as he said, "to be of help to their embattled kin in Israel" was something to be grateful for, not contemptuous of. So the Marxist Schappes worried about Israel: "Who can credit the claim of Premier Anwar Sadat that his war aim is only the recovery of Sinai? Any one war lost by Israel is seen to mean the end of Israel and survival is the issue." And he went on to quote with approval the declaration of the left-wing Yiddish daily *Morgen Freiheit:* "For the Jewish people, the eruption of the war evoked the specter of a new holocaust. It looked like an attempt to wipe out the Jewish State once and for all—through a war on all sides. . . . And that fear cannot be stilled so long as blood is being shed. . . ." Schappes, of course, belongs to what we would have to call the Old Left, but the Old Left has not yet departed the American scene. Schappes, too, does not speak for himself alone.

Among secularist Jews for whom Jewishness, Jewish identity, is more than a decayed memory, more than a relic of a distant and unappealing past, Kristol and Schappes represent extremes of the political and philosophical spectrum. Yet they seem to be, if not precisely in the same camp, at least in the same perimeter of concern for Israel's survival. Kristol wrote of being "glued" to his transistor; Schappes wrote of "the hearts of American Jews . . . thumping loudly in rhythm to TV scenes of artillery bombardments. . . ." Neither, notwithstanding an alienation from the synagogue and a lack of enthusiasm for Israel's political orientation, could regard with even minimal equanimity the prospect of Israeli defeat and extinction.

That Jews of the Western world who were secure in their freedom responded to Israel's plight was comforting and reassuring and maybe even expected, but that Soviet Jewry, perhaps the most assimilated and de-Judaized Jewry in the world today, would rise, slowly at first and then surge as a mighty stream—this was a genuinely revolutionary development. Here was the hard proof that there were Jews in growing numbers living under abject tyranny but not in abject fear, Jews who asserted even under house arrest and from prisons, "cancer wards," and "mental asylums," to which they had been committed in their moment of greatest lucidity, that they were Jews and that their homeland was Israel.

Israelis and other Jews throughout the world, who not so long ago had tended to see Russian Jewry as a lost cause, experienced a revelation which dramatized the indissoluble oneness of the Jews as a world people. No matter how that configuration of a world people might be distorted at particular moments in history, here it was again for all the sceptics to see. However dormant our underlying unity of national or ethnic and religious consciousness might be, the old rabbinic dictum of *kol Yisrael arevim zeh ba-zeh*, proved most enduring and insightful. While Jews had always responded tellingly to threats against the physical and spiritual welfare of their brethren, the response to the threat of Israel's extinction from May 23, 1967, when Nasser closed the Gulf of Aqaba, to the end of the war on June 10, was qualitatively different.

Even more intense and sober was the Diaspora reaction to the Yom Kippur War. It is clear that the Yom Kippur War heightened the sense of interdependence among all parts of the Jewish people. The events of May 1967 had revived the memory of the Holocaust. But the Yom Kippur War gave that prospect even greater focus. How that sense of a common fate galvanized American Jewry is cogently exemplified by the Reform movement in American Judaism.

Response within the Reform Movement

Yom Kippur day I worshipped at the Plum Street Temple in Cincinnati, Ohio, the cradle of American Reform Jewry. This synagogue, which was nurtured on non-Zionist ideology, slowly became electrified as the realities of the attack took hold. Not since the Japanese assault on Pearl Harbor, on December 7, 1941, was such a sense of outrage felt. The very nature of this war made it ominous from the outset; it seemed to tear at the very fiber of Jewish existence.

Reform Judaism in the United States includes within its ambit a million of the nearly six million members of the American Jewish community. When the Egyptians and Syrians launched their attack on Israel, the entire movement marshalled its forces for support of the Israeli cause. As a widely distributed pamphlet issued by the Union of American Hebrew Congregations put it: "It is incumbent upon every Jew to offer financial support to the fullest extent of his capabilities, and to solicit further assistance from all men who believe in freedom and the right of a sovereign state to live in peace and security." Reform Judaism, as is well known, has had and continues to have its differences with the Israeli religious establishment, which has thus far been willing to recognize the credentials of Orthodox rabbis alone. But all this was unhesitatingly set aside. "As members of the Household of Israel," said the UAHC pamphlet, "we felt . . . our obligation. . . . When Jewish life is threatened—as it is now . . . matters of internal disagreement fade into insignificance against the Jewish crisis of the day."[1]

The UAHC poured all its energies into meeting the emergency. Its national staff and its regional staffs joined forces to constitute themselves a task force. A center for fund raising, information distribution, and volunteer recruitment was set up at the UAHC's New York headquarters, and similar centers were established in every UAHC region throughout America. Not only were sizable sums raised in this fashion, but the general community was supplied with information about the war and its issues. Thousands of telegrams and letters urging government support of Israel were generated. UAHC affiliates like the Jewish Chautauqua Society of the National Federation of Temple Brotherhoods, the National Federation of Temple Sisterhoods, the Commission on Social Action, the Commission on Israel of the Union of American

---

1. *Middle East Up-Date: Questions and Answers,* Compiled by Albert Vorspan and Ira S. Youdovin (mimeograph), UAHC, New York, Nov. 1, 1973, p. 6.

Hebrew Congregations, and the Central Conference of American Rabbis, and the World Union for Progressive Judaism (the movement's international association, headquartered in Jerusalem) were all mobilized to support and intensify the UAHC effort. Member congregations also responded generously and energetically, so much so indeed that the UAHC's president-elect, Rabbi Alexander M. Schindler, could say, "The synagogue was the key."[2]

To cite responses of just a few congregations, the board of the Isaac M. Wise Temple in Cincinnati unanimously decided "to postpone indefinitely the construction of a new facility, and . . . to invest the bulk of the remaining proceeds from the sale (of its old facility) . . . in Israel Bonds."[3]

Cincinnati's Valley Temple, which had been founded in the 1950s with an anti-Zionist American Council for Judaism orientation, appealed to its membership to participate in a plan whereby all the Cincinnati synagogues would borrow three million dollars for the purchase of Israel bonds; the president of the Valley Temple urged his congregation to obligate itself for "at least $150,000 of these bonds."[4] The members of Temple Beth El in Knoxville, Tennessee, were urgently requested to contact President Nixon, Secretary of State Kissinger, and United Nations Secretary-General Waldheim in support of Israel.[5] Parallel activities and expressions of feeling were encountered in virtually every one of the UAHC's 700 congregations.

The Central Conference of American Rabbis, in addition to giving its full support to the joint Commission on Israel and endorsing participation in the nationwide Yom Kippur Sheni program, recommended that Reform rabbis of America "call on your senators and representatives to speak out publicly in strong support of the position of the President and Secretary of State in opposing Soviet blackmail and in

2. *Reform Judaism: Publication of the Union of American Hebrew Congregations,* New York, November 1973, p. 10.
3. Jacob K. Stein, President, Isaac M. Wise Temple, Cincinnati, to the members of the congregation, October 17, 1973 (files, American Jewish Archives [AJA]).
4. Bernard S. Reckseit, President, Valley Temple, Cincinnati, to the members of the congregation, October 30, 1973 (files, *AJA*).
5. Matthew I. Derby, Rabbi, Temple Beth El, Knoxville, Tenn., to the members of the congregation, Oct. 10, 1973 (files, *AJA*).

continuing to re-supply Israel with urgently needed equipment."[6] In Rochester, New York, Rabbi Judea B. Miller of Temple B'rith Kodesh wrote an article for the *Rochester Democrat and Chronicle,* in which he said that what is at stake "is really the survival or destruction of the State of Israel."[7] In a Boston suburb, Rabbi Thomas P. Liebschutz of Malden's Temple Tifereth Israel applauded the Reform movement's "profound concern for Israel" and agreed that a major emphasis of Reform Judaism had to be "a continuing concern for Israel in the aftermath of the Middle East war."[8] Such sentiments were heard from one end of the country to the other.

The faculties, students, and staffs of all four campuses of the Hebrew Union College-Jewish Institute of Religion recognized at once the ultimate meaning of the Arab attack: *being a Jew means living on a very narrow ledge of history,* a ledge from which our enemies ever seek to push us into death and oblivion. They shared Israel's indomitable will to survive. Many on its three American campuses were eager to join the thousands crowding the airports to volunteer their services in Israel, but being informed by the Jewish Agency authorities that the College's greatest service could be rendered in America, educating Jews and non-Jews about the needs of Israel and the issues of the conflict, the College complied. The Hebrew Union College community resolved "to provide whatever services we are able to perform in response to the dire needs of the hour." It was "fully prepared, if necessary, to reschedule, postpone or cancel normal academic endeavors" and "join with Jews throughout the world in a bond of commitment and action." I have no doubt whatsoever that we spoke for the entirety of Reform Jews in declaring: *"Am Yisrael Hai!* The People of Israel lives."[9]

6. Joseph B. Glaser, Executive Vice-President, CCAR, New York, to the members of the CCAR, Oct. 29, 1973 (files, *AJA*). See also Robert T. Kahn, "From the (CCAR) President: A Prayer for Israel," *Central Conference of American Rabbis Journal,* Autumn 1973, p. 2.
7.   "Arabs on Flight from Reality That's Madness," *Rochester Democrat and Chronicle,* Oct. 28, 1973.
8.   "Rabbi's Message," *Temple Tifereth Israel Bulletin,* Malden, Mass., Dec. 4, 1973.
9. See Kenneth D. Roseman, Dean, HUC-JIR, Cincinnati, "Response to the Yom Kippur War at Hebrew Union College-Jewish Institute of Religion, Cincinnati, Ohio"

Faculty members and students, in addition to contributing as much as they could themselves to the Israel Emergency Fund, made themselves available for placement in their communities and set out on a host of activities geared to fund raising and distribution of information. Some Cincinnati students drove an *Israel Action Mobile* to various shopping, recreational, and communal centers in the city in an effort to raise funds and distribute information among the general public. Student rabbis called on the biweekly congregations they serve in various parts of the country—mostly small Jewish communities which are not usually linked to the UJA's fund-raising apparatus—to support the Israel Emergency Fund. One student rabbi raised $30,000 in the Texas-Oklahoma area; another raised nearly as much in the Western Tennessee-Western Kentucky-Southern Illinois area.[10] In New York our students joined with other student groups in demonstrations before the Egyptian and Syrian United Nations delegations to demand that the Arabs give the Red Cross lists of Israeli prisoners of war. In Los Angeles students served in car pools to deliver information to various agencies in the community and to pick up large gifts which were needed without delay. They helped lead a number of community youth activities on behalf of the Israeli cause.[11] On all our campuses, there was no hesitation about suspending classes when that was necessary.

The campus in Jerusalem immediately went on a war footing. *Haga,* the civil defense force, utilized the campus as its area headquarters, and most of the College's vehicles were placed at the disposal of the Israel government. Israeli members of the Jerusalem staff were called up for military service. The students—for the most part Americans spending the first year of their rabbinical education in Jerusalem —mobilized to volunteer their services on the home front. Some volunteered for work at Hadassah and other hospitals.

(typescript; files, *AJA*). See also "President's Report to the (HUC-JIR) Board of Governors." Nov. 8, 1973. I am particularly grateful to Stanley Chyet, Professor of American Jewish History at the College, for his assessment of much of this material.
10. *Ibid.*
11. See statement by William Cutter, of HUC faculty, Los Angeles, Dec. 1973 (files, *AJA*).

Others did volunteer driving and worked at bakeries or took over *kibbutz* jobs to replace mobilized *kibbutzniks*. A group of students gave concerts at army bases as far down as Sinai. Custodial and guard duty was undertaken at a variety of institutions—among them the Kol Yisrael headquarters, the NBC Broadcasting Studio in Herzliah, the Israel Museum in Jerusalem, and WIZO's Child Care Center.[12]

Response from College Campuses in United States

What of the American collegian of Jewish origin not known to be affiliated with any established group? Did the Yom Kippur War confirm the impression held by many that he did not care? Apathy was *not* the typical response. Sherman Teichman, a graduate student at Washington University in St. Louis, is editor of a journal called *ACIID* (*A Critical Insight Into Israel's Dilemmas*)—a journal which not infrequently has been quite critical of Israeli policies. Teichman wrote that we cannot let "a perverted sense of 'progressivism' symbolized by Egypt and Syria with the support of the Soviet Union overwhelm Israel's fundamental right to exist. . . . When the survival of Israel is assured," he said, "then we can go back to the luxury of bickering among ourselves about specific policies, settlements . . . annexation, for instance."[13] Is Teichman a maverick?

Was Uri Levi, a 19-year-old art student in Boston, a maverick when he left his studies for volunteer work in Israel at Sde Boker? Levi made it clear that his work in Boston had been going very well, "but when the war broke out," he said, "it just hit me emotionally. I couldn't handle being over there (in America) any more." Levi found his duties at Sde Boker "uninteresting and . . . unglamorous," but, as he put it, "my commitment here is emotional, not political. Politically, I have a lot of objections to what goes on."[14] The fact that, by

12. Janet Kaplan, "Report to Hebrew Union College. . ." on the Yom Kippur War activities of HUC, Jerusalem. Oct. 22, 1973 (files, *AJA*).
13. Robert A. Cohn, "*ACIID*, Student Magazine, Gives Mideast Information to Campus," *St. Louis* (Mo.) *Jewish Light*, October 24, 1973.
14. Karen Heller, "Young Volunteers to Aid Israel Find Work Hard," *Cincinnati Enquirer*, December 9, 1973.

the end of October, the United Jewish Appeal could report that a quarter of a million Jewish college students were "involved in around-the-clock campaign activities all over the United States" would suggest that Teichman and Levi cannot be seen as unusual among collegians in their wish to be of help to the Israeli war effort.[15]

These examples of reaction to the Yom Kippur War in the United States illustrate that the Jews in this country tend to see themselves in a new and closer relationship to Israel. In great measure, the heightened awareness of another possible Holocaust and positive factors of renewed Jewish identification engendered by the Six Day War have created a new climate in the Diaspora of support for Israel and for grass-roots Jewish affiliation in their own countries.

But serious questions wait for answers. Everywhere there seems general agreement that the Jewish student population is an unknown quantity. Even in Israel there is reason to believe that some Israelis born at the time of the State's establishment think of emigrating and need to be convinced that life in their homeland is not meaningless.[16]

Future Relations of Israel and American Jewry

The activity of American Jewry from October 6 until today has been well charted. The political pressure, information programs, rallies, marches, demonstrations, all strengthened the foundations of community action first attempted during the Six Day War and brought to consummation during the recent crisis. The sad caveat that must be added is that, while there is every indication that American Jewry's response was overwhelming, there remained a vast sector of American Jews who showed no demonstrable concern.

There is a struggle confronting the American Jewish community. What I have described ought to be seen and evaluated in that light. American Jews—whoever and wherever they are, whatever they do—cannot be thought of as living in a vacuum. They live in a society which happens to be in

15. "College Students Mobilize for United Jewish Appeal," *UJA News*, October 30, 1973 (files, *AJA*).
16. *"Na L'Hachlit"* ("Please Decide"), in *Haaretz*, March 1, 1974, p. 13.

many respects a confusing and troubled society. Their efforts on behalf of Israel will not endear them to many of their non-Jewish neighbors. How formidable the opposition within non-Jewish ranks will be, no one can say for sure, but it is not likely to be inconsiderable. And I think that many—maybe even most—American Jews are aware of this and nervous about it. Does that mean they will falter in their support for Israel?

On the other hand, a not inconsiderable by-product of the response of organized Jewish communities was the continuing organizational integration and centralization of American Jewish life. American Jewry's religious, educational, community-welfare, community-relations, and Israel and overseas agencies, in a new-found sophistication, are moving toward a *de facto* restructuring of their communities.

In a general way, America's pro-Israel posture softened the harsh reality sensed elsewhere in the world that, when it comes to Jews and Israel, despite our normalization and assimilation we remain a "people set apart." We are one people living in concentric circles of Diaspora communities around the center, which is Israel. Perhaps this awareness of our unity despite our dispersion can lead Israel and American Jewry into new areas of understanding and agreement. What is involved at the Israeli end is the need to realize that Israel, both people and organizations, must engage the Diaspora in significant, well measured areas of relationship reflecting a partnership of rights and obligations. The equality of our partnership stems from our participation in the weal and fate of Jewry as a whole.

The Diaspora has needs which in many areas only Israel can provide. Our needs are for a fuller cultural, social, and religious participation in the life of Israel. Reform Jews recognize their responsibility to encourage *aliyah* but not on the terms of having our *olim* questioned as to whether they are really Jews. Their act of personal commitment through *aliyah* should speak for itself. Our plea is that concrete steps need to be taken to recognize the legitimacy of self-electing emancipated Jews who espouse the right of choosing the terms of their own Jewishness. All evidence of the Diaspora's response to the Yom Kippur War indicates that the notion of Jewish peoplehood should be inclusive rather than exclusive. In such a conception the legitimacy of Jewish diversity must be recognized. Israel, while remaining the *center,* must grant that legitimacy to the Jews of the Diaspora.

This is after all not such a new concept for Zionist ideology. Ahad Ha-Am had championed this view at the turn of the century and maintained it as a necessary corollary in his notion of Israel itself as a *merkaz ruhani,* a "spiritual center." As Ahad Ha-Am saw it, Eretz Yisrael was the hub of the wheel. The spokes of the Diaspora were always an important factor in his conception of Jewish destiny. Consequently, his thought was Diaspora-oriented as well. Israel continues, because of natural circumstances, to be the creator of new Jewish patterns of thought and culture. It is interesting that Ahad Ha-Am conceived of a two-fold *galut*—a physical *galut* which no Zionism could utterly obliterate and a spiritual *galut* which Ahad Ha-Am claimed could be escaped.

What purpose could there be for this center—apart of course from its being a haven for the oppressed of our people? David Ben Gurion spoke of the State of Israel as a vehicle for the redemption of man, for the implementation of the prophetic society to which Ahad Ha-Am had alluded. "Anyone who does not realize that the Messianic vision of redemption is central to the uniqueness of our people does not realize the basic truth of Jewish history and the cornerstone of Jewish faith."[17] He argued that there had to be a uniqueness to Israel, that it had to embody a difference to make it distinctive from other nation-states. Was it all pie in the sky, so to speak? Were Ahad Ha-Am and Ben Gurion expressing a sensibility which a later generation could never have claimed for itself? If so, how are we to account for the words of Chief of Staff Yitzhak Rabin shortly after the Six Day War? He spoke of soldiers who could not celebrate the victory of the Six Day War, for they had seen "not only the glory of victory, but also the price of victory—their comrades fallen beside them. . . ." And he went on, "I know too that the terrible price paid by our enemies also touched the hearts of many of our men. It may be that the Jewish people has never learned and never

17. *Forum,* IV, p. 113.

accustomed itself to feel the triumph of conquest and victory, with the result that these are accepted with mixed feelings. . . ."[18]

The time is now to begin the redemptive process within our people. We can build a living bridge of Jews who will traverse the tangents between the center and the Diaspora. Let those of us who are part of the modern world in Israel and the Diaspora write a new *K'tav Amanah,* a document of mutual trust and belief; let us try to develop a general overarching ideology in which we all can share. Jews who find their place by conviction in the camp of Progressive Judaism are ready to begin. It should be intriguing to Israelis that those who were called the most assimilated and non-Zionist of religious Jews in the Diaspora have been the first to move their international headquarters, the World Center for Progressive Judaism, to Israel. It should give them pause that this most modern of Jewish religious movements has sought to pioneer new modes of Jewish religious and national life in Israel; that its rabbis in *Zahal* serve in the tank corps and as anti-aircraft gunners and ordinary soldiers; that its Hebrew Union College in the heart of Jerusalem, in 1967 and again in 1973, functioned as a fully integrated unit within Israeli life. Thus Reform Jews are in Israel not as occasional visitors, but as a firmly planted and legitimate factor of Israeli life. Reform Judaism does not have all the answers to the future of Jewish existence. Perhaps too often to its own hurt, the question sometimes proves to be more important than the answer. But that is the nature of a liberal conception. Indeed, the time has come to take a new look at the relationships between Israel and the Diaspora and pursue the question with whatever self-searching and even agony prove necessary.

18. Address by Major-General Yitzhak Rabin, Hebrew University of Jerusalem, 1967, pp. 7-8.

United States of America: Perspectives

Norman Lamm

The events of the Yom Kippur War and its aftermath are so traumatic, that we do not yet have the mental equanimity to assess the situation in the psychological calm requisite for such judgments. Perhaps an halakhic analogy is apt: the *avel* (mourner after the deceased has been buried) is expected to grieve over a situation which he then begins to perceive and perhaps even understand. But the *onen* (mourner before interment) is released from all religious obligations to mourn because he is assumed to be so stunned that he has not absorbed the gravity of his predicament and its implications. Nevertheless, certain moods have already made themselves felt.

Reactions of Intellectuals

Among the intellectuals, in which group I include the more thoughtful American journalists, the moral issue appears to have three aspects. Some have been beguiled by Arab arguments, and build their case around earlier insults to Arab manhood and dignity, the need to acknowledge the national aspiration of the Palestinians, and the imperative to return territories won by military action. Underlying this is the question of the legitimacy of the Jewish claim to a national homeland in the Middle East. A second group is amoralistic, preferring to deal with the political issues purely on a pragmatic basis, with the major consideration being America's national interest, however that interest may be defined. A third group dismisses the amoralist position as untenable and as inconsistent with American foreign policy over the years, and sees Israel as mostly or altogether in the right.

I suspect that a good part of the uncharacteristic silence of the intellectuals derives from their acute dilemma

49

regarding the Third World. In their own way, intellectuals can be more conformist than *hoi polloi*. They are waiting to see how their colleagues will react to the astounding conduct of the non-aligned nations who have solidly joined forces with the Arabs. Third World nations became the *cause celebre* of liberal intellectuals because they were poor and weak. Now they suddenly act out of motives that are as cynical as those of any of the great powers.

Among intellectuals with a positive attitude toward Judaism, the deliberations in the United Nations and the fading away of West European support have proved a blow to conventional (or "traditional") American Jewish liberalism. This liberalism formerly looked askance at nationalisms as such, and assumed rather romantically that collectivity somehow does not possess the faults of its constituent parts: the United Nations, as the "Family of Man," will be the secular analogue of the prophet Elijah as the harbinger of the Messiah. But the ugly scenes in this vindictive and loveless "Family" have dealt a severe blow to political optimism. A sense of loneliness, deep and penetrating, has set in.

The same facts seem to have a different effect on American Jewish intellectuals less favorably predisposed to Israel in the past. The Yom Kippur War is seen as having made everything more uncertain than ever. Israel may not be viable and American Jews may no longer be as secure as they were. The ghost of American anti-Semitism has never really been laid to rest, despite the protestations of many native American Jews that they never experienced anti-Semitism. There is real concern that the energy crisis and inflation will result in a severe recession, bringing the anti-Semitic worms out of the woodwork and negating the accomplishments of American Jews since World War II. If this is indeed the case, such intellectuals will, I believe, abandon all support of Israel.

Israel's Image

For the intellectuals as well as for everyone else, however, there is another element to be considered that is more psychological and subtle than the issues adumbrated so far. The Yom Kippur War was for Jews a trauma of the order that Vietnam was for most Americans. This psychological, and perhaps spiritual, issue revolves around the question of image and the values that feed it and flow from it. I do not believe that this is the only or even the most important issue, but it is so significant that to ignore it would be irresponsible.

Heretofore, many friends of Israel of all faiths have had a somewhat ambivalent attitude to the State. On a conscious level, there was delight in Jewish self-assertion and pride, and admiration for the tough Israel-born sabra. People took vicarious pleasure in his self-confidence, brashness, even his rudeness. The *galut* mentality with its timidity, self-abnegation, and passion for invisibility, had for so long been a burden and a shame, that the successful effort of Zionists deliberately to change that image and that reality was applauded.

On a more unconscious level, however, things were not always quite that clear. In an occasional article, in a snatch of intimate conversation, one could sense a pervasive uneasiness, particularly on the part of certain Jews. Was it merely that the *galut* mentality was causing mental pain as it was being extracted and replaced by the image of the new *Homo Israeli?* Perhaps, and perhaps something more than that. A number of factors seem to have contributed to this inner malaise. There was an unexpressed fear that the bubble would burst, and the inexorable numerical superiority of the Arabs and the underlying anti-Semitism of the Christian West would eventually join forces, rise, and take revenge. There was apprehension that Israeli braggadocio was too extravagant and would unnecessarily provoke resentment. There was an uncomfortable feeling that the Jews, who had always protested militarism in American politics, who had always been hypersensitive to the influence of the military in government, were now passively accepting a situation in Israel in which military officers were taking command in the highest levels of government and industry. This discomfort was not allayed by the knowledge that Israel's was largely a civilian army, that many of its most distinguished leaders were scholars, that, in Israel's awkward and ponderous bureaucracy, the army was perhaps the most efficient organization. There was, too, an annoyance at the inversion of traditional Jewish values such as the abhorrence of bloodshed, the reluctance to rely on force alone, or at the very least, the aversion to glorifying the arms and weapons instead of the achievements of the mind, the heart, and the spirit.

It is these diverse and yet related feelings that emerged almost angrily when the Arab surprise attack "demytholo-gized" the popular image of Israel. The later successful counterattack by the Israelis, no matter how brilliant, did not make up for the sudden feeling that we had all been "taken." Jews began to look back wistfully to their youth, ended just a month or two earlier, when it seemed that everything was so certain, so clear, so secure. Dying illusions are painful, and also enraging.

Suddenly on Yom Kippur more than one American Jew became sharply aware of these and related questions. What was all that rhetoric about relying on "our own strength"? Had independence for Israel become not merely a non-negoti-able national value, worth every sacrifice, but an ideological fixation and a theological absolute, in an age when even great powers have to depend upon each other for survival, when mighty nations are often reduced to diplomatic sycophancy? This resentment—focused as much on oneself and one's own gullibility as on Israel—of course exaggerated matters, overlooked the pressure of historical circumstances, general-ized too much, and lacked intellectual sophistication and analytic depth. But it was real—it still is—and may be a major psychological underpinning for the standoffishness of many intellectuals, and for the distress of even those who rallied to the flag and labored zealously with other Jews for Israel.

One can, of course, interpret these originally inchoate feelings less charitably and more cynically, and discover in American Jews, particularly intellectuals, an inner resentment of Israeli assertiveness and pride. This would attribute to American Jews, still entangled in the tentacles of their old *galut* complex, a sub-conscious jealousy of the martial components of the Israeli charisma. Such an assertion may have only a measure of validity; but it is no less a fact for being psychological and irrational.

This erroneous and unrealistic image projected by Israel represents not only a public-relations failure (which it is

because the one-sided view neglects so many of the human and constructive features of the State), but also an educational disaster of vast proportions. What is needed is a profound reordering of priorities in creating a new conception of what the Israeli would like to be, a model for his own future development. The answer, I believe, lies in the direction of a synthesis of the new Israeli dignity of regained nationhood with the pioneering spirit and moral commitment of early Zionism, and these, above all, integrated into the continuum of the historic spiritual values of the Jewish traditon.

We can afford nothing less, because the present image can only bring us grief—witness the ludicrous "imperialism" charge so seriously and solemnly hurled at us by otherwise intelligent people. Daniel Elazar has observed that many Diaspora Jews, having lost faith in God and Torah, have begun to apotheosize the State of Israel. I subscribe to his assertion of the existence of this "Israelolatry." We have contributed to this dangerous attitude which has made the State an end in itself. In true religious fashion, its worshipers have attributed to their idol the qualities of power, wisdom, and benevolence to an absolute degree. Like all objects of faith, Israel has been exalted beyond criticism. The danger is that, ultimately, the idol will be found to have clay feet. And when that happens, the devotees will blame not their own gullibility but the limitations and inadequacy of the idol.

The figure of David has often been conjured up as the historical model or metaphor for the new Jew of Israel. It is a good symbol, provided it takes David in the fullness in which he appears both in the Bible and in the Jewish oral tradition. Little David confronting Goliath is not an incorrect image. But it is inadequate. David was the fighter and the king, but also the composer of psalms. David had not only a slingshot, but a harp. He was soldier and poet, fighter and musician, a sinner who was manly enough to accept criticism and change his ways, a brave warrior who was not ashamed to be afraid and trusted in a Higher Force, a general who prayed, a student of Torah and of political sophistication, and a man of firmness and moral magnanimity.

It is this traditional image which inspires Orthodox Jewry in all its sub-groupings. Their response to the crisis may help illuminate the wider spectrum of American Jewish feelings.

Positions in American Orthodoxy

Orthodox circles in the United States experienced a remarkable identification with Israel no matter what disagreements individual religious groups or individuals may have had with Israeli policy or society, and no matter how bitter their previous frustrations. On Yom Kippur day, political and religious differences with regard to Israel faded and all religious Jews, whether Agudah, Mizrachi, or unaffiliated, showed genuinely deep concern, worry, and a desire to help in every way possible.

Yet, despite this feeling of solidarity with Israel in its time of crisis, almost all religious groups experienced a reaction similar to the disaffection of the intellectuals. It might be called an alliance of the religious right and the political left in decrying the excessive pride that has come to be associated with Israeli statehood. The attitude is one against which Moses warned at the threshold of Israel's entry into Canaan:

> Then thy heart be lifted up, and thou forget the Lord thy God, who brought thee forth out of the land of Egypt, out of the house of bondage. . . .And thou say in thy heart: *"My power and the might of my hand have gotten me this wealth."* But thou shalt remember the Lord thy God, for it is He that giveth thee power to get wealth, that He may establish His covenant which He swore unto thy fathers. . . .[1]

It is this Biblical exhortation—and it is surely a fundamental of the whole religious *Weltanschauung* of Judaism—that makes the oft-repeated assertions that "we can rely only on our own strength" sound so abrasive and sacrilegious, even blasphemous. Traditional Judaism is by no means pacifist, but it rejects arrogance and self-assertion which ascribe power and success to arms alone.

Religious Jews were upset when the Declaration of Independence of Israel gave only begrudging acknowledgment to the Deity in veiled reference to Him as the "Rock of

---

1. *Deut.*, 8: 14, 17, 18.

Israel" *(Tzur Yisrael),* but it was forgiven, or at least accepted, in the turmoil of those difficult days. The Six Day War inspired the whole people, and religious Jews saw the hand of Providence at work. In those heady days, the issues were clear, the victory astounding, and the return to Jerusalem certainly lifted events out of the stream of ordinary, every-day history. Secularists who could not bring themselves to speak of "miracles," except metaphorically, at least testified to the uniqueness of the events of 1967.

Unfortunately, the sense of national joy and thanksgiving quickly evaporated. Maybe it is in the nature of things that such levels of religious exaltation or exquisite historic awareness must soon fade as the routines of life take over and clamor for attention. But even before the Yom Kippur War, some of the poetry and mystical charm began to vanish. Not all of it was the result of natural attrition. Humble gratitude gave way to a much less noble interpretation of the events of the war. Israeli military men who came to speak to American Jews reveled in "demythologizing" the victory and reserving full credit to *Zahal* for all the accomplishments of the 1967 war. Not Providence, not faith, not luck, not accident, but *Zahal's* superiority in power and generalship gained the victory. There was also the shameless public polemic of the generals, some of whom declared there never was a threat of massacre prior to June 1967, that all fears of another Holocaust by the Arab armies were propaganda, that the Army was in control of the situation all along. Not only the poetry and the magic, the miracle and the exaltation, but even the sense of relief (and perhaps even justice of our cause) were stolen from us retroactively. Israel's power and the might of its hand have begotten for us not wealth, but confusion and resentment—- and an image as unattractive as it is unrealistic. It was unattractive both to intellectuals and to religious Jews, although no one really bothered to talk about it. But when the Yom Kippur War showed it to be unrealistic—as well as highly dangerous—these simmering sentiments came to the fore in both disparate circles. Perhaps a good lesson for the future, when with the help of God, peace and security return to Israel, is for Israel to keep its generals and colonels and majors at home or in service, and send other kinds of spokesmen for Israel to the communities of the Diaspora.

Theological Responses

In the attempts at formulating an interpretation of these events and integrating them into a theological framework, several divergent tendencies in the Orthodox community are beginning to appear. It must be stressed that, as of this time, some six months after the outbreak of hostilities, the situation is still fluid and no crystallization of approaches has yet taken place. Our adumbration of theological responses must therefore be taken as tentative and provisional.

Three major reactions may be discerned: that of the non-Zionist Orthodox community, the one usually associated with the yeshivot; that of the religious Zionist community and its sympathizers; and that of Orthodox Jews who, despite associations with one or both of the above, take an independent approach. The writer belongs to this third group and will speak from that vantage.

The "right-wing" groups of the yeshiva and Hasidic worlds have never endowed the State with Messianic or pre-Messianic significance. The exception is the *Neturei Karta* group, whose major spokesman is Rabbi Joel Teitelbaum, the Satmarer Rebbe of Brooklyn. His demonological interpretation of Zionist and Israeli history paradoxically does invest the State with a perverse negative Messianic function: the State, as the creation of the Zionists, is an arrogant usurpation of the divine prerogative, for God alone can usher in the redemption; the State is thus a diabolical invention tempting the people of Israel away from true faith, hence impeding the coming of the Messiah. I elaborated on this in "The Ideology of the *Neturei Karta*—According to the Satmarer Version."[2] Nevertheless, the stunning events of both 1967 and 1973 have engendered a considerable amount of Messianic speculation, more evident in the general community than in official leadership.

There are groping efforts to explain the events of 1973—especially the superpower confrontation—as the beginning of the apocalyptic cataclysm that tradition predicts as the prelude to the coming of the Messiah. There was much talk abroad in these circles of "The War of Gog and Magog" being at hand, and not only *Ezekiel* and *Daniel* but a number of

2. *Tradition*, Fall 1971.

kabbalistic texts were found to contain prophetic hints of current events.

Several works elaborating these "signs" have recently been published in Israel and have had a rather wide currency. The two most notable are by Shabbatai Shilo and Chaim Shevili. In 1970, Shilo published a short book with a long title, *The Redemption and Eternity—Happy is He Who Waits for and Reaches the Days of 1973.* The outbreak of the Yom Kippur War in October 1973 was considered little short of amazing, confirming his designation of 1973 as the decisive year in the Messianic drama centering around Israel's refusal to surrender Jerusalem, thus provoking an international military expedition against the Holy City. The invading army, composed of Russians and Arabs, was to conquer Jerusalem. Then the miracle, precipitated by an earthquake, was to have occurred—the divine intervention on behalf of Israel and the appearance of the Messiah. Shilo designated Hanukkah, December 1973, as the height of the war against Jerusalem. (In his defense one must cite the "tolerance of error" of one year that he reserves for himself.)

Chaim Shevili long ago predicted that 1948 would be a fateful year in the process of redemption. In 1935 he published his *Vision of Life,* in which he calculated that the Temple would be rebuilt in 1948-49. The founding of the State in 1948 was sufficient to establish his credentials. In 1964, his *Book of Calculations of the Redemption According to the Book of Daniel and the Writings of the Gaon of Vilna and Rabbi Isaac Luria and Chapters on the Dates of the Creation* pointed to 1967 as the pivotal date in the Messianic redemption. Naturally, the Six Day War lent his thesis considerable credibility.

While most leading rabbis and heads of yeshivot have refused to endorse such Messianic speculations, at least publicly, the sense of crisis and frustration has kept these issues alive, anxiety giving rise to anticipation. The eruption of the recent war on the holy day of Yom Kippur itself has understandably underscored the Messianic nature of the war to those predisposed to such interpretations. I do not know, however, if such a tendency will develop further, for the following reasons. First, there has always been an inclination to identify the vicissitudes of contemporary Jewish life as the catastrophic fulfillment of prophecies of pre-Messianic agonies. In our own lifetime there have been several major confrontations that have evoked similar theological speculations—from World War I through World War II, to the Cold War between the nuclear powers. Second, the nuclear war that is part of the contemporary version of the Gog-and-Magog scenario, may, hopefully, not take place. Third, such an ascription of pre-Messianic cataclysm to events concerning the State paradoxically invests the State of Israel with at least some element of Messianic redemption which these groups themselves vehemently deny. Sooner or later the contradiction must become apparent.

The above approach and the one following have one thing in their favor, and that is the advantage of a ready-made pattern, exegetically elaborated, into which historic events can be integrated. The ability to relate the twists and turns of an impulsive and sometimes convulsive history to a foreordained process, by imposing a rational structure on otherwise reckless and chaotic events, decreases the anxiety of the unknown future.

The second response to Israel in Orthodox circles is that of the religious Zionists, who subscribe to the thesis that the State of Israel represents a definite and crucial stage in the Messianic process. This is identified as the *at'halta di'geulah,* the "Beginning of the Redemption."[3]

More accurately, the founding of the State is considered a key event *within* the *at'halta di'geulah,* the genesis of which is located in the first agricultural resettlement of the Yishuv.[4] Rabbi Akiva Yosef Shlesinger had already expressed his consciousness of living in *at'halta di'geulah* in 1873;[5] and thirteen years earlier Rabbi M.N. Kahanow, noticing prosperous Jewish orchards in the vicinity of Jaffa, declared this a sign

---

3. The term first appears in the Talmud, *Megillah* 17b, where, however, it clearly refers to personal salvation rather than to the collective political redemption of Israel; see Rashi, *ad loc.* The notion of the beginning of the Messianic redemption is more accurately called *ha-ketz hameguleh,* the "revealed end (of days)," referring to *Sanhedrin* 98a.

4. Rabbi A.I. Kook, *Iggerot Hareiyah,* Part III, in a letter dated 1918.

5. *Kollel Ha'ivrim,* ed. 1955, p. 19.

of the "Beginning of the Redemption."[6] For those inclined to interpret the early Zionist movement in such redemptive terms, the establishment of the State was embraced as a political validation and vindication of the Messianism implicit in Zionism. The remarkable conjunction of the declaration of statehood and the Holocaust that immediately preceded it without doubt lent credence to such exuberance. The survival of the fledgling state and its growing prosperity was further confirmation of the new plateau that had been reached in *at'halta di'geulah,* and the events of the Six Day War were the miraculous revelation of what the believers had known all along: the State of Israel was the herald of the Messianic Kingdom.

The setbacks of 1973 now become quite problematical for those who persisted in ascribing a Messianic dimension to the State. It is clear that the traditional Jewish view insists upon empirical criteria by which Messianic claims may be tested. Maimonides codified these criteria in his *Yad, Hilkhot Melakhim,* and Nahmanides made ample use of these empirical standards in his polemics against Pablo Christiani. If, therefore, one affirms a Messianic role for the State, he must explain the reverses of the Yom Kippur War. It is reasonable to assume that if success proves the truth of a proposition—if 1948 and 1967 are the validations of the Messianic claims for the State of Israel—then failures prove the opposite.

Not many of the advocates of this school have responded to the challenge of the Yom Kippur War to clarify their thinking. In the United States there appear to be two contradictory assessments of the Israeli performance in the 1973 war. The first reaction is one that has an air of unreality about it: despite the setbacks, the military performance of *Zahal* was so brilliant as to keep intact its reputation for invincibility. The contemporary Messianic calculus has its own logic: losses become gains and reversals become triumphs. At a time when leaders of the military themelves rue the day they allowed the myth of Israeli military invincibility to gain currency, the Messianists will not allow "invincibility" to give up the ghost, fearing, as well they

6. *Sha'alu Shelom Yerushalayim,* Odessa, 1861.

might, that even a minor defeat invalidates, at the very least, the evidence they had previously adduced from earlier victories for the Messianic nature of the State.

The second reaction is more compelling in its reasonableness by subjecting the theory to logical criticism. The Messiah will not come suddenly, the Talmud states, but *kimah kimah,* bit by bit, like the rising of dawn. So the State, as the political harbinger of the Messianic redemption, cannot be expected to score an unbroken string of triumphs without occasional slackening or discomfiture. There is a commendable modesty to this answer, and it allays somewhat the uneasy feeling that the *at'halta di'geulah* theory is a form of triumphalism. This may be one of the theologically salutary results of the Yom Kippur War. But while it may be acceptable to those who seek a more naturalistic and rationalistic interpretation of the belief in the Messiah, it does not any longer allow one to use successes, when they arise, as evidence of the imminence of the Messiah's arrival. To do so would be to make the whole theory of the "Beginning of Redemption" an unfalsifiable thesis and hence of questionable validity. We are then thrown back upon faith—in itself no tragedy—rather than history, in supporting our feeling of experiencing the "Beginning of the Redemption."

A third approach, with which this writer identifies, takes exception to the apocalyptic-salvific versions of current history as illustrated by the two theories described, especially the second. Some criticisms have already been mentioned and more can be added. Most important, while searching for Messianic clues has been a psychologically understandable and spiritually justifiable endeavor, the development of a formal ideology that asserts dogmatically that we are in a specific stage of the Messianic redemption may well be an act of presumption. Are those of us who are devoid of the gift of prophecy privy to divine secrets? Even to Moses, the greatest of all prophets, it was told, "Thou shalt see My back, but My face shall not be seen."[7]

God's plans may be known to man in all their magnificent detail and moral fullness only retrospectively. We

7. *Exodus,* 33:23.

may, at best, "see My back." But we have no clairvoyance into the future and even the present is concealed from us if it is considered as part of a continuum whose culmination lies in the future. The assertion that the State is *reshit tzemihat geulatenu*—another term for *at'halta di'geulah*—as so many Israelis and Diaspora Jews declare in their "Prayer for the Peace of the State of Israel," entails a certain spiritual arrogance, as if we have lifted the veil into the mysterious *eschaton* and wrested from the Messiah his deepest secret: the time of his arrival. To read the present as a historian of the future, instead of as a journalist, is the prerogative of the prophet, provided God has shared His secrets with him. Ordinary humans tread on dangerous ground when they purport to view events from a divine perspective.

I wish to make it clear that I do not *deny* the Messianic character of our times or of the State. To do so with any conviction would be to commit the same sin of presumption. What I am saying is that I *do not know,* and that I believe this form of skepticism or Messianic agnosticism is the only valid spiritual position under the present circumstances. Since the Messianic quality of present-day events is not empirically demonstrable or verifiable, the wisest way for one who is committed to the traditional belief (or, more accurately, anyone of the various traditional beliefs) in the Messiah is to "bracket" the question, as phenomenologists would say.

History bears eloquent testimony to the grief that comes in the wake of premature Messianic expectations and unchecked eschatological fervor. Professor Gershom Scholem makes the point that of all the cornerstones of traditional Jewish theology, only the belief in redemption continues in full force. All the more reason for treating the supposed Messianic dimension of the State with a great deal of caution, there being no guarantees that secular pseudo-messianism is any less dangerous than the religious kind.

It must granted that the coming of the Messiah is, by its nature, the kind of event that raises doubts, especially in the light of the history of false Messiahs, and that such skepticism can congeal into an automatic denial of any and all Messianic claims even where they might be legitimate. There is a certain amount of risk-taking that cannot be avoided. But mistakes, even honest ones, can be made—witness Rabbi Akiva and his sponsorship of Bar Kokhba as the Messiah.

I prefer to view the events of our time as providential and not (necessarily) Messianic. I accept that the rebirth of the national homeland, after the vicissitudes of our history, and especially on the heels of the Holocaust was a "miracle," in that it defied all predictability and probability.

I accept the State as an act of redemption, but not every redemption is necessarily Messianic. The terms here associated—*at'halta*, Messianic, pre-Messianic—must be reserved for that specific period of history which will culminate in the fulfillment of all the visions of the past—political autonomy, economic welfare, intellectual advancement, spiritual flowering, religious renaissance—climaxed by the leadership of a unique individual who will create these conditions and possess the leadership capacity to enable them to be enjoyed by the people of Israel, ushering in an era of peace and justice in the world. I am not trying to summarize the traditional Messianic beliefs as much as to isolate such a period from the normal, run-of-the mill, historical epoch. If we understand this, then what is to prevent us from experiencing non-Messianic redemptions, of various extents and scopes, in the course of Jewish history?

Neither *aliyah* nor solidarity of the Diaspora with Israel requires the apocalyptic-salvific hypothesis of the *at'halta di'geulah* advocates. On the contrary, the attribution of Messianic importance to the State leads, paradoxically, to two opposite and unfortunate conclusions: one, that the State, as a Messianic instrument, is beyond criticism, and hence its leaders can do no wrong; and two, that the State of Israel is disastrously delinquent in not living up to the high moral and religious standards one would expect of a Messianic state.

The Jewish commitment to the State of Israel does not require Messianic presuppositions. That commitment was forged in the fires of the crematoria; in the hatred of and indifference to Jews by the civilized countries of both West and East; in the Covenant, which has paradoxically allowed us to live without Eretz Israel for 2000 years—and for 2000 years has not let us give up our longing for it; in the knowledge that the realization of the Torah and the fulfillment of the Word of

God are more likely to be found in Israel than anywhere else
on this globe. The State of Israel is the guarantee of Jewish
survival today, whether or not it is a Messianic state.

For the Future

The suggested "bracketing" of the Messianic element
by no means implies an abandonment of the belief in the
coming of the Messiah. It asserts that the role of Israel in
history is not exclusively linked at every point with the
Messianic element. The Covenant speaks of God's *hester
panim*—His turning away of His face from us—and *he'arat
panim,* His smiling upon us. These Biblical categories, while
less emotionally charged, may ultimately be more fruitful than
exclusively Messianic terms in interpreting the great events of
our times. *Hester panim* and *he'arat panim* are relational
ideas, implying mutuality and reciprocity between God and
Israel, the two partners in the Covenant. While a fuller
development of this theme cannot be given here, I do suggest
that these concepts will serve better than *at'halta di'geulah* as
the parameters for a contemporary theological evaluation of
Jewish history.

The Messiah is only the messenger of God. It is He, and
He alone, who redeems. If He has chosen to redeem us and to
restore us to the Land promised in the Covenant, it is a divine
redemption. And a divine redemption is not that far inferior to
a Messianic redemption.

As I mentioned, the common religious reaction to
Israel's national psychology, precipitated by the Yom Kippur
War, does not end in the criticism of "my strength and the
might of my hand." Religious groups, especially the religious
right, so long critical of Israel's illusion of self-sufficiency and
its rhetoric of national self-assertion, have already begun to
articulate a constructive criticism of the prevailing mood of
the country: its sadness, depression, and pessimism. They are
consistent with their premises: just as national bluster was a
symptom of lack of *emunah* (faith) when the news was good,
so the despair and depression and sense of foreboding today
are equally inconsistent with *emunah.* If our previous error
was an unwarranted trust in our "power and might of our

hand," our present mistake is forgetting that "Behold, the Guardian of Israel neither slumbers nor sleeps."[8] Both arrogance and despair have the same provenance: a lack of faith.

What the religious groups are saying, then, is that it is time to get on with the people's business, to do what has to be done whether pleasant or not, but to do it in the humble confidence that, God willing, we will prevail.

It is a consoling and comforting summons, and one that makes good sense.

8. *Psalms*, 121:4.

United States of America: Perspectives

Mordecai Waxman

The Yom Kippur War left as its aftermath a rubble of discarded illusions and misconceptions and posed the need to rebuild the structure of Jewish life in somewhat different form. Coming as it did on the heels of the celebration of the 25th year of Israel's existence, in the midst of a climate of escalating expectations, it was doubly shocking and sobering. It was an unhappy reminder of the tenuous base on which Jewish achievement rests and of the fact that established Jewish accomplishments can be reversed in a day.

This paper reflects on some of the reactions to the Yom Kippur War and some consequences flowing from it in large segments of the American Jewish community. It does not purport to present "hard data," in the sense of statistically documented material. Rather, it is intended to reflect the mood which can be generally apprehended within the American Jewish community. It concerns itself with the attitudes of American Jewry to Israel at this point, with certain consequences which seem to result, within the community, and with some of the short- and long-range problems which have been raised by the war.

Relationship of American Jewish Community to Israel

The Yom Kippur War did not substantially alter the relationship of the American Jewish community to Israel itself. It merely confirmed an attitude which already existed and gave a slightly different perspective to questions which were already on the agenda of American Jewish life. Potentially, however, it posed questions which had been pushed into the background in recent years.

The war made clear that American Jewry is committed to Israel and is willing to expend itself financially and

65

politically on its behalf. These attitudes, however, were not born in the maelstrom of this war. Indeed, given the rapidity with which the Yom Kippur War started, the desired attitudes, emotional feelings and actions could not possibly have been developed in time to be effective, were they not already present. They were present because the Six Day War, the tension preceding it, and the catharsis and euphoria following it were a watershed in establishing the relationship of the American Jewish community to Israel.

It has been suggested by some Israelis that the Yom Kippur War should have been viewed by American Jews as potentially holocaustal. It is doubtful whether Israelis saw it in that light during the first few days and it is plain that most American Jews did not see it that way at any time. The reason for the American Jewish attitude is simple enough. The year 1973 neither created the mood of potential Holocaust in the minds of American Jews nor did it alter the attitudes already formed about Israel (although it did suggest that some attitudes are likely to change).

It was 1967 that was the decisive year for both sets of feelings. And here, too, the reason is simple enough. In the feelings of Jews, the framework for 1967 was the Holocaust; the framework for the Yom Kippur War was 1967 and its rewarding victory. Oddly enough, the full impact of the Holocaust was felt more keenly in the 1960s than it had been felt in the preceding decade. Perhaps this was partially a matter of delayed emotional response. More likely, it was due to the double fact that a significant literature on the Holocaust, both of fiction and non-fiction, began to be produced in the United States in the 1960s and that it was more widely read because this was the decade in which American Jewish writers became major figures on the American literary landscape and undertook writing about Jews and Judaism. The result was that in the long preliminary to the 1967 war, the feeling of concern that a new Holocaust was possible mounted in America, as did the conviction that this time the Jewish community must not be found wanting. Rallies for political action and a new level of monetary contributions resulted. Individuals and groups hitherto cool to, or indifferent to, Israel changed their stance. American Jewry emerged as a community committed to Israel and its survival. Even within the ranks of Jewish leftists the issue of support for Israel was largely resolved, despite the prevalent tendency, issuing from the Vietnam war, to deprecate military action and achievement.

The decisive nature of this settling of opinion and commitment may be measured in several ways. Quantitatively, it showed itself in the United Jewish Appeal campaign which jumped to a new level after 1967 and remained on that plateau until the events of 1973 pushed it to a still higher level. The more pervasive, although subtler, effects could be noted in the fact that the Council of Jewish Federations and Welfare Funds (whose origins were in the local Federations and their support of local and national Jewish institutions and which had been dominated by non-Zionist elements), increasingly centered its fund raising about Israel-oriented campaigns. The final seal was set upon this approach, on the heels of the Yom Kippur War, when the Council at its New Orleans Convention adopted a national goal of $900 million, $750 million of which was to go to Israel. And even in New York City, where the Federation of Jewish Philanthropies had never merged with the United Jewish Appeal, the two campaigns were combined after the 1973 war as a result of the sober recognition by the Federation that community interest and generosity were centered on Israel.

More subtle indications still are the fact that such groups as the Reform movement and the American Jewish Committee, which were in the past divided on support for Israel or lukewarm in their affirmation, now stand totally committed. A further straw in the wind is that the only Jewish public figures whose names are known throughout the American Jewish community are such Israelis as Golda Meir, Moshe Dayan, and Abba Eban.

Parameters of Involvement

With all its impact, there were clear parameters to the effect of the 1967 war and they have not been substantially altered by the Yom Kippur War. Concern did not translate itself into a significant movement for *aliyah.* The great bulk of

American Jews do not come out of the background of the Zionist movement and even those who do were not trained to see Zionism as a movement for *aliyah* from America. Unlike the European Zionist movements of an earlier era, the American movement was primarily directed to securing political and economic support for Israel rather than providing people for the land.

In the years since 1967 there has been a major bent towards tourism and a developing pattern for American students to spend a year of study or work in Israel. However, even though there has been an increase in numbers, *aliyah* has not been a serious item on the American Jewish agenda. There have been no significant and widely recognized circumstances on the American side which might promote *aliyah* and the pull from the Israeli side has not been very great. Nor has there been until very recently a significant and coordinated campaign in America to promote *aliyah.*

Meanwhile, the factors which have produced some *aliyah* are essentially personal. There are people who are attracted by the prospect of a different quality of life from that which prevails in America, whether it be for reasons of religion, a search for a more simple life, idealism, or Jewish patriotism. Some *aliyah* has resulted from the movement back and forth of young Israelis and Americans with resultant marriages. In the case of other people, a reasonable job in their field combined with an attraction for Israel and a distaste for certain aspects of American life constitute the inducement. For retired people, the prospect of a simpler and possibly cheaper life in Israel is the decisive element. Other factors, however, militate against these inducements, notably the rising costs in Israel, the difficulty of making a middle-class living, the problem of adjustment in Israel and what is seen, particularly by young people, as the decline of idealism in Israel.

In default of a new approach to *aliyah,* the Yom Kippur War is more likely to discourage immigration from America than to encourage it. People with growing children are likely to think several times about committing their children to long years in the army and to the possibility of recurrent and difficult wars. If, as some Israelis feel, the future of Israel can be assured only by a steady and massive immigration from America, then it is necessary to constitute a new Zionist movement whose theme will be Jewish patriotism and to assume that results will be long delayed. The Herzlian thesis that a Jewish State would eliminate anti-Semitism is not now a compelling factor for American Jews, even if it were true. The sheer existence and success of Israel have heightened Jewish pride and improved Jewish status. They have simultaneously removed Israel from the realm of fantasy to the realm of reality. Perhaps then it has become necessary to think of the factors which make for immigration to a real country rather than those which make for *aliyah* to a fantasy.

One element of fantasy, nonetheless, remains. Most American Jews want to be admiring of Israel. They see it as a source of pride, an answer to the Holocaust and a validation of Jewish history and experience. They want Israel to be everything that Jewish life ought to be and is not elsewhere. They want to be able to point with pride to an autonomous Jewish community where Jewish ideal values are fulfilled. Unfair as this may be to a real society which operates under great difficulties, it nonetheless may be a necessary factor to induce *aliyah* as an ideal.

Which American Jewish Community?

In weighting the above observation, it is important to know of which American Jewish community we are speaking. There is both an organized and an unorganized American Jewish community, each of which comprises roughly half of America's estimated six million Jews. The unorganized community is concentrated in the major cities—New York, Los Angeles, Philadelphia and Chicago—where the sheer dispersion and mass of numbers and the mobility of America make such Jews essentially unreachable. By and large, fund raisers make little effort to reach this group since they assume that it would cost them more to raise the money than they would get. The general feeling, however, is that the attitude of the non-organized to Israel is not substantially different from that of the organized community. This conclusion, which is shared by politicians as well as by other observers, has political importance, even if it does not carry weight in the financial realm.

The organized community is an overlapping community. The largest component in it is the synagogue membership comprising close to fifty per cent of American Jewry at the present time. To this number, however, must be added the many Jews who were members of synagogues until they moved or aged, or who intend to become members of synagogues at the appropriate time, and those who treat Jewish institutions like "gas stations." The last category, concentrated in large cities, involves Jews who expect Jewish institutions to be available to them when they need them, do use them, but do not labor either to create them or maintain them. Of the synagogue groups, the Conservative movement embraces almost a half and the Reform and Orthodox comprise the balance, according to the recent survey of the Council of Jewish Federation and Welfare Funds.*

The membership of these synagogue groups overlaps and is overlapped, in part, by the membership of such organizations as B'nai B'rith, Hadassah, other Zionist organizations, the American Jewish Congress, the American Jewish Committee, and such fund-raising agencies as UJA and the Federations. People may give their primary loyalty to one group or the other but, broadly speaking, on the issue of Israel and several other issues they all operate within the same universe of discourse. Nonetheless, it might be desirable to point out that the synagogues enjoy advantages which are denied the other groups. They not only embrace more members, but they are in closer contact with their members, as a result of their personal connections with both children and adults. Even if synagogue members are not "religious," they concede the right of the synagogue to contact them, to enter into their homes, and to seek to sway them to Jewish concerns and commitments. In its embracive quality, the American synagogue is far more than a place of worship, whose

---

*The indicated percentages are as follows: Reform 13.5; Conservative 23.1; Orthodox 8.9; Other .7; No membership 53.1; Not reported .6. See *National Jewish Population Study,* Council of Jewish Federations and Welfare Funds. In "Demographic Highlights: Facts for Planning," Table 7: Congregational Membership, 1971.

potentialities, perhaps, have not been fully appreciated or utilized by those concerned with Israel.

Apart from the fact that the synagogue is *the* agency for Jewish identification for most Jews, there is also the factor that the synagogue school is the *primary* agency for Jewish education in the United States. Whatever one may think of the adequacy of the Jewish education offered in these institutions, the truth is that eighty-five to ninety per cent of the Jewish children who receive some form of Jewish education receive it within synagogue schools. The other ten to fifteen per cent receive their education in parochial schools, many of which are sponsored by synagogues.

Case Illustration: The Conservative Movement

The reaction of the Conservative movement, which embraces the Jewish Theological Seminary, the Rabbinical Assembly and the United Synagogue of America, was aptly described by Seminary Chancellor Gerson D. Cohen in a report to his colleagues in November 1973. He spoke of "the spontaneity and inspiration" of the response which included financial, political, and public action. The soil out of which these reactions grew, however, was seeded many years ago. They are not necessarily a paradigm for the Reform and Orthodox movements, each of which has its special character, but there are points of converging concern.

The Conservative movement, virtually since its inception, has regarded Zionism as a central part of its ideology. It has supported Zionism *qua* Zionism, without regard to party divisions, and its members have been heavily involved in all fund-raising and political efforts, both through the medium of the synagogues and through other agencies in Jewish life. Its schools have taught Zionism and its youth groups initiated the Israel pilgrimages.

The movement has been both Herzlian and Ahad Ha-Amist in its approach. It has endorsed fully the idea of a Jewish state but has simultaneously hoped that an autonomous Jewish community would serve as a center for the creation of a revitalized Judaism which would have meaning for the Diaspora. While believing that Israel should be a central concern for all Jews, it did not and does not believe that there is no hope for Judaism in the free Diaspora. On the contrary, it seeks a vibrant Judaism in the Diaspora, and particularly in the United States, being convinced that this is necessary for American Jews and for the welfare of Israel.

Conservative Judaism is a religious movement. While its sense of peoplehood is very strong, it, nonetheless, believes that Jewish peoplehood must be based on a religious outlook. It further holds that there are varied expressions of the religious and moral outlook and that there must be resonance for all of them in Jewish life, both in the Diaspora and in Israel.

Oddly enough, the 25th anniversary of Israel, while it was a time of vast jubilation, also became a psychological watershed for many in the leadership of the Conservative movement. It became a time for recognition that the Ahad Ha-Am expectation was not being fulfilled in ways which would strengthen or revitalize Jewish religious life in the American Diaspora. Israel, it began to be felt, had been polarized between a secular nationalism and a rigid religious orthodoxy, neither of which spoke to the question of Judaism as a religious and moral outlook or contributed significantly to the strengthening of Judaism (as against Jewishness) for the bulk of American Jews. The oft-repeated formula of Israeli political leaders, "If you want your point of view represented in Israel, come and settle here" began to sound both sour and evasive. Obviously mass immigration was not in prospect, and just as obviously the question was not whether Conservative Jews could form a political party in Israel, but whether the political elements in Israel could agree that the need to strengthen Judaism all over the world should be part of the concern of a state or society which wants to be central in Jewish life.

In short, what was beginning to focus was the need for a philosophy of Jewish life and Judaism after the foundation of the State, which would unite Jews in common endeavor, outlook, and aspiration. If the Israeli rabbinate is supposed to be the bridge builder of Jewish religious unity and concern across the Jewish world, then its parochialism makes it an inadequate engineer. If other elements of Israeli society have a creative policy with regard to the American Diaspora, it must be said, regrettably, that it is a well-kept secret.

The sentiment which was beginning to develop in the Conservative movement, after a generation of Israeli existence, was that the original expectations, that Zionism would not only lead to the establishment of a Jewish State but to a revitalization and redirection of Judaism everywhere, had miscarried. This meant no diminution of concern or support for Israel, but a rather reluctant recognition that Israel was not a universal panacea for the problems of Judaism. Many Conservative Jews now ask what is the content of Judaism, the purpose of Israel, and the elements which unite the Jewish people when there is no crisis. If these questions are ignored in an hour of crisis, the problems nonetheless remain as part of the permanent agenda for both Israel and Diaspora Jewry.

Responses of Youth

In evaluating the reaction of the American Jewish community to Israel. Moreover, the evaluation must take note of the fact that this organized community is an older group and embraces a fraction of the young people in their twenties and early thirties. This is especially true in the larger cities, where young men and women and young couples are still in limbo in their commitments and in their sense of community. American Jewry has reluctantly accepted a situation it cannot control and lives with the hope that as people enter their mid-thirties and find their place economically, socially, and geographically, and begin to cope with the problems of raising children, they will make their commitment to the organized Jewish community. While this has been true in the past, it is by no means certain that it will be true for the "revolutionary generation" of the late 1960s.

In this context the reaction of high school youth who are still at home and function as part of the family was not discernably different from that of their parents. College youth and young people beyond the college age belong to another category. A great many of them are away from home and belong to no community, since neither the college nor the large, anarchical city provides a community for them. In consequence, they are neither seriously influenced by the community nor do they contribute to it. This stage in their lives is likely to last well through their twenties and in consequence the organized community neither mirrors nor reacts to their feelings or needs. Since the "college revolution" of the mid-sixties, the Jewish community has not known how to cope effectively with its young people and, indeed, is afraid of them. The percentage of intermarriage among them is now recorded as thirty per cent and their Jewish attitudes are thought to be a mystery. However, Jewish youth is not monolithic. There is a nuclear group of highly committed young people who follow establishment patterns; another group, also committed, exploring such new directions as the *havurot;* and there are peripheral segments, some alienated.

Several facts should be noted about young people. One is that they have grown up in an atmosphere in which anti-Semitism has been at its lowest ebb and the urge for integration in American life has been at its greatest. This situation has made for a lowered sense of danger of religious repression and, perhaps as a consequence, for a greater tendency to think in terms of political activism. Paradoxically, while the intermarriage rate is high, the Jewish identity level is also high. In consequence, there is little conversion by Jews in their intermarriage to people of other faiths, while twenty-five per cent of the non-Jews convert to Judaism, and another twenty-five per cent or more identify themselves with the Jewish community, without conversion. There is also a fringe group in the Jewish community involved in spiritual search centered about Eastern mysticism and a smaller group with New Left propensities.

There is no adequate way of measuring the reaction of this widely dispersed college youth, numbering some 400,000, and the larger group lost in the cities and outside the community, to the Yom Kippur War. It is clear that there was a strong, emotional positive reaction on many campuses by considerable numbers of Jewish youth. It expressed itself in rallies and money raising. It conceivably could have expressed itself in considerable volunteering, had volunteers been asked for on other than a six-month basis and had the sense of crisis been more prolonged. It would be reasonable to hazard the guess that most Jewish young people have positive feelings about Israel, a concern with it, and a pride in it. In short, they are not markedly different from their parents in this matter, but have far less opportunity to engage in the primary form of expression of this concern which, in America, is fund raising.

Some Consequences of the Yom Kippur War

The long-range consequences of the Yom Kippur War are still to be recognized, but there are some immediate results which command our attention. The war has changed the Arab image in the eyes of American Jews. Despite the fact that Israel succeeded in winning a military victory in the face of great odds, the total result of the war emerges as an Arab victory. The feeling was already abroad, before the war, that the Arab international terror campaign and the refusal of all nations to deal with it represented a kind of Arab triumph. When to this are added the facts that the Arabs achieved some military gains, succeeded in isolating Israel diplomatically, are in control of huge funds with which to affect world economy, and are able to mount a sophisticated propaganda campaign in the American media, the picture is exacerbated. Granted that governments and many elements of the public know that the connection between the Arab oil embargo and the position of Israel is spurious and that blackmail and economic greed are involved, the situation is still dangerous. Although the Arabs are not united, they emerge as a major power factor capable of manipulating a disorganized world.

While this has not affected American Jewish support for Israel and indeed has heightened the awareness that Jewish support may be Israel's indispensable asset, it has left a feeling that Israel's position is extremely tenuous. It has also left the impression that the Arabs are able and willing to engage in ongoing wars which Israel can only lose. Simultaneously, the war has changed the image of Israel. It revealed that the notion of Israeli independence may be a chimera, since Israel is increasingly seen as a client state strongly dependent on its one patron, the United States. While the Arab powers also appeared to be client states dependent upon Russia, the march of events since the war has made it clear that, by virtue of their oil and money, they can supply themselves with arms and aid from anywhere in the international community.

The problem of Israel as a client state is further complicated in the eyes of American Jews by a feeling that American policy is by no means fixed or unalterable. The ambivalence which has always existed in American government support for Israel is likely to be increased, it is felt, by the weakening of the American international economic and political position, by the energy crisis, and by internal political and economic problems. When to this is added the post-Vietnam War syndrome, an unwillingness to engage in foreign adventures, including perhaps the peripheral aspect of arms sale, the dependence of Israel upon one patron state seems even more serious.

While these factors are not likely to weaken Jewish community support for Israel, they, perhaps, ought to lead to a reexamination of the nature of American Jewry's activity. This has been geared primarily to fund raising for Israel. But the problems of the near future are increasingly likely to be political problems and the organization of American Jewry for such purposes is singularly inadequate. Another reaction in the American Jewish community to the Yom Kippur War and the oil embargo, was that the situation might lead to anti-Semitic reaction in the United States. It was at once a recognition that the destinies of American and Israeli Jewry are related and a statement of commitment despite all prospects.

In the ensuing months the American public focused its concern on the general energy crisis, on Arab behavior and most recently on the manipulations of the oil cartels. However, there are still echoes in political and newspaper statements of a linkage between the Israeli-Egyptian Geneva negotiations and the relaxation of the oil embargo. This continues to afford grounds for uneasiness as a long-range energy crisis looms and the prospects of economic dislocation grow.

Still another development in American Jewish life which was underlined by the Yom Kippur War was the political stance of American Jews. There has been a significant move away from the conventional Jewish liberal position in the last few years. On the local scene, this shift was seen as due to crime, busing, Black anti-Semitism and similar factors. However, on the national scale, the question of support for Israel clearly has played a part. Thus in 1972, Mr. Nixon received thirty-five per cent of the Jewish vote rather than the fifteen per cent which went to him in 1968; and one reason for the increase was his support for Israel. Of equal significance is the erosion of Jewish community support for the U.N., since the 1967 war made it clear how much that body was controlled by Arab and Russian forces.

Some Problems—Ideological and Sociological

As one of its aftermaths, the Yom Kippur War left an uneasy feeling among many American Jews that a group of dimly perceived or suppressed problems would have to be dealt with in the near future. So long as Israel seemed to be on the upswing, there was a mild hope that time and serendipity would resolve these questions. In the current situation there is a feeling, as yet unfocused, that several issues need to be reexamined and that new and deliberate formulations of policy may be called for. One major problem is that organized American Jewry feels itself in a crisis situation with regard to its internal life. The sharp increase in intermarriages within the last decade and the ambiguous Jewish attitudes of young Jews has raised the question of whether American Jewry is devoting enough effort and time to its own needs. The results of a quarter of a century of post-World War II effort have created a markedly stronger and better organized American Jewry. But it has become clear that all these efforts have not been enough to cope with the increased threat of assimilation in a world whose standards and values are in disarray. Nor has the existence and drama of Israel, significant as they have been, provided enough of a counterweight to the problems which have developed.

If the American Jewish community regarded itself as a community in transit to Israel, this problem might not be significant. If Israel were the cultural center which Ahad

Ha-Am envisaged, capable of providing new directions and
new dynamism to Diaspora communities, the problems might
not have arisen. At this stage neither of these alternatives is
true. American Jewry sees itself—barring major anti-Semitic
developments—as a permanent feature of the American
landscape, but fears it will dwindle in numbers and force as a
result of assimilation. On the whole, it does not feel that Israel
either understands it or speaks to its needs. Israel, therefore,
does not serve it as a central dynamo or reviving force, even
though the sheer existence of Israel adds strength to Jewish
life everywhere.

One major example of the distance between the two
communities is provided by the fact that the reachable
American Jewish community is organized by means of
synagogues and organizations which have no real parallel in
Israel. As cited, seventy-five per cent of organized American
Jewry is connected with the Conservative and Reform
movements in Judaism. Israel Jewry, in religious terms, is
dominated by an Orthodox establishment which not only does
not talk the same language, but does not speak to these
movements, and has little if anything to contribute to them.

By the same token, the Jewish Agency which should be,
in part, a liaison body between Diaspora Jewry and Israel, does
not embrace all the currents in American life. The Zionist
organizations, Hadassah apart, are not very strong in America
today and include a small fraction of the people who are
concerned with Israel. Inevitably, then, just before the war,
American Jews were beginning to talk of devoting more of
their energy and funds to the improvement of the quality of
Jewish life in America. Israel seemed to be soundly
established and American Jewry seemed to be in trouble. The
conclusion was obvious. The shock of the war presented the
further development of that feeling and the necessary
resultant actions. But there is no doubt that, when the sense of
crisis wears off, that feeling will return and with it an effort
will be made to reallocate American Jewish funds and
energies.

Perhaps what is necessary is a truthful rethinking of the
pattern of relationships between Israel and American Jewry.
The existence of a vibrant Israel is necessary to American

Jewry. But the existence of a vital American Jewry is increasingly necessary to Israel, as the diplomatic isolation of Israel should make more and more evident. Some medium must be created which is capable of starting with the premises that there are two foci in Jewish life today and that their problems—social, spiritual, cultural, financial and political— are interrelated.

The war made it increasingly evident that political support for Israel is at least as necessary as financial support. In this crisis, fortunately, intense political action in the United States was not vitally necessary, since the attitude of the American administration was already formulated. However, it can very likely be an important subject of contention in the future, and the American Jewish community is not at present geared for meaningful and prolonged political action. It may be that the mixture as before is the best that we can or should undertake, but the Yom Kippur War has raised the issue of whether the political activism of the Jewish community should be reexamined.

A related area is that of public relations and the image that Israel projects. It is the general feeling in American Jewry that Israel has done too little that is new in that area and has not been as effective as it might be. The reliance upon tried and true methods and media were justified when Arab and oil propaganda were muted. More sophisticated presentation of Arab viewpoints (plus other factors) have diminished the sense of moral concern for Israel. Unfortunately, the moral climate in the world is such that people no longer seem capable of moral outrage and thus fail to react both to the war and to the extremes of Arab terrorism.

The problem thus becomes one of reestablishing Israel as a matter of general moral concern. There are two aspects to the matter. One involves the quality of Israeli society and the image with which Israel was born, as a nation in quest of social justice, alive to social experiment and idealistic in tone. The other involves a serious attempt to establish contact with religious and intellectual groups of other countries in the moral terms to which they might respond. Obviously, here again a joint effort by Israeli and American Jews is called for.

A crucial ideological point to be considered is the

current state of Zionism as an idea. Reality seems to have overtaken ideology. Israel exists and so for Jews abroad classical Zionism has been fulfilled. It is true that in the light of the reactions to the war and the oil embargo, neither Pinsker's nor Herzl's vision of the disappearance of anti-Semitism has been validated. Israel is still a "peculiar" rather than a "normal" nation. But since the Ahad Ha-Am vision does not seem to be fulfilling itself either, classical Zionist ideology is left devoid of meaningful content. In Israel, too, in the light of the stresses of normal nationhood, Zionist ideology seems to be fading out. And the war has brought into focus the question whether Zionism, as an unfulfilled ideal, and as a goal for achievement within the State of Israel, has to be revived and given new content. Certainly, if *aliyah* is a major concern it must march under the banner of some greater ideal than a mere change of place.

United States of America: Perspectives

Marie Syrkin

After a rash of initial statements in which friends and foes took up predictable positions, the immediate reaction of intellectuals, Jewish and non-Jewish, to the Yom Kippur War and its aftermath can best be described as one ranging between muted concern and indifference. On the whole there was far less discussion of the basic causes or the rights and wrongs of the Arab-Israeli conflict than in 1967. A good bellwether of the intellectual climate was the *New York Review of Books.* Immediately after the Six Day War the magazine had carried an article by I. F. Stone which created a sensation at the time because it marked the beginning of the anti-Israel campaign launched by progressives and leftists not formerly identified as dogmatically anti-Israel, like the various communist sects.[1] In 1973, on the other hand, the sole reaction of the *New York Review of Books* to the new conflict was to print the statement of twenty-one Hebrew University professors in one issue, with a lengthy rejoinder, addressed by David Amitai to Professor Talmon, one of the signatories of the statement, in the following issue. These two communications, appearing in the back of the periodical among letters to the editor, were as of mid-December the sole comment on the war in the *New York Review of Books.*[2]

Similarly *The New Yorker,* which generally manages to discuss topics it considers noteworthy, was silent on the subject except for a comment on the interdependence of oil and politics, and a subsequent, non-committal *Letter* on Israel. It would be safe to say that in general magazines there was no

---

1. "Holy War," *New York Review of Books,* August 3, 1967.
2. See Appendix I, pp. 351–354.

immediate outpouring of either overt sympathy or hostility in the measure elicited by the Six Day War.

The daily press, on the other hand, not only in its reportage but in letters to the editor and columns, gave some clue to the state of mind of the intellectuals. Shortly after the outbreak of hostilities, a brief letter in the *New York Times* expressed sympathy for Israel and opposed Arab aggression. The communication was notable for its signatories: Saul Bellow, Irving Howe, Alfred Kazin, Michael Harrington, Meyer Schapiro, Lionel Trilling. Each of these names could be counted on to turn up singly in one or another of the various appeals issued by artists, writers, and academicians; appearing together they represented, with the exception of Michael Harrington, a not inconsiderable segment of the leading Jewish intellectuals.

Were one to examine the illustrious signatories of various pro-Israel statements one might readily assume that the intellectual community had rallied behind Israel. Many Nobel Prize winners, university presidents and scholars of international renown forthrightly called for a secure Israel with defensible borders and condemned Arab aggression. Intellectuals of the extreme left, of course, continued to call for the destruction of "the Zionist state" in their accustomed style. Nevertheless, while individuals went on record in 1973 as in 1967, the overall impression was one of lesser ferment and agitation.

This sense of greater apathy may be attributed to two causes: the first, to the conviction that all the arguments *pro* and *con* had repeatedly been made in the intervening years; the second, to an overwhelming sense of helplessness. When I asked a leading Jewish intellectual, who while not a Zionist could certainly be viewed as sympathetic to Israel and committed to Israel's survival, why his fellow intellectuals seemed inert in the present crisis, he answered, "Because we feel impotent."

By this he meant that in 1973 the array of international forces had become such as to dwarf the specific Arab-Israel confrontation. Geopolitical considerations, American-Soviet competition for the Middle East, the introduction of oil as a weapon on a massive scale—these factors served to give the struggle dimensions in which particular points appeared minor; there seemed little to argue beyond a demand for Israel's survival. This sense of assisting at a foredoomed spectacle in which the given moves of the supposed chief actors would not alter the finale created melancholy apprehension rather than an impulse to debate, demonstrate, hold meetings, or engage in the usual activities open to intellectuals who enlist in a cause.

In 1967 the feeling that Israel's actions shaped her destiny had been dominant. From it sprang the euphoria that followed upon Israel's extraordinary victory in the Six Day War. Now, despite a victory against even greater odds, the assurance that another Israeli victory would appreciably alter the outcome was gone. It was taken for granted that even if the war were to be renewed and Israel succeeded in completing the rout of the Arab armies, Great Power insistence on Israel's withdrawal from occupied territories would not thereby be lessened. Regardless of protestations to the contrary, the assumption remained that the United States would exert pressure on Israel to make concessions large enough to assure some kind of accommodation with the Arabs. In that case re-arguing the justice of the Zionist case seemed as futile as the labor of Sisyphus.

This comparative apathy did not reflect a less favorable evaluation of Israel's moral stance. In 1967 the heated discussion of the *pros* and *cons* of the claims of Arab refugees, subsequently Palestinians, was something of a novelty. By 1973 unaligned intellectuals—those who were neither Zionists nor subscribers to an ideology which automatically called for the "dismantlement of the Zionist entity" on every possible occasion—fell into two groups: some who soberly, and without malice, recommended that Israel withdraw from occupied territory because Arabs could not be expected to endure foreign occupation indefinitely; and some who, while appreciating what such withdrawal entailed and aware of the history which led to the Israeli presence beyond the June 1967 borders, no longer had the heart to argue the case.

Irving Kristol, editor of the influential intellectual quarterly *Public Interest,* writing on the Yom Kippur War, limited himself to confessing his gloom at the course of events: "Things have not been going so well for Israel, as in my bones, I had always feared might be the case. . . . I am one of those Jews who has never been able to take Jewish good fortune seriously, but rather suspect it as a deception. Only misfortune is real."[3] His article, appearing in a national newspaper where some suggestion of policy might conceivably have been useful, was wholly couched in this reflective, elegiac vein.

Professor Hans Morgenthau, surely a friend of Israel, in a widely publicized TV interview with William Buckley outlined the future of Israel in the darkest terms.[4] His prognosis shocked Mr. Buckley into inquiring as to how Professor Morgenthau felt about the prospect of Israel's demise. Professor Morgenthau assured his interlocutor that though he deplored what he foresaw, he was objectively outlining a possible international scenario. Professor Morgenthau's prognostications aroused dismay and criticism among his colleagues. What point was there in forecasting the possible end of Israel? Professor Morgenthau answered such criticism by stating that his purpose had been to alert the public and the American government as to the likely outcome of present policies. The sense of doom communicated by such Jewish intellectuals as Kristol and Morgenthau, whose goodwill toward Israel need not be questioned, was symptomatic of a pervasive state of mind.

In this context the passionate words of a British journalist, Max Hastings, appearing originally in the London *Evening Standard* but reprinted in the United States by the American Zionist Federation, seemed particularly stirring: "In this atmosphere it takes a moment's thought to remember how contemptibly we Western Europeans have responded to the events of the past three weeks. For the first time in my life on Golan and at Suez I have felt ashamed to be a mere reporter of events. The sight of the Western Powers attempting to appease the Arabs' genocidal ambitions has seemed to me one of the most humiliating of my short life."

In the editorial pages of the *New York Times* Friedrich

3. *Wall Street Journal,* October 18, 1973.
4. November 25, 1973.

Dürrenmatt, the Swiss playwright, took occasion to stricture the silence of the intellectuals. Indeed, the silence had been resounding, if we seek to find more than formal declarations of support such as have already been mentioned. One missed the sense of personal involvement such as characterized the immediate post-1967 period. Dürrenmatt's indignation was sufficiently rare to be noteworthy. He highlighted what I have already mentioned: the failure of the intellectual community to rally strongly and openly to the cause of embattled Israel in the fall of 1973 though the fate of the Jewish state hung in the balance. The chief reason for this failure was not that the Arabs had made wholesale converts since 1967. This explanation might hold for a minority. For the larger number the cause had to be sought in a psychological retreat before the march of what appeared to be irreversible events. Among sympathizers of Israel, as distinct from Zionists, there were signs of battle fatigue.

One striking change in reaction should be noted. Up to the outbreak of the Yom Kippur War the image of invincible Israel still dominated much of the rhetoric even among intellectuals. Whatever the odds against the small Jewish state, it would prevail against the Arab hosts. It must be admitted that this notion was fed not only by the previous record of Israeli triumphs but by the confidence of Israeli spokesmen in their analyses of Arab military capacity. The view of Israel as the "strongest military power in the Middle East" able to take on all comers gave way to a more realistic estimate of what might be expected of two and a half million people pitted against one hundred million Arabs armed by the Russians with the deadliest weapons of modern technology. Not that the former legend was either flattering or reassuring. Few bothered to point out that a state routinely expected to perform miracles in order to justify its existence was being measured by a yardstick applied to no other people. By virtue of this thinking, because Israel in 1973 suffered heavily, its successful repulse of the Arabs was interpreted as a defeat and the actual Arab defeat as a victory. In the view of the general public the "myth of Israeli invincibility" was supposedly shattered; nor did the intellectuals, who presumably had a more sophisticated estimate of the course of the war, trouble to note that considering the disparity of forces and the introduction of Russian SAM Six missiles into the fighting, the Israel Army's accomplishment was no less remarkable than before.

So much for the sympathizers. For a notion of the reactions of that sector of the Jewish Left that granted Israel's right to exist while espousing the rights of the Palestinians and the justice of Arab claims, a piece by Arthur Waskow, author of "The Bush Is Burning," could be viewed as representative.[5] He called for Israel's total withdrawal and for the surrender of its claim for a Jewish Jerusalem. In a similar vein, Paul Jacobs indulged in routine attacks on the Israeli "establishment" and urged the recognition of a Palestinian state on the West Bank and Gaza.[6] In the same issue of *Ramparts* Noam Chomsky reiterated his concern for the Palestinian nationalists, whom he viewed as the "most tragic victims of the endless conflict." While championing Palestinian nationalism, the writer with incorrigible optimism continued to recommend "socialist internationalism" as the panacea for the ills of the Middle East.

The well known socialist author, Michael Harrington, who has consistently championed Israel, presented what could be viewed as a progressive liberal position which showed an understanding of Israel's vital interests as well as those of Palestinian nationalism:

> In the long run—which the Yom Kippur War makes me believe more than ever before must begin as soon as possible—a negotiated peace with the Arabs, involving their acceptance of Israel as a Middle Eastern state, is crucial. That, obviously, cannot be a matter of relying on promises or "world public opinion." It requires provisions which will really lift from Israel the tragic burden of constantly being in readiness to send its sons and daughters out to die in the struggle for national life itself. Moreover, it will have to resolve a tangle of conflicting interests: Israel's right to a secure and recognized existence (which, among other things, is not compatible with Arab arms poised on the pre-1967 frontiers); the Arabs' right to a settlement of their claims on the territories occupied in 1967; the Palestinian right to national self-determination.[7]

5. *New York Times*, November 24, 1973.
6. *Ramparts*, January, 1974.
7. *Midstream*, December, 1973.

Significant in this statement was Harrington's straight-forward declaration that Israel's security was "not compatible" with the pre-1967 borders. Harrington concluded his article with the warning that the oil weapon had made the defense of Israel more difficult than before the Yom Kippur War because the effects of an oil shortage would eventually affect American policy as it had that of Europe. At the same time, Harrington urged Israel's supporters not to turn to the American right because of their disenchantment with the Soviet Union's patronage and incitement of the Arabs.

The effect of the oil weapon on American thinking as reflected by the intellectual community is worth examining. The Arabs astutely motivated their oil blackmail with the demand for Israel's withdrawal from Arab land. The whole thrust of Arab propaganda concentrates on the return of occupied territory. While bloodcurdling calls for Israel's extermination still resound on the home front, as any monitoring of the Arab press or radio indicates, these cries have been muted for foreign audiences. In 1967 the Arabs learned that their candid zeal to "drink Israel's blood" was counter-productive in enlisting public opinion. There is no denying that the present Arab stance is more persuasive. When Arab spokesmen soberly, almost gently, voice their natural longing to regain their lost lands, the patrimony of their sons, the uninformed listener is not likely to quarrel with this desire. Many a good church-goer wonders why the stubborn Israelis do not implement U.N. Resolution 242 and go back peaceably to their borders, so giving everybody, including a weary world, a break. The Arab grievance, if taken at face value, can be formulated in one sentence: "Leave Arab lands." The rejoinder, compelling though it be, requires explication, perhaps even a glance at a map to bring the points home. It is all too easy for Israel's adversaries to exploit this advantage on the simplest grass roots level. And fears of an oil shortage or of American involvement provide fertile ground for cultivating anti-Israel sentiment.

Stalinist writers sought to exploit the situation along lines that could be gauged from an advertisement of the Communist Party. It said in part that continued occupation can only mean: never-ending warfare; escalated U.S. involvement leading to a new Vietnam with the danger of nuclear war and scrapping the promise of U.S.-U.S.S.R. détente; billions from U.S. taxpayers and severe cuts in spending for schools, housing, health and child care, etc.; a faster inflation and a long cold winter without fuel; promotion of anti-Arab hysteria in the U.S., and with this a growth of racism; growth of anti-Semitism as more and more people reject the costs of the war and wrongly blame all Jews rather than the Zionists and other U.S. monopoly interests who benefit from annexation. This hodgepodge indicates the ingenuity with which the extreme left managed to harp on every conceivable alarm and prejudice from the "growth of anti-Semitism" to "a long cold winter." Nothing was missed.

The extreme American right has also sought to inflame American opinion against Jews and Israel. (Automobile stickers bearing the legend "We need oil not Jews" appeared in various parts of the country.) To date the effect of such propaganda has been negligible. American intellectuals have taken the lead in stressing the need for America's independence and opposing surrender to Arab blackmail. The warning of eight distinguished American economists against such surrender has been taken seriously not only by academic and intellectual circles. The following extract from the *Wall Street Journal* is instructive:

> The U.S., for its part, has followed a correct policy in response to the Arab oil embargo. It has done its allies a great favor by not responding to suggestions—from the French, for example—that it join in appeasing the Arab states. Although they may not yet see it that way, it may well be doing the Arabs a great favor as well by warning them at the outset about the dangers of overreaching. Mr. Kissinger's threat of possible countermeasures against the Arab states if they become too persistent in wielding the oil weapon was entirely appropriate, given the gravity of the present situation. . . .
>
> If Mr. Kissinger is to play a firm, constructive role, he needs political support at home, such as that provided last week by eight leading American economists, Messrs. Samuelson, Arrow, Kuznets and Leontief, all Nobel laureates, and Messrs. Fisher, Solow, Galbraith and Peck. These eight urged the U.S. to resist "oil blackmail." Further urging along the same lines came on "Meet the Press" over the weekend from Walter J. Levy, one of the nation's foremost oil economists. It is particularly important that totally unrelated issues, such as Watergate, not be allowed to weaken the U.S. political stance.

A firm stand by the U.S. is vital at this juncture. And the Arab leaders in Algiers would be well advised to demonstrate some flexibility. We doubt that Western civilization is quite yet ready to be plunged into cold and darkness without uttering a peep in its own defense. . . .[8]

Among the most spirited demands made by American intellectuals that the United States preserve its moral integrity as well as economic independence in the face of Arab threats was that of the historian and former diplomat, George F. Kennan:

The relatively minor adjustment we would be obliged to make in order to get along without Arab oil, or at least without the oil of those who have cut us off at the present juncture, should be seen only as a beginning on a much wider process of self-emancipation from dependence on foreign-controlled sources of energy which we ought anyway to be putting in hand, with vigor and determination, at this stage in our national life.

We can be grateful that we were kicked into such a beginning. If we quail at this minor inconvenience, it will be a bad omen for our prospects for coping with the larger problem, for it will mean that our addiction to the wastage of energy, particularly through the medium of the automobile, is so abject that we prefer to face the loss of a considerable portion of our independence of policy rather than make even a minor effort to overcome the addiction. This would represent a humiliation which earlier American statesmen would never have accepted, and for which future generations of Americans would be unlikely to forgive us.[9]

Nevertheless, despite the restrained and principled position on oil blackmail for the most part taken by the intellectual community as represented by economists and political analysts, the question of the uninvolved intellectuals—Jew and non-Jew—remained. The fact that they allowed the use of their names on pro-Israel advertisements, or even signed a brief letter to the editor, could not be viewed as an adequate response in a time of crisis. Aharon Megged, observing the scene during a short stay in the United States, asked: "I have been appalled to witness the silence of American intellectuals in the face of the latest events. . . .

8. November 28, 1973.
9. *New York Times,* December 2, 1973.

Will not a few voices of courageous and conscientious intellectuals be heard at this troublesome time?"[10]

While reporting on Israel for *New York Magazine*, Nora Ephron, a feminist writer, also commented on the virtual abandonment of Israel by the world intellectual community. To the question, "Where are all the writers?" she answered:

> I have no idea what the answer to that question is, but I wonder whether part of it has to do with the effects of the Vietnam war, which, if it accomplished anything at all, managed to give war a thoroughly bad name. In any case, that is true for me.
>
> I constantly have to remind myself that the Israelis have had little choice but to fight, that it is inevitable for them to have become as chauvinistic and militaristic as they have.[11]

This explanation might have held good for some, particularly those like Miss Ephron, who though well aware that Israel was obliged to fight for survival nevertheless expected Jews to react differently from Egyptians, Russians or Syrians when in peril, but the basic reason for the failure to speak out at length and repeatedly lay in what has already been mentioned—a sense of impotence before a developing drama. It was the silence of passive complicity in a forthcoming sacrifice the bystanders felt unable to avert.

Such was the initial stunned reaction—a lack of response sufficiently notable to prompt distinguished critic Irving Howe to rephrase the questions of Megged and Ephron:

> Various intellectual prominences are silent. Some leaders of the Vietnam opposition, with trained capacities for public speech, have not said a word in behalf of Israel. Where is the great poet, conscience of America? Where is the sensitive psychiatrist who studies collective brainwashing? Where is the brilliant novelist, champion of the new, darling of the young?[12]

The significant element in Howe's protest was not the reiteration of a query already posed, though he did so in more

---

10. "Letter to the Editor," *New York Times*, December 14, 1973.
11. "Israeli Notebook: Thoughts With the Cease-fire," *New York Magazine*, December 3, 1973.
12. "Thinking the Unthinkable About Israel: A Personal Statement," *New York Magazine*, December 24, 1973.

pointed terms directly applicable to specific individuals who could be identified by literate Americans. Howe's article marked a new phase in the feeling toward the Yom Kippur War in that he went beyond interrogation. The writer called for action in behalf of beleaguered Israel on a scale commensurate with the activities intellectuals had carried on for other causes such as the Black revolution or the campaign against the Vietnam War. Concluding eloquently that silence was "intolerable," Howe urged his fellow intellectuals to resume their role of keepers of the conscience in behalf of Israel's independence:

> A time may come when it will be necessary to turn to more dramatic and militant methods, perhaps a march on Washington. A time may come when the traditional Jewish outcry of *gevalt!*, provoking scorn and worse, may be necessary. Let us keep our voices in readiness, but meanwhile there is the work of politics, pressure, persuasion.

As the strategy of the great powers became clearer, as the full scope of the oil weapon emerged, the sense of helplessness gave way to a greater militancy. The stakes were so high, the nature of a new world order with a fresh alignment of forces so much in the balance, that the fate of Israel, like the fate of the Jewish people throughout history, was again perceived as the barometer of international morality. To curry favor with Arab potentates by sacrificing Israel was so blatant a collapse of moral pretentions that whatever the dictates of expendiency, it aroused protest.

Furthermore, it became obvious that Israel still remained a considerable factor in shaping its future. The United States was not pressing Israel to make territorial concessions Israel found unacceptable. Serious negotiations were under way and despite an urgent desire for a Mideast settlement, the mediators understood that the autonomy and vital interests of Israel were not negotiable. This assurance was translated into serious discussion as to the terms of settlement, rather than capitulation—a discussion bound to involve the intellectual community once it had overcome the paralysis of initial shock.

The faithful band of Zionist intellectuals, who could not be accused of silence at any moment in the aftermath of the Yom Kippur War, continued the task of exposition they had set themselves. Among these, the writers associated with the Academic Association for Peace in the Middle East were particularly effective in refuting challenges to Israel's "legitimacy" raised by Arab propagandists, and through the publication of scholarly articles on various aspects of the energy crisis.

The new mood indicated a heightened awareness of Israel's exposed position. This sobering awareness was accompanied by an equally intensified realization of the fact that an independent Jewish state was an integral part of the modern world, and would so remain barring a total collapse of the world order, in which case the fates of large as well as small states would become uncertain. Politically and psychologically there was no going back to a "homeless" Jewish people. Israel's flourishing existence for over a quarter of a century had created a reality which even the Arabs were grudgingly beginning to acknowledge. Those hostile to Zionism understood, if reluctantly, that the map of the Middle East could not be redrawn to exclude Israel, while Zionists and their sympathizers appreciated more profoundly than ever at any time since the establishment of Israel that Jewish national independence constituted an irreversible historical development. All this was reflected in the writing of the intellectual community.

In a leading article in the *New York Times Magazine*, Norman Podhoretz wrote that American Jewry was at last wholly committed to Zionism and the survival of Israel.[13] The editor of *Commentary* described a degree of commitment among American Jews not all Zionists were able to perceive. But whether or not the writer's estimate of Zionist fervor among American Jews was a shade rosy, Podhoretz's article was another indication of a depth of feeling in regard to Israel not readily gauged by the first probings.

It should be noted that intellectual debate in the United States has been marked by a disconcerting reluctance to assert moral values. In the post-Vietnam era words like "justice" and "morality" are suspect. They have become depreciated

13. February 3, 1974.

currency. At the same time violence, individual or national, has become so familiar a staple of contemporary experience that a treacherous attack on the life of a small state or the most vicious excesses of Arab terrorism, do not arouse the large-scale revulsion that might normally have been anticipated. This blunting of sensibility is further complicated by the intellectual climate of the United States in which criminal acts are explained in terms of the supposed grievances of the perpetrators. Hence the most monstrous outrages find their defenders.

The foregoing makes the reassertion of the morality and justice of the Zionist case all the more imperative. The argument cannot be left solely to the exigencies of *reálpolitik*, potent though such considerations be. As long as Israel is under brutal attack, military or political, silence is culpable. This, many in the intellectual community are realizing with increased force.

Canada: Overview

Saul Hayes

An introductory comment on the Canadian setting will be helpful to this summary of Jewish reaction to the Yom Kippur War. Canada's politics, legal system, constitutional background, and history in international affairs can be encapsulated as follows:

1. Canada's Department of External Affairs, under late Nobel Laureate Lester B. Pearson, took an active part in Middle East affairs from 1946 to 1956. After 1957 it restricted its role to the U.N. Peace-Keeping Force. Since the "expulsion" of this force by Nasser, Canada's interest has waned.

2. Canada is really two worlds—French Canada and the rest of the country. French-Canadian leadership is not interested in foreign affairs, particularly the Middle East. This is true of its politicians, union leaders, churchmen, and media policymakers. Recent exceptions have been Quebec's warmth for the French-speaking countries of France and Belgium and those of Africa. One of the interesting features of Quebec's national isolationism is that French Canadians form 22.7 per cent of the Liberal Party in the House of Commons, and, in the Cabinet of thirty members, they number nine. (Not all are isolationist, but many prairie non-French Canadians are.)

3. Canadian leadership in English-speaking Canada is more concerned about foreign affairs. A White Paper issued by the Department of External Affairs, outlining the bases of Canada's foreign policy (1970), dealt with many areas of the world and international organizations of importance to Canada—U.N., Nato, Atlantic Alliance and the Commonwealth —but mentioned not a word on the Middle East, leaving us to conclude that, for them, it is a peripheral matter.

4. Oil is not a factor in Canada's foreign policy, since it

is one of the few industrialized nations which is self-sufficient in sources of energy.

5. Canada's political system is based on Cabinet responsibility, making it responsive to pressures by special-interest groups.

6. Canada's policy on arms, effective since the late 1950s, rules out gifts, loans, or cash sales of arms to countries in areas of the world where armed conflict exists or putatively exists. This made it impossible to submit petitions for arms for Israel. It is particularly difficult, if not impossible, to change this policy since all parties support it.

7. There are very few constituencies where a Jewish vote is decisive. Curiously enough, the Jewish vote does matter in Eglinton in Toronto, the seat held by Secretary of State Mitchell Sharp, and in Mount Royal of Montreal, the home base of Prime Minister Pierre Elliott Trudeau. Jews traditionally vote Liberal in federal elections and, short of hostility to Israel's cause, Jewish voters in the two ridings are not likely to repudiate their representatives.

8. Canada's total Jewish population, spread over 4,000 miles, numbers less than 300,000. Whatever political influence the Jews have is due not to numerical strength but to their position in Canadian society and among policy-makers. In Canada under the system of one man, one vote, bloc-interest voting has little significance.

Canadian Public Opinion

There never has been a serious problem of "dual loyalties" in Canada, because just as Jews have a single loyalty to the integrity and sovereignty of Israel so do the government of Canada and the opposition parties. The Canadian Jewish Congress (CJC) monitored the French and English newspapers very carefully and found nothing on the issue of the political viewpoint of Jews being inconsistent with their status as Canadians.

However, the question of dual loyalties appeared subliminally during the fund-raising campaign. Certain Canadians are very much concerned for native low-income groups, such as the Indian and Eskimo populations, which suffer from poor housing and insufficient diet, and the thousands in metropolitan areas living below the poverty level. These social-welfare partisans cannot understand why Canada has to worry about starvation in Biafra, or Nigeria, or Ethiopia, or other places. Similarly, such people cannot understand why Canada's relatively small Jewish population is willing to contribute large amounts of money to a foreign country when Canadian poor and disabled need help. Double loyalty is an accusation made not only by malicious anti-Israelis but also by serious, decent people. The theme is not that Jews should not help, but, as one recent editorial in a nationalist French Canadian paper asked, why Jews are not doing the same thing, in the same measure, for the poor of Canada. The phrase "double loyalty" is not used, but the inference is clear. The allegation also appeared in an editorial which praised the Jews for maintaining the integrity of Israel as a State, then asked why they did not support, equally, Quebec's independence. But these are not dominant views in Canada.

There was a certain amount of agitation by Canadian Arabs and Arab propaganda agencies, asking the government to investigate where Israel appeal money was going, alleging it was being used to purchase arms. The Congress dealt with this accusation by stating the actual facts—that the money was supporting the total economy of the country.

Official Government Policy on Israel

The government of Canada is in the hands of the Liberal Party and foreign policy is directed by Secretary of State for External Affairs Mitchell Sharp, whose constituency, as was mentioned, has a large proportion of Jewish voters. Government policy on the Middle East recognizes Israel's right to its integrity and its sovereignty. U.N. Resolution No. 242, calling for secure and defensible borders, remains the cornerstone of government policy, which means support of the resolution in the General Assembly and through other diplomatic channels. Canadian spokesmen have recognized that the October war was instigated by the Egyptians and Syrians, who were supported by Jordan and Iraq, and subsequently helped by

Algeria, Libya, and Kuwait. Canadian policy has been consistent, and has always acknowledged that an accommodation would have to be made with the Arab states in accord with Resolution 242. Public speeches made by prominent persons were all in favor of Israel, but when the oil-energy crisis became a world-wide issue, Canada was in a dilemma since it felt that it was friendly with both Israel and the Arab states.

In what is essentially a bi-cultural country, the Jewish entity flourishes and develops its group life and institutions. Jews in Canada are community-oriented. Consequently, any national representative organization was bound to be built beyond the religious interests of the Jews, and to concentrate on their status, welfare, and socio-cultural concerns. When the war broke on Yom Kippur day, the Canadian Jewish Congress, official representative organization of Canadian Jewry, was in contact with leaders of the government and major political parties. Canadian Jews wanted assurances that Canada would hold steadfast in its policy on Israel. Leaders met with government officials, with the Secretary for External Affairs, with members of Parliament, and with groups made up of representatives of the three pro-Israel parties. Congress representatives were also in constant touch with the senior civil service, and committees of the House, providing material favorable to the Israeli cause, a form of propaganda which was effective because it was straightforward factual information.

Community Activities for Israel

Following October 6, there were many meetings, mostly attended by members of the Jewish community, but with a sprinkling of representation of others who, like British non-Jewish Zionists of old, had a Zionist or theological philosophy. The principal rallies took place in the areas of dense Jewish population, Montreal and Toronto. Montreal has approximately 125,000, and Toronto 115,000 Jews. There were also many well-attended meetings in Winnipeg, Vancouver, Edmonton, in the Atlantic provinces, Ottawa, and other communities. These were held for two purposes: to manifest the community's solidarity with Israel and with the people of Israel; and to try to get sufficient coverage for the Israel point of view in all the public media. Most synagogues had special solidarity meetings.

During the first few days Canadian Jewish leaders were in an ambiguous situation. On the one hand, they were asked not to embark on an emergency campaign; on the other, they received calls from all parts of Canada asking, "When are we going to have a national fund-raising campaign?" But they did as advised and collected all previous pledges before going into the emergency campaign.

Just after the war broke out, Israeli Minister of Finance Pinchas Sapir, Mr. Arye L. Dulzin, Acting Head of the Jewish Agency, and General Haim Laskov came to Toronto and Montreal to meet with representatives of twenty-eight Canadian Jewish communities. They launched an Israel Bond Sale and the Emergency Campaign. Canada's response on a proportional population basis was very high, among the highest in the Jewish world. It was more than an act of philanthropy. It was a statement by the Jews of Canada, proudly expressed, that the war was not only Israel's war, but the war of the entire Jewish people.

The 1967 results amounted to about $30 million; afterwards there was a decline in fund raising. But as of January 1974, donations totalled about $70 million, over twice what the 1967 campaign produced. The response was more generous in 1973 because people realized that the situation was different from 1967; then the troops were disengaged very quickly and went back into the economic mainstream of life. This was not true in 1973. Israeli economic life is still not back to normal; and needs for social services are enormous.

As for personal identification, there is always a great out-pouring of voluntarism when Israel is in trouble. In 1967 and 1956 young people rushed to Israel not knowing where they were going or what they were going to do. In fact, in 1967 Israel was unable to deal with the thousands who arrived and could not be placed in useful tasks. This time a different type of volunteer came: doctors and engineers, who gave up several months of their practice at home, and performed extremely useful functions. The big hegira of young people from Canada to Israel which took place in 1967 was neither encouraged by the Jewish Agency, nor was it repeated on the part of the young in 1973, who are much more apathetic.

As for *aliyah*, there is not the same feeling that there was in 1967, because then Israel was a winning cause. In 1973 the war was a standoff, and while the need may be greater, the response is less.

However, on other fronts, all of Canadian Jewry rallied to the cause of Israel. We had felt we shared in the success of June 1967, and we felt as one in the tragedies of October 1973. There was the need to express feelings by fund raising, by bond purchases, by vigils and demonstrations, by insisting on the good offices of our government, by enlisting ecumenism, by soliciting avowals of friendship for the Israeli cause from our friends of the non-Jewish community, by telling the story of the historic right to Jerusalem as often as we could, and by countering the propaganda of Israel's enemies. In a word, by feeling for Israel's cause as the Israelis themselves did.

Canada: Overview

Irwin Cotler

In any analysis of Canadian Jewry's response during the Yom Kippur War one must necessarily consider a wide spectrum of themes. Among them I would include: the forms and manifestations of public identification; the character of political advocacy; the "politicization" of Jewish academics; the media and the "message" of Canadian Jewry; the "Winnipeg Experience," a case study in symbolic interactionism; and ultimately, the "delegitimization" of Israel—an agenda for Canadian Jewry. For the purpose of this volume we select two subjects.

The "Politicization" of Jewish Academics

During the Six Day War, the involvement of Jewish academics *qua* academics was negligible if not non-existent. Apart from several noteworthy—but individual—efforts, the Jewish professoriate in Canada received the anonymity it sought. Unlike their American counterparts, who were instrumental in the formation of the American Professors for Peace in the Middle East(APPME) and participated in the organized communal effort on behalf of Israel, the Jewish academics in Canada possessed neither an academic framework for involvement *qua* academics, nor integration in the organized Jewish community.

The response, or lack of it, of the Jewish academic in Canada, and the contrast with his American counterpart, has larger implications both in terms of what it suggests about the different relationships of the United States and Canada to Israel and the Middle East, as well as the political sociology of American and Canadian university faculty. The Middle East holds little interest for the Canadian academic, dovetailing with and reinforcing the observation made by Saul Hayes, that the Middle East is a low priority issue for Canadian foreign policy as a whole. On an intellectual level, there is very little writing on this subject; on a political or policy level, there are no "committees for new alternatives," nor submissions before Parliamentary Committees. Canadian academics, then, unlike their American counterparts, see no possibility—or even any need—of trying to influence a "non-policy." Moreover, Canadian academics—Jewish or non-Jewish—tend to be indifferent to, if not eschew, organizational involvement. The academic "lobby" has been a rather unknown, and, one might suspect, a rather unwelcome phenomenon in Canada.

The Yom Kippur War, however, may have generated a new orientation among faculty people. Indeed, as some have suggested, it may yet signify a new departure in their involvement and the beginning of organizational activity on the part of academe as a whole. The following summarizes the activities of Jewish academics in the immediate aftermath of the war.

1. Canadian Professors for Peace in the Middle East (CPPME) was organized to provide a framework of action for Jewish professors and their non-Jewish colleagues and to educate and inform public opinion in general, and academics in particular, of the underlying issues in the conflict.

2. A major educational project was undertaken to circulate a statement of principle signed by over four hundred Canadian academics, the large majority of whom were non-Jewish. It was important because it was the first time that Canadian academics had ever expressed themselves on the Arab-Israeli conflict.* Moreover, the very process of circulation and discussion of the statement had an intrinsic educational value, in terms of the "feedback" it offered about perspectives on the Arab-Israeli conflict amongst intellectuals.

3. Jewish academics not only participated but exercised a pivotal role in both the manifestations of public solidarity with Israel and on-going political advocacy. In the former, they delivered the keynote addresses at many of the

*See Appendix II, p. 355.

assemblies and demonstrations; in the latter, they prepared the working papers on political advocacy and formed part of the delegations making representations to government.

4. Unlike 1967, when fund raising (as distinct from private contributions) as an organized activity was resisted by Jewish academics, the Yom Kippur War prompted not only an increase in contributions, but participation in the fund raising itself. At many of the universities, Jewish academics organized the fund-raising effort in conjunction with the local Jewish welfare structure; at other places, such as Osgoode Hall Law School at York University, a contribution of over $8,000 resulted from the spontaneous initiatives of faculty members themselves.

5. Faculty members are often perceived as "significant others" by various students, particularly as concerns "politicized" questions. They may become the reference norm for students' behavior, whether it be in the initiation of political activity or forbearance from it. Unfortunately, Jewish academics have too often been perceived as indifferent to, if not benignly neglectful of, Jewish concerns, a posture which has tended to dissuade students from involvement, or to suggest that "pro-Israeli" activity was somehow "unacademic" or "illegitimate." The public expressions of Jewish academics, therefore, may have served as a "rehabilitation" not only of the Israeli position, but of the advocacy of that position, which had become increasingly discredited in intellectual circles.

The response of Jewish academics to the Yom Kippur War, as outlined above, appears to "deviate" from the tradition of Canadian academe as previously described. It may well be that, however encouraging the indicators appear to be, the activity is more representative of Jews who happen to be academics rather than the emergence of a collective consciousness amongst Jewish academics as a whole.

The "Winnipeg Experience": Operation Outreach

One of the more unique dimensions of Canadian Jewry's response to the Yom Kippur War—a useful case study of impact and response—is what has come to be known in Canada as the "Winnipeg Experience." This refers to a series of informal discussions between a group of prominent Winnipeg Jews and their non-Jewish counterparts on the Yom Kippur War, the opinions expressed therein, and the initiatives taken in consequence thereof.

A small group of Winnipeg Jews shared a number of common characteristics. First, they were unusually distinguished in the field of public service, e.g., two Leaders of the Opposition Parties in the Manitoba Legislature, a former executive assistant to the Secretary of State for External Affairs, and the Chairman of the Canadian Consumers Council. Secondly, they were not affiliated with any of the Jewish organizations, nor did they work through or on behalf of the parent organizations or any of their affiliates. Finally—and perhaps most importantly—they were linked by their identification with and commitment to Israel and the Jewish people. The non-Jews in the interaction included their counterparts in politics, business, and public service, and embraced a formidable cross-section of the leadership of the various "publics" in the city of Winnipeg and province of Manitoba —representing thereby a microcosm of the general Canadian community.

In the course of these "informal encounters" between the Winnipeg Jews and their non-Jewish counterparts—most of whom were either sympathetic or benignly neutral to the Israeli cause—a number of prevailing attitudes emerged.

1. The Yom Kippur War was not perceived as a "war of survival," but as "just another round" between the combatants.

2. The Yom Kippur War was seen as a continuation of the Six Day War. Accordingly, since Israel was the "aggressor" in the Six Day War and unlawfully seized Arab territory, the Arabs had only gone to war to regain their lost territory.

3. The war was not unrelated to the "intransigence" of Israeli policy. Israel should be less inflexible and more conciliatory—including the return of the occupied territories—if Israel genuinely wants peace.

4. The legitimacy—rather than the fact—of Israeli statehood was not understood. Palestinian "homeland" was believed to have been "usurped" in the creation of the State of Israel. A compensatory initiative—such as the creation of a

Palestinian state—was now necessary.

5. Israel was perceived as ignoring the plight of the Palestinian refugees; no mention was made of Jewish refugees from Arab lands.

6. The Russian involvement in the Middle East was not appreciated, either as an ominous threat to the State of Israel or to East-West relations.

7. There was very little understanding of the "asymmetry" of United States aid to Israel in comparison with Russian aid to Egypt and Syria; rather, the prevailing belief was that United States aid to Israel—and the financial support of world Jewry—greatly outstripped assistance to the Arabs and Arab oil wealth. Indeed, the discovery that in fact American aid to the Arabs had been greater than its aid to Israel was a shock.

8. There did not appear to be much disturbance about Canadian Jewish fund raising for Israel. Many Canadian non-Jews had responded financially and politically to other overseas causes (Biafra, Bangladesh, etc.) but they had never been asked to contribute either financial or political support for Israel.

9. The Israeli prisoner-of-war problems with the Egyptians (formerly) and with the Syrians were not felt to be particularly important or compelling issues. All wars were deemed to have prisoners-of-war problems and the Middle East situation was not unique.

The Winnipeg group tested these attitudes with friends in other parts of Canada, particularly in governmental, industrial, and professional circles, and the opinions expressed were surprisingly similar; the dominant motif in all cases seemed to be either mis-information or lack of information.

Accordingly, the Winnipeg group undertook a series of initiatives designed to explain and represent the case for Israel in Canada. These included parlor meetings in the homes of prominent non-Jews; over fifty speaking engagements at general service clubs and groups throughout metropolitan Winnipeg; a "speakers' briefing seminar" for Jews and non-Jews, at which background presentations were made on the major discussion areas of conflict; over seventy-five speaking assignments to Jewish groups in order to "brief"

Jewish leadership so that the advocacy for Israel would be both informed and informing; and small group "counterpart" meetings with media, politicians, academics, students, labor, and other influence makers and conveyors of opinion.

The immediate responses were encouraging. News coverage of the Middle East became more informed and editorial opinion more enlightened; prominent politicians joined in demonstrations and voiced their support; clergymen, academics, and other "publics" expressed their concern. And, perhaps most important, a significant number of non-Jews who had attended parlor meetings with the Winnipeg group volunteered to host similar gatherings in their own homes with other participants, thus introducing a "multiplier" effect into the information campaign.

The Winnipeg experience is both instructive and significant in several respects. It provides a useful case study of attitudes and perceptions held by non-Jews considered sympathetic to Israel; it reveals, as indicated, that these attitudes and perceptions are grounded fundamentally in both mis-information as well as lack of information; it suggests that there exists a responsive "latitude of acceptance" for the Israeli case; and it demonstrates that an informed presentation of Israel's case, made by "significant others" with an understanding of the target group, and an appreciation of communications dynamics, can disabuse "publics" of half-truths and mis-information.

What is needed, therefore, is a repetition of the "Winnipeg Experience" in many communities—and not only in Canada—involving the public affirmation of Israel's case as well as the case itself; the enlisting of widely respected non-Jewish spokesmen who will be prepared to promote the Israeli case; and the "people to people" counterpart approach in advocacy for Israel, organized on a "small groups" basis, media with media, academics with academics, etc.—the whole with a view to generating a "critical mass" of élite and popular support for Israel.

Canada: Perspectives

Emil L. Fackenheim

If historical events rarely prove anything decisively enough to *force* intellectuals to reappraise their previous positions, the Yom Kippur War may seem to illustrate this fact more dramatically than most other events in recent history. At the time of the Six Day War few could deny that the Arabs aimed at the destruction of Israel, and only after the event could the legend find credence that they had never meant to go beyond "mere words" or, indeed, had been "sucked into" the war. In contrast, the Yom Kippur War produced opposite reactions from the start, and these persist to this day. To one group of intellectuals this war is proof of the wisdom of Israel's refusal to withdraw from the 1967 lines. (Had she done so, the war would have been fought in Tel Aviv and Jerusalem, and Israel might have perished.) To another, this same refusal is proof of the folly of Israel's "intransigence." (Had she withdrawn, the war would never have started.) These conflicting reactions extend to non-Jewish and Jewish intellectuals alike. One Toronto Protestant minister (who was forced to change his previous position) confessed that for the first time he understood how fragile was the existence of Israel, and how she must necessarily consider her security before all else. (He was appalled that he had not seen this before, and hoped—though not very hopefully—that his colleagues would now understand.) Yet a well-known American Jewish scholar (who saw no need to change *his* previous position) confessed his sin of not having criticized Israel for *her* sins against the Arabs more harshly, and vowed to do better in the future. Thus, it may well seem to the bystander that this war has proved nothing.

Yet the opposed views are so far from being equally well-founded that we are not faced with a situation in which nothing has in fact been proved, but rather with what may be called a "nothing-is-proved" syndrome which stands in need of scrutiny. To this must be added another—what we may term the "war-is-over" syndrome. No one would have guessed during the Yom Kippur War how quickly and thoroughly nearly everyone—intellectual and ordinary citizen, Jew and non-Jew—would return to business-as-usual. And if it be replied that such is normal human behavior one must immediately ask whether such "normalcy" is responsible when the war obviously is *not* over: not only may *actual* war break out again at any moment, but also, to reverse Clausewitz, politics, as currently conducted at Geneva and elsewhere, is war carried on with different means—with dangers to Israel which are extreme.

In view of the "nothing-is-proved" and the "war-is-over" attitudes, it is well to ask at the outset whether, as the result of the Yom Kippur War, *something has really happened* in the consciousness of intellectuals (so that the "nothing-is-proved" attitude only touches the surface, and the "war-is-over" attitude is mere escapism), or, on the contrary, *nothing* has happened, business-as-usual is real, and this crisis, like others before it, has come and gone without a trace—except, of course, for the Israelis who must live with its consequences. This question involves not only one particular historical judgment but also a philosophical view of history as a whole. Does the consciousness of intellectuals *ever* matter in history? And is it possible for the conscious responses of a few to have large consequences? Are there events after which, business-as-usual notwithstanding, history is not the same?

We hold that something *has* happened to the consciousness of intellectuals under the impact of the Yom Kippur War, yet espouse that view aware of its fragility. There are those who maintain with some plausibility that even the Six Day War has changed nothing in the minds of Jewish intellectuals, to say nothing of their non-Jewish colleagues. On our part, we shall be able to illustrate and corroborate our view but cannot demonstrate it. Only generations hence—if then—will conclusive answers be given to what we take to be the essential questions of this essay and, indeed, of the whole volume of which it is a part: Exactly *what* have been and continue to be the significant intellectual responses to the Yom Kippur War? And, more radically still, have even these responses been *ultimately* significant, that is, part of a new page in Jewish if not world history, so profound as to change the minds and even lives of men?

Canadian Response

Intellectuals are said to know no borders. This view has only limited truth. Compared to the United States or France, Canada has had little public intellectual debate in the wake of the Yom Kippur War. It is true that Canada has few Jewish intellectuals, and also that she is widely regarded as an intellectual backwater. We dig deeper, however, when we look for an explanation to the emerging Canadian national character.

For better or worse, the Yom Kippur War has caused national character to emerge (or re-emerge) in many countries. (Holland is still Holland, Belgium is still Belgium, and as for France—shades of Petain.) Canada has been no exception. Rather than *being* a nation, this country is still in the process of trying to become one, under circumstances which cause intellectuals generally to consider Canadian nationalism a good thing when elsewhere they might consider nationalism a bad thing.

A prominent feature of the emerging Canadian nationhood is her self-image—well- or ill-founded—as an honest broker among the nations, an image first taking shape when Canada, hardly freed from the old colonial dependence on Great Britain and rightly fearing to fall into a new neo-colonial dependence on the United States, began to struggle to carve a role for herself as a bridge between these two countries. This role has found its most authentic reality thus far in the person of Lester B. Pearson, a towering figure in the United Nations activities leading to the endorsement of a Jewish State, and winner of the only Canadian Nobel Peace Prize for his part in settling the 1956 Arab-Israeli conflict. It is thus not outlandish to suggest that the issue between Israel and the Arabs and Canadian identity are not unconnected.

Against this background the general Canadian response

to the Yom Kippur War becomes intelligible, which is not to say, however, that it is admirable. For there has been a general decline in national purpose since the Pearson era. At the outset of the war the former leader of the Opposition challenged the Government to condemn Syrian and Egyptian aggression. Evading the challenge, the Government in the days and weeks to come promised support, now to one side, then to the other, only to end up scrambling furiously to achieve "neutrality"—a neutrality which was acknowledged as such by a representative Arab delegation on their next visit.

The extent to which the Canadian Government yielded to Arab petro-colonialism is dismaying in view of the fact that, alone among all the non-communist industrial nations, she is wholly self-sufficient in this area, and suffers only a temporary problem of distribution, the solution of which costs money, patience and, above all, a sense of national purpose. Much encourages the depressing conclusion that in the present crisis Canada has lost its national purpose altogether and sunk into a crass self-seeking materialism which threatens to balkanize the country, a threat evident in the current feud over profits between the provinces which have the oil and the rest of the country which needs it. However, it is probably more correct and more just to say that the national purpose has not vanished but is rather in a state of crisis. This crisis of purpose manifested itself in the frantic search—as if desperately seeking to recapture better days—for the prestige of becoming part of a new United Nations Peace-Keeping Force; and the search not only started while the war was still raging but also gripped, if not the people, the media as well as the Government. The slightest sign of a possible role for Canada was enough to create headlines and editorials across the country, eclipsing the actual life-and-death struggle in the Middle East even as it was still taking place. For actual news of the war (rather than its potential effect on Canada) one more often than not had to switch from Canadian to U.S. media, and the prestigious Government-owned CBC was the worst offender. It is the considered opinion of the present writer (who has spent virtually all his adult life in Canada) that rarely have the very factors which have helped to shape the as yet uncertain and insecure Canadian national consciousness—the urge to mediate all conflicts at home and abroad, the fear of U.S. domination, and others—prevented Canada so thoroughly from rising to national greatness at a moment when she had the chance. And the moment has passed.

In this setting the Canadian Jewish community—more cohesive and of more recent origin than its U.S. counterpart, and for these reasons alone generally more strongly committed to Israel—found itself, when Israel's very existence was at stake, in a state of being torn between bitter frustration with its own Government and gratitude for small mercies. As for its intellectuals, they to a degree shared the general tendency of shifting attention from the war itself to the possibilities of a mediating Canadian role in the conflict. To be sure (as will be seen), those Jewish intellectuals who are committed to Israel spoke and acted more firmly than ever. However, if there was not much heated or high-level debate among Canadian intellectuals, Jewish or non-Jewish, the conditions described in this section may well be as good an explanation of the phenomenon as can be given.

Non-Jewish Intellectuals

This account of the reaction of non-Jewish intellectuals must begin with an action of Jewish intellectuals. In 1967 Jewish professors at the University of Toronto hesitated how to approach their non-Jewish colleagues, wondered whether a petition headed by a Jewish professor might do more harm than good, and (after a few attempts to find a non-Jewish colleague to head a petition had failed) did nothing. (At other universities the situation was probably much the same, or worse.) This time, all such considerations were swept aside as irrelevant, and Jewish professors did not hesitate to approach or even confront their non-Jewish colleagues openly and frankly. This difference is all the more remarkable since before the Six Day War the whole Jewish people perceived the specter of a second Holocaust, whereas during the entire period of the Yom Kippur War it was never realized, for reasons to be given below, that this time the actual danger was far greater.

It would seem that this difference in response—to be

sure, by a minority of Canadian Jewish intellectuals, perhaps even a small one, but a minority which counts and will continue to count—can be understood only in terms of the Six Day War experience, reinforced by the Soviet Jewish struggle. There are now Jewish intellectuals and professors in Canada for whom certain things Jewish are no longer subject to debate. Among these are Israel's right to live; the duty of Jews outside Israel to back this right; and·the exercise of this duty with apologies to no one.

Jewish professors discovered that the reactions of New Left and similar anti-Israeli intellectuals were either over-estimated during the last few years, or had become weakened, and were in any case wholly predictable, increasingly ludicrous as petro-colonialism reared its ugly head, and certainly overshadowed by far more real dangers. The Canadian New Left has in any case always had an air of unreality, unable to rid itself of the contradiction of following its U.S. counterpart to the point of borrowing issues virtually non-existent in Canada, while at the same time trying to be second to no one in Canadian nationalist fervor. This unreality fully displayed itself during the Yom Kippur War crisis. (A meeting of Arab students at the University of Toronto called to counter our meeting of several hundred attracted only a handful of forlorn Arab and New Left sympathizers, until through misguided zeal about two hundred Jewish students came to argue with them.)

The above is not to deny that New Left anti-Israel ideologies do not continue to have their effect, and perhaps the most frightening recent proof is that a man of spiritual stature such as Father Daniel Berrigan can preach the most vicious anti-Israel propaganda, largely couched in New Left terminology. However, perhaps precisely such extreme examples may help solve a riddle inherent in the New Left anti-Israel stance all along. How could anyone—let alone an intellectual—ever seriously classify *kibbutzim* as outposts of imperialism and at the same time consider Saudi or Kuwaiti oil sheiks as true (if unwitting and unwilling) representatives of socialism? This riddle finds at least a partial solution if outpourings such as Berrigan's are understood as dialectical transformations of Christian theological anti-Semitism. The elements are all there: the identification with the crucified Jew at Auschwitz; the hostility to the Israeli soldier who refuses to be crucified in physical fact or theological thought; and, above all (as at least one critic otherwise sympathetic to Berrigan has noticed[1]), the sweeping and even savage refusal to consider any hard evidence which does not fit into, and might disturb, the neat framework.

Far more serious than the New Left (although, if the above is correct, not its hidden mainspring) is what has been called the "steady process of delegitimization of Israel" since the Six Day War, both in the community at large and among intellectuals. Neutral and even friendly non-Jewish colleagues approached by Jewish professors often came up, in obvious sincerity, with propositions such as:

> "How can you argue with a man thrown out of his house who wants it back?"
> "It is fair enough if they were the aggressors this time; you were the aggressors last time."
> "Israel is intransigent as regards territory, refugees etc."

Can learned professors have forgotten the closing of the Gulf of Aqaba, Nasser's encirclement, the Khartoum conference, Egyptian agreements broken days after they were made concerning Russian missiles at the Suez canal? One may wish to explain the delegitimization of Israel presupposed in the above statements in terms of the increasingly subtle, world-wide Arab propaganda. But this only raises the deeper question of why, for all the unlimited wealth at its disposal, this propaganda should have been so effective, and the delegitimization of Israel so shockingly easy.

Canadian Jewish professors may have touched this deeper question with a petition circulated at universities (see Appendix II) which made these points: 1. Israel's right to exist in security; 2. the need for direct negotiations; 3. the characterization of the Arab aim as the destruction of Israel, not merely the recovery of territory lost in 1967.

Few of our non-Jewish colleagues balked at the first and

---

1. Paul Cowan, "The Moral Imperialism of Dan Berrigan," *Village Voice*, January 31, 1974, pp. 22–23.

second of these points. Many, however, balked at the third. They in all honesty refused to believe that Israel's existence was in any danger. In view of consistent and uncompromising threats for a quarter of a century, backed by ever-more formidable armaments and now, all of a sudden, vast, oil-based political power, this refusal may seem incredible. Yet it is real.

To a degree, Israel's public stance may itself be to blame. If *everyone* (this writer included) failed to realize the *full* extent of the danger during the first few days of the war, it was because the Israeli government kept this fact a secret. At a meeting of Toronto Jewish leaders on October 8 the local Israeli consul gave us the following message, as coming directly from Jerusalem: "Victory is ours."

It could be argued that this policy decision, whatever its higher necessities, will have a deleterious effect on the public mind for a long time to come; that now in hindsight only the most imaginative among Israel's friends can relive the danger, while all the less friendly and imaginative fail altogether; and that thus the perversion of the David-Goliath imagery which first took root after the Six Day War survives unscathed after the Yom Kippur War, along with the devastating view that Israel is both morally obliged and physically able to make all the concessions.

However, this line of reasoning cannot withstand closer scrutiny. In the months since the Yom Kippur War the Arab pseudo-David has given world-wide proof of being in fact a super-Goliath, able to shake countries and continents and showing no scruples in doing so. Yet this proof has not noticeably affected the perversion of the imagery. Nor has it produced among intellectuals a rash of articles, meetings, and the like, the content of which is opposition to petro-colonialism and affirmation of Israel's right to live with secure boundaries, the same right—no more and no less—as is enjoyed by every other nation. One asks: Precisely *what* would have to happen to produce the universal recognition among intellectuals that—alone among existing nations—Israel has been faced with the threat of extinction during her entire life?

The pondering of what is behind this refusal to believe in the face of all the evidence drives one to the grim conclusion that its other side is found in statements (also heard at the time when our petition was circulated) such as "The danger of nuclear warfare is too high a price to pay for Israel." (This writer heard of a lady in Ottawa, prominent in Liberal party circles, who during the war was trying to obtain land in Canada for Jewish refugees from Israel who were sure to come when the State was destroyed.) In short, there is a frightening ambivalence in the mind. In one corner, it refuses to face the possibility of a mortal threat to the existence of Israel; in the other, it has already sold out. This ambivalence would seem to be one source of the "nothing-is-proved" syndrome referred to at the outset.

A few of us found much the same ambivalence among a group of Quakers who visited Toronto two years ago, on a tour to argue the merit of their book on the Middle East with Jewish leaders. Their spokesman opened the session by stating that peace was essential, and that the obstacle was Arab technological backwardness. However, he soon reversed himself under sharp questioning. ("If technology is the key, why does your book not say so?") Peace was still of the essence. The obstacle, however, was no longer technology or the lack thereof, but the existence of a Jewish state.

Maximally, this ambivalence calls to mind the attitude of those who first refused to believe that a Holocaust was happening, and, when forced to accept the fact that it *had* happened, asked Jews with the most indecent haste to "forgive and forget." Even minimally, however, it reflects a conscious or unconscious moral cynicism to which the mere *fact* that Israel's right to exist is not universally accepted suffices to make this right *itself* "controversial." Yet the same intellectuals who display such cynicism vis-à-vis Israel would presumably not hesitate to condemn South African apartheid, despite the fact that many or most South African whites consider it right.

In the above we have dwelled—perhaps more than is warranted by the evidence—on the negative. It is necessary to give the positive at least equal emphasis.

In their approach to their non-Jewish colleagues Canadian Jewish professors came upon some surprising opponents but also, more importantly, on some surprising friends. Not a few of these latter considered the three propositions in the petition as self-evident, and the fact that Jewish professors should ask their support the most natural thing in the world. If these included men who had never before stood up for Israel it is probably *because they had never been asked.* And if *this* had never been done, the probable cause is that even in Canada Jewish intellectuals dare not yet quite believe that they have many colleagues so totally free of anti-Semitism that Israel's right to live requires in their eyes no defense. (Among those wholly free of anti-Semitism one should count also those genuinely troubled by the complexities of the moral issues, so long as they were willing to face the threat to Israel's existence, and pay more than lip service to her survival.)

We move into an entirely different realm when we turn to a response to the Yom Kippur War made by a group of prominent Canadian Christians. In 1967 our Christian friends, except for a handful, responded with a silence probably due to confusion; and our Christian enemies took the initiative with attacks which went on for years. In 1973 there was no confusion among our friends; it was *they* who took the initiative, and their statement was outstanding, not to say unique, for these reasons. First, its fourteen signatories included eminent Roman Catholic and United Church heads of colleges and theologians. Second, the statement was produced entirely spontaneously, without any Jewish requests and, one gathers, as a result of soul-searching ever since the Six Day War. Third, the statement itself has a quality which to the best knowledge of this writer has been achieved by no similar Christian statement. It includes the following points: (1) Zionism is an early modern liberation movement. (2) By its very existence Israel is "both a reminder and a rebuke to Christians for their role in the Jewish plight in the twentieth century." (3) Israel is to Jews "a resurrection symbol following the near extinction of the Jewish people within living memory." (4) For Christians "the option of remaining neutral .   does not exist . . . in a conflict where the object is apparently not merely the recovery of territory but the destruction of the Jewish political community." (5) While obviously obligated to act in sympathy with the Palestinian refugees, the churches have no right to abuse this sympathy to assume a posture of moral objectivity or a mediatorial role, for both of which they are long disqualified by their past record toward the Jewish people.[2]

This initiative by our Christian friends not only put our Christian enemies on the defensive but also made them look sick. A letter by fourteen University of Toronto professors stooped to accusing the above statement of "virulent antisemitic prejudice against the Arabs," since they too were "Semites and cousins of the Jews"[3]—as if learned professors might not be expected to know that "antisemitism"—a term concocted in nineteenth century Germany—had nothing to do with "Semites."[4] And a letter by United Church officialdom accused the statement of serving to "polarize local feeling."[5] That very officialdom had boasted of "not being a monolithic body" whenever it was asked why, since 1967, it permitted its official magazine, *The United Church Observer,* to follow a policy consistently hostile to Israel. Now that United Church leaders of far greater prominence than the *Observer* editor made a pro-Israeli statement the great United Church virtue-of-not-being-a-monolithic-body suddenly became a vice.

Jewish Intellectuals

We have already referred to Canadian Jewish intellectuals willing to stand with Israel with apologies to no one, and attributed their new stance to the Six Day War experience and the Soviet Jewry struggle. We must now add, more precisely, that while such intellectuals have always existed, they were

2. Toronto *Globe & Mail,* October 19, 1973. See Appendix III, pp. 356–358. ·
3. *Loc. cit.,* October 24, 1973.
4. On May 17, 1943 a certain Hans Hagemeyer of the Nazi Foreign Office gave the following directive concerning the use henceforth of the word "antisemitism":
> When the Grand Mufti visited *Reichsleiter* Rosenberg the latter promised to instruct the press to eliminate henceforth the word "antisemitism." The use of this word always hits the Arab world, arñd this latter, according to the Grand Mufti, is overwhelmingly friendly to Germany. Our enemies abroad exploit our use of this word in order to give the false impression that we look on Arabs as we do on Jews.

Poliakov-Wulf, *Das Dritte Reich und die Juden: Dokumente und Aufsaetze,* Berlin, 1955, p. 369.
5. *Loc. cit.,* October 30, 1973.

not organized prior to the Six Day War, and even the *ad hoc* committees formed before that war vanished when it was over. However, it would seem that while the organizations vanished the experience itself did not, for this was doubtless the major cause why the Soviet Jewish struggle produced, to this writer's knowledge for the first time in Canadian Jewish history, a professorial organization which is more than *ad hoc* in character. And this history in turn at least partly explains why the Yom Kippur War, unlike its predecessor, has produced an organization which bids fair to last. Together with its many weaknesses—relative lack of leadership, insufficient organization, political inexperience, and of course, above all, smallness of size—it has virtues which bid fair to outweigh them. Among these are impatience with ideological and other nonsense; a willingness to act rather than remain with words; and some signs of readiness for what is sure to be a long haul.

This last characteristic is the most important, and the best promise that what has been begun will last. This is a sober perception that the war is *not* over, and this perception may well carry in train the development of Jewish leadership coming from academic circles; and—it is important to add in view of problems to be tackled below—academic Jewish support for Israel abroad is sure to spill over into academic Jewish support for Jewish causes at home as well.

If some Jewish intellectuals perceive that the war is not over, there are others (and here we have in mind Americans more than Canadians) who speak, argue and act as though it had never taken place. Even while the war was still raging there were intra-Jewish intellectual quarrels as to the nature and destiny of the Jewish or Israeli soul which seemed almost totally oblivious to the fact that there were Arab enemies and Russian missiles attacking Jewish bodies. To each side the war proved the correctness of its own ideology, and the main concern seemed to be, not Israel's survival and the chances of peace, or even bridges between themselves and the Israelis, but whether they, in their ideological conflicts, could still speak to each other.

It is a well-known intellectuals' weakness to insert ideological castles in the air between themselves and realities, and ideological unrealism may well be the partial cause of this extreme manifestation, on the Jewish side, of the "nothing-is-proved" syndrome which we have already come upon on the non-Jewish side. In both cases, however, it seems too unspecific to explain it wholly. What additional factors are at work? Probably many, among them the following: a delegitimization of Israel among Jewish as well as non-Jewish intellectuals; a demand that—of all nations—Israel alone be perfect and, as the ideology may demand, either commit no moral sins or make no military and political mistakes; and, finally, an inability to face the possibility of a second Jewish catastrophe in a single generation.

Of these factors the deepest would appear to be the last-named, for it has affected far wider circles than the narrow one hitherto referred to, and done much to produce what we have called the "war-is-over" syndrome. Even serious communal leaders have expressed such views as "Now that the war is over we can go back and worry about our domestic problems," or "Since Israel's decisions affect us all, a new framework should be created which permits American Jewish leadership to participate in major Israeli political decision-making." These responsible leaders would not hold either of these opinions if they realized that the "war-is-over" view is so far from the truth that in every major political decision taken now or in the foreseeable future Israel risks her life. Then why is this *not* realized by some otherwise responsible Jewish leaders in North America? Surely it is less plausible (as well as less fair) to blame a lack of identification or political imagination than what may be described as a shrinking from an unprecedented shudder which shook the whole Jewish world. This shudder occurred in those terrible days and weeks when Israel was in virtually total isolation—*and so were Jews the world over.* The shades of the fearful thirties were with us again, and there was a well-warranted fear of a new anti-Semitism, this time lent explosive power by the world's need for oil.

Happily the fears have proved unfounded (which is not to say that they do not still lurk underneath, and that the evils feared have wholly vanished). The moment of shudder has passed. But it is not implausible that the whole complex of traumatic events and traumatic fears is now not only fogotten by the indifferent but also blocked by some of the most committed.

This interpretation is lent further support if we recapture an experience which was ours at the height of the crisis and in the midst of the shudder—an experience which can be likened only to a moment of apocalyptic truth. In that moment Jews normally united were divided.

One group felt an identification with Israel which had grown far beyond what was manifest in the Six Day War: her shock was theirs; her questioning as to what had gone wrong was theirs; her mourning was theirs; her transistor addiction was theirs. Above all, when Israel was fighting for her life, they knew that they could not expect her to pull the Diaspora's chestnuts out of the fire, but, on the contrary, had to fight on Israel's behalf where they were.

The feeling of the other group found expression in sentiments such as "Israel is not all of Judaism," or "The Jewish people has survived the destruction of the Second Commonwealth and would survive the demise of the third." One Toronto father told his son who wanted to go to Israel as a volunteer that, in case Israel went down, Judaism would require committed young Jews in the Diaspora.

We refer here not to the indifference of the uncommitted or the abandonment by the semi-committed, but rather to what may be described as a "hedging of bets" on the part of those considered genuinely committed, both by others and by themselves. No one ever said that Israel was all of Judaism. Then why the need to deny it at the time of Israel's greatest peril? No father can be blamed for fearing for his son's life. But why connect his personal fears with a catastrophic view of the Israeli—and Jewish—future? At the moment of shudder some of the most committed of Israel's Jewish friends found themselves able not only to consider the possibility of Israel's demise but also to think—however fragmentarily and guiltily—of the day after. The Six Day War, if but for a moment, united the whole Jewish people, including some of the most marginal. The Yom Kippur War, if but for a moment, divided the most committed.

This experience in the moment of shudder may help

explain the emergence since that time of otherwise totally puzzling organized efforts to reconsider the priorities in North American Jewish life. In these organized efforts, the question is being raised of "whether an almost exclusive concern with Israel has not caused a withering away of Jewish life in the Diaspora," and concern with Israel is described as "vicarious participation in the life of Israel." The description goes on:

> Support of Israel has so captured the energies of American Jews that many have abandoned hopes for the development of vigorous and creative Jewish communities in the Diaspora.

It concludes:

> Due to the Yom Kippur War, the present time is critical because for the first time the question of Israel's and the Diaspora's security has seriously arisen.[6]

How can we understand these organized efforts? Even if the issues were the perennial financial ones—say, the relative allocation of funds to Israel and to educational institutions in North America—one should be puzzled, not only by the unnecessary and indeed obfuscating ideological terminology, but above all by the *timing* of the proposed reappraisal. Can the North American Jewish community seriously consider cutting down its financial commitments to Israel at the precise time of her gravest financial crisis? After the Six Day War such a move might have been intelligible. After the Yom Kippur War the reappraisal, if any, should be the reverse.

The puzzle deepens as one recognizes that the issues transcend the financial; that the cited views are apparently seriously held, and, according to their proponents, are receiving a wide response. But how *can* they be serious? To be sure, one who does not know what it has meant to be a Jew these forty years may accept readily enough that it is one thing to be over there, another thing to be over here, and that for a Jew living here to act as though he were there is to live vicariously. But let him *learn* what it has meant to be a Jew

6. *Canadian Jewish News*, February 15, 1974.

since the year 1933—and he no longer understands distinctions of this kind. A generation ago the world was divided into one half bent on the murder of every available Jewish man, woman and child, and another half which reacted half-heartedly when it reacted at all. After this event, what would the surviving Diaspora be without an Israel? Except for a few pockets of the faithful, a remnant in total disarray, with assimilation, self-hatred and despair rampant everywhere! The Diaspora's "participation in the life of Israel" is a merely "vicarious" affair, a "concern" which may have caused a "withering away of Jewish life in the Diaspora" and robbed its communities of "creativity" and "vigor." One requires only historical imagination to recognize that the exact opposite is the truth! Israel has made even Jews indifferent to her more wholesome, more at peace with their past and future—and better Jews. After the Holocaust, it is Israel, more than any other single factor, which gives Diaspora communities such "vigor" and "creativity" as is theirs. Israel has produced the miraculous resurrection of Soviet Jewry from almost certain extinction, a fact which in itself proves there is not, or at any rate need not be, anything "vicarious" about the bond between her and the Diaspora. Israel needs the giving done by the Diaspora. But the Diaspora receives more than she gives.

One should have thought that these were agreed-on matters among committed Jews ever since the debates between Zionists and non- or anti-Zionists died in the ashes of Auschwitz. Then why should anything even faintly resembling them have come to haunt us in the wake of the Yom Kippur War? We are told that "for the first time the question of Israel's and Diaspora's security has seriously arisen"—a statement utterly absurd about Israel but having an element of truth about the Diaspora. Could it be that the moment of shudder of the Yom Kippur War, still living beneath the surface, has produced, not only a well-warranted sense of danger for *both* Israel and the Diaspora, but along with this, a despairing response that if the one were to die, may at least the other live? If so, this despair must be brought to full consciousness—and defeated.

Let us recapture the darkest moments of the Yom Kippur War and its aftermath. A shudder unlike anything since the

Holocaust went through the *entire* Jewish people, with Israel in well-nigh total isolation by her enemies, and the Diaspora faced with the specter of oil-fed anti-Semitism. As the moment passed and the shudder went underground, the vast majority not only of non-Jewish but also of Jewish intellectuals saw no serious danger either to Israel or themselves, or, if reaching the verge of that insight, blocked or rejected it, and thus the "nothing-is-proved" and the "war-is-over" syndromes were born.

In that dark hour those few Jews committed to Israel who perceived a mortal threat were—if but for that moment of apocalyptic truth—divided into those who were on the verge of planning to rebuild Jewish life in case the catastrophe should occur, and those who could and would think no further than being prepared to do anything to prevent the catastrophe from happening, and were bitterly frustrated by how little they could do.

The moment is past. The task of the hour is to bring it to consciousness and master it. And to master it is to perceive that the first response was a lapse into weakness and failure of nerve, while the second was a decisive step forward in the common Jewish destiny in our time, with historic consequences which have yet to unfold.

Latin America: Overview

Natan Lerner

Anyone who attempts to analyze the reaction of Jewish communities in Latin America to the Yom Kippur War will encounter a number of difficulties, primarily since Latin America is not a homogeneous entity. Its twenty republics have much in common, but the intrinsic differences between them are numerous enough to preclude an overall monolithic survey. The "atypical" nature of political regimes and social structures, the interplay of internal forces, and the patently salient differences in foreign-relations patterns in Latin American countries exert a variety of pressures on the Jewish communities within them.

This review covers the attitudes of the non-Jewish public and their possible impact on the attitudes of the Jews, as well as the attitudes of Jews themselves. The first group includes governments, the general public, intellectuals, the Church, trade unions, the army, and political and intellectual circles. The second group consists of communal organizations, youth, intellectuals, and, in some cases, specific sectors of the population. Our sources of information are the Latin American press; Jewish publications and *ad hoc* information bulletins issued by a number of Jewish institutions; reports by representatives of Israeli and international Jewish organizations; interviews with several local Jewish leaders or with Israelis who visited the Latin American continent; and informal assessments by reliable local observers.

Government Attitudes[1]

According to some observers the Yom Kippur War served to define the extent of Israel's diplomatic isolation on the Latin American continent. All that could be expected from most of the governments was neutrality. An exception, not surprisingly, was the attitude of the then President José Figueres Ferrer of Costa Rica, who made a strong pro-Israeli statement. (His wife campaigned for Israel and his son enlisted as a volunteer.) The Foreign Minister of Costa Rica referred to the war in two speeches (delivered in October and November) in which he evinced a clearly pro-Israel attitude.[2]

Uruguay with a Jewish population of 50,000, was among the countries subjected to intense Arab pressure and, in an interview, an Uruguayan journalist is quoted as saying that a Libyan diplomat "agreed to provide all the oil Uruguay needs provided that all the Jewish members of the Cabinet resign."[3] Uruguayan General Hugo Chiappe Posse allegedly reacted with an indignation not shared by all his colleagues, and Jewish Cabinet Minister Moisés Cohen was in office when these lines were written. But the incident is indicative of a trend that cannot be ignored.

An extreme example is Cuba, which broke off diplomatic relations with Israel after the Algiers Conference and has never resumed relations.

It would be a purely academic exercise to venture a guess on the stand Chile would have taken had Allende not been overthrown. A prominent member of the Jewish community in Chile asserted that, despite his personal feelings, Allende would eventually have had to sever diplomatic relations with Israel. At any rate the Chilean

1. This section is based on reports from Dr. Paul Warszawski, of the Buenos Aires office of the World Jewish Congress, *Peulot Hafederaztziot Hatzioniot Be'et Milhemet Yom Hakippurim*, Jerusalem, November 1973; the Executive of the World Zionist Organization and its Information Department; the Office of Jewish Information (OJI) *Bulletin* of the Buenos Aires office of the World Jewish Congress; and interviews with such personalities as Yaakov Tsur, World Chairman of the Keren Kayemet Le-Yisrael; Ezra Shapiro, World Chairman of the Keren Hayesod; and Isaac Goldenberg, Chairman of the Latin American Jewish Congress. Yosef Govrin, of the Israel Ministry for Foreign Affairs, provided us with important information.
2. OJI, October 22, 1973; *Semana*, Jerusalem, November 20, 1973.
3. *Latin America*, Vol. VIII, No. 6, London, February 8, 1974, p. 46.

Under-secretary for Foreign Affairs simply stated that his government would maintain a strictly neutral attitude.[4] During the war the largest countries on the continent maintained an attitude of strict neutrality. Argentina and Brazil carefully avoided any statement on the war and President Perón made it abundantly clear to a Jewish delegation which visited him that Argentina would not budge from her neutral stand.[5]

The attitudes of the governments concerned are no doubt influenced by the main trends in their respective foreign policies. Recently some Latin American countries have adopted definite anti-American positions. Pro-Israel statements can hardly be expected to abound in such countries at a time when the identity of interests between the United States and Israel seems firmer than ever before. But, on the other hand, no country has resorted to measures which might be interpreted as an attempt to prevent Jewish communities from helping Israel.

A strikingly unfavorable trend, as far as Israel is concerned, was revealed in the recent votes of Latin American countries at the United Nations on issues concerning the Middle East, e.g., concerning the Palestinians. No less relevant is the impact of Arab propaganda which intensified considerably. The Arab League sponsors a wide range of heavily-financed activities and engages in cloaked anti-Semitism. For example, late in 1973 the Pan-American Congress of Arab Communities took place in Buenos Aires. During the weeks of fighting in the Middle East, Arab Week celebrations were held at Tucuman and an Arab Cultural Center was opened in Buenos Aires.[6] The impact on Latin America of the Arab oil policies prompted a news weekly to write that, while a major oil-deficient country like Brazil is making arrangements with the Iranians and the Nigerians rather than with the Arabs, "there is no doubt that the Israeli cause in Latin

---

4. Comité Representativo de la Colectividad Israelita de Chile, *Informaciones de Prensa*, November 9, 1973.
5. Statement by Delegación de Asociaciones Israelitas Argentinas (DAIA), Buenos Aires, November 8, 1973.
6. News items in OJI and in the general local press for October 1973.

America is now at a low ebb, in spite of the support that it still receives from a number of leading newspapers."[7]

Some pronouncements by prominent government officials deserve to be quoted on their own merits and due to their influence, direct or indirect, on Jewish institutions. President Perón's statement to a Delegación de Asociaciones Israelitas Argentinas (DAIA) group on November 8, in the presence of the Foreign Minister, the Vice-President and the Minister for Economic Affairs, a Jew, warrants special attention. The President of DAIA expressed serious concern over the proliferation of anti-Semitic pamphlets and publications exploiting the concept of "Sinarquia," devised by Perón to represent the five main evils afflicting mankind—capitalism, communism, Judaism, free masonry, and pseudo-Catholic lodges. The head of the DAIA delegation conveyed the concern of the Jewish community over the tension in the Middle East, suggesting that the President intercede in favor of a just and lasting peace based on the principle of defensible borders to be recognized by all states of the region.

Replying, Perón asserted that it would be absurd to apply the term "Sinarquia" to the Jewish community of Argentina. (It can thus be inferred that in the case of Jewish communities outside Argentina the application of the term may not be quite so absurd.) Yet he expressed stern opposition to any manifestations of anti-Semitism in connection with the Middle East conflict and repeated a favorite charge, that the countries involved were victims of collusive manipulation by the superpowers. He again emphasized that Argentina would maintain her neutrality, and expressed gratification over the determination of the delegation to prevent the conflict from extending to the Latin American continent. He hoped that the two communities—Jewish and Arab—would continue their harmonious and peaceful co-existence on Argentinian soil.[8] Two weeks earlier, after the outbreak of the war, Perón had received Yaakov Tsur, Israel's special representative at the inauguration ceremony, granting him definite precedence in protocol over the Arab delegates. The Argentinian press gave

7. *Latin America*, Vol. VII, No. 6, February 8, 1974, p. 46.
8. DAIA statement, November 8, 1973.

extensive coverage to the statements made by the Israeli delegate on that occasion.

More recent developments show the growing impact of the oil situation on the political stance of the Argentine government. In February, President Perón's personal secretary and a member of the cabinet, José López Rega, suggested, after signing several economic agreements with Libya, that the presence of Jews in the Argentine government has put the country at a disadvantage in negotiations with the Arab nations.[9] The Argentine news media, many of them controlled by the Peronist Government, gave extraordinary prominence to López Rega's visit. His remarks stirred a general controversy and created deep uneasiness among Argentine Jews, particularly since Finance Minister José Ber Gelbard is Jewish.

The oil crisis also affected Brazil policies vis-à-vis the Middle East and, consequently, engendered uneasiness amongst Brazilian Jews. The *New York Times* reported that the Arab countries were engaged in a "discreet courtship" of Brazil, and that the *"sine qua non* condition" for Arab friendship was a declaration of support for the Arab stand in the Middle East conflict.[10] Jewish quarters, according to the same source, noted with concern recent changes in official attitudes as well as in the press. On February 24, the Brazilian Ambassador to Israel wrote a letter to *Haaretz* stating there is no change in his country's stand on the Middle East conflict.

In Peru Prime Minister and Commander-in-Chief of the Armed Forces General Edgardo Mercado Jarrin wrote a military review of the Yom Kippur War for a local newspaper, in which he declared that the political objectives of the two belligerents were aimed at territorial conquests to be used for bargaining purposes. Peruvian Foreign Minister General De la Flor Valle publicly expressed the hope that peace and tranquility would be restored to the Middle East and, on the eve of his departure for Cuba, alleged that the countries of the Third World were staunch supporters of peace, as had been clearly reflected in the draft resolution submitted by them to the Security Council.[11]

9. *New York Times*, February 21, 1974.
10. February 3, 1974.
11. OJI, October 30, 1973, November 13, 1973.

Another declaration expressing deep regret over the war was that of Dr. Rafael Caldera, then President of Venezuela, a major oil-producing country. The Jewish community of Venezuela, which numbers 15,000, cabled the President expressing appreciation of his stand. Dr. Caldera referred to Venezuela's "friendship" with all the countries involved in the conflict, stating: "We are particularly anxious to preserve that atmosphere of mutual understanding which has at all times prevailed here between the descendants of Jews and Arabs." These prudent presidential statements coincided with a spate of violent anti-Jewish and anti-Israeli propaganda appearing in articles and pamphlets published by Arab organizations or by Arab or pro-Arab politicians.[12]

The small Caribbean nations adopted a neutral though generally friendly attitude, with Barbados emerging as the most sympathetic.

Public Opinion and Reactions of Non-Jewish Groups

As a rule editorial positions adopted by the news media indicated traditional political trends, but the pressures of the conflict were often visible.

In Uruguay, for example, each time a group of Jews called at the offices of the local paper or appeared at a radio station to publicize support for Israel, it almost invariably encountered Arabs who had come for propaganda purposes of their own. There was an active "war of declarations," in which the two sides tried to outdo each other in publishing paid political statements. It was not unusual to see statements by the Israeli Embassy and those of Arab groups appearing side by side in the very same paper. There are, in addition, such anti-Semitic publications as the Peronist *Primera Plana* of Buenos Aires, a vehicle for pro-Arab propaganda. The Communist press invariably sided with the Arabs. Throughout the Latin American continent there was a considerable intensification of popular propaganda, not only anti-Israeli, but basically anti-Semitic.

---

12. OJI, on Venezuela, October 30, 1973.

The general daily press gave extremely wide coverage to the war. The sources of information of the daily press were confined to the international news agencies, with the exception of a small number of daily papers, which employ their own correspondents. The pro-Israeli information increased in volume considerably after the first few days of the war. The larger Buenos Aires papers, such as the traditional *La Nación* and *La Prensa* and the influential *La Opinión* (sarcastically dubbed "the Zionist Opinion"), and some Peronist papers gave extensive coverage to Jewish demonstrations organized in the Argentinian capital. Some television programs presented one-sided reports which the DAIA protested.

In Chile one of the consequences of the revolution was the closing down of the leftist press. Well-established papers presented unbiased information about the war. *El Mercurio,* for instance, defined its stand as that of a "neutral observer." All papers expressed hope for the maintenance of peace and peaceful development of all peoples in the Middle East. Expressions of sympathy for Israel were evident in numerous cases.

In Uruguay the liberal and democratic press and that of the center parties usually sided with Israel. *El País,* for instance, castigated the Soviet Union for its anti-Israel attitude and its domestic policy with regard to the Jews. *El Día* and *La Mañana* also published numerous pro-Israeli articles and public declarations, including statements by the Israeli Embassy. The leftist press assumed a distinctly pro-Arab stand. *El Popular, El Oriente,* and *Ahora* attacked Israel, publishing declarations and editorials stemming from Arab sources. Television presented a balanced view.[13]

In Ecuador anti-Jewish leaflets were distributed and some papers, as for example, *El Comiercio,* declined to publish pro-Jewish articles. *La Crónca,* a daily in San Salvador, frequently published anti-Jewish articles. In Venezuela some Caracas papers published violently anti-Israeli

---

13. The review of the Uruguayan press was provided by the Israel office of the American Jewish Committee. *Repercussions of the Middle East Conflict in Uruguay ,* Buenos Aires, October 30, 1973.

statements, to which the Confederation of Jewish Organizations replied. Local politicians published anti-Israeli articles. The press in Costa Rica, with the exception of its Communist paper, adopted a clearly pro-Israel stand.

Organized groups, such as political parties, the Church, and intellectual circles, published numerous expressions of solidarity with Israel. In Argentina, a group of liberal intellectuals issued a pro-Israel manifesto. In Buenos Aires a Committee for Peace between Jews and Arabs was set up, comprising prominent political and intellectual figures, among whom were a number of leftists. The interreligious Confraternity declared its friendship for Israel. The Bishop of Avellaneda and the editor of the Catholic magazine *Criterio* sent messages of solidarity to the Israeli Embassy in Buenos Aires. Opposition deputies in the Argentinian Parliament submitted a draft resolution calling for peace in the Middle East. The Social Democratic Party issued a statement condemning the Arab aggression. Occasionally some newspapers published pro-Arab articles.

In Uruguay the Judeo-Christian Confraternity issued an appeal for peace. A women's organization issued a manifesto openly supporting Israel and a manifesto signed by numerous Uruguayan intellectuals confirmed Israel's right to exist and to develop in peace (for text, see Appendix IV, p. 359). The liberal Colorado party groups issued pro-Israel declarations, as did the Israel-Uruguay Cultural Institute.

Brazilian support for Israel was expressed in the Congress and a group of writers launched an appeal for direct negotiations for peace. Non-Jewish intellectuals, including the Mayor of Sao Paolo, participated in pro-Israel demonstrations. In Colombia distinguished public figures, including four former Presidents, published a warm pro-Israel declaration on November 24. The Panama-Israel Cultural Institute issued a statement condemning Arab aggression and calling upon the Panamanian people to support Israel. Writer Miguel Angel Asturias (Nobel and Lenin Prize Winner) expressed his support of Israel in a cable sent from Guatemala to Yaakov Tsur.

The foregoing serves as evidence that not everyone maintained silence about the war and that some non-Jewish groups did express pro-Israeli feelings. Despite this, in 1973 there was a diminution of the spontaneous feeling expressed in 1967. In Latin America public opinion did occasionally reflect expression of solidarity with Israel, while government pronouncements were conspicuous by their absence. Attitudes towards the war reflected naturally enough the political views of various groups and organizations.

Reactions of Jewish Communities

The war which broke out on Yom Kippur and took the State of Israel by surprise found Jewish communities of the Diaspora no better prepared. In the case of the approximately 800,000 Latin American Jews a lack of psychological preparedness was further complicated by the tensions of local internal and political crises.

The quality of Jewish life in Argentina, for example, has slowly been deteriorating because of such factors as the decline of Jewish credit cooperatives, alleged cases of financial squandering, and certainly, because of the generation gap and the gap between traditional communal leadership and Zionist parties. The reasons for such conflicts seem to be ideological as well as generational. A case in point is that the President of the Zionist Federation of Argentina did not join the group of Jewish leaders who were received by President Perón during the Yom Kippur War.

By and large the Yom Kippur War has brought about a consolidation of the different groups in Argentina, as well as in other countries of the Latin American continent. This was reflected in the creation of Coordinating Committees representing the leading communal organizations (the Zionist Organization, the Kehilla, DAIA, the United Jewish Appeal and the Youth Confederation).

The general political crisis in Chile has deeply affected many facets of life. The Jewish community of 30,000 is now most anxious to emphasize its identification with Chile and its participation in her national reconstruction. This patriotic zeal found expression in a fund-raising campaign—highly commended by the authorities—which reached its climax in the midst of the Yom Kippur War. All this coincided with extensive anti-Marxist purges carried out at universities and other institutions.[14] This had a marked effect upon some sectors of the community—particularly academic circles. Some commotion was stirred up in the American press by rumors that Jews in Chile were being persecuted. The Chief Rabbi deemed it expedient to send (November 1) messages to rabbinical institutions the world over, assuring them of the religious freedom of the Jewish community of Chile. Subsequent reports from that country indicate that Jewish community life continues its normal course.

Such pressures, arising out of the economic and political situations, have most definitely influenced the attitude of the Jewish community of Chile to the Yom Kippur War and its consequences. However, regardless of difficulties, Chilean Jewry did its utmost to respond to Israel's needs. A joint Emergency Committee, comprising representatives of the central institutions, has been functioning uninterruptedly from its inception and has maintained permanent contacts with Israeli representatives. Relief action was organized and political measures taken, particularly with regard to Israeli prisoners of war.[15]

In Brazil and Uruguay the authoritarian political atmosphere and existing legal restrictions clearly affected the nature of the reactions of the Jews to the Middle East War, particularly as far as material aid was concerned. In Uruguay, friction between the Zionist federation and the Jewish Central Committee was created by the former's decision to publish a manifesto defining the goals of the Zionist movement as a result of the war. The Central Committee, apparently supported by Israeli factors, opposed this publication and was criticized by the Zionists.[16] In Mexico the first conference of Jewish communities was convened in November, at which the deliberations were devoted primarily to the Middle East situation.

14. *New York Times,* November 14, 1973.
15. See, for example, in Santiago, *Ultimas Noticias,* October 26, 1973 and *El Mercurio,* November 1, 1973.
16. Report of the Organization and Information Department of the World Zionist Organization Executive, Jerusalem, November 19, 1973.

Beyond any doubt the war has brought about a revival of Jewish solidarity in sectors that in the past kept aloof from the conventional communal frameworks, particularly professional groups linked to the left. These are now active in organizing public meetings and promoting the publication of pro-Israel statements by non-Jewish associates.

The response of Jewish youth on the whole was positive, at least in countries like Argentina, Chile and Uruguay—a fact which ought to be stressed, considering its lack of enthusiasm in general for local Jewish communities and because of the tension between the age groups. The main task of young people was to promote pro-Israel opinion among the general public and to assist in the enrollment of volunteers. In Buenos Aires, for instance, "information tables" were set up in the city's main streets and leaflets and materials were distributed widely in public places. A public demonstration in that city arranged by youth groups was attended by 10,000 people and received extensive coverage in the press. Large crowds were also drawn to the commemoration ceremony for those fallen in the war (a public gathering attended by some 6,000 participants was organized by the Argentine Jewish Youth Confederation). Large numbers participated in a demonstration held in front of the Soviet Embassy, in the course of which clashes were reported and several people arrested.

In Montevideo, Lima, and Santiago similar meetings were held, drawing large audiences with significant youth participation. It is difficult to assess whether this implies a real increase of young Jewish activism for Israel. Nevertheless, it is estimated that, in Argentina alone, 5,000 young people volunteered for emergency work in Israel.

Unaffiliated Jews

A large number of Jews who are not active within the framework of Jewish institutions are yet connected to some degree with them. There is evidence indicating that such persons cooperated in activity on behalf of Israel. Jewish anti-Israeli leftist circles do not seem to have changed their position. In Buenos Aires the Yiddisher Cultur Farband

(ICUF) issued a press statement attacking the United States, criticizing Israel in more muted but still violent tones. Declarations by similar groups appeared in the Argentinian provincial press.

It would be interesting to know the reaction of those Jewish youths who had joined the leftist ranks within, or close to, the Peronist movement. Such groups are now undergoing an ideological crisis and it is fair to assume that they are at present re-examining the problem of their identity and identification. The impact of the Yom Kippur War on young people whose complete identification with Argentina had caused them to drift away from the Jewish community is a complex intellectual and psychological phenomenon and of obvious organizational significance. Such young adults are searching for a way of life, are susceptible to ideological influences, and vulnerable to the contradictory pressures of a non-Jewish environment on the one hand, and communal Jewish life on the other. Many of these young people are associated with Israel through family links and personal connections. They undoubtedly cannot be indifferent to the fate of Israel, but they are exposed to strong environmental pressures which, particularly on the university level, are influenced by pro-Arab sentiments of their peers.[17]

One obstacle to efficient activity by the communities was a lack of up-to-date information from Israel. The one exception was Caracas, where a Jewish Information Center published some one hundred bulletins, and daily briefings were given by an Israel Embassy official. In Argentina, Peru, Uruguay, and Brazil special publications were put out, including some dailies. *T'nuat Aliyah* also published daily communiqués. The Eighth Plenary Session of the Latin American Jewish Congress, held in Buenos Aires at the end of October, proved to be an appropriate occasion for the exchange of information and for the pooling of coordinated efforts between the representatives of the participating communities—those of Argentina, Bolivia, Brazil, Colombia,

---

17. See, for instance, article in the Peronist left-wing *El Descamisado*, November 6, 1973, where Arnoldo Liberman attempts to define his stand as an "Argentine Jew."

Chile, Mexico, Paraguay, Peru, Uruguay, and Venezuela. What was originally planned as a routine gathering developed into an emergency rally that provided a continental view of the situation. From all reports, representatives of Israeli institutions and the World Zionist Organization were particularly active. The Venezuelan community stands out as an example of mutually rewarding cooperation between the Embassy of Israel and delegates of world Jewish institutions.

As we review government attitudes, the reactions of non-Jews, and the response of the Jews themselves in turbulent Latin America, the diversity of political futures facing the communities is ominously clear. The internal character of these communities, necessarily influenced by the dominant trends in each country, are equally turbulent. It may be that some solutions to the internal problems of Latin America will have to come out of changed, but intensified, long-range relations with Israel.

Latin America: Perspectives

Haim Avni

Jewish communal life in Latin America was always seen to be closely identified with the State of Israel. Jewish cultural institutions were modeled after those of Israel, and community leaders continually asserted that the inner life of Latin American Jewry depended on the prosperity and welfare of the State of Israel. The communal structure of Argentine Jewry, for example, is based on the Zionist party system; thus, changes which occurred in Israeli politics during the last two decades were reflected in parallel parties in Buenos Aires. Similar patterns can be found in other communities in Latin America.

Character of Latin American Jewish Communities

To understand this distinctive development in the Jewish society of Latin America, one must remember that the predominant elements of Jewish identity there are the cultural and national aspects of Judaism rather than the religious ones. The tendency of the host societies to identify minority groups with their ethnic origins also contributed heavily to self-identification. In countries that welcomed immigration, new immigrants created a cultural and ethnic heterogeneity which allowed the Jews to strenghthen their group consciousness and reinforce their ethnic loyalty. In countries which did not welcome immigration, all immigrants and their descendants were marked as aliens; and this too encouraged Jewish identification and organization. A case illustrating this dual relationship is recorded by former Israeli Ambassador to Peru and Bolivia, Nathanel Lorch, who wrote that non-Jews of all walks of life considered him not only the Ambassador of Israel but also the head of the respective Jewish communities.[1]

---

1. Nathanel Lorch, *HaNahar HaLochesh*, Tel Aviv, 1969, pp. 132-133.

In this climate it would be reasonable to expect that the reaction of Latin America Jewry to the Yom Kippur War would be outstanding among world Jewish communities. The certainty of a successful and short war should conceivably have been replaced by an enveloping concern as soon as it became apparent that the results of the fighting during the first days were devastating to Israel. The grim reality reported in the media and extensive familial ties with settlers in Israel should have alerted Latin American leadership to the true danger.

Natan Lerner's article details the various events which took place in the Latin American Jewish communities during the war and its aftermath. While a great deal of anxiety was felt, it becomes clear from existing evidence that despite the shock, public support for Israel did not affect large segments of the Jewish population in Brazil or Argentina, and in some of the smaller Jewish communities indifferent Jews continued to remain apathetic towards Israel. Compared with the Six Day War, at which time the events in the Middle East brought about a considerable increase in financial support for Israel, inspired many young people to come to Israel as volunteers, and brought out masses for public demonstrations and rallies, the Yom Kippur War had, in most communities, a lesser effect. Evidence gathered indicates that the general concern and willingness to sacrifice diminished even before the fighting was over, or very soon afterwards.

Dr. Isaac Goldenberg, President of the Latin American branch of the World Jewish Congress, who chaired the emergency meeting of the heads of the Congress local chapters convened in Buenos Aires in November, said: "Jewish identification with Israel was revealed despite manifest eroding elements in the Jewish communities. For the first time some Jewish leaders hesitated to express Zionist conceptions. This is a slight tendency, but if ignored might create profound divisions in the Latin American community."[2] This observation is important, particularly if we remember that for Jewish leadership in Latin America, unlike other communities,

2. Shazar Documentation Unit, Latin American File, Institute of Contemporary Jewry, December 1973.

"Judaism" was almost unanimously identified with "Zionism."

How can we interpret the considerable gap between what could have been expected and what Lerner's overview reveals?

Political Climate of Latin America

The first factor to be considered is the political constellation in some of the major Latin American countries during the second half of 1973.

In Argentina, home of almost a half-million Jews, national political agitation reached its climax precisely during the first days of the Yom Kippur War. On October 12 General Juan Domingo Perón was reinstalled as President of the Republic, after eighteen years of exile, including two years of extreme political machinations. Committed Jews, as well as the indifferent and alienated, who participated ideologically in the Argentinian political struggle, were absorbed by these important events which were then seen to be the beginning of a new and better era in Argentinian history.

As for Brazil, the present military government frowns upon political activism, and political demonstrations are controlled. An economic boom, which benefited mainly the middle class during the last decade, also enhanced the economic and social conditions of the underprivileged classes. The combination of economic prosperity and political controls, in addition to uneasiness regarding the immediate future, may very well have contributed to the timid and disappointing response of some Brazilian Jews described by observers.[3]

When the Yom Kippur War broke out, the Jewish community in Chile was still trying to adjust to the rightist military revolution of the previous month. Terror, shortage of food, rumors about executions and killings, along with an appeal made by the authorities for patriotic sacrifice, may have subdued natural Jewish reactions to the events in the

---

3. Yitzchak Harkabi statement and correspondence with Israeli emissaries in Sao Paolo, Shazar Documentation Unit, December 1973.

Middle East. Uruguay, once considered the "Switzerland of Latin America," was in the throes of political oppression—the violence of guerrilla activity there and the suppression of such activity have been dealt with in great detail in the foreign media. Thus, to some degree, Uruguayan Jews may also have been deterred from open support of Israel.[4]

Reactions of Jews

In judging Jewish response the first factor to be considered is the ever-increasing gap between the Jewish Establishment and various elements within the Jewish population. In spite of the large number of organizations in each Jewish community, only a minority of the population is affiliated. The impact of existing institutions on the young people has been a subject of grave concern in recent years. It has been reported that approximately forty per cent of Jews are assimilated or on their way to assimilation. Many of the younger Jews are totally unconcerned with Jewish tradition or Judaism as a whole and the rate of intermarriage is high.[5] The need for reform and change has been recognized and much energy has been devoted to attracting university students to Jewish life and institutions, but with minimal results. The atmosphere of militant leftism and opposition to the United States which characterizes Latin American youth as a whole, along with changing attitudes towards Israel during the last few years, have undoubtedly deterred a spontaneous and positive identification of young Jews with Israel's struggle.[6]

Another factor to be remembered in evaluating the expressions of identification with beleaguered Israel is the position of leadership held by Israel's official representatives in Latin America. The Israeli embassies and legations are not only a focal point for Jewish identification but also a source of guidance and leadership accepted by the community in matters concerning world Jewry in general and Israel in

4. Shazar Documentation Unit, December, 1973.
5. *American Jewish Committee Report*, January 1974.
6. For an analysis of Latin American Jewry at the beginning of the 1970s, see Haim Avni, "Latin America," *World Politics and the Jewish Condition*, Louis Henkin (ed.) New York, 1972, pp. 238-274.

particular. Evidence indicated that there was confusion and lack of orientation in the field of political action. "Everything which has been done," states Isaac Goldenberg in the questionnaire about the role of Jewish communities, "was a result of spontaneous initiatives. . . ."[7] This contrasted with the efficient mobilization of fund raising organized by Israeli emissaries.

Implications

What then are the lasting implications of the Yom Kippur War for the individual Jews who contributed money, who demonstrated, and who volunteered their personal services? To what extent can Jewish leaders inspire greater commitment from affiliated members and to what degree can existing institutions establish viable contact with the non-affiliated and the indifferent? Can Latin American Jewry mobilize itself for continuing and multi-faceted efforts?

One can best answer such questions in the context of the world Jewish condition; and as regards the future of Latin American Jewry, the increasing influence of Arab power is crucial. Arab hostility has long been directed toward local Jewish communities. During the last several months, however, Arab propaganda has been more effective and widespread. Argentina's efforts to secure necessary supplies of oil and to attract Arab capital investments for development of its own oil resources resulted in mutually beneficial agreements with Libyan Colonel Muammar Qaddafi. The strengthened influence of this vehemently anti-Israel ruler on the Argentinian government cannot but endanger the Jewish community. The emergence of a united Arab organization of Argentinian and Latin American Arab immigrants, which coincided with the Yom Kippur War, will undoubtedly bear watching by the Jews. Brazil's urgent need for oil, supplied by African countries, and the close contacts of other Latin American countries with the Arabic world through OPEC and the Third World are an additional menace and conceivably could influence Latin America's relationship with Israel negatively.

7. *Loc. cit.*

Furthermore, because of the tendency of the host societies in most of Latin America to identify the local Jewish communities with Israel—an identification which originates *inter alia* with the similarity of the terms "Israelita" and "Israeli"—any deterioration in the relationship with Israel might *ipso facto* affect negatively the general attitude toward the Jews of Latin American countries.

In view of all these factors, the relationship between Latin American communities and Israel is undergoing radical change. The reaction to the Yom Kippur War was merely symptomatic of the ongoing process.

Great Britain, Oceania, South Africa: Overview

Ernest Krausz

This survey considers the effects of the Yom Kippur War on the 600,000 Jews found in the Commonwealth communities of Great Britain, Oceania, and South Africa, with specific interest in the phenomenon of Jewish identification and group solidarity evoked by the crisis.

Britain's Jewish community of 410,000 is the oldest, largest, and most complex of this group, in terms of its history (going back some three centuries) and the origins of its members. South Africa's Jews numbering nearly 120,000, and those of Oceania some 70,000, represent relatively younger communities, dating from around the middle of the last century. All three communities, however, have certain common characteristics, stemming from the British Commonwealth links between them, certain Anglo-Saxon cultural characteristics, and some linkage and uniformity in communal organization.

Great Britain

Britain's position, and therefore that of its Jews, is a special one. The very establishment of the State was strongly influenced by Britain's relation to the Jewish homeland. At first there were positive factors, such as the Balfour Declaration (November 2nd, 1917); later, particularly towards the latter stage of the Mandate period (prior to 1948), there were negative attitudes; and later still, there were fluctuations

For help in preparing this article I wish to thank Dr. J. Braude, British Jewish communal leader; P. Glikson of the Institute of Contemporary Jewry; G. Gromer of Bar Ilan University; Chief Rabbi Dr. I. Jakobowits; Ald. Sir Samuel Fisher, J.P., President of the Board of Deputies of British Jews; Greville Janner, Q.C., M.P.; Professor E. Kedouri; M. Davis, Secretary of the Chief Rabbi; H.S. Langton, Vice-President of the Reform Synagogues in Britain; and D. Sonin, Director of Publicity, Joint Israel Appeal.

in Britain's policy towards the new State of Israel, the most recent being a completely pro-Arab stance. These fluctuations have frequently created awkward and ambivalent feelings among Jews in Britain. Ever since the establishment of the Zionist movement, Zionism has been strongly embedded in Jewish life in Britain, but British Jews labored under the burden of doubts raised regarding their loyalty to Britain, particularly at the time of the Mandate period.

Perhaps because of this, in the first years after the establishment of the State of Israel, many British Jews rejected identification with the Jewish homeland. For years after 1948, they regarded Israel merely as a haven for refugees from Nazi Europe and from the Arab countries. They were, however, prepared to provide financial and moral support. This kind of support did act as a catalyst and, as Anglo-Jewish communal leader Michael Sacher has pointed out, it was the continual physical contact with Israel, over the years, that created in world Jewish communities, including that of Britain, a clear realization that they had a close relationship both with the Jews in Israel and with each other. As Sacher says, involvement in fund raising and other activities in support of Israel meant that Jews in England actually helped to create the State of Israel, and they realized that their thoughts were not very different from those of Jews in Atlantic City, or Marseilles, or Mexico City, or wherever they were.[1] This kind of involvement obviously led to a strong identification with Jews in Israel and in other countries. The events of the Six Day War in 1967 heightened the identification of the majority of Britain's Jews with Israel for two reasons. First, as a result of the Six Day War the very image of the Jew had changed; this image now reflected a resoluteness to continue to exist in the ancient homeland. Second, the religious element in identification which had declined in the post-World War II period, was now renewed through stronger national identification, with definite religious undertones and implications.

The Yom Kippur War with its Holocaust specter has further heightened the British Jew's identification with Israel. First, there were spontaneous gatherings in huge numbers in

1. Interview in Jerusalem, November 1973.

the streets of London, which proved that for many Jews Israel was the backbone of their existence even outside that country. Some 20,000 Jews gathered in Trafalgar Square, the center of London, on October 14, 1973, to show solidarity with Jews of Israel. Another similarly large demonstration took place on November 11, 1973. The annual parade of Jewish ex-service-men, held on November 18, was turned into a solidarity march for Israel, which concluded with a memorial service for Jewish soldiers who fell in the two world wars. The number of those in the parade and of those who came out in support was double the numbers that turned out in the previous year and the largest turnout since 1952.

A second manifestation of solidarity concerns volun-teering. Out of a total of some 50,000 volunteers from world Jewry, more than 5,000 were registered in Britain. Nine hundred volunteers actually went to Israel, some for three months, others for six months. Another 200 students went as volunteers to the agricultural settlements during the winter holidays. Considering Britain's Jewish population, this is proportionally higher than in other countries.

Third, the financial support that British Jews gave on this occasion, when looked at proportionally, surpassed all other countries. Some seventy million pounds were given in this campaign, that is, approximately one hundred and fifty million dollars. This, coming from a Jewish community of just over 400,000, compares more than favorably with contribu-tions made in the United States, where a community numbering over five and a half million Jews contributed $750 million. The reports show that in most countries the contributions in this campaign were about two and a half times higher than the contributions at the time of the Six Day War. In Britain, however, the contributions this time were nearly six times higher than at the time of the Six Day War. It is even more significant to note that the number of contributors rose from 65,000 in 1967 to over 100,000 in 1973.

Fourth, Jews in Britain rushed to contribute to the war effort in terms of blood and medical supplies. The number of blood donors was 10,000—many more volunteered but were not accepted.

Fifth, responsible organizations attempted to influence

the views of Members of Parliament, and many Jews both in official capacities and as private citizens wrote letters to the press in order to influence public opinion in a direction favorable to Israel.

There is evidence that many less identified Jews came into the various campaigns quite spontaneously. Students collected 15,000 signatures for a petition to the Prime Minister on the arms embargo issue. By and large, the majority of organized Jews reacted with tremendous zeal. The explanation for this strong reaction probably lies in a feeling of alienation from the larger society that developed quickly amongst Jews in Britain, despite the fact that public opinion polls and other information suggest that nearly half, and possibly an even greater proportion of the British people, including large numbers of Members of Parliament, were sympathetic to Israel and felt uneasy about the official policy.

But official and semi-official antagonism to Israel was very clear. In the first place the British Government refused to charge Egypt and Syria with aggression. In addition, it put an embargo on tank parts which had been paid for and were ready to leave port, an embargo affecting primarily Israel.[2] At the same time the British Government allowed the training of Egyptian pilots in Britain to continue during the fighting. Britain also sponsored and joined the European pro-Arab declaration regarding political arrangements in the Middle East and refused landing rights to U.S. aircraft airlifting arms to Israel.

Secondly, anti-Jewish sentiments were expressed in a number of quarters. For example, Foreign Secretary Sir Alec Douglas Home in Parliament raised doubts regarding the loyalty of a well-known Jewish member of the House of Commons. This occurred on November 28, 1973, when Gerald Kaufman, Labour M.P. for Manchester Ardwick, asking about oil supplied to Holland, described that country as "Britain's loyal and steadfast ally." Sir Alec replied: "I am not sure that the words of loyalty and steadfastness come very well from the

2. The Foreign Secretary announced in the House of Commons on January 21, 1974, that the British Government had lifted the arms embargo to the Middle East, and that the criteria for selling arms to the region would be the same as before the Yom Kippur War.

honorable gentleman."[3] The BBC provided its share of anti-Jewish sentiments, quite apart from labelling a number of House of Lords and House of Commons members as "the Jewish Lord" or "the Jewish M.P." Thus, some of its reports had clear anti-Semitic undertones. Another commentator stated on December 3, 1973, in the 24-hour program carried by the overseas broadcasting service, that one reason for Holland's pro-Israel policy was that Jews *control* (my italics) the trade of Amsterdam, a statement which is patently false. In the same program on another date, a commentator stated that Japan was able not to follow a pro-Israel policy because it had *no Jewish problem* (my italics).

Thirdly, there were a number of newspaper articles containing at best anti-Jewish innuendoes, at worst simply anti-Semitic remarks, describing how Jews in control of big business and the City were contributing large sums of money to Israel, with adverse effects on the British economy.

On October 17, 1973, three articles appeared. A *Daily Mail* article entitled "The voice from Tel Aviv talks to the men of money . . . direct" related how, at the behest of the Israeli Ambassador in London, wealthy sympathizers gathered at the City stronghold of banker N.M. Rothschild, and were called upon by the Israeli Prime Minister to provide funds. Those present included senior members of the Rothschild family, members of the Sieff family, who control the Marks and Spencer department stores, and Sir John Cohen, head of the Tesco supermarket chain. (It should be noted that J. Edward Sieff was subsequently shot by an Arab gunman and Sir John Cohen was similarly threatened by an Arab terrorist organization.[4]) The second article, by the city editor of the *Daily Mail*, writing on "What the war means for our money," pointed to the concern in some circles about the effects that large Jewish monetary contributions would have on Britain's financial affairs. The third example is an article by Robert Bolton in the *Sun*, entitled "Check on Jews' Cash." In it he describes how large sums were raised from London Syna-

3. David Lennon, "Home Slurs Jewish M.P.'s Loyalty," *Jerusalem Post*, November 30, 1973.
4. The Popular Front for the Liberation of Palestine claimed responsibility for the shooting. See report in *Jewish Chronicle*, January 4, 1974.

gogues, and stresses that the Bank of England was "making sure no illegal methods are used to export some cash." The *Manchester Guardian Weekly* carried an article on December 1, 1973, entitled "Bad Taste—More Inconvenient Facts," which claimed that a sizeable proportion of funds (supposedly raised for the war effort) go not in the form of gifts but to buy into the booming Israeli property market.

Fourthly, in this category we find the *Manchester Evening News* article of December 1973, which claimed that Britain's Stock Market was being ruined by huge sales of shares carried out on behalf of wealthy Jews who wished to contribute to Israel. Several Jewish leaders in Britain commented that this article was reminiscent of the anti-Semitic articles in the German press in the 1930s. The mischievous nature of these press reports is that, through part truths and part falsehoods, they are able to incite the general public at a time when Britain is experiencing a seriously deteriorating economic situation.

Finally, the Church silence was significant, particularly considering that the Arab attack was launched on the holiest day of the Jewish calendar. There were, however, some pro-Israel reactions from Christian quarters which came mainly from Fundamentalists, but even here there was nothing like the support initially forthcoming in 1967. The Church and its leaders, and even the Council of Christians and Jews, failed to make any statement throughout the duration of the fighting. Similarly no steps were taken by Christian leaders concerning Jewish prisoners of war and their torture and murder at the hands of the Egyptians and Syrians. Leading rabbis and communal leaders came to the conclusion that "The Christian leaders in Britain on the whole do not appear to have come to terms with the Jews and their stay in Israel."[5] Again, commenting on the unsatisfactory nature of the meeting with Christian leaders, one well-known and responsible communal worker stated that "Many Christians probably shared an unspoken feeling in the political world, of

5. Quotation from material taken from interviews held in Britain during November 1973 with communal leaders and communal workers.

satisfaction that the Israelis (and Dayan) had been taken down a peg or two!"[6]

The Jews in Britain reacted to this pro-Arab stance and to the anti-Semitic signs with a call for closer identification with Israel. As one leading Jewish member of the community on a visit to Israel stated: "It is wrong to call our endeavors, that is, the work the Jews in Britain and other parts of the *galut* carry out in connection with Israel, a partnership. We are united into one people, a union which you cannot break, whilst a partnership could be broken."[7] It is also the case that more and more Jews have relatives in Israel and that therefore there was personal concern quite apart from the general identification with Israel which has become part of the communal make-up. Yet, despite this close identification, strengthened by the alienation which has befallen the Jews of Britain during and immediately after the Yom Kippur War, there was also an effort by the Jews to square this identification with Britain's own interest.

The arguments are best summed up in a London *Jewish Chronicle* editorial entitled, "Britain's Real Interest."[8] The paper argued that surrender to Arab oil blackmail could not be in the interest of Britain; it reminded its readers that the British Foreign Secretary was one of the "men of Munich," who has again practiced appeasement. Furthermore, Britain's so-called "even-handed policy" had reduced that term to a mockery and had damaged Britain's interest in another respect, that is, her credibility as an honest trader. The article went on to point out that more important than the calculations of profit or loss is the duty to maintain the quality of civilization for which Britain has fought, and which could be maintained only within the framework of NATO and in cooperation with the United States. It was also the case, the paper said, that Britain could have had a role in promoting Middle East peace, a role she has forsaken through her pro-Arab stand. The article concluded on a note concerning

6. *Ibid.*
7. Mr. Henry Knobil, interviewed by the writer at Bar-Ilan University.
8. November 2, 1973.

the moral aspect of Britain's policy, quoting from a speech the week before by a non-Jew, Reginald Paget, in the House of Commons, who had this to say: "One may sometimes take too narrow a view of British interests. Among British interests may be placed honor and self-respect. These are intangible interests. It is these intangible interests that enable the State of Israel to live. She has them. I wonder whether we do."

The need to link support for Israel with an expression of allegiance to Britain and a care for her interests was clearly evinced by the Anglo-Jewish Association. In a letter to the *Times* on December 22, 1973, twelve members of the Council, which includes leading Anglo-Jews and members of the oldest established Jewish families in Britain, wrote: "With our sympathy for Israel reinforced by a shared historic experience, we believe that this onslaught sustained by Soviet equipment must inevitably damage the strategic interests of Britain, the country of our allegiance."[9]

A general assessment of Jewry's reactions in Britain during the Yom Kippur War may be set against the reaction at the time of the Six Day War. The views expressed in special interviews for this survey carried out in Britain with members of the Jewish community suggest that the periods to be compared should be the few weeks *before* June 5, 1967 with events *after* October 6, 1973. Such a comparison would show that the intensity of feeling by Jews about the survival of fellow Jews in Israel was the same in 1967 as in 1973. However, there were also differences between the two situations.

On the occasion of the Six Day War many people *awoke* to the fact that they were Jews, whilst on this occasion those who had previously awakened were not thrust one stage further. This was a stage at which a deep fear arose that individual Jewish survival would not be possible in a world where Israel disappeared. As one member of the community put it: "For the first time after two thousand years, in 1967 the Jew in the Diaspora was respected because of the achieve-

9. The names of the signatories were: Victor Lucas, Leon Bagrit, Isaiah Berlin, Maurice Edelman, Louis Gluckstein, Toby Jessel, David Kessler, Ewen Montagu, Frances Rubens, Neville Sandelson, Harold Sebag-Montefiore, Harold Soref.

ments of his brethren in Israel. He was able to walk with his head up. In a brief period of a few days in 1973 this whole image was changed. We had something in the last six years that we did not have for two thousand years."[10] It was, however, not only the feeling of pride but also that of security which was shattered to some extent. The majority of Jews, with the exception of those moving fast towards complete assimilation and substantial numbers of Jewish students influenced by the New Left, felt that their future depended on the existence of Israel. The Jewish response was, therefore, stronger than some of the communal leaders anticipated, and its intensity surprised even the Jewish community itself.

Oceania: Australia and New Zealand

The historical developments of Australian Jewry are well characterized by the changes which have overtaken its largest component, the Jews of Melbourne, over the last fifty years. Earlier in this century, when the community was very small, the Jews were engulfed socially in a process of rapid assimilation. This situation has been altered radically: a flourishing network of communal institutions and activities has been established; the intermarriage rate has declined; and Jewish rituals have become more commonly observed than half a century ago. Above all, "Zionism has become a focal point of communal existence."[11] Melbourne Jews and their brethren are now characterized by "group survival," a process in which Israel, and the wars Israel has gone through, play a major role. The small community in New Zealand enjoyed the favorable reaction of their government to Israel, but Australian Jews were in a similar position to Jews in Britain regarding the government attitude to the Middle East conflict. The Australian Government refused to condemn the Arabs as aggressors and came out with statements favorable to the Arabs. At an emergency committee meeting held on October 12, 1973 by Jewish leaders, it was reported that the Australian

10. J. Braude, interviewed by the writer in Jerusalem, January 3, 1974.
11. P.Y. Medding, *From Assimilation to Group Survival*, Melbourne, 1968, p. 2.

Prime Minister declined to see them and indicated that he was not prepared to make a pro-Israel statement as requested by the Jewish community. On the other hand, in a statement by New Zealand's Prime Minister, that country declared itself in support of "Israel's safe, secure and defensible frontiers" from the first day of the war.[12]

Jews in Australia and New Zealand reacted as did those in Britain. Their energies were directed primarily to fund raising, lobbying in favor of Israel, and demonstrating openly their identification with Israel. It is worth noting, from a long report in the *National Times,* that organized Jewish students were very active and expressed views, such as those of the Victoria Union of Jewish Students, that, "most Jews in Melbourne . . . feel their security has been shaken by events in the Middle East."[13] The same paper also reported, however, that to some extent in Melbourne, but even more in Sydney, a number of young Jews cut themselves off from the Jewish community and did not identify with Israel's struggle, many of these being of extreme left-wing views.

Much more reliable indication of Australian Jewry's reactions is given by the systematic comparative surveys undertaken by Ronald Taft and his associates in Melbourne, both after the Six Day War and after the Yom Kippur War. The salient conclusion reached on the basis of these surveys is that the high degree of involvement in the crises and identification with Israel were maintained in 1973, but did not surpass the intensity of feelings aroused in 1967. The Six Day War produced lasting effects, which the 1973 war changed only marginally, as for example, in the greater disappointment felt vis-à-vis other nations and heightened feelings of vulnerability.[14]

It may be added that there was also some evidence,

12. Information *re.* Australia contained in Minutes of meeting held on October 12, 1973; *re.* New Zealand in letter from Dr. Julius Stafford, dated October 25, 1973.
13. *National Times,* October 29–November 3, 1973.
14. The latest survey also showed that involvement and identification were at a higher level among older and East European born Jews than among the younger more Australianized Jews. R. Taft and G. Solomon, "The Melbourne Jewish Community and a Revisitation of Middle East War, 1973" (forthcoming); R. Taft, "The Impact of the Middle East Crisis of June 1967 on Melbourne Jewry," *Jewish Journal of Sociology,* 1967, Vol. IX, pp. 243–262.

gleaned from other material, that the smallness of the communities in Oceania, particularly New Zealand, and the great distance from Israel and other major Jewish population centers, may be additional factors causing feelings of anxiety during crises.

Union of South Africa

South Africa differs from Britain basically, both with regard to the general society and, to some extent, to the internal composition of the Jewish community.[15] Whilst in Britain the concept of Britishness is a clear one, the concept of South Africanism remains problematic to this day. White South Africa is divided into two distinct sections, the Afrikaans-speaking and the English-speaking. Although the cultural reference group of the Jewish population is mainly the English-speaking section, Jews are, in many respects, regarded as a separate ethnic group. In addition, the Jewish community in South Africa is extraordinarily homogeneous in composition. The vast majority of its nearly 120,000 Jews stems from the Lithuanian region of Eastern Europe. As a result of this background as well as the dualistic character of white South African society, Zionism has long been the major focus of Jewish identification and the Zionist organizations have been the primary elements of communal life. This has made the South African Jewish community the most Israel-centered in the English speaking world. One expression of this has been the fact that this community has always been amongst the largest, if not the largest, per capita contributor, to the Jewish Agency.[16]

In this context, neither the Six Day War nor the Yom Kippur War may be said to have had a revolutionary effect on the pattern of Jewish group identification. In a community already committed so strongly to identification with Israel, material support of Israel, and recognition of the centrality of

15. I am indebted to Gideon Shimoni of the Institute of Contemporary Jewry, Hebrew University, for the information and evaluations in this section.
16. S.N. Herman and G. Shimoni, *The Jewish Community in the Apartheid Society of South Africa* (Hebrew), Institute of Contemporary Jewry, 1973.

Israel in the life of the Jewish people, these events dramatically reinforced, rather than changed, that commitment. As elsewhere in the Jewish world, the news of the Arab invasion on Yom Kippur electrified the Jewish population and filled it with immense anxiety and an overwhelming desire to help. In Johannesburg a protest meeting, called before the war to protest the Austrian government's decision to close Schoenau to Russian immigration, turned into a massive demonstration of solidarity with Israel in the face of the Arab attack. As in past crises, both in 1948 and 1967, the Zionist Federation, which encompasses all of the Zionist groups from the youth movements and women's organizations to the Maccabi sports clubs, effectively galvanized the entire community's resources on behalf of fund raising for the Israel United Appeal (IUA). Synagogues were crowded to capacity to hear sermons on solidarity with Israel and every type of Jewish organization, including the sports clubs with their large membership, mobilized itself for the combined fund raising effort. Shortly before the outbreak of the war, the Israel United Appeal had completed its last campaign. It now went back to contributors and got them to double and treble their previous commitments.

Nearly a thousand applications for volunteer work in Israel reached the Zionist Federation from young Jews within a short time. In the past, not only during the war of 1948, but also in the period of the 1956 Sinai campaign and again during the Six Day War, South African Jewry had sent relatively the largest groups of volunteers to Israel. With a view to the long-term encouragement of *aliyah,* the Zionist Federation set up a strict selection system, with the participation of psychologists and persons with experience in past volunteer schemes. As a result, a total of about three hundred volunteers, mostly students, and many of them graduates of Jewish Day schools, were sent in an organized scheme for the period of the university vacations from the end of November 1973 until the end of March 1974. Youth movement leaders and students were asked to remain in South Africa in order to ensure the conduct of the large Zionist youth camps which take place in December. Thereafter, some were sent to join volunteers already in Israel.

In South Africa the contributor to the IUA does not benefit from tax deductions and one of the distinguishing features of the IUA campaigns is their distribution over the entire Jewish population, from the small contributor who gives a bank order for a few Rands a month (one Rand equals approximately one and a half dollars) to those who make large contributions. The leaders of the Israel United Appeal estimate that they had already reached over ninety per cent of the community's potential contributors after the Six Day War, when their campaign rose from an average of about two million Rand per campaign ($3,600,000) to about eighteen million Rand ($26,000,000). It is expected that the Yom Kippur War campaign will reach the forty million Rand mark ($58,000,000), a figure which maintains this relatively small community's high record per capita.

Since the beginning of this century, South African governments have displayed a sympathetic attitude towards Zionism, particularly in the long period of Jan Christian Smuts' political leadership. The Nationalist Government, which has been in power since 1948, adopted a similarly sympathetic attitude until it was disturbed by Israel's U.N. votes against South Africa's Apartheid system. Between 1961 and 1967 the South African Government retaliated by refusing to permit the community to transfer funds, raised by the IUA, to Israel. Under the impact of the Six Day War, when Israel's cause had the overwhelming sympathy of people in South Africa, this restriction was waived. But, thereafter, tensions continued to emerge from time to time, as in 1971 when Israel made a small symbolic donation to the Organization of African Unity, much to the chagrin of the government of South Africa.

However, the Yom Kippur War broke out at a time when the relationship between Israel and South Africa had greatly improved, one sign of which was the establishment of a Consulate in Tel Aviv. Israel had long had diplomatic representation in South Africa. Against this background, the outbreak of the war stimulated an enormous upsurge of pro-Israel sentiment in the white South African public. In the South African situation, it is difficult to know how the African, Coloured, and Indian non-white majority of South

Africa's population reacted to the war. The little evidence there is indicates that the vast majority remained quite unaware and unconcerned with the events surrounding the Arab-Israeli conflict. However, it is known that many urban Africans who are in the employ of Jewish business firms, or have come into contact with Jews, expressed sympathy for Israel. On the other hand, there were some signs that Moslem Indians supported the Arabs.

As for the white population, different as the internal social purposes of the Israeli and South African societies may in fact be, the war highlighted the fortuitous congruence of strategic interests between Israel and South Africa. The Afrikaner press, as well as the English press, pointed out that South Africa and Israel were both struggling for survival in a hostile world. Israel was the northern bulwark in Africa against Russian imperialism, whilst South Africa was the southern. Great admiration for Israel's stand and deep concern that she succeed were compounded by the feeling that if Israel were to fall South Africa would be the next victim. Official sympathy for Israel's cause was also forthcoming from a number of government ministers. The Minister of Defense was reported as saying:

> Israel is the guardian of the important strategic gateway of the free world. This is well understood by most South Africans. Further, Israel is bound to South Africa by historical ties of blood and religion. There is a deep feeling of sympathy on the part of tens of thousands of South Africans towards Israel in its struggle against the forces supported by Communist militarism. It is also a threat to us.[17]

Actually, the Jewish community has never experienced an atmosphere as sympathetic to its passionate devotion to Israel's welfare. As was shown by the community's perseverance in responding to campaigns even during the 1960s when the government frowned upon this activity, there is no reason to doubt that it would have supported Israel to the hilt even if the atmosphere had not been so conducive. Still, there can be

17. A. Goldberg, "War and the Middle East—Review of South African Opinion," *Jewish Affairs*, October 1973; L. Hotz, "South African Sympathy for Israel," *loc. cit.*, November 1973.

no doubt that the positive attitude of the non-Jewish majority greatly encouraged Jews to express their deep commitment to Israel's welfare.

The impression gained, in the absence of any systematic study, is that the sudden threat to Israel's existence, in conjunction with this sympathetic atmosphere within South Africa, has heightened the self-esteem of South African Jews and reinforced the conviction that their identity and status are dependent, above all, on the fate of Israel. It is quite possible that this will have the effect of drawing more of the "young adult" generation into Zionist activity, as happened after the Six Day War. This will further guarantee the strength of Zionism and its centrality in the life of the Jewish community.

On the other hand, there is the fact that the apartheid policy of the South African Government has been anathema to many of the younger generation of Jews who have imbibed left-wing views and identified themselves with the struggle of the black population and with the Third World rather than with the struggle of Israel. Perhaps this explains why the vice-chairman of the South African Zionist Federation faced a half-empty great hall at the University of Witwatersrand, Johannesburg, during the second week of the fighting when he addressed what he termed "one of the most important meetings of the past few days," directed at obtaining the support and closer understanding for Israel in the student community. Some six hundred students were present, but as the national chairman of the South African Federation of Jewish Students remarked, "There are four thousand Jewish students on campus." The speaker talked to this audience about the sense of complacency and indifference, and even hostility to Israel's just cause, that many students have developed in recent years.[18]

Nevertheless, the overall impression one gains is that Jewry in South Africa maintained an extremely high level of support for Israel. At the same time, precisely because no sense of alienation from South African society resulted from the events of the Yom Kippur War, there is little reason to assume that these events will have a marked effect on the

18. *Jewish Herald*, October 23, 1973.

number of *olim* from South Africa, a number which presently averages a steady five hundred per year.

Observations on Immediate Jewish Identification Trends

For the vast majority of the Jews in the countries surveyed in this paper, the Yom Kippur War, as other staggering events in recent Jewish history, have evoked a need to reappraise their Jewish identification. This appeared to be the case even amongst those students and intellectuals who have in recent years been linked only tenuously with the Jewish community, or even amongst those who have cut themselves off from other Jews. It is true that reports from British universities indicated a lack of support among large numbers of Jewish students, and many were even taking anti-Israel positions. But, at the very least, some confusion has arisen amongst these younger elements and some intellectuals, a confusion due to the realization that Jews were, in the last analysis, singled out for differential treatment on an international scale. For the Jews who closely identified with their communities, the Yom Kippur War has evoked a tremendous feeling of solidarity which occurred spontaneously. As Michael Comay, the former Israeli Ambassador in London, said, "Apart from the fact that Jews were giving their support out of loyalty and complete conviction, they also felt the need to be regarded by Israel as genuine partners."[19]

This partnership became even more real when Jews in Britain found themselves on the "front line" as evidenced by the shooting and serious wounding of J. Edward Sieff. When other well-known Jews were similarly threatened, the threats were met with renewed and staunch declarations of continued support for Israel. Compared to the Jews in the United States and the Soviet Union, the Jews in Britain were in an in-between position on this occasion. They felt alienated, mainly through the actions of the British government, from the larger society in which they lived during this crisis situation, but were not faced with a hostile regime, either so far as their own safety was concerned or as regards intentions

19. Interviewed on November 14, 1973 by Geoffrey Wigoder in Jerusalem.

vis-à-vis Israel. On the other hand, they and Australian Jewry were not enjoying the kind of congruence of interests of the larger societies and the positive attitudes of the governments of the United States and South Africa, which ameliorated somewhat the effects of the crisis for Jews in the latter countries. But there was a common denominator functioning at a very high level in all the communities surveyed. This was the strengthening of identification with Israel for the majority of Jews, a factor which appears to have reached such heights that we may now assume that many regard Israel as their true homeland. This was expressed succinctly by a Jew writing to the *Jerusalem Post* from London: "It is becoming increasingly clear that there can be only one real home for us Jews in the light of our experiences over the last 2,000 years and the past two months. However, Home has its (Diaspora) outposts which can send vast sustaining forces, spiritual and material."[20]

Ethnic minorities invariably face the test of the necessity to choose their links between what may be termed the "ethnic homeland" and the society in which they actually live.[21] In terms of group identification this may be expressed symbolically and in certain deeds: the kind of manifestations we have come across among the communities that we focused on. Some take this process of identification to its logical conclusion, namely, physically leaving the society in which they live and returning to their "ethnic homeland." Yet even this crisis situation has not had a real impact on the Jews we have examined.[22] It may be too early to predict the longer-term effect of the Yom Kippur War in this respect. But the strong impression one gains is that the meanings of "peoplehood" and "homeland" have become crystallized and reinforced through a closer identification with Israel and world Jewry.

20. Letter by Stafford Lone, written on December 9th, 1973 and published in *Jerusalem Post* on December 19, 1973.
21. Marshall Sklare, *America's Jews*, New York, 1971, p. 210.
22. It should be noted that although there were no indications of a substantial increase in *aliyah* from Britain, the 79 *olim* in October 1973 was a relatively high figure. It was also reported from the Youth and Pioneering Department that there were no cancellations by candidates for *aliyah* whose cases were under review and that among the new applicants were many who never before thought of *aliyah*.

Great Britain: Perspectives

Maurice Freedman

What I am capable of saying, on the basis of my knowledge and experience on the reactions in Britain to the present crisis with special reference to opinion among intellectuals, is in reality rather little; but I have let my imagination play upon that limited stock in order to fulfill what I take to be the intellectual's chief role: to seek truth through scepticism.

Attitudes of British Intellectuals

I shall begin by commenting upon a statement by intellectuals. During the fighting, a letter signed by twenty-one teachers at the Hebrew University, a few of them my friends, was circulated among British academics, to call for our support in "bringing home to the Arab countries the demand of the world that the language of hate and vilification, and the dialogue of war, must be replaced by the dialogue of peaceful coexistence." That was a *cri de coeur* uttered at a very dangerous time, and it merited, and still merits, great respect. But, at the risk of appearing brutal, I shall use it as an example of some of the difficulties my Israeli colleagues face in speaking to the world, or rather, to intellectuals in Britain, for I should clearly not venture too far beyond that limited field. The first point to make is that in being asked to post up that letter on university notice boards (although I am not sure that was the intention of the signatories themselves) we were being invited to engage in the kind of instant propaganda that many of us (especially those of us who have taught in the more turbulent universities) have on principle systematically condemned. There are two sides to the objection. The first is that a university is not a place for political propaganda, least of all when conducted by teachers. The second is that if we are in any way to be associated with political argument, it had better be sophisticated. I hope it will not come as a surprise to my Israeli colleagues that the reply to the October letter which appeared on November 29 in the *New York Review* by Professor Daniel Amit was heartily commended to me by one of Israel's firmest supporters in the British universities. And since I look upon myself as a faithful friend of Israel, I had better add that I consider Professor Amit's letter a much better argument on Israel's side than that contained in the letter to which it responded.*

One may think that judgment perverse, but consider the context in which the debate has to be conducted. No intellectual, however friendly his disposition towards Israel, is going to believe that right is all on one side. The Arabs have a case and it is against that case that Israel's has to be measured. The argument in favor of the Arab side has been skillfully made by many intellectuals—and I stress that not all of them are anti-Semitic. (It is absurd to impute to non-Jews the same evaluation of the link between pro-Jewishness and pro-Israel sentiment as that made by Jews themselves, especially those in Israel.) That pro-Arab argument needs to be countered by dialectic of an equally subtle kind; and it is no use speaking as though Israel were evidently right in all respects. To talk self-righteously and adopt a high moral tone is, in intellectual circles, to lose the argument.

I make this point in the context of a general proposition that support for Israel is less secure among intellectuals in Britain than in the mass of the population. There are several reasons why that should be so. Toughness and military efficiency (both, by the way, seen to be in evidence in the fighting despite the initial setback) are not qualities that the modern intellectuals much admire, especially when those talents are pitted against representatives of that Third World which has come to occupy a special position in the social cosmology of the liberal imagination. We all recall a time when Israel was a prominent part of the furnishings of that

*For the content of both statements, see Appendix I, pp. 351–354.

imagination, when an ascetic utopianism could be vicariously enjoyed by long-distance contemplation of the kibbutzim. Those days are gone, and the normalization now realized in Israel (although perhaps not quite as the founding fathers of Zionism imagined) makes Israel far too much like a developed country to allow it to continue to be worthy of sentimental investment. Indeed, the very fact that Israel is a democracy is paradoxically to its disadvantage: that it is a democracy makes it mature, and its maturity shifts it into the other camp; Israel has moved over into the democratic-imperialist camp from which a large part of the intellectual world is eager to disassociate itself. The raw facts of history (if such there be) have not changed, but men's perception of them has. What once was brave and struggling, poor and dignified, is now arrogant, expansionist, and too rich by half. Criticism and denigration of Israel are a form of self-criticism and self-denigration, and just as some intellectuals could once live out their hopes in Israel, they now live out their hate in it. Alas for Israel, it has come to be a symbol of the detested imperialist past (Was not the creation of Israel the last major act of imperialism in the old form?) and of what is taken to be the obscene prosperity of the West. This is one kind of intellectual reaction. Another, springing also from the imperialist past, expresses itself in weariness with the foreign world, a world from which Britain has learned to expect nothing but trouble, and issues in an indifference to Israel's problems. I have, of course, left out of account those British intellectuals whose extreme leftist political opinions make them, fortunately, a small minority, and, unfortunately, unamenable to argument.

I do not, however, wish to be understood to be saying that Israel lacks intellectual supporters in Britain. Obviously, and happily, that is not the case; and the success that some of us had in getting the signatures of university people during the second week of the fighting to a statement against British government policy bears witness to that support. But it rests, in part, on a conservative irritation with Israel's enemies, in part on personal and academic loyalties to Israel, and in part, on the older view retained by older people, of Israel as the struggling orphan. I stress this last point, the obverse of that I made earlier about the modern liberal imagination. In this regard, time is not on Israel's side. If it were simply a matter of New Left ideology, as some might think it to be, then perhaps there would not be much to worry about; after all, the New Left in Britain is in eclipse. No: there is a much more general and relatively political view of the world among the intellectual young that leaves Israel unqualified for sympathy. Not being a member of the Third World, Israel is at best boring. I imagine that, being used to strong sentiments of love or hate, Israelis must find it astonishing that to some people in the outside world, they are bores.

I have said that some of the support for Israel has sprung from personal and academic loyalties. I am not alone in having been struck during the recent conflict by the relative ease with which support would be rallied for Israel among those academics who have visited the country—provided, that is to say, that they were not Jews. It is a sad paradox. Jewish academics who visit Israel go there as Jews and react as Jews; a fraction of them do not like what they find. Their emotions are in any case necessarily complex. Non-Jewish academics appear to react simply as academics, and liking what they see, respecting what they discover, remain loyal to the society that produces it. May I point the moral? If Israel wants non-Jewish academics as supporters in Britain it could easily have many more by bringing them to Israel. It must be a relatively inexpensive way of making friends.

But I turn now to question the very purpose of making intellectual friends and seeking intellectual support for Israel. Is it really necessary? If the aim is to keep open Israel's intellectual lines to the West and to maintain its intellectual standing in the world, well and good. But if it is thought that intellectual support for Israel in Britain is a commodity with a high political value, then I suggest that we need to be sceptical and cautious. It may well be (but I tread warily here) that the Israeli perception of political life in Britain may be distorted by Israel's view of how their own society works and of how a modern democracy ought to work. It is important to stress that, however active and fruitful its intellectual life, however good its writers and universities, British society is not an intellectual society in the sense in which France, and to a degree, the United States are. That is to say, authority does not strikingly flow from intellectual excellence and standing; intellectuals do not shape public opinion.

British society is a Philistine society (I hope I may use that adjective without risk of being accused of Jewish chauvinism); intellectuals are in positions of power to the extent that they are deintellectualized. Watch the behavior of excellent men in the bureaucracies and politics. (Incidentally, British students misread their own society when, looking upon themselves as young intellectuals, they imagine that they are in a position to shake their country up. They cannot.) Government and politics in Britain are swayed by other forces—as perhaps Israelis may have already concluded from observations of British Jewry which, in its unintellectual and political behavior, will have given a clue to the nature of the society within which it is embedded. No: the great mass of Britain's scientists, writers and academics might raise their voices in Israel's favor without political action being materially affected. If that rough analysis is accepted, it follows that Israel should not waste its time and money in the attempt to affect Britain's response by trying to influence its intellectuals. There are much more important targets: the political élites, the trade unions, the industrialists, and so on.

And I am led by these reflections to wonder how far Israel's leaders and representatives abroad have taken the measure of the societies they have sought to influence in their favor. How much understanding, at other than a superficial level, is there in Israel of the outside world within which it must struggle to maintain itself? What institutional arrangements does Israel have for informing itself of the world? Is its diplomatic service of the sort that seeks out knowledge of the societies where it operates and learns to put its case in the several languages of the several groups that compose a complex society? In between crises, how much hard work of that sort is undertaken?

Thinking about that basic question, I happened upon an interesting and encouraging piece of information in the course of turning over the pages of the volume called *Hebrew University General Information 1972/3*. On page 49 there is mention of a project called "Documentation of the Israeli Experience in Africa" under the direction of Professor

Nehemia Levtzion. The rubric says: "Israeli experts who have served in Africa are being interviewed, and the information gathered will be catalogued and indexed to serve future researchers." It is not for me to join the chorus of people shouting "diplomatic disaster in Africa," for it is, I should have thought, far too early to say—although one is bound to wonder whether Israelis have ever faced up to the difficulty posed to them by their being inevitably *not* in the Third World in the eyes of those they have sought to influence, and the further difficulty which any social scientist could explain, that aid to underdeveloped countries is more likely to lead to resentment than gratitude. I raise the matter only to express the hope that the kind of research to which Professor Levtzion's project points is made much more general. Certainly, Israel will not be successful in influencing Britain if it does not have a deep understanding of that country.

But I must not leave the matter of British intellectuals without adding the qualification that they are not entirely useless in Israel's cause. Clearly, there are some limited ways in which they may serve. During the war crisis it was correctly seen by some of Israel's friends in Britain that intellectuals may be rallied in an informal way to bring pressure to bear on political leaders in such matters as the maltreatment of prisoners of war. That is an important enough matter, and if only a little can be done, it is still worth doing. But I repeat my more general point: there is no great political job for the intellectuals to do.

British Jews and British Public Opinion

Let me now turn to the Jews. I shall suggest that the war of 1973 has, for the Jews of Britain, not been simply a sequel to that of 1967, a sort of projection of one line of history, but a new point in that history. I can perhaps best make my case by referring to one of my memories of the so-called Suez campaign of 1956. I recall a conversation I had with a Jewish colleague in the midst of the fighting. What, we asked each other, would happen if ever the day came (and why should it not?) when Jews in Britain were confronted with a wide divergence between British and Israeli interests? (It may be said that the divergence had earlier existed, during the struggle with Britain as Mandatory power. But, in fact at that time, British Jewry was not yet committed as a whole to the Zionist cause.) The year 1967 did not see the conflict of interests, and British public opinion was then largely pro-Israel. (On June 12, 1967, the National Opinion Poll [NOP] reported 55 per cent of the public as blaming the trouble on the Egyptians; 3 per cent blamed the Israelis.)

But 1973 has realized (or at any rate begun to realize) the possibility envisaged by my friend and myself in 1956: there is still a large body of public opinion in Britain in favor of Israel, and I am pretty sure that it is larger than the pro-Israel opinion among the intellectuals; but the current opinion polls, while showing that pro-Israel sentiment is still vastly greater than pro-Arab, demonstrates that general interest in the conflict has declined. Half of the people in Britain appear to support neither side. (I shall cite data from the NOP. In May of this year, 23 per cent supported the Israeli side, 2 per cent the Arab; but 35 per cent had no opinion, and 34 per cent took neither side. On October 13, 1973 at the beginning of the second week of the fighting, 47 percent took the Israeli side, 5 per cent the Arab, while 33 per cent took neither side, and 15 per cent had no view. In a *Daily Express* poll taken in the same period, 50 per cent appeared to take neither side, 36 per cent were pro-Israel, and 7 per cent pro-Arab; presumably, the remaining 7 per cent had no views. In that poll, 56 per cent were in favor of Britains's embargo on arms to the Middle East. Finally, in the NOP poll taken in the last week of November, 43 per cent were pro-Israel, 7 per cent pro-Arab, while 31 per cent took neither side, and 19 per cent had no view.) British public opinion is not strikingly out of alignment with government policy. In any case, even if, in circumstances we cannot foresee, British public opinion were to be once more decisively in Israel's favor, government policy might very well not reflect the shift, and Jews would then be left to speak out against the official line.

Let me add my personal view that a change of government would make no or little difference to the situation. As far as their public supporters are concerned, the major political parties are not clearly differentiated on the

Middle East struggle, although the Labor voters, while being no more pro-Arab than Conservative or Liberal voters, are more indifferent, markedly more so than the Conservative voters. In this situation, facing a perhaps increasingly indifferent public opinion, and an official policy that, while not being enthusiastically pro-Arab, has the effect of being anti-Israel, the Jewish minority in Britain begins to look as small as its numbers. It is a fragment, less than one half of one per cent, of the total population of Britain. I do not myself believe (although of course, in that I speak with no authority) that the enormously greater Jewish population of the United States can expect constantly to wield political influence in its society; in Britain, certainly, the Jews can do practically nothing. I do not mean that they will not try. On the contrary, we are now, in my view, past the point of brushing the dual loyalties problem aside as though it were unreal. By and large, British Jews are by now so caught up in the implications of their past support for Israel, that they will learn to accommodate themselves to being a minority in a much more forceful sense than they have been for a long time.

The analyses made of Anglo-Jewry between the end of World War II and the recent past were not wrong to stress the comfortably successful niche British Jews had found for themselves; but events have overtaken the analysis—or so it seems to me as I face the future. However, there is of course quite a different side to the relations between Anglo-Jewry and Israel. British Jews may be of little political help, but Israel presumably has interests in Anglo-Jewry as a source of funds and immigration. On the former score, the evidence is clear enough that money is forthcoming, and it could well turn out that as British Jews feel themselves increasingly isolated by their support for Israel, they will be all the more willing to contribute.

Emigration is another question altogether; and we here come up against one of the most difficult problems in the mutual understanding between Israel and the Diaspora (not only in Britain). I do not think that it is an exaggeration to say that, if it were politically and militarily possible, great numbers of young British Jews would rush to Israel to fight whenever the guns open up. And, just to add a third condition, if it were possible for the not-so-young to fight, there would be thousands more. I think the Israelis know that, and it must puzzle them the more that so few choose to settle among them. Indeed, it must seem almost insulting that someone will take the gravest of risks to come to your aid but not be willing to be your neighbor.

In the absence of serious research (or in my ignorance of any that may have been conducted), I cannot say why immigration from Britain languishes, but I shall suggest some possibilities. Let me begin where most people would: with material considerations. It may be that it is not the differences in standard of living between the two countries that is the crucial point; perhaps it is not the fact the British Jews are better off but that they are predominantly middle class that constitutes the difficulty. For their experience of that middle-class life creates a set of attitudes to work and organization that may not go too well with attitudes in Israel. Naturally a marked economic decline in Britain may send more Jews to Israel as it sends more people to Australia, Canada, South Africa, and even Rhodesia. I could hardly be expected to welcome that prospect. But setting economic considerations aside, I think there are other important ones to take into account. British Jews like Britain. I myself would not hesitate to assert that no country in the world (I make no exceptions) has managed to create and, so far, to maintain so high a standard of public decency and urban civility as Britain has. Such a civilization is hard to abandon. After all, Israel is a rather rough-and-tumble society. I am not naive enough to imagine that Britain must continue to be so pleasant a society, and Israel might be one of the beneficiaries of a decline in British social amenities—a decline even to the point of anti-Semitism, for no such tragedy is precluded in history yet unmade.

Image of Israel

Let me turn away from that unpleasant possibility to a matter that, I suspect, concerns Israelis more immediately: the image of Israel in the minds of young British Jews and the effects of that image on migration. Again, I do not speak upon the basis of well collected data, but I hazard the guess that what many Israelis fear as New Left hostility is really unimportant, and that what Israelis do not fear (for they are not well aware of its existence) is highly important. I mean: a generalized view of the world, more marked certainly in the better educated, which incorporates the attitudes to the Third World I tried to characterize earlier in my paper, in the context of the general British population. (To my brief statement about the New Left, may I just add that the only overt anti-Israel Jewish opinion I was aware of in Britain during the recent fighting came from *Israelis*.) The Third Worldism of the Jewish young does not turn them against Israel to the extent of making them anti-Israel, but it induces an uneasiness in them about Israel's role in the world and about their relationship with a country that would otherwise be less problematic. The view they hold makes them come down firmly on Israel's side when its existence is threatened, or appears to be threatened, but falters on the threshold of identification with Israel. It is in part based upon the liberal historiography of our times: Israel is an intrusion upon the Arab world and adds insult to injury by its total rejection of the culture about it and by its contempt for what it is pleased to call Levantinization.

Israelis are not required to take such views into account when shaping their own destiny; certainly, nobody from outside has the right to tell Israelis what they must do; but it might be worth considering the possibility that different facets of Israeli life and culture might be presented to the young of the world (and not only the Jews) so that the image of the swaggering Western Israeli, contemptuous of the oriental both within and outside his boundaries, might be balanced by an image of a more pleasing sort: the Israeli at home in an oriental world. It has long been noticed that "Zionism" is a pejorative; if the name "Israel" is also in some danger of accumulating the wrong connotations, it might be made more acceptable by being tightly packed with the rich meaning of that country's cultural diversity. I do not say that a more orientalized Israel would be an unambiguous benefit (it might put off some potential immigrants, after all); but I am thinking of the possibility of an improved atmosphere in which the young Jews of the Diaspora would be more willing to experiment with the idea of coming to grips with Israel at first hand. I realize that the Israeli authorities are likely to prefer clear-cut decisions and wholehearted commitments (Who can blame them?); but it seems to me that young Jews in the Diaspora need to be treated with the utmost gentleness and tact while they feel their way to an appreciation of where their duties and interests lie. What if large numbers of those who sojourn in Israel leave? The last thing to do, I should think, is to write them off as deserters. Even if they do not come back at once, they are a pool upon which Israel may need at some time to draw. If Israel denigrates Jews who will not definitely opt for it, then it is cutting itself off from large numbers of Israelophiles, whom one might have supposed to be a precious asset. For one reason or another, Israel is not going to be able to contain all well-wishing Jews. Why should it not look with favor and understanding upon those Jews in the Diaspora who have had some firsthand experience of the country? Is it not better that Jews pass and repass through Israeli life than that, once having left, they are not encouraged to return? In its national pride, Israel wants to be a fulltime fatherland for all Jews. Better, one might suggest, that it consider being a part-time fatherland for some of them.

A Recommendation

When I referred earlier to Israel's perception of foreign societies, I raised the matter of its arrangements for gathering knowledge about them; and I want now to return to the point in the context of Israeli views of young Jews abroad and of those who sojourn in Israel. Israelis see the world through lenses ground to their prescription. That is not a criticism; one recognizes the limits put upon all countries by their peculiar positions and problems. It takes a great effort of imagination and much courage to see beyond one's normal range, to question one's assumptions, and to put oneself in someone else's position. What systematic effort is being made to try to appreciate the problems and potentialities of young Jews arriving in Israel? It would be useless to look at them only from an Israeli point of view; the observer must know not only what they are reacting to, but the background against which they are reacting. To understand British Jews, you must know about Britain, and you must know it well.

In closing, I suggest that one of the saddest parts of Israel's relations with the Diaspora (at least as seen from Britain) is the low level of the interchange between the social scientists on the two sides. Why that should be so is a problem separate from anything in my brief; I want merely to note it, underlining the consequences for our understanding of what happens to Jews from the Diaspora when they make the experiment of living in Israel, as well as, more broadly, for our understanding of what happens when Israelis face the world in foreign countries. There is a need for an Institute of Contemporary Jewry as exists in Jerusalem. There is another need for an Institute of Contemporary Israel, manned by scholars able, by their being freed from the pressures of Israeli life, to stand away from what they study and see it clearly in its relations with the greater world. Perhaps such an institute should not even be in Israel.

Great Britain: Perspectives

S. M. Schreter

There is a widespread opinion that since the Six Day War the links between Diaspora Jewry and Israel have never been stronger. I found this proposition wanting in my own milieu, the University. While October–November 1973 found me in London, my previous academic wanderings had taken me to Canada and the United States. I therefore cast my remarks in a slightly broader context. Why has student response to the Israeli situation undergone changes between 1967 and 1973?

First, there are situational differences. In 1967 there was a period of build-up and anticipation which riveted the attention and anxieties of Jews of all ages on the Middle East. In six days, the feelings of anxiety gave way to a sense of incredible deliverance. In 1973 Jews were first stunned, then deeply depressed by the human cost of Israel's victory.

This may be formulated in a slightly different manner. One of the things Zionism is about, and which Diaspora Jews have little understood, is power. Only through power could Zionism approach its fundamental goals, namely, to achieve the security and dignity of the Jewish people. The combination of the Holocaust, the policies of the British Mandatory Government in Palestine, and the relentless intransigence of Arab leaders made this an unavoidable reality. But political power, and its manifestation in state power, is at best a harsh, often ambiguous, and costly affair in many senses.

What could Diaspora Jewry appreciate of all this? Their notions about Zionism and Israel were largely romanticized in the crucible of fund-raising appeals and Leon Uris. Their fantasies were scarcely diminished by the propaganda/information policies of the Israeli Government and the Jewish Agency over the years, or by the apparent effortlessness of the

Israeli military victories in 1956 and 1967. Their comprehension of power did not reach beyond the attempts of some leaders to act as a pro-Israel pressure group on the Middle East policies of their respective governments. In 1973, these issues were recast in a more realistic light, and the new realizations of what it can mean to have and to hold power had a sobering and, I should think, ultimately healthy effect.

Second, there are the general unarrested processes of acculturation and assimilation acting on many Diaspora Jews, weaning them further and further away from their ethnic loyalties and attachments.

Third, mention should be made of changes in that admittedly amorphous entity called "student culture." Until 1967 the student culture was significantly influenced by the fresh and non-ideological stage of the New Left. As such, it had few preconceptions and less information about Israel, which still enjoyed a considerable credit rating among liberals of all sorts. This situation was rapidly transformed by the static situation in the Middle East, while Israel became more dependent on American arms. Much of the international left swung decisively into a pro-Arab posture, supporting what appeared to be the righteous struggle of the Third World against imperialism.

Today, no matter how great the decline in conspicuous New Left activism on campuses, the political consciousness of the evolving student culture is still largely influenced by its perspectives. It has become part of the "general wisdom" in the student culture to assign a villainous and pernicious role to Israel in the Middle East; it is hardly more controversial to assert this than it used to be to attack the perfidy of America's policies in Vietnam. The superficiality of the anti-Israel stance is not so significant as its potential scope. To swallow such assertions one would not have to be ideological or even very politically concerned at all, or anything but a relatively ignorant Jewish student equipped with a fund of background hysteria and misinformation about Israel, a regulation liberal conscience, and an anxiety to be "with it."

Fourth, the difference in student reactions must be seen in the context of increasing cynicism in many circles about Israel, its foreign policy, and what it stands for. This has two aspects: what Israel herself does, and how the established Diaspora Jewish communities respond.

On the first aspect, there is widespread opinion that Israel's post-1967 foreign policy has been unimaginative and disastrously inflexible. The myth of Israel's military impregnability and the "time-is-on-our-side" axiom of complacency contributed to this cynicism. The Israel that many Jewish students find when they visit is a disappointment, for they are not seeking inadequate facsimiles of New York and London, but idealism, commitment and community. (The kibbutz, by the way, in which less than four per cent of Israel's population lives, is no panacea.) The old pioneering and egalitarian values seem rather antiquated and quaint for most Israelis, and pragmatism and consumerism reign supreme. Pragmatism may be useful as a technique but it is certainly not an ideology capable of motivating action and self-sacrifice, or of conveying to the young Diaspora Jews *why* Israel is. There is also deep discomfort over the Israeli approach to the Palestinians, and a feeling that the Israelis are denying the self-determination to another people that they demand for themselves.

On the second aspect, Israel has become associated inseparably with the emptiness of Jewish life as many students perceive it in the suburbias of North America and Western Europe. The hysteria provoked by criticism of Israel or her policies is a less than reassuring influence. A more fundamental issue is that the obsession with fund raising has so pervaded Jewish communal activity in the Diaspora as to have virtually pre-empted all other communal activities in terms of frequency or intensity. But a sense of Jewish community and values will not successfully be transmitted to new generations if that community defines itself more and more by virtue of raising money. The old question is still applicable: survival for what?

In this context, I can only view the unprecedented fund-raising activity of American Jewish students with mixed feelings. I am glad they did it, because Israel needs the funds, but I think that the 1967 student response was far healthier, more personal. It seems as if in 1973 committed Jewish students simply appropriated the adult Jewish pattern of fund raising, with accompanying superficiality. This time round they will not reach out to present the Jewish views of the Middle East conflict to their fellow students. The Jewish student movement will not miraculously revive and eclipse its former achievements; the Jewish student newspapers will enjoy a brief respite owing to renewed interest in the Arab-Israeli conflict, but will continue declining as spontaneous expressions of grass-roots Jewish student feeling, and as agencies of local mobilization. The basic apathy seems unlikely to abate, barring extraordinary change in the Middle East situation and in the degenerative trends within Diaspora Jewish life. I am saying, then, that Israel is in trouble with the "children of the checkbook" generation and that, in the wake of the Yom Kippur War, there is no cause for celebrating the Jewish student reactions.

What Israel means to Diaspora Jews in general should be considered carefully. Marshall Sklare has written of Israel's centrality to the basic sense of meaning and order in life of American Jews, suggesting that Israel has thereby taken on religious or spiritual significance with immediate psychological implications for them. Without Israel, the events of twentieth-century Jewish history become too monstrous and overpowering to bear. "In sum, if Israel were to be destroyed the American Jew would fall prey to *anomie*—the breakdown of social norms and values. By acting as he did (in support for Israel in May and June 1967) the American Jew was not only assisting his fellow Jews abroad; he was also protecting himself from the bottomless pit of *anomie.*"[1]

Charles Liebman goes further, arguing that Israel is not so much a spiritual, ideological, or cultural center for American Jews, as it is the very *content* of their Jewishness. Support for Israel has replaced endogamy as the primary boundary-defining criterion of membership in the Jewish community. Previous Jewish foci, such as Yiddish culture, synagogue activity, theology and belief, the Jewish "social justice" ethic, anti-Semitism, and sense of peoplehood, have

1. Marshall Sklare, *America's Jews,* New York, 1971, p. 217.

become seriously attenuated—leaving Israel as the residual Jewish attachment.[2]

The current generation of young Jews, however, has not shared the same socialization experiences. The Holocaust and Israel War of Independence are ancient history to them. It is probable that most of today's Jewish undergraduates have only unclear memories of the Six Day War. This is not an age when historical consciousness has fared very well. If Israel is to "make it" with them, we will have to recognize that the basic *raison d'être* of the State—as a home for persecuted Jews and the instrumentality through which Jews become the subject rather than the object of their history—is not enough for young people, though it was for their parents. The flag and the anthem and the Jewish army may have been revolutionary for one generation, and perhaps taken for granted or disregarded by another. How, then, *can* the loyalty of today's young Jews to Israel be consolidated?

I have no small-scale answers to suggest. Of course, programs such as the World Union of Jewish Students (WUJS) Arab Institute or Sherut La'am should be expanded or improved. But these will never affect more than a very small minority. Nor is the answer to be sought in better public relations. The complacent assumption that the young Jews of the Diaspora will eventually transcend the essentially adolescent form of rebellion and comfortably settle into the same roles as their parents with regard to Israel is counter-productive and dangerous. It fails to take account of serious social dynamics or to begin coping with them. And it also relates to the complex of complacent attitudes, constituting an updated version of the good old anachronistic *shlilat ha-golah*, negation of the Diaspora, which threatens, if unchecked, to distort the relationship of Diaspora to Israel into that of host to parasite.

In other words, it is the basic quality of life and the justice of the society Israelis build which will have most influence on the attitudes of young Jews to the State. This is

2. Charles S. Liebman, *The Ambivalent American Jew*, Philadelphia, 1973, pp. 88–108.

not because they are highly informed and critical observers of social developments within Israel, or because they are in any sense more morally discriminating than their parents. They are not. It is simply a realization that socialization seems not to have instilled in them as deep an emotional attachment to Israel as that of their parents, and that their future support will likely be more conditional on Israel's attainment of certain social and moral standards.

The lines of argument at this point should be clear. I have been describing student attitudes to Israel, and attempting to forecast what will influence them most in the next period. I have not suggested that Israel's policies should be carefully planned so as to avoid bruising the tender sensibilities of Diaspora Jewish youth. These "sensibilities" may be a factor, perhaps an utterly irrelevant one, entering the decision-making process. But when, for example, the decision is taken that American arms and funds are vastly more important than the sympathies of liberal young Jews, or Afro-Asian diploma ` relations for that matter, then the consequences in either case ought to be faced squarely, without wasting time and dignity crying "self-hating Jews" or "foul." There simply is not much use, and perhaps considerable harm, in appealing to the Jewish loyalties of the under-25 generation as if they were their parents. They are not.

Is it possible, then, to specify which areas of change in Israeli society and policies are most likely to effect positively overall Jewish student attitudes to Israel? In the absence of concrete data, obviously not, but having gone this far, I will indulge in brief speculation.

Foreign policy in general and the pursuit of peace in particular are, in my opinion, the most important issues. Many Jewish students are looking for a moderate and flexible Israeli stand at Geneva, and for an abandonment of unrealistic views about the Palestinians. They wish Israel's desire for peace and compromise to become more manifest and energetic. They are not convinced by the argument of "no alternative." The attainment of even an interim peace, Israel's participation with other nations in the humanitarian task of rehabilitating the Palestinian refugees, and the political task of dealing seriously with the Palestinian national question, would do much to shatter the image of an amoral, obstinate, and militaristic Sparta/Israel.

There are domestic issues, in reality much dependent on Israel's security situation, which also have significant impact. The intractable nature of Israel's political life, the *"protektzia"* system, the drift away from the old egalitarian principles of democratic socialism and toward American-style consumerism and entrepreneur-ship, the low social status of "Oriental" Jews and Arabs within Israel, are all cases in point. I would not want to emphasize these too much, however, since they presuppose a familiarity with Israeli society which most Diaspora Jewish students lack.

On a deeper level, however, I believe the basic ideological confusion and apparent loss of national purpose and direction in Israel today have percolated through to many Jewish students abroad. On the intellectual level, the old argument about how Jews should relate to political power remains an issue. Just having power for its own sake will not satisfy many of today's young Jews, who lack their parents' sense of the bitter necessity underlying it. I think they are more preoccupied with the moral quality of the uses to which Jewish power is put.

Great Britain: Comment

Sir Isaiah Berlin

In my own rather narrow experience at Oxford in connection with the Yom Kippur War, I have had young men come to me who have complained that when they applied to go as volunteers, they were in fact discouraged and rejected. Now I perfectly understand that Israel wants serious people who come for a certain length of time and who are useful while they are there. I feel, however, that these applicants will be frustrated if they are not encouraged sufficiently, and may turn in an anti-Israeli direction. It is very desirable that young men should come to Israel, even if it be for a fortnight or three weeks and even though some of them may be disappointed. Visits to Israel sow seeds which in the majority of cases actually sprout.

It may be true that the majority, perhaps, of the Jewish student population in England has recently been less eager and less responsive to Israeli needs than they might have been fifteen or twenty years ago. But it seems to me on the whole that this recent war produced a passionate and fairly unanimous reaction among Jewish students, at least among those I've walked. Some of them were explicit, some of them were not; but, so far as my experience goes, they are all troubled. They all think about nothing else. They have all kinds of ideas. But the thought that they are indifferent, or couldn't care less, or that they are inclined, in some kind of New Left way, to think of Israel as a semi-imperialist country, acting as an American satellite, and directed against the Third World—that kind of thing can be exaggerated. I should have thought that the importance of bringing people over to Israel, even for short periods, is very great indeed. It must not be overlooked, even at the cost of some inconvenience to the country, even at the cost of getting some superficial characters, and even at the cost of antagonizing a few of them.

I think there is now some degree of shame in England, as far as public opinion—even official opinion—is concerned about the degree of knuckling under to Arab blackmail, which has occurred. Some degree of embarrassment and national humiliation is felt. This ultimately creates a climate which is more favorable to pro-Israel feelings than there has been in the past.

If one asks how can this be of help to Israel, I say that the more persons of an uncommitted kind in central positions in British life, who can be brought to Israel in some reasonable way—because somebody wants to discuss something with them of common interest, or because there are institutions in which they are likely to be interested—the better the effect in England. Broadly speaking, I believe in two propositions: one is that most non-Jewish visitors are moved by what they see, particularly if they are encouraged to wander freely, and come back friends; the other is that so far as Israeli propaganda in England is concerned, the people who are listened to are the moderate doves.

What one has to project is the image of a people which recognizes that their situation is complex and realizes that there are all kinds of incompatible values involved, which in some sort of way have to be solved in a humane manner, and that what one wants to achieve is the least degree of injustice. It must not be projected as a black and white situation, in which the Arabs are all barbarians and murderers, and the Jews are all virtuous and innocent victims, set upon by violent and unprovoked aggression from without. Even if this were true, it is not likely to be believed. About all this, I am in complete agreement with Professor Freedman.

Western Europe: Overview

Itzhak Sergio Minerbi

In Western Europe the most outstanding difference between the effect of the Yom Kippur War and that of the 1967 Six Day War is to be found in the general political situation. Today the grave isolation of the State of Israel is deeply felt; not one state in Europe, not even Holland, took a clear pro-Israel stand. Some countries, led by France, took a blatantly pro-Arab stand.

Much has already been written about the attitude of many groups in Europe, which gave their full support to Israel in 1967 so long as they were under the impression that the Jewish State was on the verge of annihilation, but changed their attitude drastically at the moment it became apparent that Israel had triumphed. According to historian Saul Friedlander, "June 1967 cancelled out the weight of the Holocaust. In the Western conscience the Jews, identified with the victorious Israelis, have become strong and cruel and the others are the victims."[1] To this should be added the

The author wishes to express his gratitude to Dr. Joel Fishman for his assistance in the preparation of data; to M. Willy Bok of the Centre Nationale des Hautes Etudes Juives, Brussels, for his comments; to Francine Kaufman who conducted interviews with M. Pierrot Kaufman, Director of CRIF, and M. Castro, Secretary of the European Council of Jewish Community Services; to Sophie Rosenberg who interviewed M. Boulawko; to Fanny Minerbi who interviewed Signor Luciano Tas, editor of the Rome Jewish monthly *Shalom*; to Professor Chaim Perelman and M.J. Malfait of Brussels for materials they gathered; to the Centre de Documentation Israël et Moyen Orient, Paris, for press cuttings; to the Ministry for Foreign Affairs in Jerusalem for free access to reports from European capitals. All interviews are filed in the Shazar Documentary Unit of the Institute of Contemporary Jewry, The Hebrew University of Jerusalem.

1. *Réflexions sur l'avenir d'Israël*, Paris, 1968, pp. 156–157.

irreparable damage done by General De Gaulle in the notorious press conference of November 27, 1967, in which he described the Jews as "self-assured and domineering."[2] Israel's image became that of a military power with superior military strength. This image was built up to an extent by Israel itself after the Six Day War and fostered in Europe by the Gaullist propaganda machine.[3] The various leftist groups over the years enlarged on the image of the State of Israel as "a satellite of American imperialism," and "a capitalist wedge in the midst of the Arab progressive forces." Or, as it was phrased in a poster seen in Paris in 1968: "An expansionist state attempting to oppress the poor Palestinians who were expelled from their homes 25 years ago."[4]

In Italy the unholy alliance between the Catholics and the Communists is also having an impact. The influence of Amintore Fanfani, formerly Prime Minister and today Secretary General of the majority Christian-Democratic Party, is powerful and he undoubtedly wants to strengthen ties with the Arab states in order to safeguard the interests of the national oil company (ENI). For this reason Italy took a neutral stand at first, but in January 1974 supported the pro-Arab interpretation of Resolution 242.[5] In a debate on the Middle East which took place on October 17 in the Italian Senate, eleven days after the outbreak of the Yom Kippur War, Foreign Minister Aldo Moro stated: "The right of existence of the State of Israel is not a matter for discussion and the goal is the

2. The text of President De Gaulle's press conference of November 27, 1967, and Ben Gurion's letter to De Gaulle of December 6, 1967, are in D. Ben Gurion, *Israel, A Personal History,* Tel Aviv, 1972, pp. 792–806.

3. *L'Arche,* No. 200, October–November 1973.

4. On the anti-Israel attitude of the participants in the May 1968 riots in Paris, see *L'univers contestationnaire,* Paris, 1969: "The conflict in which the leftist intellectual finds himself forces him to reject the anal phase, prevents him from accepting the individual who has done everything necessary to succeed . . . at the same time the idea of the Jew as a martyr is erased; the Jew has once more taken on the ancient character of the exploiter in contrast to the Arab who is poor, unrealistic (and thus pure and innocent), in short proletarian" (p. 151).

5. *Maariv,* January 24, 1974. Italian Foreign Minister M. Moro declared on January 23 in the Senate that his government stands for a complete Israeli retreat from all occupied territories and backs full rights for the Palestinians, as well as the existence of the State of Israel.

coexistence of the Arab states in conditions of real and reciprocal security. This requires the solution of the Palestinian problem, which is not only an economic-social problem but a political one."[6]

The recognition by the majority of the states of Western Europe of the political rights of the Palestinians is a political development worthy of note. The Vatican, which exerts a strong influence on all the Christian parties throughout Europe and has not yet granted official recognition to the State of Israel, advocates a special status for Jerusalem. No opportunity is missed to stress the Palestinian problem as the background to and justification for terrorist activities.[7]

An additional factor contributing to the negative influence on the attitudes of the governments towards Israel is their unfriendly, even hostile, attitude towards the United States. The extent to which this attitude has had a detrimental effect on Israel was pointed up when a number of European countries refused to grant landing rights to American planes flying arms to Israel during the Yom Kippur War.

The current oil shortage has exacerbated the situation. It is not just a matter of "central heating," but of the actual well-being of the industry of Europe, dependent to a large degree on oil. The submission of the European countries to Arab extortion was swift and total, possibly even greater than the Arabs themselves had dared to hope for. On November 6, 1973 the Council of Ministers of the European Community passed a resolution urging Israel's return to the position held

---

6. Ministero degli Affari Esteri, *Italia e Medio Oriente, 1967–1973*, Roma, 1973, p. 170.
7. After the Munich massacre of Israeli participants at the Olympic Games in 1972, the unofficial monthly *Civiltà Cattolica* published an article excusing the motives of the "homeless Palestinians." Professor Alessandrini, the official spokesman of the Vatican, wrote after the Yom Kippur War in the weekly *Osservatore della Domenica* that Israel has the right to exist, but the same is true of the Palestinians, and while the Arabs are fighting with the arm of oil, on the other side there is "the mobilization of international high finance to the side of Israel." Quoted by R. Marciano, "Le Vatican et la morale," *Journal des Communautés*, No. 538, December 14, 1973, p. 10. On December 22, 1973 the Pope received the Emperor of Ethiopia, the President of Sudan, the Vice-President of Liberia, and the Foreign Minister of Zambia who expressed their views about the Middle East conflict, the legitimate rights of the Palestinians, and the problem of Jerusalem.

on October 22, stating that a peace agreement should be based on the inadmissibility of the acquisition of territories by force and on the legitimate rights of the Palestine people.[8] The presence of six Arab foreign ministers in Copenhagen at the time of the European summit between December 14 and 15, 1973 symbolized a further step in the process of the surrender of the Europeans to the pressure of the oil sheiks.[9] This occurred despite evidence that England, France, Italy, and possibly other European countries, were not being harmed by any reduction in the quantity of crude oil reaching them even after the embargo was officially declared.[10]

Attitudes of Political Parties and Other Organizations

In contrast to the almost united stand of the West European governments, there was visible diversity in the attitudes of the political parties and also among members of the same party within the respective countries.

In France the Comité de solidarité française avec Israël (Committee for French Solidarity with Israel) issued a call for direct negotiations between Israel and the Arabs, stating that Israel was having to face aggression for the fourth time in twenty-five years. The call was issued by the presidents of two parliamentarian groups of "France-Israel" friendship and two other organizations. Among the personalities who signed the call were 120 Parliament members, thirty-six belonging to the UDR, the Gaullist party.[11]

---

8. Point 3 of the Resolution said: Ils estiment qu'un accord de paix doit être fondé notamment sur les points suivants: i) l'inadmissibilité de l'acquisition de territoires par la force; ii) la nécessité pour Israël de mettre fin à l'occupation territoriale qu'elle maintient depuis le conflit de 1967; iii) le respect de la souveraineté, de l'intégrité territoriale et de l'indépendance de chaque Etat de la region et leur droit de vivre en paix dans des frontières sures et reconnues; iv) la reconnaissance que, dans l'établissement d'une paix juste et durable il devra être tenu compte des droits légitimes des Palestiniens.

9. *Bulletin Europe*, Brussels, December 1973.

10. *Economist*, December 8, 1973.

11. Leaflet, "La voix de la France" issued by the Comité de solidarité française avec Israël. See Appendix V, p. 359. Cf. also "Apres la prise de position des groupes parlementaires d'amitié France-Israël," *Le Monde*, October 14–15, 1973.

Public opinion polls in France revealed that within the Socialist party opinions were divided equally between supporters and detractors of Israel. Even within the French Communist Party about one quarter of the members came out in support of Israel. This revelation is particularly surprising in light of the fact that the Communist parties in Europe adhered strictly to the official line and took the classical Soviet anti-Israel stand.

In Belgium on October 15 the Rassemblement Belge pour Israël was established, headed by Gaston Eyskens, a former prime minister, and other Belgian political leaders. They published a proclamation asking for "understanding and support for the State of Israel."[12] In Italy, too, differences of opinion were evident within most of the political parties, although a number of small parties gave unwavering support to Israel, principally the Social Democrat party, the Republican party (both in the government), and the Liberal party.

A comparatively new phenomenon, whose origin can be traced to May 1968, is the existence of numerically insignificant groups not represented in the parliament, belonging to the Trotskyist or Maoist extreme left. Although small in number, these groups are influential in France and Italy and, despite their fragmentation, they have taken control of a number of university campuses. The Communists themselves are afraid of them, are forced to take them into consideration and make allowances for them, and their hostility on the campus is in many cases so overt that it endangers the physical well-being of Jewish students at universities.[13] Such groups joined forces with extremist Arabs who are investing large amounts of money in propagandizing the universities.

On the other side of the political spectrum are various groups who have expressed support of Israel. In Milan the Unione democratica amici d'Israele (UDAI) held a mass rally on November 20 attended by the Socialist mayor and

---

12. The proclamation by the Rassemblement Belge pour Israël was published in full in the *Jerusalem Post*, November 18, 1973.
13. See section on *Youth and Volunteers*.

representatives of all parties, except the Fascists and Communists.[14] In Marseilles Mayor Gaston Defferre, also a Socialist, participated in a pro-Israel demonstration organized by the local Jewish community and published a statement expressing personal support of Israel on the front page of *L'Arche Provençale*.[15]

In Berlin Mayor Klaus Schütz, a well known friend of Israel, participated in a public meeting of solidarity after the start of the war.[16] In Brussels six mayors also played an active part in the appeal campaign to raise money for the purchase of ambulances for Israel.[17]

In Paris on November 16 an impressive meeting of members of parliament from eleven European countries was held in support of Israel and a European Parliamentary Committee of Friendship with Israel was created.[18] Two voices were almost silent: those of the Catholic and Protestant Churches, which not only neglected to express condolences to the families of the war victims but took no part in any of the purely humanitarian activities for the speedy exchange of prisoners of war.[19] Sole exceptions in France were the Reverend Michel Riquet, who participated in numerous rallies in support of Israel, and the Archbishop of Grenoble, Monseigneur Matagrin, who organized a mass for Israel's welfare.[20]

14. Pamphlet, *Per la pace e l'amicizia tra i popoli*, Teatro dell'Arte, November 15, 1973, Unione democratica amici d'Israele. See Appendix VI, p. 360.
15. October 1973, No. 49, p. 18. Defferre states that the Egyptians and Syrians initiated the war and that the Arab leaders publicly stated their desire to destroy the State of Israel; Israel is a democratic state while her enemies are dictatorships.
16. Nahum Orland, "German Jews identify themselves with Israel" (Hebrew), *Davar*, January 8, 1974.
17. "Communiqué de Presse" du Comité d'Action pour Israël, Brussels, October 30, 1973. On the same day the burgomasters of Anderlecht, Etterbeek, Forest, Ixelles, Saint Gilles and Schaerbeck personally gave the Israeli Ambassador the sums collected in their areas for the purchase of ambulances.
18. The group met again on December 13, at the National Assembly in Paris, and a declaration was issued. "Déclaration de Parlementaires Européens."
19. The Chief Rabbi of France revealed that the Catholic and Protestant Churches in France refused to participate in a joint protest against Syria's refusal to release Israeli POWs. *Jerusalem Post*, February 1, 1974.
20. Michael Bernheim, "Le silence complice des dignitaires de l'église," *Israelitsches Wochenblatt*, November 23, 1973, No. 47, p. 55. See also: "Christian views on the Yom Kippur War," *Christian Attitudes on Jews and Judaism*, No. 33, December 1973.

In Belgium a joint Catholic-Protestant Commission for Relations with the Jews published a leaflet stating *inter alia:* "Our choice for peace must pass through a deep communion with the Jewish people in its concrete relation with the State of Israel. . . . We invite our fellow Christians to show their solidarity with Israel."[21]

Public Opinion

Various public opinion polls indicate that the "silent majority" of the public supported Israel.

In Germany 57 per cent of the persons polled in October 1973 expressed their support of Israel, while 8 per cent supported the Arabs.[22] In Austria at the same time 41 per cent of Austrians over the age of 16 came out in support of Israel and only 3 per cent supported the Arabs.[23]

In France according to a poll held in mid-October, 45 per cent expressed their sympathy for Israel and only 16 per cent for the Arabs; 47 per cent were convinced that the French government was giving preference to the Arabs, while 60 per cent were in favor of a neutral policy. Surprisingly, among the Gaullists 56 per cent sympathized with Israel against 7 per cent for the Arabs.[24] In Italy 43 per cent of the persons interviewed were pro-Israel and 18 per cent pro-Arab. But among the women, only 39 per cent were in favor of Israel, and among the 18–34-year-olds only 41 per cent came out in support of Israel.[25]

These surveys were conducted by different centers using different methods, and it is therefore difficult to determine the extent to which they are comparable. At the same time, the general impression is that in most countries of Western Europe today, supporters of Israel outnumber

21. "Témoignage de solidarité de groupes chrétiens de Belgique avec Israël pour la paix," *Service de Documentation pour les relations entre Chrétiens et Juifs,* November 19, 1973, Brussels. See Appendix VII, pp. 361–362.
22. "Fifty-seven percent of the inhabitants of Germany sympathize with Israel," *Al Hamishmar,* October 22, 1973 (Hebrew).
23. *Ibid.,* quoting the Austrian paper *Kurier,* October 21, 1973.
24. Polled by S.O.F.R.E.S.; commentary by P. Thibon, *Le Figaro,* October 17, 1973; quoted in Supplement, *JTA Bulletin,* No. 690, October 19, 1973.
25. *Shalom,* Rome, October–November 1973, p. 29.

opponents, but unfortunately the government policies do not reflect majority sentiment.

The attitude of the press is more sympathetic than the government policy, but even newspapers which purport to be independent, and are not spokesmen for specific parties, have been careful to balance reports coming from Israel with an equal number of articles from Arab countries. Moreover, perhaps because of the regimes existing in the Arab countries and the working conditions of the correspondents there, reports sent from Cairo or Damascus were fanatically pro-Arab and could not realistically be balanced by reports filed from Tel-Aviv.

A special problem is that of radio and television services, which in most countries of Western Europe are government institutions. These are often influenced by leftist journalists. Especially blatant in its lack of objectivity was Belgian radio, which in its coverage of the events consistently came out on the side of the Arabs.[26]

In any event, the deterioration of the attitudes of Europeans towards Israel since the Six Day War cannot be ignored, and not least because of the effect on the activities of the local Jewish communities. The impact on them as readers of the local press and listeners to the radio was direct, and since they were constantly aware that they were carrying out their activities in a hostile, or at least indifferent, environment, there undoubtedly was an indirect effect.

Reaction of Jews

If we compare the reaction of the Jews to the Yom Kippur War in 1973 to their reaction to the Six Day War in 1967 we can define it as less emotional and more reflective, accompanied by a deep concern for Israel's fate. It is possible that the reactions did not reach the same emotional heights as in 1967, but there was a deeper awareness of the importance of the events. Some were particularly affected because the attack against Israel came on the holy day of Yom Kippur, a fact that deeply shocked even non-religious Jews.

26. Maurice Elbaum, "Lettre au Directeur de la R.T.B.," *Regards*, Brussels, November 1973, No. 79, pp. 29–31.

In addition, in certain cases the prevailing political and economic conditions, as described earlier, determined reactions. For example, in Mainz, Germany, the Jews did not go out into the streets to demonstrate, primarily because they felt that the environment was not as friendly as at the time of the Six Day War.

George Friedmann, eminent French sociologist, wrote of the Six Day War that it strengthened the mutual feeling of dependence and the recognition of the common fate of all Jews, that it was a Jewish war, and not just the war of Israel alone. [27] As so many have observed, this was true sevenfold in relation to the Yom Kippur War. The feeling of isolation—as Jews in an environment relatively indifferent to Israeli political developments and as a group opposed to the policy of their country of residence—generated among many Jews the feeling that the Jewish people as a whole was in danger. Many Jewish leaders felt that if Israel lost the war, Jewish life could not possibly continue in the Diaspora. Eloquent expression of this was given by Chief Rabbi of France Jacob Kaplan, who stated: "There is within us a tiny flame which consumes us when Israel is in danger. Israel's danger is also that of Jewish religious life in the entire world."[28]

The war revived in all its intensity the problem of the Jewish identity of every Jew in Europe. Sociologist Charles Liebman has pointed out that Jewish support of Israel is not support for some distant state but a symbolic expression of Jewish identity.[29] For many Jews, writes Liebman, support of Israel is the only Jewish focal point left, since other forms of expressing Jewish identity have lost significance. Thus many expressed pride in their ties with Israel, in defiance of the unjust policy of their government, and saw this struggle for justice for Israel as giving profound content to their life. It is of interest to point out that, after having had no contact over a long period, many Jews returned

27. "Israelis and Jews," in *Dispersion and Unity* (Hebrew edition), No. 60/61, Summer 1972, p. 97.
28. At the opening of the Jewish seminar in Paris on November 1, 1973. Cf. *Journal des Communautés*, November 9, 1973, No. 536, p. 12.
29. "American Jewry and Israel," *Dispersion and Unity* (Hebrew edition), No. 60/61, Summer 1972.

to synagogues. In Rome, converted Jews or children of converted Jews, second or third generation, suddenly felt some impulse to express their identification with Israel and to give to the Israel Appeal. In addition to an expression of their Jewish identity, this served as recognition of the undying memory of the Holocaust. Professor Friedlander wrote that the Six Day War in 1967 seemed to be the announcement of a new Holocaust and "the memory of Auschwitz rose from the depths of the Jewish soul and through Auschwitz suddenly the Diaspora Jews identified themselves with Israel," since they realized that the destruction of the State of Israel was synonymous with the annihilation of the Jewish people.[30] In 1973 this was evident especially in Rome, where many Jews of the ghetto gathered spontaneously on October 16, the same date on which in 1943 the Nazis carried out their mass round-up of the Jews of Rome. They collected 100 kilograms of gold, symbolic of the 50 kilograms of gold demanded by the Nazis as a ransom for the lives of the Jews. "This will be our oil," said the Jews of the ghetto who came in masses and gave everything, down to the last golden earring, traditionally pawned only to prevent starvation.[31]

A similar idea was expressed in France by Daniel Mayer, president of the Ligue des Droits de l'Homme, who wrote: "Yesterday they wanted trucks in lieu of Jews, today it is Jews for oil."[32]

Italian Jews reacted strongly to expressions of anti-Semitism, and felt their isolation from an environment becoming increasingly hostile to them. In countries like Italy, where there was no real anti-Semitism even at the time of the Fascist racial laws, a new kind of anti-Semitism appeared.[33] It

---

30. *Op. cit.*, p. 150.
31. *Shalom*, Rome, No. 9, October–November 1973, p. 3.
32. "Des Juifs contre du Pétrole," *Le Monde*, November 8, 1973. This article was stencilled and distributed in large quantities by Jewish students in Brussels.
33. On new anti-Semitism in Italy, cf. A. Di Nola, *Antisemitismo in Italia, 1962/1972*, Florence, 1973; L. T., "Antisionismo è Antisemitismo?" *Shalom*, October–November 1973, p. 21. The Di Nola book was violently attacked by the Communists, but its author did not dare to react strongly. See also: G. Zincone, "I nemici nostrani degli ebrei," *Corriere della Sera*, August 14, 1972, and "Il vago malessere del ghetto," *ibid.*, August 18, 1972.

became more and more apparent that an anti-Israel attitude was identical with an anti-Jewish attitude and anti-Zionism was synonymous with anti-Semitism.[34] For the Jew in the Diaspora, as for the Israeli, Parisian sociologist Edgar Morin explains, to abdicate his role as victim is to risk losing the sympathy of those who give him protection.[35]

Such is the rationale expressed by the paper *Il Manifesto,* the extreme leftist Rome daily: "The fate of the prisoners is becoming more and more the basic problem: Israel considers it unbearable that 400 of the members of the superior race be held as prisoners by filthy infidels."[36] Even more pernicious are the various detective novels and comics aimed at an audience which has little information and is generally lacking in education. They provide a distorted picture of the Jewish religion in the days of Abraham, or of the Israeli in our day, and always in a clearly anti-Semitic manner.[37]

There is no evidence yet that the oil crisis has increased anti-Semitic feelings in Europe, but it is still possible that this will happen as society finds itself in need of a scapegoat and "once again it will be the Jews who will be blamed as the cause of all the disasters."[38] On November 12 and 13, the Netherlands Institute for Public Opinion (NIPO) found that 65 per cent of those questioned thought the Arab countries responsible for the oil troubles, 59 per cent held the Dutch government responsible, while 27 per cent thought Israel was responsible.

Reactions of Jews According to National Origin and Socio-economic Class

The material at our disposal does not give us an accurate sociological analysis of the reactions of Jews. The

34. P. Giniewski, *L'Antisionisme,* Ed. de la Librairie Encyclopédique, Brussels, 1973.
35. *La rumeur d'Orléans,* Paris, 1969. He writes: Le Juif "pour une fraction toujours plus grande de l'intelligenzia de gauche, il demeura de moins en moins le martyr de l'hitlérisme, et il deviendra de plus en plus le soutien de l'impérialisme."
36. *Il Manifesto,* Rome, November 3, 1973.
37. *Shalom,* Rome, No. 6, June–July 1973, p. 3, giving a reproduction of a comic strip printed by *Cabalà,* No. 26, May 1973.
38. Saul Friedlander, *op. cit.,* p. 157.

general impression is that again those in the lower economic groups reacted more enthusiastically and spontaneously and gave more, proportionately, to the emergency appeals than did the richer strata of society. This was noted by observers in Rome, Paris, and West Germany. In addition, there is a distinct difference between Jews who have recently immigrated to their country of residence and those who have been living there for a number of generations and have succeeded in assimilating to a large extent.

In Sweden the active role played by the Jewish immigrants from Poland and others who had settled in that country at the end of the 1950s was particularly evident. In France the process of assimilation has been going on over centuries among certain groups who consider themselves "Frenchmen of Jewish origin" and have endeavored to become integrated into French culture, which is particularly attractive to intellectuals. This process, as a result of the two recent wars, has apparently slowed down or may even be moving in the opposite direction. In certain cases it is felt that the sudden identification with Israel may have awakened Jewish feelings. In any event, today few advocate assimilation as the solution to the Jewish problem in France.

A subject of special significance is that of Jews with leftist leanings. Large numbers of young intellectuals or students apply to the Middle East situation models familiar to them from the internal struggles in Europe between the "progressive" and "reactionary" forces. Many of these Jews realized on October 6 that the State of Israel was in real danger. The ensuing diplomatic isolation stressed this danger even more strongly and led to a change in attitude: today these young French Jews are prepared to participate actively in the struggle for the existence of the State of Israel, even though they are critical of its government's policy. Jewish members of the French Communist party, who remained within the party despite the various crises it has undergone—such as the Soviet invasion of Czechoslovakia—demonstrated their solidarity with Israel in opposition to the official party line and in certain cases even contributed money anonymously. Professor Vladimir Jankelevitch of Paris stated that he does not consider himself as belonging to any community other than that of

France, whose language he speaks and teaches. Despite this, he acknowledged a feeling of solidarity with Israel, which impels him to act on her behalf.[39]

At the same time, there exists a small, vociferous Jewish minority which expounds an anti-Zionist line, support of the Palestinians, and calls for the creation of a "secular, free and democratic Palestine," according to the proclamations of the Palestine Liberation Organization.[40] A similar phenomenon exists in Belgium[41] and Italy.[42]

In Belgium a group of leftists organized themselves as the Union des Juifs Progressistes de Belgique and published two anti-Israel declarations in *Le Soir*. When a group calling itself "the Blue Hand" circulated a letter castigating some wealthy Jews for not participating in help for Israel, the Union condemned the writers of the letter for using "Nazi" methods and demanded that the Comité d'Action pour Israël disassociate itself from this group's accusations. The leftists showed themselves sensitive to being ostracized by influential Jews, while at the same time they rejected affiliation with the Jewish community.

A new political point of view, to be found among non-Jews as well, calls for the existence of an independent State of Israel alongside an independent Palestinian state.

Who are the Jews who still belong to the anti-Zionist left? Some are those who resent Zionism as an obstacle preventing their complete integration into French society; they reject the idea of "two fatherlands," and the ambiguity they find in a Zionism which links state and religion.[43] The

39. *L'Arche*, No. 201, November 26–December 25, 1973, p. 15.
40. The Paris leftist daily *Libération*, October 24, 1973, published a declaration by anti-Zionist Jews.
41. *TJ-Belgique* of November 16, 1973; Professor Marcel Liebman, "A Jew from Brussels who supports the ideas of the Palestinians." The same Professor Liebman wrote a letter to the weekly *Nouvel Observateur*, against Israel: "Israël: sympathie et complaisance," December 31, 1973, p. 4.
42. G. Valabrega, *Il Medio Oriente dal dopoguerra ad oggi*, Florence, 1973; cf. interview by A. Santini with Leo Levi, "Il passaggio del Mar Rosso 35 secoli dopo," *L'Europeo*, November 20, 1973.
43. Interview with René Remond, President of the University of Nanterre, *L'Arche*, No. 200, October 1973, p. 30.

Jewish minority which supports the Palestinians generally belongs to the most assimilated group of French Jews. These have severed their ties with the Jewish community or the Jewish religion and are consequently torn by the polarizing pressures of their Jewish origins and French society. On the other hand, the North African Jews, of whom the majority reached France between 1950 and 1962, and who constitute almost half the Jewish population in the country, were the most active supporters of Israel. French Jews from North Africa are more likely to settle in Israel and, since many have academic professions and belong to a higher socio-economic group, there is a strong likelihood that they will redress the balance between Ashkenazim and Sephardim in Israel.

Jewish Activities on Behalf of Israel

The activities of the Jews of Western Europe on behalf of Israel can be divided into the following categories: fund-raising appeals; demonstrations and mass rallies; political intercession with the governments of countries of residence; activities in synagogues and special prayers; information activities; and youth activity and volunteers.

In all these activities one important phenomenon common to many European Jewish communities was that all activities were carried out under the aegis of a single umbrella organization. In France it was the Conseil Représentatif des Institutions Juives de France (CRIF), and in Belgium the Comité d'Action pour Israël.[44] In both countries there was harmonious coordination between the functioning bodies. In Austria it was not possible to reestablish the Solidarity Committee set up after the Six Day War, and the absence of coordination was evident. This made it difficult to exploit fully the goodwill and readiness of local Jews to act on behalf of Israel.

The various fund-raising appeals were undoubtedly among the most important and best organized activities carried out by Jewish efforts. In the first place, this was because fund appeals encompassed all strata of the Jewish

---

44. The Comité d'Action pour Israël, established on October 7, 1973, consisted of representatives of most Jewish organizations.

community, both as donors and organizers, and the emergency activated many persons who were generally far removed from Jewish life. In Paris it is estimated that the number of donors reached between 65,000 and 70,000, and the number of active workers, 7,000.[45]

The appeal in France was organized immediately by the Appel Unifié Juive de France (AUJF), which acted as the coordinating organization for this purpose. Even the Consistoire, traditional communal organization of French Jewry which was never particularly pro-Zionist, raised money for Israel and encouraged the committee of synagogues to organize the sending of volunteers to Israel. Fund-raising activities were carried out by institutions set up during the Six Day War, and the division of donors by region or by profession proved most effective.

The younger generation in France also took an active part in the appeal; over one thousand young people were involved in collecting donations and organizing special appeals in forty-three high schools and twelve university faculties, even though, as has already been pointed out, the universities were often the strongholds of the extreme left. Large numbers of people in France offered to donate blood despite the fact that no such need was expressed by Israel.

In Belgium the organization of the appeal was carried out under the direction of the Comité d'Action, and from the first days of the war donations flowed into the Solidarity Fund. It is estimated that the sum raised in 1973 doubled that donated at the time of the Six Day War.[46] Thousands of postcards bearing the symbol of a heart and the words "Israël, je t'aime" were sold, and the proceeds sent to the Fund. These postcards were forwarded to the Knesset in Jerusalem as a symbol of esteem for the people of Israel.

In addition to the general appeal in Belgium, a special appeal for medical equipment was organized by women in Antwerp. An action which deserves special mention was carried out on the weekend of October 20–21, 1973 in the streets of six of the most important districts of Belgian for the

45. *L'Arche*, No. 201, November–December, 1973, p. 27.
46. *Emergency Bulletin*, Paris, No. 15, December 19, 1973, p. 4.

purpose of purchasing ambulances for Israel. A week in advance of the fixed date the six heads of these districts were asked for their help, and the action was carried out through the work of hundreds of young people, who even asked for contributions from people leaving their churches at the conclusion of the Sunday services. In addition to the financial success (over two million Belgian francs were raised) the impact on the non-Jewish public in Brussels was also politically effective.[47] On October 10 the collection of blood donations began and on October 14 some 2,000 persons in Brussels donated blood for Israel.[48]

In Holland on November 4 a public auction of art works was held, at which actress Elizabeth Taylor appeared, and 500,000 Dutch florins (800,000 Israeli pounds) were collected on behalf of Israeli war widows and orphans.[49] Up to the beginning of December, a sizeable sum was collected and pledges for supplementary amounts were offered.[50]

Demonstrations and Mass Rallies

In general, the atmosphere after the Yom Kippur attack was different from that in 1967. There was no time to plan giant parades such as the 1967 march along the Champs Elysées in Paris displaying Israeli flags, but the result was still very impressive. A series of demonstrations and rallies were organized in Paris and other towns in France. On October 7 a large parade was held in the vicinity of the Israeli Embassy in Paris with the participation of Baron de Rothschild, Professor Ady Steg, President of CRIF, Paul Elkan, President of the Consistoire in Paris, and singer Enrico Macias.[51]

On October 9 some 10,000 persons arrived for a meeting at Mutualité Hall in Paris, which could hold only 2,000. Again, on October 16, in spite of rain, some 5,000 persons attended a rally at the municipal square in Paris.[52]

47. Report of the Comité d'Action, "Action enterprise en Belgique," covering the period October 2–22, 1973.
48. *Regards*, No. 79, November 1973, p. 22.
49. Organization-Information Department, *Activities of the Zionist Federation during the Yom Kippur War*, November 19, 1973.
50. *Emergency Bulletin*, December 19, 1973.
51. *Journal des Communautés*, No. 535, October 26, 1973, p. 3.
52. *Ibid.*

On October 8 three cities had rallies. In Marseilles between 5,000 and 10,000 people (led by Gaston Deferre, mayor of the city and chairman of the French Committee in support of Israel [Comité Français de Soutien à Israël], Rolland Amsellem, regional chairman of CRIF, and Israel Selzer, the Chief Rabbi of Marseilles) marched to the synagogue where they sang *Hatikvah*.[53] In Avignon 1500 persons participated in a rally at the municipality, where they were addressed by the mayor. In Montpellier there was a parade through the streets of the city.[54]

In Brussels on October 9 the Comité d'Action organized an impressive demonstration beginning with a prayer service at the synagogue. After the service about 10,000 people marched to Madeleine Hall, on the platform of which were eight representatives of the main political parties, Catholic and Protestant priests, the Chief Rabbi of Belgium, a representative of the Antwerp community, and the chairman of the Comité d'Action.[55] In Rome thousands thronged to the Great Synagogue on the evening of October 7 and held an all-night vigil as a sign of solidarity with Israel.

In Amsterdam on October 13 some 2,500 persons gathered outside the Stock Exchange building and were addressed by the Israeli Ambassador and several representatives of Dutch political parties.[56] In Stockholm 2,000 persons marched to the Israeli Embassy where they sang *Hatikvah*.[57] The Israeli Ambassador, members of the Swedish Parliament, and the Bishop were present at a rally in the central synagogue.

Political Activity

A number of attempts were made to exert pressure on certain governments. In France Chief Rabbi Kaplan and CRIF President Steg issued a joint declaration on October 8 in which they condemned the desecration of Yom Kippur and expressed the support of French Jewry for the people and government of Israel. They called upon the French govern-

53. *Le Provençal*, October 9, 1973; quoted by *L'Arche Provençale*, No. 49.
54. *L'Arche Provençale*, No. 49, October 1973, p. 19.
55. *Regards*, November 1973, No. 79, p. 18.
56. *Jerusalem Post*, November 5, 1973.
57. Organization-Information Department, *op. cit.*

ment to impose a strict embargo on arms shipments to all Arabs countries. "It is impossible to conceive of French arms killing the refugees from the Nazi camps," the declaration stated. President of the Consistoire Baron de Rothschild and the Chief Rabbi sent a joint cable to the Israeli Prime Minister expressing the support of French Jewry.[58]

On October 17 the Chief Rabbi and the President of CRIF met French Prime Minister Messmer to express "how upset and bitter" the Jews of France were at the unbalanced policy of the government of France. The French branch of the World Jewish Congress demanded the imposition of an embargo on arms shipments to Arab countries, and a similar demand was made by Rabbi Selzer and the president of the regional section of CRIF.[59]

Under the direction of CRIF political action was taken on a local scale in many provincial towns in France. Most of the mayors participated in demonstrations and prayer services. Local Jews met with the prefects, sent announcements to the local newspapers, posted placards, and distributed leaflets. In a few localities, because of the known hostility of the authorities, it was impossible to carry out activities of this nature. In general, however, in most areas of France Jews were able to express public concern for Israel.[60]

In Belgium the Action Committee began to organize a "national petition" in support of Israel on October 11. It was signed by 1,000 persons, including members of Parliament and the Senate, journalists, and academics, many of whom are non-Jews.[61] A few days later the Belgian Committee for Peace Negotiations between Israel and the Arab States was set up; its first action being to send letters written by professors at the Hebrew University of Jerusalem to 2,000 professors at Belgian universities.[62]

58. *Journal des Communautés*, No. 535, October 26, 1973, p. 5.
59. The cable included a demand to prevent the sending of arms to Libya on board the Méjean II which was due to leave Marseilles during the next few days.
60. These activities were carried out in the following cities: Lourdes, Periguell, La Rochelle, Colmar, Menton, Lyon, Grasse, Besançon, Strasbourg, Nice, Le Havre, Toulouse, Libourne.
61. *Jerusalem Post*, November 18, 1973, p. 4. The petition appeared on a full page of the paper. See also leaflet: "Petition nationale du Comité d'Action pour Israël."
62. "Action Enterprise en Belgique," report of the Action Committee for the period October 6–22, 1973. See Appendix I, pp. 351–354.

Later, action was taken on behalf of the Israeli prisoners of war in Syria. Hundreds of letters were sent on December 21 by the Action Committee to Belgian ministers, members of Parliament and the Senate, together with statements by Nobel Prize winner René Cassin, and noted author Simone de Beauvoir, calling on the Syrians to cease their violation of the Geneva Convention.[63]

Similar action on behalf of the prisoners was taken in Italy, and a number of parliamentary questions were submitted to the Italian government on the need to speed up the exchange of prisoners. Earlier, leaders of the Jewish community in Rome had condemned the release of two Arab terrorists suspected of being involved in the plan to shoot down an El Al plane. with ground-to-air missiles.

In Sweden, the representative of the Action Committee asked for a meeting with the prime minister, but was received instead by his Chief of Cabinet.

The joint declaration of the nine states of the European Community on November 6 was regarded by Jews as a submission to oil blackmail by the Arab states, and there were strong reactions on the part of Jewish institutions in Western Europe.[64] The European Council of Jewish Community Services, a non-political organization whose members include the Jewish communities of Rumania and Yugoslavia, expressed its condemnation of the EEC declaration.[65]

Synagogues and Special Prayers

Fervor and solidarity on behalf of Israel were unanimously expressed by rabbis in synagogues throughout Europe. News of the outbreak of hostilities generally became known during the Yom Kippur service and the reaction was immediate. Prayers were recited for the State of Israel, its people and the Israeli Army.[66]

In Paris Chief Rabbi Kaplan recited a special prayer between the *Yizkor* and *Musaf*, and on October 21 called for a national fast day.[67] Synagogues became centers for the

---

63. Simone de Beauvoir, "Le Syrie et les prisonniers," *Le Monde*, December 18, 1973.
64. See footnote 8.
65. *Exchange*, Paris, No. 12, February 1974.
66. *L'Arche Toulouse*, No. 32, December 1973, p. 7.
67. *L'Arche Provençale*, No. 49, p. 21.

collection of money, for rallies of solidarity with Israel, and for special prayers for the State and army. In Vienna Chief Rabbi Eisenberg announced on the eve of Succot, that a ban *(herem)* would be placed on Jews who did not give to the appeal according to their means.[68] In Rome Chief Rabbi Toaff recited a special prayer for the welfare of the State of Israel on October 6, and one day later launched an appeal in the Great Synagogue.[69] Many of those present went up to the Torah to announce their contributions publicly.

Youth Activity and Volunteers

The response on the part of youth was impressive and surprising in all the countries of Europe. It was said that "our youth can no longer be described as coffee house habitués, but as responsible Jews with a national conscience."[70]

In France the Collectif de la Jeunesse Juive (Jewish Youth Council)—representing thousands of young people from Zionist movements, the Youth Services Division of the Fonds Social Juif Unifié (FSJU), and other organizations, whose programs were mainly educational—adapted itself to the emergency needs of the war. Zionist youth and people from the community centers, both religious and non-religious, students and workers, organized the mass demonstrations held in the Place de la République described in a previous section.[71]

In Marseilles a group of young people belonging to the Collectif entered the offices of "Marseilles-Fret" in protest against the sending of arms to Libya from Marseilles harbor. Two days later they held an impressive demonstration outside the offices of the port management in protest against the departure of the *Heelsum* with eleven AMX tanks bound for Saudi Arabia. Earlier, 20,000 leaflets were distributed in the streets of Marseilles, protesting the sending of arms to Libya.[72]

68. *"Freierlicher Aufruf des Oberrabbiners," Die Gemeinde,* October 22, 1973, p. 1.
69. *Shalom,* Rome, October–November, 1973, p. 2.
70. "Antisemitismus in Österreich," *Profil,* No. 23, November 9, 1973. See also: "Antisemitism in Austria," *Patterns of Prejudice,* London, Vol. 7, No. 6, November–December 1973, p. 17.
71. Supplement, *JTA Bulletin,* November 16, 1973.
72. *L'Arche Provencale,* No. 49.

On October 17 some 200 young people from Toulouse demonstrated in the Tarbes-Laloubère airport where Iraqi military pilots were being trained. They distributed leaflets signed by the Collectif against the unilateral embargo of the French government.[73]

Young people also assisted in fund-raising appeals in France and Belgium. In the latter country Jewish students were very active at the Free University of Brussels; on October 8 they distributed leaflets in the entrance hall at the campus explaining Israel's position. Two days later, Arabs, with the help of professional thugs, savagely attacked Jewish students and fifteen of them were injured.[74] The Jewish students protested to the University rector and made public their distress at the attack against freedom of speech within the walls of the university, an unusual occurrence, since confrontations of this nature are not common in Belgium. In Switzerland observers noted that young people and students took a more active part in affairs than in 1967, and in Germany young people distributed leaflets and posted handbills. In Holland pupils were active in soliciting blood donors and explaining Israel's position to non-Jewish students.[75]

As in 1967, the immediate and intense desire of thousands of young people was to go to Israel and place themselves in the service of the State. But the government of Israel had learned from the experience of the previous war that the utilization of volunteers, to have any significance, must be planned with great care. By the end of November, 120 volunteers were accepted from France. When there was a need for citrus fruit pickers in December the regulations for length of service were relaxed and young people with a month's school vacation were accepted for that period of time.

Conclusion

To all outward appearances the Yom Kippur War did not cause such a drastic change in the attitude of West

---

73. *L'Amitie, Combat Sioniste* (Toulouse), No. 55, October 1973. "Tarbes, ou le pourquoi d'une action."
74. *TJ-Belgique*, supplement to *Tribune Juive*, November 16, 1973.
75. *Jerusalem Post*, November 5, 1973.

European Jews as that which occurred after the Six Day War. If, however, the reaction in general was less emotional than in 1967, it was more profound and durable. In this respect the Yom Kippur War may well have far reaching effects on the activities of Jewish communities and their institutions in the foreseeable future.

For community life two developments may have a permanent impact: the remarkable unity with which Jewish institutions worked together under central organizations (although they were created *ad hoc* and may disappear), and the enthusiastic response of youth. Recognizing this, programs must be devised to sustain this solidarity, to encourage the feeling of participation, to provide outlets for practical action which are not merely fund raising.

The feeling of isolation, the cool and sometimes hostile attitude of the various European governments towards Israel, may continue for a long time. European Jews may discover that thirty years after the Holocaust it can again be fashionable to express anti-Semitic feelings, whether under the guise of the so-called anti-imperialistic struggle of the left, or because of the strong residue of hatred still to be found among Fascists and Nazis.

Intimations of this may be found in the almost incredible case of Arrigo Levi, editor of the Italian daily *La Stampa*, whose dismissal was requested by the Arab Boycott Office in Beirut after two journalists published a satirical article about Libyan president Muammar Qaddafi in *La Stampa*, a daily owned by the Fiat concern. It so happens that Levi is a Jew who fought for Israel in the War of Independence. While the affair provoked a general outburst in Italian papers against suppression of freedom of the press, some weeks later Fiat surrendered symbolically to the Boycott Office by declaring it had no plant in Israel.[76] Some days later the well-known French journalist Eric Rouleau of *Le Monde*, an old friend of the Arabs who was due to accompany French Foreign Minister Jobert to Saudi Arabia, was denied a visa because he was a Jew.

76. *Maariv*, January 1, 1974.

This appears to be a time when West European Jews need support and encouragement. It may be the best time to build a new kind of partnership between Israeli and European Jews, to give them the feeling that while Israel needs financial help, it also needs their advice, their technical skill, their moral support. Perhaps the activities of the various Israeli and Jewish bodies often working in the same field should be better coordinated, especially in matters concerning exchange of information and public affairs.

France: Perspectives

Adolphe Steg

It is perhaps arbitrary, when talking about intellectuals, to separate the reactions of Jews and non-Jews in France, since a large number of Jewish intellectuals barely participate in Jewish communal activities, living in total symbiosis with their non-Jewish colleagues. Furthermore, in French politics, especially on the extreme left, Jews whose religious origin is seldom acknowledged hold significant and influential positions.

Nevertheless, recognizing that distinction we shall consider first the reactions of non-Jewish intellectuals in France, and then those of Jewish intellectuals.

Reactions of Non-Jewish Intellectuals

If we must characterize the behavior of non-Jewish intellectuals during the last war, apparent indifference seems the most appropriate definition. This indifference is all the more surprising if it is contrasted with the general involvement of the same circles at the time of the Six Day War. We find this reaction very different from the emotions and passions displayed then. The events of May 1967 with their dramatic progression and the spectacular pace of the Six Day War stirred feelings and inspired intense emotional reactions. When the war began on Yom Kippur no one really believed that Israel's existence was in danger.

This absence of real anxiety for Israel was certainly the determining factor in the attitude of a good number of intellectuals and academics in France, but it was not the only one, and other motives played an equally large part. First of all there was a widespread feeling that all these events were not foreseeable and that one should wait to see the results. It is this conviction which explains why Foreign Minister Michel

Jobert's aphorism "Does trying to set foot in one's own territory truly constitute unforeseen aggression?" provoked so little opposition. There was also a conviction, occasionally cynically expressed but more often unacknowledged, that it would be good if the superman were taken down a peg, that it would make him more amenable to reason. Above all there was a very general feeling that in this war no one could boast of absolute innocence. Even the most ardent supporters of Israel could not dismiss the problems of the "occupied territories" or the "Palestinian refugees," and we must recognize the weight that these arguments carry in intellectual circles.

Apart from those who have deliberately chosen their stand, the majority of intellectuals have refused to become openly involved. Faced by what they consider to be a "complex," "sad," or "dirty" affair, they have preferred to remain silent. One can therefore see that the apparent apathy was not a real lack of interest, but a painful concern and inability to choose.

It is interesting to note, however, that even the reactions of those who overcame these hesitations and made their choice came through in a more subdued manner than during the Six Day War. While the opponents of Israel showed themselves less virulent, Israel's friends revealed themselves less enthusiastic; and it is the behavior of both that I now describe.

Since 1967, and even more since May 1968, circles of the extreme left have expressed hostility to Israel; in fact, it is a dominant theme in their programs. But, compared with the customary unbridled hatred they display as soon as the subject of Israel is discussed, their reactions to the Yom Kippur War were relatively cautious or moderate. Undoubtedly, the mere possibility that Israel might really be destroyed checked the animosity of the leftists, who always harbor a certain sympathy for "victims." Also, without doubt, the arrogant display by Arab countries of their fabulous wealth and oil power came as a surprise to those for whom the Arabs, by definition, were the "poor." Whatever the explanation may be, during the Yom Kippur War the opponents on the left expressed far less hostility than they had previously. In addition, even the unanimity of these circles was affected by events. Thus, for example, *Liberation,* the leftist pro-Palestinian daily, reported in an editorial that there were serious differences of opinion among its editorial staff, some of whom were siding with Israel.

Still more significant was the attitude adopted by the monthly review *Les Temps Modernes,* founded by Jean-Paul Sartre and Simone de Beauvoir and regarded as the rostrum for leftist intellectuals. The November 1973 issue carried an editorial obviously inspired by Sartre and clearly divergent from the fundamental tenets of leftist doctrine. In it the writer denounces and ridicules those who label Israel "an agent of American imperialism" and identify the Arab countries as "progressive and socialist states." He challenges the theory that Palestine is fundamentally Arab, and the Jews intruders. Zionism originally developed, the writer says, in an Ottoman Palestine centuries ago, and if the Jews forced the British government to renounce the Mandate, "no preexisting Arab State was subdued or harassed by the formation of Palestine." The writer takes a clear stand against the claim of the Palestinians to a secular state, because it would mean offering "the Jews the status of a cultural minority paternally tolerated as long as they remain obedient." He energetically rejects the pretensions of the Palestinians that "the Israel they acknowledge is an Israel which does not exist and which could exist only . . . without the Israelis." This attitude would seem to illustrate a real reversal among leftist circles.

Even the Communist intellectuals have behaved with relative discretion. Although the Communist daily *L'Humanité* vigorously supported Soviet and Arab arguments, Communist intellectuals made no move to issue a declaration and called for no demonstrations, in contrast to their public protest against Chile and Greece in a similar period.

Perhaps the most remarkable change of tone was to be found among those intellectuals of the left who are neither Communists nor political activists but are important and influential in the press and French public opinion. These molders of opinion, who until then had been so critical of Israel, seemed to rediscover abruptly an "Israel with a human face," i.e. one which is vulnerable and fallible. Thus criticism became less harsh and views more flexible. "As long as Israel was invulnerable," an influential journalist told me, "one could well criticize it severely and condemn it, because after all in practice this was of no consequence. But now, it is no longer the same; Israel is in danger, we must therefore weigh our reactions in a way which cannot be interpreted by the Arabs as approbation by the left of their plan to destroy Israel."

These circles were rather impressed by the solidarity shown by Israeli intellectuals, and the statement expressing deep anxiety for Israel's continued existence, sent by twenty-one professors of the Hebrew University of Jerusalem, had a significant impact upon them.[1] Until then, it was considered chic for an opponent of Israel to base his position on a particular statement by an Israeli, and considerable harm was caused by irresponsible statements claiming that in May 1967 the State of Israel had not been exposed to real danger.

A further evidence of the relative lessening of hostility among French intellectuals was the general calm prevailing in universities during the Yom Kippur War. Not only was there no pro-Arab agitation, but fund raising for Israel could be publicly organized, and was actually carried out at Nanterre University, the main center of pro-Palestinian activity. Similarly, Zionist groups were able to demonstrate in most high schools without interference.

The relatively moderate reaction of Israel's opponents was matched by equal moderation on the part of Israel's friends. Many non-Jewish intellectuals showed their unshaken solidarity with Israel during these events. All the same, these sympathizers—socialists, centrists, and many from the majority—did not manifest the depth of emotion and determined involvement which moved us so in 1967. Also, many of the declarations of the intellectuals on Israel's behalf did not so much reflect a concern for Israel as shame and anger at the "Munich"-like behavior of the French government when faced with Arab demands.

However, even among the staunchest friends of Israel a consensus existed concerning the necessity to make conces-

1. See Appendix I, pp. 351–354.

sions, and sometimes (unexpressed) disapproval of Israeli "intransigence." One can thus generally say that non-Jewish intellectuals showed at least some understanding and often a profound sympathy for Israel, but that these feelings rarely led to strong action on Israel's behalf. For example, when non-Jewish physicians of the Paris region known to be sympathetic to Israel were asked to come to express their solidarity with Israel (thousands of invitations were sent) only a very small number actually accepted the invitation.

My own feeling is that this dampened enthusiasm on the part of people who essentially wish Israel well denotes a fundamental lack of understanding for Zionism. Even intellectuals who cannot in any way be suspected of anti-Semitism constantly ask: "Why has the Jewish State been established in the heart of the Arab world? Why was this powder keg created? Wasn't there (isn't there) really any other solution?" It seems to me that a considerable effort toward ideological explanation and information is indispensable at the present time when most intellectuals no longer follow a rigid ideological line in relation to the Israel-Arab conflict. They are accessible to reason; they ask the question of why the Israeli government's political policy did not appear to develop with events but gave the semblance of intransigence. They were disappointed that no project for future relations between Israel and her Arab neighbors was proposed. A genuine friend of Israel wrote to me in this context: "Our faith in Israel was not shaken, but it couldn't be communicated."

French Public Opinion and Anti-Semitism

A poll of public opinion taken soon after the war revealed that the majority of the French people were pro-Israel. When asked if they approved of the French government breaking off relations with Israel as a result of the Arab threat to stop oil deliveries to nations who maintained diplomatic relations with Israel, 63 per cent did not approve. Only 18 per cent were in favor of breaking off relations. Nevertheless there remains within France the residue of right-wing classical anti-Semitism, which received renewed impetus from General De Gaulle's opprobrious description of the Jews. Such Gaullists profess to believe that Israel is the center of a Jewish conspiracy aiming to undermine the so-called traditional friendship between France and the Arabs. Continuing in this vein is a comparatively recent publication, the *Carrefour*, which in December published an article questioning the status of the Jew in France and the right of Jews to act as functionaries of the French government.

On the left, the only intellectuals who have not softened their attitude toward Israel, are those who belong to the *Témoignage Chrétien* (Christian Testimony) group, consisting of Catholics whose enmity toward Israel seems to be the principal justification for their existence. I fear that this group is incurable, but having discussed the matter with numerous Protestant and Catholic friends and colleagues, I can say that the *Témoignage Chrétien* is considered to be a marginal group, with no influence on the mainstream of French Christianity.

Reactions of Jewish Intellectuals

The behavior of Jewish intellectuals did not differ from that of the rest of the Jewish community. They displayed the same level of anxiety, the same identification with Israel, the same desire to act.

Perhaps most remarkable was the reaction of anti-Zionist Jewish intellectuals, who from 1967 on have often spearheaded the ideological opposition to Israel. Nothing comparable emerged during or after the Yom Kippur War; the Jewish anti-Zionist voices were remarkably discreet or silent. The majority of Jewish intellectuals frankly took the side of Israel, and if anything definitive in their attitude, as compared with the rest of the community, can be gauged, it is perhaps in the following three aspects:

First of all, like their non-Jewish colleagues, Jewish intellectuals expressed their conviction that after this war it is imperative that Israel consider important concessions.

Second, their analysis of the behavior of the French government concerning the Israel-Arab conflict was particularly severe because they not only regarded government policy as a victory for the "spirit of Munich," but also as a prelude to the "spirit of Vichy," i.e. submission to blackmailers: a belief that one must surrender the expendable (and the

Jews are always expendable) in order to save the "essential."

Above all, Jewish intellectuals could not dismiss a certain feeling of isolation and lack of empathy. Their anxiety for Israel found only a faint echo in their environment, and the silence of their colleagues during those terrible days was painful. Not only did their colleagues remain silent, but when appealed to, they could not help showing irritation with the problems of the Jews, which they defined as an obsession.

It is fair to say that if the Yom Kippur War weakened the reactions of hostility or reserve of non-Jewish French intellectual opponents of Israel, it has also dulled the enthusiasm of those who are her friends. On the other hand, these events have not only accentuated the identification of Jewish intellectuals with Israel, but they have had an effect which was undoubtedly less spectacular but perhaps more profound than that of the Six Day War. Indeed, by making French intellectuals aware of their non-conformity to the surrounding intellectual milieu, by obliging them to reflect upon this non-conformity of feeling and behavior in a milieu from which they thought themselves indistinguishable, and by uncovering the extent of the lack of comprehension shown by these circles to their deepest concerns, the Yom Kippur War may have slowed the rush toward assimilation in France.

The French Jewish Community and Israel

In reality, as regards the Jews of France there are two types of problems: one is that of communal Judaism, and the other that of peripheral Judaism. The question is, how does one reach peripheral Jews? If they were not won over to our cause in 1967 or after the Yom Kippur War, it may be because they are not to be influenced. They reject Jewish social institutional ties and have no interest in Zionist activities and we have not learned the technique of winning over such people.

As for those French Jews who are vitally attached to their ethnic roots, and these comprise about fifty per cent of the total number of Jews in France, they are seeking some form of organizational structure which will engage their interests and serve their needs. But what happened on Yom Kippur day in Israel and the reactions of the many committed French Jews gives us reason to hope that Israel and the Jews of the Diaspora will share a spiritual relationship. Perhaps this relationship will guide French Jewry to some solutions for its internal problems.

As far as *aliyah* is concerned, one cannot attract Diaspora Jews to Israel simply by telling them: come here, you can help us rebuild after this war. I feel uncomfortable about giving Israel advice on how to convince Jews that they should come to Israel—but it seems to me the way to do it is through ethical values. These have always been the basis of Jewish teaching:

> Behold, the days come, sayeth the Lord God,
> That I will send a famine in the land,
> Not a famine of bread, nor a thirst for water,
> But of hearing the words of the Lord.[2]

Those days have arrived. People are hungry. People are thirsty. And what they are hungry and thirsty for is something Israel *can* give them: it is a sense of being part of the Jewish people. This is something Israel must understand—that one of its goals must be the Judaization of the Diaspora. Once we in the *golah* who feel ourselves close to Israel, feel that we are also part of the same Jewish people, and that what is asked of us is not merely money or help with the agricultural harvest, but that we be Jews, then our natural destiny will be *aliyah*.

2. *Amos*, 8:11.

Belgium: Perspectives

Chaim Perelman

How European Jews reacted to the plight of their fellow-Jews in Israel can be seen only in the context of their status within European society. For today, West European Jews are very much part of their countries of residence, involved in local and national politics, in university life, in business, in the arts and communications. In that sense, Belgium can serve as a model both of Jewish behavior during the days of crisis in October 1973, when the Jewish *community*, rather than any organization or combination of organizations, became the partner of Israel in its struggle against aggression. The following evidence elaborates on this thesis.

Reaction of the Jewish Community

There are 40,000 Jews in Belgium, of whom 25,000 live in Brussels, 13,000 in Antwerp, and 2,000 in the towns of Liège, Charleroi and Ghent.

The Six Day War aroused tremendous sympathy for Israel, seen at the time as a tiny beleaguered state about to be crushed by Arab hordes. In Belgium the Jews were joined by fellow Belgians in mass meetings, at which former prime ministers, ministers, and representatives of major political parties spoke up in behalf of the "victim," Israel. Following the period of victory and jubilation there was a reaction against the "victim" turned victor and Arab propaganda was successful in creating in some part of the public mind an image of Israel as a tool of American imperialism, a military aggressor, and the barrier to the creation of a Palestinian state. This was the atmosphere when the dreadful blow struck on Yom Kippur.

The immediate impact of the war was directly opposite to that of the 1967 war. There was no sense of jubilation or self-congratulation. As the magnitude of the Arab attack was revealed, people became increasingly aware of the danger to Israel and Belgian Jewry mobilized itself to provide every means of support.

Early in 1973 a committee had been formed to celebrate the 25th Anniversary of the State of Israel. The day after the attack this committee was enlarged to include organizations and community leaders from every sphere, and became the Comité d'Action pour Israël (Action Committee). It organized an imposing demonstration in the streets of Brussels, in which more than 6,000 people took part. Three thousand filled the largest public hall in Brussels and heard support for Israel expressed by members of both Belgian Houses of Representatives, with the exception of Communist Party and Flemish National Party representatives. The funds raised on behalf of Israel were estimated to be seventy times more than those raised in 1966, and about two or three times greater than in 1967. As indicated in my opening statement, for the first time the *whole* of Belgian Jewry was represented within a single organization, an outstanding accomplishment for a community which had never been able to unite because of divergent views.

Perhaps most significant among the activities of this Committee was the petition circulated immediately upon the outbreak of the war, alerting Belgians to the extremely grave situation in Israel, in which the total resources of the Arab nations, backed by Soviet arms, menaced the existence of Israel.

In part the petition read:

> We demand that moral and religious authorities, political organizations, democratic institutions, trade unions, and the Parliament condemn the aggression and offer their support and help to Israel in its struggle for survival.
>
> The government and people of our country cannot remain indifferent to the tragedy now taking place.
>
> When you sign this petition you will demonstrate your wish to see our government take a clear stand faithful to our national tradition.

Hundreds of eminent personages—government officials, university professionals, leaders of labor, church, and industry—signed their names to the document and made large financial contributions. The Centre Communautaire Laïc Juif de Bruxelles (CCLJ), the major Jewish communal organization in the country, issued a special edition of its publication *Regards,* expressing its desire to cooperate with all other Belgian Jewish groups, and urging financial contributions and moral support to prevent the "destruction of the State of Israel and the annihilation of its people."

Those Jews who did not join the Action Committee in essence detached themselves from the Jewish community. These were members of the Union of Progressive Jews, which includes the hard-line Communists, Maoists, Trotskyists and other leftists, whose only bond appears to be their opposition to Israel. The Communists compose the most moderate elements, while the extremists go so far as to support Palestinian organizations publicly. These leftists number about a thousand, approximately the membership of the Zionist parties in Belgium, including the youth movements.

Attitudes of Non-Jews

Belgian public opinion towards Israel has always reflected its attitude toward the United States. Those in favor of closer ties with the United States are favorably disposed towards Israel. This includes the Liberal Party, which is the most conservative of Belgian political parties, the majority of the Catholic party, with the exception of its left wing, and the Old Guard of the Socialist party. The young Socialists, the Communist Party, and the extreme left, i.e. Maoists, Trotskyists, and anarchists, are pro-Palestinian. The pro-Israel left confines itself to one goal, to promote peace negotiations between Israel and the Arab states; it opposes the slogans of the Arab summit at Khartoum, which denounced recognition of Israel, negotiations, and peace.

1973 Public Opinion Poll

In general, the non-Jewish population of Belgium should not be identified with the image reflected in current government pronouncements. A month after the Yom Kippur War broke out the Action Committee commissioned a public opinion poll which was administered in November by the Société Belge D'Economie et de Mathématique Appliquées (SOBEMAP). The survey studied attitudes related to the Middle East conflict. A random sampling of 1,000 men selected from different geographical areas of the country were asked questions based on these themes: sources of information about the Middle East; attitudes towards President Nixon's alert of American troops; views of the self-interests of the major powers; and perceptions of which countries desire peace.

People questioned came from different educational levels and from Flemish, Walloon, or Brussels communities. An analysis of the responses indicates that French-speaking persons of a high academic level generally are more interested in the Middle East conflict and more sympathetic to the cause of Israel. One or two enlightening results of the poll should be mentioned. While a fair percentage (32 to 41 per cent) of persons had no opinion regarding their country's political behavior vis-à-vis the Middle East conflict, of those remaining, the next largest group, 33 per cent, felt that Europe was wrong not to protest the massive shipment of arms by the Soviet Union to the Arabs. On the question of who might have won the war had neither the Soviet Union nor the United States intervened, 56 per cent selected Israel, 8 per cent chose the Arabs, while 36 per cent had no opinion.

Thus we see that not only Jews thought Israel an indomitable military power but more than half the Belgian people were convinced of this same fact. And, with the exception of Communist Party members, few are deluded by the role the Soviet Union plays in the Middle East.

Christian Support for Israel

On November 19 the document "Témoignage de solidarité de groupes chrétiens de Belgique avec Israël pour la paix" was circulated by a major interfaith group in Brussels, Les Commissions Catholique et Protestante pour les Relations entre Chrétiens et Juifs en Belge. It affirms a Christian theological recognition of Israel as the home of the Jewish people; it acknowledges Christianity's obligation to work for a just peace between the Jewish State of Israel and the Palestinians; and reminds the world that when Israel is harmed, the entire Jewish people mourns. It concludes:

> As Christians let us be aware of our responsibility and let us recognize that the West is totally implicated in the conflict and the search for peace. . . . We put ourselves on record against any political declaration which condemns without judgment and we invite our Christian brothers to demonstrate their solidarity with Israel, even to make the concrete gesture of helping financially.*

The implications both of my thesis and the supportive evidence relate both to the inner structure of the Jewish community and to the role that such a community can play when it is united by and around the *élan vital* of contemporary Israel.

*See Appendix VII, pp. 361–362.

Soviet Union: Overview

Mordechai Altshuler

Attempting to deal with the implications of the Yom Kippur War for the Soviet Jewish community we focus on two groups: the nationalist-Zionist and the non-Zionist Jews. For the Soviet Union, perhaps more than for any free nation, such an examination must take into account internal developments among Jews during the last decade, the political stance of the government in regard to the Middle East, and the reaction of Soviet society to the Yom Kippur War.

To examine this subject in so short a period of time after the event itself presents many obstacles, but being aware of these may, to some degree, permit a balanced approach. One obstacle is that the proximity of events and the intense emotional feeling toward them may lead to a description of what is desired rather than what actually occurred. Another obstacle, which every Sovietologist encounters, is the paucity of information available, and particularly on the non-Zionist Jewish population.

It should be clear from the above that the writer does not see the Soviet Jewish community of over two million people as a monolithic body. In the last decade a polarization, unparalleled in Russian Jewish history, has occurred in the nationalist outlook of the Soviet Jews: there are those who claim that Jews, as Jews and as human beings, have no place in Russia, and those who oppose this position.

A portion of the Jewish population which has decided to resolve the debate by leaving the country is here identified as the "nationalist-Zionist community." The use of this definition does not mean that we ignore the fact that, for some of this group, leaving the U.S.S.R. has been more significant than fulfilling the Zionist dream, to settle in Israel. For another segment, the desire to be freed from life under a totalitarian regime and anti-Jewish discrimination has become so identified with a craving for a full national existence in Israel that it is difficult to determine which has been the dominant factor in the decision to leave the Soviet Union. A precise examination of motivations is not the subject of this paper as far as Soviet society and the government is concerned, and every Jew who asks to emigrate to Israel is here defined as nationalist or nationalist-Zionist.

The position of the nationalist-Zionist community is not uniform either in respect to the attitude of the Soviet government and society toward it, or the intensity of its reaction to recent events in Israel. Thus, for this discussion we have divided the nationalist community into sub-groups. Although such a division is schematic, with an overlapping among sub-groups, we believe that this division will help to focus the discussion and facilitate a clearer and more precise analysis.

I. The Nationalist-Zionist Group

Activists

The first nationalist-Zionist sub-group includes individuals whose requests for emigration permits have been denied and who are engaged in an open struggle to achieve the right to leave the Soviet Union. "The most tragic are those whose requests for exit visas have been refused," according to 42-year-old physicist Moshe Gitterman, who himself was one of that group and has only recently arrived in Israel. Gitterman reports, "They face economic persecution, and, morally, they are in need of encouragement, since they are cut off from the very breath of life."[1] These Jews have burned their bridges, and Soviet society and the government suspects them of being guilty of incitement. The vast majority of this sub-group, sometimes called "*aliyah* activist," are under constant surveillance. Ida Nodel, a 42-year-old economist who submit-

---

1. *News Bulletin* of the Scientists Committee of the Israel Public Council for Soviet Jewry, October 21, 1973, p.6.

ted her request to emigrate in May 1971, expressed this attitude in a letter she sent to Communist Party First Secretary Leonid Brezhnev:

> Give me a visa and it will not be necessary to have me followed through the streets of your town by a man acting in the most provocative and disgraceful manner. Give me a visa and it will not be necessary to take me off the streets when I am going about my lawful business. Give me a visa and it will not be necessary to undertake constant day and night surveillance of me and my home by several men in a car who follow my every footstep.[2]

Although not altogether ignoring Nodel's arguments, the government does not act consistently. The result is that the voice of the smallest sub-group in Soviet Jewry is heard most strongly via the media outside the Soviet Union. This group regards every appeal to the Soviet government, every publication of a message in the foreign press, as part of the personal struggle of its members and the fulfillment of its public duty toward all of Soviet Jewry. Indeed, *aliyah* activists create their own momentum and by force of circumstance form the élite of the nationalist-Zionist community in the Soviet Union.

Their reaction to the Yom Kippur War was characteristically rapid and open, although they clearly recognized that in fact they were supporting an "enemy" country. Immediately after the outbreak of the war, telegrams, letters and telephone calls expressed unambiguous identification with Israel and hopes for its victory.[3]

Forty-five Moscow Jews, among them Professor Aleksandr Lerner, Professor David Azbel, Dina Belina and Yuli Veksler sent a letter to the government and residents of Israel:

> Dearest brothers and sisters: Another tragic military adventure of the war-mongering Arab leaders began on Yom Kippur and is destined to end in a catastrophe for their nations. Both sides embroiled in this war, Arabs and Jews, will suffer bloodshed. We cannot describe in words our shock at these events, nor to what extent we identify with the inhabitants of Israel. We will only say that we do not have the least shred of doubt concerning the bravery and dedication of our men and

2. *Ibid*, November 7, 1973, p. 3.
3. *Haaretz; Davar*, October 8, 1973.

their ability to resist aggression, as has already been proven in previous cases. We are with you in these crucial moments.[4]

Leningrad Zionists followed the example of the Moscow *aliyah* activists. Thirty of them sent the following telegram to Knesset Speaker Israel Yeshayahu:

> Our hearts are full of fear. Men are again dying in our homeland, our enemies are again threatening our land and our brothers are once more compelled to defend with arms the land promised to us. We are restrained from being with you to share the pain and hardships and our distance heightens our fear. All our thoughts and emotions are with you. Circumstances do not permit us to unite with you today, but we live with the hope that the day is not distant when our wishes will be fulfilled. We believe with total faith that the enemies of Israel will be defeated this time. Our greatest desire is that the number of losses be small and victory near.[5]

Three former officers from Minsk—Yefim Davidovich, Lev Ovsishcher, and Naum Alshansky—sent the following telegram to Israel's Prime Minister and Defense Minister on October 7:

> From the first moment of the new fascist Arab attack on the State of Israel, we are together with you, prepared to sacrifice ourselves to defend the righteous cause of our people. We want to send our greetings to our sons and brothers defending the independence and existence of our State in Sinai and Ramat HaGolan. We do not doubt victory for one moment. Long live Israel.[6]

From the city of Kishinev fifteen Jews wired this telegram to the President of Israel:

> We ask you to pass on our warm regards and good wishes to the sons and brothers fighting to defend the honor, independence and very existence of our State. We do not doubt our victory. Long live the people of Israel.[7]

4. *Haaretz*, October 10, 1973.
5. *Davar*, October 17, 20, 1973; *Nowing i Kurier*, October 22, 1973.
6. *Nasha strana*, October 22, 1973.
7. *News Bulletin* of the Scientists Committee of the Israel Public Council for Soviet Jewry, November 7, 1973, p. 2.

Five Tbilisi Jews cabled the following message:

Our hearts are with you. We wish we could be with you in your battle, but unfortunately are unable to do so.[8]

Thirty Jews from Riga sent a telegram to the Prime Minister in which they stated, "We are all with Israel in this hour." And twelve Jews asked Foreign Minister Abba Eban by telegram to grant them Israeli citizenship, saying, "Now when the blood of our brothers is being spilt, it is very hard to be far away from our people. . . ."[9] Eight Jews from Talin, capital of the Estonian S.S.R., also sent a telegram identifying with Israel.

When the International Congress of Peace Forces opened in Moscow, eight Soviet Jews asked Congress representatives to support their requests for exit permits from the Soviet Union.[10] After this appeal, a similar petition was presented by another twenty Jews from other cities. Several Soviet *aliyah* activists also turned to the chairman of Amnesty International, who was in Moscow for the Congress, and asked for his guarantee of the release of twenty-seven Prisoners of Zion in the U.S.S.R., who had been sentenced because of their desire to emigrate to Israel.[11]

The intellectuals within the Soviet activist group did not content themselves with identification alone. In the first week of the war, scientists Mark Azbel, Aleksandr Voronel, Aleksandr Lunts, and Viktor Brailovsky published a call to the world, asking, "Must millions of Jews be destroyed to make peace in the world?" [12]

The wave of open and public identification expressed through these letters and petitions involved several hundred Jewish families. However, more important than the quantity of those who openly identified with Israel is the quality of their standing within the Jewish community of the U.S.S.R.

8. *Ibid.*
9. *Al Hamishmar,* October 16, 1973.
10. *Nowing i Kurier,* November 5, 1973.
11. *Nasha strana,* November 5, 1973.
12. *Maariv,* October 1973.

Telegrams and letters of identification with Israel were sent from eight cities, the largest centers of Jewish population. According to the most recent Soviet census of 1970, approximately six hundred thousand Jews live in these cities, that is to say, over a quarter of all Soviet Jewry. It is reasonable to assume that there are a few hundred who dare to appeal openly and disseminate information about Israel.

As the experience of the recent past demonstrates, the influence of these individuals far exceeds their numerical size and extends beyond their cities of residence. Their struggle and their stand strengthen the position of the undecided and perhaps even influence some of the non-Zionist Jewish category.

In addition to declarations of solidarity with Israel, the activists did not ignore the second front, namely, appeals to central Soviet governmental bodies. In recent years such appeals have become an accepted weapon in the struggle of Soviet Jewry. At the end of October a group of Jews from Kishinev sent a cable to the President of the U.S.S.R. stating, "As citizens of Israel, we cannot remain at a moment when the blood of our fathers and brothers is flowing. We demand immediate permission to go to Israel, our homeland, to be with our people at this moment."[13]

Aliyah activists also protested one-sided Soviet reporting of events in the Middle East. In mid-October, a group of twenty-five Soviet Jews contacted the official news agency Tass, and complained about the biased reporting of the Yom Kippur War. They appealed to the Soviet Union to cease sending weapons of destruction to the Arabs and to use its influence to make peace and guarantee the security of all states in the region.[14] Although some of the demands listed in the letter do not contradict Soviet Middle East policy, for Soviet citizens to express publicly views on Soviet foreign policy involves considerable risk.

Any view which does not agree with the official Soviet line causes the government to react aggressively. The reaction of the Soviet government to Andrei Sakharov's declaration on

13. *Jerusalem Post,* October 15, 1973.
14. *Haaretz; Letste Nayes,* October 25, 1973.

the subject of U.S.A.-U.S.S.R. relations is an example of this.[15] Those who sent the letter to Tass were undoubtedly aware of this fact; nevertheless, the Jewish activists dared to speak out.

In addition to sending telegrams of solidarity, a tactic that did not provoke governmental retaliation, some members of the group organized demonstrations. In Moscow, on October 13, Yona Kolchinsky of Kharkov, who had been drafted against his will into the Soviet Army, staged a demonstration with Aleksandr Slepak and Yevgeniya Kerzhner, near the offices of the Central Committee of the Communist Party. The three protestors carried a placard with a short and meaningful message: "Either Exit Permits to Israel or to Prisoner of War Camps." The last part of the message implied that the demonstrators regarded themselves as citizens of an enemy country, who, if not permitted to leave, should be treated as prisoners of war. This demonstration, like those held several days before the war, was halted by Soviet authorities; the demonstrators were beaten, arrested, and sentenced to fifteen days in prison for hooliganism.[16] After reading notices at universities and elsewhere calling on Soviet citizens to give blood for the Arabs, eighty-eight Jews from Moscow, Novosibirsk, Vilna, and Tallin asked to donate blood to Israel. Soviet Jews applied to the International Red Cross headquarters in Geneva, asking for representatives to come to Moscow to enable them to donate blood. The International Red Cross replied that if the Soviet Red Cross transferred blood to them for Israeli wounded they would forward it to its destination; however, they were not empowered to act independently in the U.S.S.R.[17] It must have been clear from the start to the Russian Jews who asked to donate blood for Israel's wounded, that this action would be impossible but, despite the risk, they wanted to demonstrate loyalty to Israel.

Acts expressing loyalty to Israel were repeated after the cease-fire, and scores of immigration activists in the U.S.S.R. continued to send messages to Israel, emphasizing their joy

15. *Zarya vostoka; Pravda vostoka* October 20, 1973.
16. *Jerusalem Post*, October 15, 17; *International Herald Tribune*, October 15; *Jewish Chronicle*, October 19, 1973.
17. *Jerusalem Post*, October 25-26, 28; *Jewish Chronicle*, October 26; *Haaretz*, October 25, 1973.

that the Arab armies had failed despite wide support and a vast supply of modern armaments.[18] The reaction of Soviet authorities to this bold activism within Zionist circles was swift. The fact that the International Forces of Peace was then holding its convention in Moscow was no doubt an additional motive for Soviet action. It has long been the practice of the Soviet Union to neutralize, terrorize, and otherwise silence Zionist activists just before international conventions.

On October 11, the Soviet police detained Professor David Azbel, a 62-year-old chemist, and Vitali Rubin, a Sinologist, who had asked to speak to Western journalists regarding restrictions on Jewish immigration to Israel and to express their identification with Israel at war. On the same day, journalist Benjamin Gorakhov, aged 50, who had signed telegrams of solidarity with Israel during the Yom Kippur War, was arrested.[19] On the eve of the opening of the Conference of the Forces of Peace, the telephone lines of many Soviet *aliyah* activists were cut and others were called to the Security Police offices and warned that if they dared to demonstrate or make declarations while the Congress was being held they would be severely punished by the government.

Other activists were arrested while walking in the street. Thus, for example, Solomon Reiser was arrested in Leningrad while on his way home from the emigration office, and did not reappear for several days.[20] These arrests were not confined to the major Soviet cities of Moscow and Leningrad, but took place in other cities as well. At the end of October, in Sverdlovsk in the Urals, 32-year-old Leonid Zabelishensky was arrested and sentenced for parasitism. His home was searched and evidence was allegedly found indicating a transfer of money to Israel via Czechoslovakia.

The anti-Jewish activists campaign also spread across the Ukraine. On October 18, 26-year-old Aleksandr Feldman, whose requests for an exit permit had been refused several times and who had signed a number of petitions, was arrested in Kiev. Before this last arrest, Feldman had been twice

18. *Haaretz*, November 5, 1973.
19. *Maariv*, October 12, 1973.
20. *Ibid.*, October 31; *Haaretz*, November 5, 1973.

apprehended for the "crime" of Zionist activities, and sentenced to fifteen days imprisonment for hooliganism on both occasions. In a search of his home after the last arrest, evidence of illegal gold trading was allegedly discovered. On November 24, Feldman was tried behind closed doors. His family was not permitted to attend, and he was sentenced to three and a half years' imprisonment for assault, according to reports reaching the West early in December.[21]

In October, some of the Zionists imprisoned for their beliefs began hunger strikes in protest against their prison conditions and in solidarity with Israel. News of these strikes reached the world public and encouraged world Jewry to intensify its struggle on behalf of the prisoners. In response, the authorities transferred certain prisoners (Vladimir Mogilever, Oleg Prolov) to different prisons without informing their families, so that they were cut off from communication with the outside world.[22]

These arrests indicate that following the war government pressure on the most active sub-group in the Soviet Jewish community has increased. It is probably safe to assume that Soviet policy in relation to the Middle East War resulted in intensified repression of Zionists in the U.S.S.R. The Soviet government undoubtedly counted on the Middle East trouble to distract the attention of world Jewry from events in the U.S.S.R.

Intensified suppression of the Jewish Zionist group must also be seen as part of Soviet internal policy toward dissident groups. The bitter attacks, threats, and pressure exerted recently upon the courageous fighter for human rights, academician Andrei Sakharov, are well known. During the Yom Kippur War Sakharov called upon the Western nations to protest the massive Soviet supply of armaments to the Arab countries. This enraged the Soviet press, which published a sharp condemnation of Sakharov taken from the Italian Communist press.[23] Suppression of the democratic movement in the Soviet Union, which has been almost totally destroyed, can also be seen in the warning received by Nobel

21. *Nowing i Kurier,* October 28; *Haaretz,* October 31, 1973.
22. *Ibid.,* November 28, 1973.
23. *Trud,* October 16; *Pravda Ukrainy,* October 17, 1973.

Laureate Aleksandr Solzhenitsyn that plans were being made to murder him under the pretext of an accident. Finally, but most importantly, there is the verdict incarcerating Yuri Shokhanovich in a mental hospital, after interrogations apparently did not succeed in breaking his spirit as they had in the case of the dissident historian Piotr Yakir. These cases, and the intensified suppression of Jewish activists, belong to the same campaign and reveal the contradictory attitude of the Soviet government, in which growing détente with the U.S.A. is accompanied by increased Soviet suspicion of Western influences on public opinion in Russia. This policy may also be an external manifestation of internal struggles among different groups within the government itself. Although the timing and severity of the increased pressure on nationalist-Zionists was undoubtedly influenced by the Yom Kippur War, this pressure may not necessarily result in a reduction of the number of exit visas.

The problems confronting Jewish scientists who belong to the disintegrating "dissident movements" as well as to the militant nationalist-Zionist sub-group demand special analysis. An article published recently in the Soviet journal *Literaturnaya gazeta* deserves our special attention here because of its author, its date of publication, and especially, its contents.

The article was written by historian Itzhak Ben Israel Mints, a member of the Soviet Academy of Sciences and of the editorial staff of various publications dealing with the history of the Communist Party. Mints wrote a number of books on the October Revolution, the Civil War, and international relations and is, without a doubt, a leading academic figure in the Soviet Union. The article referred to was published in the holiday edition of *Literaturnaya gazeta* of November 7, commemorating the October Revolution, a date of great ideological significance to the Soviet people.

Entitled "The Alma Mater of a Man of Science—What Stands Behind the Legend of Free Migration," the article disputes the view that there is an international community of scientists; instead, it states, there are "national schools of experts in different scientific fields." If one of these schools is weakened, scientific progress in the world will be harmed. Mints suggests that capitalist countries, under the pretext of endorsing freedom of movement, are using Israel to entice brains away from Russia. The activity of "enticing scientists," says Mints, seriously harms the country the scientist leaves, since in addition to ethical implications, national capital has been invested in his training. When he leaves, the scientist takes with him "not only his personal knowledge but also part of the combined knowledge, a large portion of joint scientific achievements." Thus, claims Mints, the attitude of society toward the emigrating scientists must be one of scorn and reproach.

The significance of this article can be seen from the vantage of two interrelated dimensions: the Jewish and the general. In the Jewish dimension, this is the first attempt to make public the real reason for Soviet opposition to the emigration of Jewish scientists to Israel; one that makes more sense than the unconvincing allegation of betrayal of defense secrets. In general, the article is also meant to respond to the few democratic circles in Soviet society, for whom freedom of travel for scientists and unrestricted exchange of information throughout the world is one of the outstanding expressions of human rights. Seen as an omen of views on future Soviet scientific international relations, the article does not bode well.

The Soviet policy makers must be aware that the struggle of the *aliyah* activists is an organizing and unifying factor for world Jewry, which determines its stand toward the Soviet Union in the context of the latter's attitude toward free migration. Insofar as the Soviet Union considers American Jewry, rightly or wrongly, a highly significant factor in forming public opinion, the *aliyah* activists are surely seen as affecting the attitude of the United States. This might be one reason for the ambivalence in Soviet attitude toward them. On the one hand, the authorities show their anger in the form of suppression—imprisonment, trials and the like—while on the other, they display a greater relative tolerance toward them than toward the democratic movement.

Prospective Emigrants

The second sub-group in the nationalist-Zionist community comprises those Jews who had applied for exit permits and were expecting to receive them, or who had already received permits and were engaged in final preparations for immigration to Israel when the war broke out. According to Soviet procedure it is impossible to keep an application for an exit permit secret. Every applicant must request a *kharakteristika* (testimonial of character); thus his decision becomes public knowledge. Every application for an emigration permit is akin to applying for a divorce from Soviet society and the state and is regarded as an expression of hostility to the regime.

The time lapse between the application for an exit permit, its receipt, and the last days prior to leaving the U.S.S.R. is a difficult one for all prospective emigrants to Israel. In the words of a Vilna orthopedist, "That was one of the most difficult periods in our lives, for we were preparing for the trip and preparations are always difficult, and just at that time we suddenly learned of the outbreak of the war."[24] In this connection we should note that information was received by nationalist-Zionist circles in the Soviet Union via direct reports from broadcasting stations abroad and from commentaries by official communications media. "The very fact that the war began on a day as holy to the Jews as Yom Kippur," states a recently arrived physician from Vilna, "speaks for itself. To us it was absolutely clear who had started it." An engineer from Lvov concluded that the Arabs had begun the war, "We were convinced, and not only we ourselves but everyone I met, even non-Jews, that the Arabs started the war. Israel had no reason to be in this war, particularly on such a day." A man from the Bukharan Jewish community, who had heard the news of the outbreak of war while in the Tadzhik S.S.R., and who had no news aside from the official Soviet communications channels, also arrived at the same conclusion from the following analysis: "Since I knew that Israel was in a position to enter into discussions with the Arabs, I understood that Israel had nothing to fight for. She has no need to begin a war against the Arabs. Thus I became convinced from an analysis of the situation that they were

24. Testimonies quoted are from the Shazar Documentation Unit, Oral History Division, Institute of Contemporary Jewry.

speaking of Arab provocation. If Israel had opened the war against the Arabs, she would not have retreated but advanced, and since I knew that the Egyptians were on the east side of the canal I said to myself: the Arabs are the ones who began the war."

These few testimonies seem sufficient to indicate that Jews expecting to receive exit permits, or preparing for emigration to Israel understood that Israel had been attacked by the Arab states, regardless of Soviet news reports. Despite their realistic and somewhat pessimistic evaluation, the majority did not renounce their applications for exit permits although that would have been possible. An economist from Kishinev related that when they came to Ovir—the office that grants exit permits—clerks appeared saying, "Where are you going? There's a war raging over there." They were told that they could cancel their applications and remain in the country as Soviet citizens enjoying all the privileges it offered them. However all those present, numbering some one hundred, answered with one voice, "Let us out as fast as possible." An immigrant from the Ukraine relates a similar reaction. On the third day of the war, October 9, twenty-two families from one small town were called to Ovir to receive exit permits. The clerks expected that some would renounce their decision to leave the Soviet Union during the war but no one did.

In addition, Soviet border officials attempted to frighten the émigrés. The following conversation, characteristic of the line taken by customs official took place at the frontier, where one family was asked, "What are you going for? All the property that we're examining now is just going to sink in the Mediterranean." One of the officials turned to a doctor, "You will fall into the hands of the Arabs and your daughter"—a third-year student in medical school—"will be drafted to work somewhere in one of the hospitals. Why are you going?" Having heard about conscription of the Soviet population during World War II, many believed that immediately upon their arrival in Israel they, or at least the younger ones, would be conscripted. They imagined that there were shortages of essential commodities in Israel, and were surprised to find shops open in Israeli towns and goods being sold normally.

Nevertheless, while the Soviet Jews imagined the situation in Israel to be far worse than it was in reality they did not give up their right to leave; in fact, they attempted to accelerate their departure. We are told by a mathematics teacher from Chernovits, "Perhaps at another time we would have postponed our departure." (The interviewee's father was confined to a hospital and was about to undergo an operation, so it would have been possible to delay departure without relinquishing the exit permits and wait for developments in Israel.) But the interviewee and her family, including a 19-year-old son who, they believed, would be drafted into the army on arrival in Israel, did not exploit this possibility. She decided to remove her father from the hospital and leave immediately while the war was in progress. Further, all the interviewees testified that they were anxious to leave the Austrian transit camp and were happy when they could do so.

The question that naturally arises here is, what motivated the nationalist-Zionist sub-group to continue their immigration to Israel in the midst of a war? Similarly, what considerations prevented the Soviet authorities from halting Jewish immigration to Israel during the war as was done during the Sinai Campaign and the Six Day War? Although no comparison can be made between the dimensions of the potential Jewish immigration on the eve of those two wars and that today, the answer to the first question seems to involve the following three motivations:

The first and perhaps the most important is concisely expressed in the Biblical verse (Exodus 1:12): "When you afflict him then he will multiply and spread abroad," namely, the feeling of national unity at the moment of danger. This was expressed by a physician who stated in his testimony, "We grasped that the situation was most serious but we thought precisely because of that reason we were immigrating in order to bind our lives to our people." This was articulated in other words by an engineer from another city who said, "Seeing all the contemptible deeds and understanding that the whole world, or nearly the whole world, treats us without sympathy, we became convinced that they think we do not need a state and our own land, that we are only needed for the gas chambers. This is what the Jews understood and thus their will to immigrate grew." Hence the feeling expressed by the Psalmist (118:17), "I will not die, but live . . ." was one of the decisive motivations for these Jews.

The second motive that propelled the same group to hasten to reach their country of destination was the personal and family connections between many of them and persons living in Israel. Most interviewees testified that they were thinking of and anxious about their friends and relatives in Israel, who were perhaps even then fighting at the fronts. It is natural that friends and family seek to unite during hardship and war, and the sense of "togetherness," of closeness, and common action in times of suffering, is a source of security.

The third motivation that hastened their departure was the experience of the Six Day War. The tiny group of prospective immigrants, a very small number indeed, was completely halted with the outbreak of hostilities in June 1967. Several of our informants stated that they suspected that the borders of the Soviet Union would be completely closed after the war, and they therefore feared to delay their departure even one day. According to newspaper accounts, in October 1973, 4,200 Jews left the Soviet Union for Israel, as against 3,600 in September.[25]

To our second question, namely why the Soviet authorities continued to grant exit visas during the war, we can only answer by conjecture. Apparently, three principal arguments could have been considered by the Soviets in their decision to permit Jewish emigration to continue.

If a sudden halt to emigration, or even a significant curtailment, had been ordered, the great majority of the group under discussion, that is Jews who had requested exit permits or even those who had already received them, would have joined the Jewish sub-group which was pressing for the right to emigrate. This was a small group. Understandably, the Soviet government was not indifferent to the possibility that an energetic fighting opposition would have been created to activate international public opinion. Moreover, in principle, the Soviet Union was prepared for the overwhelming majority of those Jews to leave the country. The Arab reaction to Jewish

25. *Maariv*, November 2, 1973.

immigration to Israel during the war was not vocal enough to force the Soviet Union to provoke unrest of this nature merely to please the Arabs. Indeed, the dependence of Arab countries on the U.S.S.R. during the war, especially those fighting Israel, increased to such an extent that they could not raise an effective voice against Jewish immigration.

The second consideration likely to be weighed by the U.S.S.R. was its relations with the United States. Soviet-U.S. relations reached a state of tension during the war; however, the Soviets never ignored the fact that they would be forced in one way or another to arrive at a *modus vivendi* with the United States. Thus it was logical not to burden this relationship with the issue of Jewish emigration which the U.S.S.R. had permitted for several years and was not a crucial factor in internal policies.

The third consideration concerns Soviet options regarding Israel. The Soviets wanted to bring about a settlement in the Middle East, though obviously one favorable to the Arabs. Thus their main objective was to sponsor some form of settlement and thereby create a strong Soviet presence in the area. For this, open options were necessary, even if they were restricted in the case of Israel. Obviously, if Jewish emigration had been halted, or drastically reduced, in addition to having no diplomatic relations with Israel, the fragile Soviet connection with Israel would have been completely severed. Thus it would seem to be illogical for the Soviet authorities to halt the Jewish emigration during the war.

Potential Immigrants

The third sub-group in the nationalist-Zionist community in the Soviet Union is composed of Jews who have not yet applied for exit visas. This sub-community includes two elements. In one category are those who have received *drishot* (applications) from Israel which are necessary when applying for a visa. The request for *drishot* and their receipt are presumably known to the Soviet security services, so that this group is considered suspect or even hostile.

The other category consists of those who keep their decision to leave the U.S.S.R. a secret within the family circle and close friends. These individuals are regarded by their non-Jewish acquaintances and the Soviet government as loyal Soviet citizens, insofar as any Jew is considered a loyal Soviet citizen. They delay their exit visa applications for various personal reasons, such as completing higher or secondary education for their children, waiting for professional openings, differing views among family members, etc. These Jews live in two worlds—externally they behave as Soviet citizens, while in their inner hearts and their narrow circle of friends they identify with Israel, where they see their future. This duality of feeling increased during the Yom Kippur War and the spiritual burden was difficult to bear. They faced a crucial dilemma: whether short-range considerations were preferable at this time, or the needs of the land and community with whom their future and that of their children were bound.

On Yom Kippur the Lithuanian television network was already showing photographs, that were probably seen throughout the U.S.S.R., of the hurried mobilization in Israel, the advance of the Arab armies, and their capture of Israeli strongholds. TV cameras focused on the Israeli bunkers captured at the Bar-Lev Line, on the burning tanks and on the fallen of Israel's army. The programs were accompanied by commentaries rejoicing at the calamity. A similar picture was given in the accounts of Soviet military commentators from Arab countries. A reporter for the *Krasnaya zvezda* (Red Star), a Soviet military journal, in an article published on October 13, described his visit to the east bank of the Suez Canal giving special emphasis to the burning Israeli tanks and the remains of an Israeli airplane in which the pilot had been killed. These descriptions, in addition to continuous reports on the course of the battle from Arab sources, made the Jewish community realize fully the terror of prolonging their residence in a hostile country.

Indeed, during the first days of the war, when the burden of anxiety became unbearable, many of these Jews tried to relieve the tension by making their decision public. There were long lines of applicants for exit permits in front of the Ovir offices. The relatively large emigration from the Soviet Union at this time indicates that applicants were not deflected from their goals by the war. It can therefore be assumed that there will not be a decline in immigration to Israel from the U.S.S.R. in the immediate future. Perhaps it will grow, if there are no drastic changes in the Soviet emigration policy.

II. The Non-Zionist Community

Jews who still see their future and that of their children in the Soviet Union apparently comprise the vast majority of Soviet Jewry. Any assessment of feelings and trends within this sector must be based on conjecture and analogies. Indeed, the information available on the Jewish sub-communities in the Soviet Union is in inverse proportion to their size. Ironically, we have more information on the nationalist-activist sub-group, which is numerically the smallest, while the great majority of the Jewish community is largely silent. However, even if we are forced to base our treatment of the non-Zionist community on supposition, it must not be ignored.

Assimilationists

The non-Zionist Jewish community in the Soviet Union may also be divided into sub-groups, the smallest of which includes those desiring, whether consciously or not, to rid themselves of their Jewishness. These Jews, who have experienced the Holocaust, the persecutions at the end of Stalin's regime, and the discrimination against Jews of the past twenty years, have decided to eliminate "the Jewish problem" by a personal solution, to expedite their own and particularly their children's disappearance as Jews. When they themselves or their children marry they do not register themselves on their identity cards as Jews; they eliminate family names that suggest Jewish origins; and so on. There is no reason to assume that events in Israel would influence their decision to be absorbed into Soviet society. Only severe measures by the authorities to restrict or prevent their assimilation might stop this process, but there seems no likelihood that this process of absorption will cease at present.

Jews by Identity

The large majority of the Jewish community which does not plan to leave its country of residence consists of individuals who define themselves as Jews. This definition, articulated in the population census, for example, is a result of psychological, social, and political factors. From a psychological perspective, the forces of habit and inertia almost certainly operate, that is, the inclination to say,"I was born a Jew and therefore I define myself as one." This tendency is accentuated by a surrounding society disinclined to accept Jews and seeing them as a foreign element, even when they barely retain any trace of Jewish identity. Meanwhile, the regime imposes a national definition on Jews by registering their nationality on identity cards and by a discriminatory policy towards them. Many individuals who define themselves as Jews do not think that this is a reason for them to leave the land of their ancestors. This group is broad and variegated. It includes those who understand and speak Yiddish, and who consider it a mark of their Jewishness that they attend performances of the few theatrical companies performing in that language or that they read Yiddish books, Russian translations of Yiddish literature or the Yiddish literary journal *Sovietish Heymland.* This group includes individuals who observe some of the outward signs of Judaism, i.e., festivity on certain Jewish holidays or personal association with victims of the Holocaust. It also includes Jews whose Jewishness is simply the knowledge that they are Jews and that their forefathers were Jews, without any expression of this fact in daily life. These people show interest in the appearance of Jewish names in the Soviet press, particularly when they appear in a favorable context. Many are aware of events in world Jewry and even attentive to what is happening in Israel.

A surprisingly large number of this community took a specifically Jewish interest in what was occurring in Israel during the Yom Kippur War. Indeed, the testimonies that we collected indicate that during the war many Jews, upon opening their Soviet newspapers, looked first at the section reporting on the Middle East. This interest has been heightened because, in many cases, relatives or personal friends have recently emigrated to Israel. Thus the interest shown in Israel by Soviet Jews, especially during the war, increased because they had direct ties linking them with Jews there. Some apparently felt a sense of guilt for being in the Soviet Union and not in Israel during the war, as one witness testifies: "I feel now as if I were evading my duty because I am living here. But when the war ends and turns out well, I won't want to go because my immersion in my work has influenced all my other feelings and emotions. But, at this moment, while the war is in progress, I am unable to sleep, I am unable to live, because I see myself as evading my responsibility. I shouldn't be here now." When the fighting ends, however, as this man himself testifies, he and many like him will return to their usual routine.

A dramatic turnabout within this group might occur as the result of exceptional events in the Jewish world or in the Soviet Union. The latest war in the Middle East was depicted by the Soviet media and others as being a continuation of the Six Day War and as a struggle by the Arabs to recover conquered territory, without emphasizing the danger of Israel's destruction. This war did not serve as a traumatic event, shaking the foundations of Soviet Jews and convincing them that they must leave the Soviet Union at this time. For the majority of the community, the gap between the emotional identification with Israel and the personal decision to remain in the Soviet Union still exists.

Soviet Newspaper Treatment of the War

We examined four major Soviet newspapers: *Izvestiya, Trud, Krasnaya zvezda,* and *Literaturnaya gazeta;* and four newspapers from different Soviet republics; *Pravda Ukrainy, Zarya vostoka* (Tbilisi), *Pravda vostoka* (Tashkent), and *Sovietskaya Latviya.*

This survey revealed that few differences exist among the various newspapers. The entire Soviet press reported on the course of the fighting and violations of the cease-fire according to Arab sources and Soviet reporters in Arab states. The papers stated, during the first days of the fighting, that Israel had started the war. On October 7 the events in the Middle East were headlined "Israeli Attack on Egypt and Syria." The government newspaper *Izvestiya* on October 9 even carried an account by a sailor serving on a Bulgarian boat stuck in the Bitter Lake since the Six Day War who testified that he actually saw the Israelis start the war. In due course, Soviet papers retreated from this position and contented themselves with calling Israel an aggressor for holding Arab lands. The question of who opened fire became completely blurred. Although the coverage was indubitably hostile to Israel, the reports appeared on the inside pages of all the papers, and the few commentaries repeated mainly official Soviet government announcements.

A significant difference could be distinguished in the Soviet press between its treatment of the first weeks after the Six Day War and of the Yom Kippur War. This difference is conspicuous by the number of anti-Israel and anti-Jewish cartoons published in the wake of the Six Day War. In the newspapers we examined, seventeen anti-Israel cartoons were published after June 6, 1967, whereas this time we found only one such cartoon.[26] In contrast with the Six Day War, excluding several instances which will be dealt with below, there was no derogation, even implicit, of Jews as Jews, nor were they compared to the Nazis. As far as we could determine, this analogy, once very popular, disappeared from the Soviet press. It is worth noting that the comparison between Israel and the Nazis was not even made by the most virulent articles which reported Israeli attacks on the civilian population of Damascus—those bombings which, it will be recalled, hit the Soviet Cultural Center and killed Soviet citizens.[27]

In contrast to the weeks following the Six Day War, as far as we could determine, only isolated meetings were called to denounce Israel.[28] The notices for these meetings, in

26. *Pravda vostoka*, October 17, 1973.
27. *Trud*, October 18, 1973.
28. *Pravda Ukrainy*, October 13, 21; *Pravda vostoka*, October 16, 23; *Krasnaya zvezda*, October 21, 1973.

contrast to their placement after the Six Day War, were tucked away in corners of the newspapers and it is difficult to regard them as expressing a widespread, organized anti-Israel campaign. In all the newspapers studied in recent months, we found no vulgar attacks against international Zionism, as occurred in 1967. The exception was an article in the *Pravda Ukrainy* and a brief reference in the military journal *Krasnaya zvezda*. The article, by M. Kogan, entitled "Shantazh" ("Blackmail") condemns Zionists for inviting innocent Soviet citizens who have not been thinking about leaving the Soviet Union to go to Israel.[29] Another treatment of Zionism is found in an article denouncing Radio Free Europe. It mentions that this program has a Zionist section employing Soviet émigrés who slander their former homeland.[30]

Thus, Soviet propaganda, whatever the reasons, has not subjected the non-Zionist Jewish community to the harsh challenges which followed the Six Day War, when a vigorous campaign was launched demanding that Jews should publically denounce Israel, and saying that the Soviet public expected them to state unambiguously with which side they identified themselves. This situation created a heavy burden for the non-Zionist Jew who was not prepared to condemn Israel. It seems that after the last war, at least as revealed in the Soviet press, the non-Zionist Jewish community did not encounter such difficulties to the same degree.

At the same time, one must not ignore recent incidents of violent anti-Semitism. For example, a group of young anti-Semites attacked a group of Jewish boys in Moscow, and Jewish youths were beaten up in front of a Moscow synagogue by members of the secret police.[31] In spite of these acts of violence against individual Jews, we may conclude that no significant change leading to a massive transfer of Jews from the non-Zionist to the nationalist-Zionist group in the U.S.S.R. is to be anticipated as a result of the recent war.

As things appear now, it is difficult to see the Yom Kippur War as a factor in changing the direction of Soviet

29. Pravada Ukrainy, October 18, 1973.
30. *Krasnaya zvezda*, November 23, 1973.
31. *Jerusalem Post*, October 12; *Nowing i Kurier*, October 28, 1973.

Jewry. However, the overwhelming majority of Soviet Jews—Zionist and non-Zionist together—were transfixed by the events in Israel. If they could have given expression to their attitude by donating funds, their response would not have been less than in the United States. The non-Zionist group displayed concern through its intense interest and inner stirrings, and the nationalist-Zionist community found practical expression for its identification with Israel by hastening to apply for exit permits and to emigrate.

East Central Europe: Overview

Ezra Mendelsohn

The once imposing Jewish communities of Eastern Europe are today but a shadow of their former selves. They have been drastically reduced numerically, as a result of the Holocaust and subsequent emigration. Today there are approximately 90,000 Jews in Rumania, 80,000 in Hungary, 14,000 in Czechoslovakia, 8,000 in Poland, 7,000 in Bulgaria and 7,000 in Yugoslavia.[1] What unites these Jewries perhaps more than anything else is the Communist nature of the regimes under which they live. This has meant, historically, that the Jews have not been permitted to establish autonomous institutions, that those Jewish organizations which do exist are firmly under state control, that East European Jewry has remained isolated from Jewish centers in the West and Israel, and that severe assimilatory pressures have been applied. All this is standard Communist procedure regarding the Jews.

Anti-Semitism, drawing more on traditional East European sources than on Marxism-Leninism, has also characterized the East European scene since World War II. Jews have gradually, or not so gradually, been removed from positions of importance in political, cultural, and economic life. The emergence of the State of Israel and the Soviet Union's pro-Arab policy have added a new dimension to traditional Communist anti-Zionism. The small Jewish communities of Eastern Europe now find themselves subject to pressures resulting from totalitarian Communist Soviet policy in the Middle East, and native East European nationalism.[2]

1. All estimates should be regarded with caution. These are taken from the *American Jewish Year Book*, Vol. 74, p. 524. For example, according to the official 1966 census in Rumania, based on "nationality" rather than religious identity, there were only 42,888 Jews.
2. For historical background see Peter Meyer *et al.*, *The Jews in the Soviet Satellites*, Syracuse, 1953.

Rumania stands out as a special case, since there the native national impulse has led, fortunately for Rumanian Jewry, to the successful implementation of an independent foreign policy. The implications of this independent policy will be discussed later.

The reaction of the Communist states of Eastern Europe to the Yom Kippur War may be summarized as follows: the governments of Hungary, Yugoslavia, Bulgaria, and Czechoslovakia adopted a harsh anti-Israeli line, accusing Israel of being the aggressor, identifying Zionism with imperialism, and so on. Widespread anti-Israeli propaganda was carried on in these countries; demonstrations called for pro-Arab resolutions. Poland's reaction, in contrast to her position following the 1967 war, was more moderate. The Polish government emphasized the need for a peaceful settlement of the Middle East conflict and appears to have refrained from the more extreme brand of anti-Zionist propaganda.[3]

The position of the governments of Eastern Europe, however, almost certainly does not reflect the position of the peoples of that region. The well known Yugoslav dissident Mihajlo Mihajlov, writing shortly after the cease-fire, states: "If my impressions of Yugoslav public opinion are an accurate measure . . . the populations within the Soviet sphere do not feel any enthusiasm for the Arab cause. Everyone here knows that Israel is a democratic country where opposition parties (two of which are Communist) freely exist, while a majority of the Arab nations are run by one-party dictatorships." East Europeans also know, according to Mihajlov, that "the liquidation of Israel would mean the liquidation of a little island of democracy in the Middle East, which would, in turn, boost the power of world totalitarianism and lead to greater oppression within the Communist bloc."[4] If Mihajlov's attitude may be taken to represent that of the East European intelligentsia, popular anti-Soviet feeling in the region probably also contributes to a certain amount of pro-Israeli sentiment, as was the case after the Six Day War. Israel's identification as a "European state," in a region which is

3. See survey by Israel Foreign Office, *Skira al t'guvot artzot mizrah eiropa le-milhemet yom-ha-kippurim (Survey of the reactions of East European countries to the Yom Kippur War)*, November 26, 1973.
4. "Israel's Silent Supporters ' *New Leader*, November 26, 1973, p. 5.

particularly insistent on its own "European" character (often contrasted to the Soviet Union's "non-European" nature), may also contribute to pro-Israeli sentiments among the peoples of Eastern Europe.

The Rumanian government has, for some time now, developed an independent foreign policy with regard to the Middle East. Rumania was the only Communist nation in Eastern Europe not to break off relations with Israel in 1967, and since then has developed close economic ties with the Jewish State. Its economic interests dictate good relations with Israel, and its moderate policy has also been motivated by fear of too great Soviet involvement in Middle Eastern affairs, which might bear unpleasant implications for Rumania's freedom of action in Europe.[5] In the wake of the October war the Rumanian government called for the implementation of the 1967 United Nations resolution 242, and refrained from branding either side as the aggressor. The government called for the "respect for security, national independence, territorial integrity and the right to free existence of each state in that region [the Middle East] including Israel," and for "the establishment of a just and equitable peace, of a climate of good coexistence" between Israel and her Arab neighbors.[6] The most striking example of Rumania's independent line was the invitation of Israeli Foreign Minister Abba Eban to Bucharest in early November. Prior to his trip Mr. Eban praised the Rumanian government's position in these words: "Thanks to its foreign policy, which adheres to the principle of universality in international relations, Rumania has the opportunity of carrying on a fruitful dialogue with powers and states locked in conflict. . . . Its ability to speak openly both to Israel and to the Arab countries is without a doubt a stabilizing influence in the international arena."[7]

We know very little about the response of East European Jewry to the Yom Kippur War. The Polish Jewish organ *Folksstimme* published a statement on the war issued by the Israeli Communist party, Rakah, without any comment.

5. Michael Shafir, "Rumania and the Soviet Involvement in the Middle East," *Wissenschaftlicher Dienst Sudosteuropas* (to be published). Seen in manuscript.
6. Quoted in official Rumanian news agency *Agerpres*, No. 46, October 1973.
7. *Jerusalem Post*, November 5, 1973.

It also published a series of articles on the situation in the Middle East which reflect the generally moderate Polish line mentioned above. The articles emphasize the tragic aspect of the war and the need to arrive at a peaceful solution. The author praises the "extraordinary diplomatic talent of Henry Kissinger," which led to the talks at the 101st kilometer, and concludes that both sides can only gain from these negotiations and from an eventual peace treaty.[8] Leopold Trepper, famous as the Polish Jewish head of the "Red Orchestra" spy ring during World War II, was finally allowed to leave Poland in October. Arriving in London, he wrote to an Israeli friend: "In these moments of personal happiness my thoughts turn to the Israeli people, to the fathers and mothers mourning their sons, and my only hope is that this will be the last war. Let us hope that Israel will achieve peace and good relations with her neighbors."[9]

In Hungary the official organ of the Jewish community, *Uj Elet*, did not mention the war at all. This silence reflects the regime's position on the Arab-Israeli dispute, as well as the success of the Jewish community in withstanding possible pressure to issue anti-Israel statements. There is some evidence, in fact, that Hungarian Jewry followed the news of the war with great interest and concern, but this concern could not be publicly expressed.[10] However, the leader of the Hungarian Jewish community did express his support of the Geneva peace conference.[11]

The Jewish organ in Yugoslavia, *Jevrejski Pregled*, commented on the war in its October edition. "On October 6th," it stated, "armed conflict started between Egypt and Syria, on the one side, subsequently joined by other Arab countries, and Israel on the other." Neither side is branded as the aggressor, and the paper goes on to call for a speedy cease-fire and peace. "The Jewish people, and we the Jews of Yugoslavia as its part (*sic*), sincerely and wholeheartedly wish

8. A. Hirsh, "A guter shans farn shulem" ("A good chance for peace"), *Folksstimme*, November 10, 1973; "Di hofning oif shulem" ("The hope for peace"), *Ibid.*, November 17, 1973.
9. *Maariv*, November 25, 1973.
10. I am indebted to Dr. Yehuda Marton for this information.
11. *JTA Bulletin*, January 2, 1974.

these cease-fire efforts to bear early fruits and to see the bloodshed stopped. May this be followed by genuine, complete and lasting peace to the benefit of all nations in the region making it possible for them to devote themselves to the building of their better future. Be there (*sic*) an early *Shalom* to the well-being of all nations of the Middle East and to the benefit of all the world."[12] It should be noted that these are remarks that differ considerably from the extremely hostile line taken by the Yugoslav government toward Israel.

The situation of Rumanian Jewry, thanks in large measure to Rumania's special relationship with Israel, is unique in Eastern Europe. The community is well organized; synagogues are well kept; there are some ties with international Jewish organizations; and the attitude of the regime towards the Jewish minority is friendly. Rumanian Jewry possesses an energetic spokesman in the person of Chief Rabbi Moses Rosen. Rumanian Jews are able to come to Israel as tourists, and the Rumanian *aliyah* to Israel continues. Rumanian Prime Minister Nicolae Ceausescu visited the United States in December 1973, and met with Jewish leaders. He said at that time that Rumanian Jews may go to Israel if they so desire, although he personally hoped that they would remain in Rumania. He emphasized the government's good relations with Rumanian Jewry, while the Jewish representatives at the meeting praised Rumania's enlightened attitude.[13]

Rabbi Rosen visited Israel in late October, bringing with him the Torah scrolls donated by Rumanian synagogues to the Israeli Defense Forces.[14] During Mr. Eban's visit to Rumania, in early November, the Israeli Foreign Minister spoke at a special prayer meeting in the main synagogue in Bucharest, which was attended by an overflow crowd. "The members of the Israeli delegation," the Israeli press reported, "could not control their emotions at the sight of the spectacle before them. Mr. Eban also reacted very emotionally and his voice shook as he spoke to the Jews. Senior officials of the Rumanian foreign office who were present at the ceremony told me that

12. Belgrade, September–October 1973.
13. Reported in *Viata Noastra*, December 9, 1973. Subsequently it was reported that *aliyah* was stopped, at least temporarily.
14. *JTA Bulletin*, November 6, 1973, p. 4.

they were astonished at the degree of warmth and love with which the Rumanian Jews received the Israeli guest and his party."[15] The ceremony began with a prayer for the well being of Rumania and of Israel, and with a memorial prayer for the Israeli war dead. A choir of Jewish youth sang Hebrew songs, among them "Jerusalem of Gold." Rabbi Rosen, in his speech of welcome to Mr. Eban, expressed Rumanian Jewry's solidarity with Israel's struggle. According to a report in *Davar*, the Rabbi eulogized the heroes of Israel who inaugurated a new era of bravery and "who spilled their blood in order to defend the survivors of Auschwitz who came to build a new life in Israel."[16]

A number of Rumanian *olim* arrived in Israel during the months of October and November, and several were interviewed by the Oral History Division of the Institute of Contemporary Jewry. From their testimony several aspects of the Rumanian Jews' reaction to the war may be ascertained. For one thing, it is apparent that virtually all Rumanian Jews, whatever their degree of Jewish identification, were concerned with what was happening in the Middle East. All the Jews took an interest in the war, listened to the radio day and night, telephoned each other with information on the war, and spoke among themselves in a special way so that non-Jews would not understand. The war stirred up considerable fear among Rumanian Jews, both regarding the ultimate fate of Israel and the attitude of the Rumanian government. There was a moment of "panic," according to one immigrant, when it was feared that the Rumanian government would break off relations with Israel. Judging from letters received in Israel from Rumanian Jews, it appears that even the most assimilated reacted very strongly to the Arab threat, and felt "useless" in Rumania.[17]

Despite widespread concern and fear, the Rumanian Jews interviewed by the Institute do not feel that the war will

15. *Yediot Aharonot*, November 8, 1973.
16. November 8, 1973. The ceremony was reported in detail in the trilingual organ of Rumanian Jewry, *Revista cultului Mozaic*, November 15, 1973. Aside from this, the *Revista* did not mention the war.
17. Professor Bela Vago of Haifa University and the Hebrew University was kind enough to summarize the contents of letters he received from Rumania during the war.

have a decisive impact on *aliyah*. "There are two categories of Jews in Rumania. There are assimilationists, who ignore their Jewishness, and there are those whom the war will not dissuade from going to Israel. The war will have no influence. Those who want to leave will leave, and those who don't, won't." The respondents all remarked on the favorable attitude towards Israel which exists in Rumania, both within government circles and among the Rumanian people. Israel's existence, one said, has raised the prestige of Rumanian Jewry. "In the eyes of the Rumanians the prestige of the Jews has risen because of Israel, today the Rumanians respect the Jews because of the Israeli's courage. Now Jews are not held in contempt." Nonetheless, anti-Semitism has not disappeared, and the impression that there is no future in Rumania for young Jews seems to be the dominant motive for *aliyah*. A letter received reads: "For the youth there is a future only in Israel. The main thing now is the children. It is too bad that I gave all my good years to Rumania, but what is left I shall give to Israel. Perhaps I'll be able to contribute something."

Even from the meager data presented here it is obvious that Rumanian Jewry, on the whole, remains vitally concerned with the fate of Israel. As for the other Jewries of Eastern Europe, whose governments have sentenced them to silence, we have no way yet of telling what their response has been.

Soviet Union: Perspectives

Don Roginsky

My knowledge of the reaction of Jews in the U.S.S.R. to the Yom Kippur War is limited in several respects. I was not in Russia during the war, having arrived from the U.S.S.R. just two days before Yom Kippur; also I am a physicist, not a specialist in social sciences. Thus I can offer some observations rather than first-hand information. These considerations are based on certain sources of information available to me. They include frequent telephone conversations with my friends, Jewish activists in Moscow, meetings with recent *olim* who came during the war or after it, and general acquaintance with the state of affairs in the U.S.S.R., especially with the Jewish repatriation movement, in which I took part for the past two years.

Concerning opinion among the various strata of Soviet society towards the war, most of its members, for various reasons, are denied self-expression, so I can describe the reactions of only a few.

Among the social forces which do express themselves, there is one that does so all too clearly: the Soviet authorities. Their reaction to the Middle East war revealed itself in a new wave of repression against Zionist-oriented Jews. There was more shadowing of Jewish activists, more telephones were disconnected, Jews who gathered near the Moscow synagogue were brutally beaten up, and some severely injured. There have been new administrative arrests, with cruel mistreatment of the detainees. One has to know the overall picture well to understand the difference made by the war. There had been arrests, beatings and dispersal of gatherings before—but now there was a new spirit of savagery, a complete lack of restraint on the part of the U.S.S.R.; Feldman in Kiev, Zabelishensky in Sverdlovsk, and Pinkharov in Derbent—all three have been since condemned to long terms of imprisonment. The most important innovation is the apparent preparation for a trial of Jewish activists in Moscow; the defendents are three women: Dina Belina, Tamara Galperina, and Ida Nodel. This is significant because formerly Moscow Jews lived in relative safety compared to others, since in that city Jews are more visible to the outside world.

The main intention of renewed Soviet reprisals was to exploit the Middle East situation. During the war and the cease-fire negotiations the media devoted less space to Soviet Jewry. The authorities apparently intended to use this situation to break the Jewish movement in the U.S.S.R. Fortunately, they have not yet achieved this goal, but the danger still exists. Another factor which might play a role could be the emotional reaction of the Russian government to the war, which they had inspired against the Jewish State, and which gave them an outlet for their traditional anti-Semitic sentiments.

In the first days of the war the information media throughout the U.S.S.R. carried stories of Arab bombardments of Tel Aviv, destruction of Haifa by air raids, and an Arab victory. Attempts were made by officials to frighten the repatriates and in this way to dissuade them from leaving. Thus, in the border city of Brest, a group of repatriates was shown a film picturing Israel destroyed with crowds of refugees fleeing down the roads. A few families influenced by the film decided to stay, but not many.

I would like to comment on some reports we have heard that the number of people who arrived in Israel from Russia in October was greater than previously. First, if compared with the monthly average, the October figures do not indicate that the growth was very great. Second, this increase is apparently something of a seasonal phenomenon, as the number of visas granted in the autumn for the last three years has been much greater than in summer. This may be caused by purely technical bureaucratic reasons, such as the holiday season among the officials; possibly also they hurry to fill their annual quota in the later months of the year. Another reason why more visas were granted may have been reluctance on the part of the authorities to increase the chance for passage of the

Jackson amendment in the United States Congress. I have no doubt that my permission to leave, which I received in the middle of September, was connected with the debate on the amendment just then in progress. Most of the people who came to Israel in October obtained their permission in September. All in all, there is no evidence that Soviet Jews changed their minds about Israel when the war broke out.

Among the activists, demonstrations in support of Israel, and not just for its right to exist, were a new feature. There were many requests to permit the Jews in the U.S.S.R. to donate blood to Israel and letters of protest and solidarity were sent during the Yom Kippur War. In view of the dangerous situation in the U.S.S.R., where it seemed quite possible that the authorities were resolved to stamp out the Jewish movement, it should be especially noted that the repatriation activity did not flag but even intensified during the war. There were new demonstrations and hunger strikes, notably the prolonged hunger strikes of Valeri Panov and his wife in Leningrad and of Miron Darfman and his wife in Kishinev.

During this period Moscow activists sent a letter to the American people and Congress urging them not to heed statements that too active support of Soviet Jews by the world public might be a source of danger to them. The letter emphasized the fact, well known to the Jews in Russia, that the attention of the Western public is the source of whatever safety they have, while any slackening of this attention spells danger, as shown by events during the war.

In what way did the war influence the mass of potential Jewish emigrants? Despite urgings by the Soviet authorities and propaganda stunts like the film mentioned, there have been few cases of people refusing to go. A few families tried to prolong the term of the visa. At the same time the number of people applying for visas apparently rose significantly, according to reports by activists on the spot. One may tentatively conclude that if the war had little pronounced immediate effect on emigration, at any rate it did not have a negative one.

Indirectly, the reaction of the *olim* from Russia in Israel may also have some bearing on the problem. I do not know of a single new immigrant who did not volunteer his services in one way or another, and all took some part in the war effort. When I returned to my absorption center on Yom Kippur, a civil defense station had been set up there, and many new immigrants offered to take part in its work. Blood donation was universal; Soviet Jews who had been in Israel for sufficient time went into the army. Not a few of them are among the wounded and dead. In the middle of December a new *moshav* was founded by Russian immigrants on the Golan Heights. While reflecting a certain revival of the pioneering spirit, this may also be considered an effect of the war.

Among the reactions of other groups of Soviet society, I would like to mention that of a very small one—the dissident movement of Soviet intellectuals. It was expressed by Professor Andrei Sakharov, who proclaimed his full support for Israel, exposing himself not only to fierce attacks by the official propaganda, but also to a KGB-inspired assault by the Black September group.

While the war has apparently had little direct impact on the Jewish repatriation movement from the U.S.S.R., its indirect effects are perhaps yet to be felt. There appear to be three main factors determining the development of the movement: 1) the situation inside Russia, especially as it affects the Jewish minority; 2) the degree of difficulty in obtaining an exit visa; and 3) the success of absorption of the new immigrant in Israel and the degree of satisfaction with the Israeli reality. In the long run, all three factors could be influenced by the war and the post-war situation. Personally, I feel that now, after three years of large-scale immigration of Soviet Jews, the third factor has gradually become the most important.

The first two factors are important in determining how many Jews leave Russia, but the third consideration influences both the number of those leaving and also the proportion of those who go not to Israel but to other countries. At present the proportion going to other countries is not large. The number of Soviet immigrants who emigrate from Israel to other countries is comparatively small, too. In this respect, the extent to which their absorption is successful could have important consequences which could be called indirect after-effects of the war.

The consequences of the war need not all be negative. The war brought about mutual understanding between new immigrants and the older settlers. The importance of immigration for the country became still more evident, and this may have influenced the lifting of the age barrier for loans granted to new immigrants to obtain apartments. Aside from absorption failures, post-war difficulties affecting the country as a whole may lead to a difference of approach among Russian Jewry. Some may be more anxious to come to Israel and help while others may be deterred.

Anti-Semitism in Russia will probably be increased by this war, especially as it may lead to Israel's leaving occupied territories. The Six Day War by contrast had the opposite effect. Then it was said in Russia that instead of the saying, "Beat the Jews," one should say, "Beat like the Jews." This reflects the traditional Russian respect for force; sympathy for the underdog is alien to Russian popular feeling. Growth of anti-Semitism could be an additional stimulus to emigration, unless it leads to much greater measures of repression against the Jewish applicants. If too many concessions are made to the Arabs, this might also have a dampening effect on the morale of the Jewish population.

One of the indirect effects of the war, and in particular of the perfidious role played in it by Russia, was that it created a new argument in favor of the Jackson amendment. The amendment is a factor of the first magnitude for the problem of free emigration; it should especially improve the chances of those who had already been refused visas. If a breakdown occurs in the Soviet-American détente, this could lead to a general deterioration in Soviet internal policy, and an intensified anti-Jewish policy. The overall effect on the Jewish movement would then be unpredictable.

Asia and Africa: Survey

Hayyim J. Cohen

Today approximately 160,000 Jews live in North Africa and the entire continent of Asia, excluding Israel, where a quarter of a century ago some 1,100,000 Jews lived. The Jewish population in this part of the world now consists of remnants of communities, none of which even before this period could be considered large. The majority of Jews in Asia and Africa are living in countries whose governments are either hostile or unfriendly toward Israel; it has been impossible, therefore, to maintain contact with Jews or to assess their reactions to the war. This explains the limitations of the material.

Jews in Extremist Arab Countries

The four Arab countries with military regimes—Libya, Egypt, Syria, and Iraq—had a population of approximately 270,000 Jews in 1948; there now remain about 5,000. Most Jews left these countries because of hostile acts toward them before and after the establishment of the State of Israel (mob outbreaks against the Jews in Egypt in 1945 and 1948, in Syria in 1947, and in Libya in 1946 and 1948). In Iraq thousands of Jews were arrested and imprisoned in 1948 and 1949. Many were tortured in Iraqi jails, and some were publicly hanged.[1] The remnant of Jews in these communities left after the Sinai Campaign and the Six Day War, because to remain would mean to risk being arrested, imprisoned, tortured, and degraded after every outbreak of fighting between Israel and Arab states.

1. On this period, see Joseph B. Schechtman, *On Wings of Eagles,* London-New York, 1961, and H.J. Cohen, *Jews of the Middle East (1860-1972),* Jerusalem-New York, 1973.

The sufferings of the Jews in Egypt have been movingly described by Yuri Miloslavski, a Russian-born Jewish writer who lived in Egypt for many years, and was himself arrested in 1967. His book *Scapegoats* has been translated from French into Hebrew. In Libya there were also mob attacks after the Six Day War. As a result, thousands of Jews still living in Libya fled the country leaving all their possessions and property behind. In 1970 the government confiscated everything, though promising to pay compensation by way of fifteen-year bonds.

It is only in Syria that a relatively numerous group of Jews has remained. Out of 30,000 Jews living there in 1947, there are between 3,500 and 4,000 today, while out of 240,000 Jews living in Egypt, Iraq, and Libya in the same period there are now less than 1,000. Syria has been the only Arab state which, apart from a brief interlude, has not permitted the Jews to leave the country legally. The many Jews who did leave Syria, did so in danger of their lives. Since 1967 only a few Jews—mostly young men—have managed to escape. The severe restrictions placed on the movements of Jews inside Syria, the identity cards specifying in red print their "Mosaic" origin, and other measures make it difficult for even the most courageous to leave the country.[2]

In these circumstances, and from past experience, it seems obvious to those who follow the position of Jews in Arab countries and especially in Syria, that they will suffer severely if the war continues. These Jews must be afraid both for their own fate and that of the State of Israel, but they have no means of organizing themselves against attacks. They dare not pray for the welfare of Israel or their own safety in the synagogue lest they excite the attention of the authorities. They exist in mortal terror.

Nevertheless, to the surprise of Jews the world over, during the October fighting they were not harassed by either the authorities or the local Arabs. In none of the four countries mentioned were Jews arrested, beaten up, tortured, or

2. For details see A.S. Karlikow, "Jews in Arab Countries," *American Jewish Yea⸱ Book 1968*, Vol. 69, pp. 131–144; H.J. Cohen,"Jews in Arab and Moslem Countries," *American Jewish Year Book 1971*, Vol. 72, pp. 443–449.

murdered because of the war. According to one Israeli prisoner who returned from Egypt, the authorities even allowed him to visit a synagogue in Cairo and join the *minha* and *maarib* services on Shabbat, and to talk freely with the congregation. According to him, the congregation, consisting mainly of elderly people, seems to be living comfortably. They are largely professionals—doctors and lawyers—and well-to-do businessmen. He understood that they did not want to leave Egypt, since all of them are Egyptian-born, excepting one who was born in Russia. But others testified that though Jews are not harmed in Egypt, they have no feeling of security.

Jews in "Moderate" Arab Countries

The number of Jews in the remaining Arab countries (Yemen, Lebanon, Morocco, Tunisia and Algeria) amounted to approximately 600,000 in 1948; today some 45,000 remain. These communities did not suffer the persecutions described in the above-mentioned Arab states in the last two decades, either by the authorities or on the part of the local population. There were no arrests or imprisonments, property was not taken over, and they were not hampered in their business activities. Although some Jews left these countries during this period, it was not because of fear. But in October many were afraid that this time the Jews who remained would suffer, especially in Morocco, because of the extremist stand of the government toward Israel. In fact, no Jews were attacked either in Tunisia or in other Arab countries.[3] Nevertheless, the Jews there did not dare to demonstrate solidarity with Israel, or express their support or concern. They did not even allow themselves to hold prayers for its welfare, and feared for their own existence.

---

3. In a radio address on October 8 President Bourguiba of Tunisia warned his citizens against maltreating the Jews in Tunisia. He said: "I don't want Tunisia to display a false image to the world, and I don't want a single Jew in Tunisia to suffer physical harm or damage to his property. You all know that the instructions I give are for the good of Tunisia, and the people know that Tunisia's enemies are in Israel, with whom the war is being fought. If after what I say here, any subversive attempts are made, I am able to stop any who try to represent their country in an inappropriate manner, while Tunisia respects the rights of all her citizens and defends them with every means at her disposal. . . ."

Jews in Non-Arab Muslim Countries

In 1948 approximately 175,000 Jews were living in non-Arab Muslim states in Asia, Turkey, Iran, Afghanistan, Pakistan, and Malaysia. Today there remain about 100,000 Jews in these countries: some 65,000 in Iran, some 35,000 in Turkey, and several hundred in the remainder. The fact that the number of Jews living in these countries decreased by only forty per cent, instead of by ninety-five per cent as in the Arab countries, shows the difference in their situation. Jews living in the Muslim countries of Asia did not and do not live in fear of their existence. These countries have not declared war on Israel. Turkey and Iran did not change their relations with Israel. Some permit emigration to Israel.

Yet the Jews in Turkey and Iran made their fears felt during the Yom Kippur War. All the communications media—radio, television, and press—reported the Arab version of the fighting for the first few days of the war, either because the Israeli reports were unclear or because there was a feeling of identification among some of the Muslim population with the Arab world. Despite the centuries-old derogatory attitude of the Turks and Persians toward the Arabs, during the war against Israel they could not overlook the common religious factor. One Iranian newspaper during the first days of the war carried headlines announcing the advance of the *Muslim* army (not Egyptian, or Syrian, or Arab) on Tel Aviv. Neither the authorities nor the local population in any of these countries interfered with Jews. Although the Jews had no doubt that the government would prevent any anti-Jewish violence, they did not feel secure. When the Israeli army began its counter-attack and the danger to Israel receded, the anxieties of the Jewish population lessened, and they returned to normal life. During the war there were some who thought it better for the Jews to leave these countries; fewer thought so after the war ended.

The position of the Jews in Muslim countries is obviously different from that in Arab countries. The former feared for the existence of the State of Israel rather than for their own lives. Despite Jewish fears, and the ban in most of the Muslim countries on organizing demonstrations in support of Israel, fund-raising activities were initiated in some countries, and Jews contributed money, and volunteered blood and manpower. However, both monetary contributions and expressions of solidarity were on a small scale, not only to avoid aggravating the authorities and the Muslim population, but because of the lack of an organizational framework to meet such an emergency.

Jews in Non-Muslim Countries in Asia

The largest Jewish community east of Pakistan is that of India, where there are some 15,000 Jews in a population of 550,000,000. The decrease in the number of Jews and their differences in origin (Iraqi, Cochin, and Bene Israel) have prevented the establishment of a strong Zionist organization. During the Yom Kippur War fears for Israel's existence were widespread among the Jews in India, but the lack of organization and low financial means at the disposal of most of the community could not produce much in the way of monetary contributions. Some Jews volunteered to serve with the Israeli army or to work in Israel. Support for Israel was expressed publicly. President of the Bombay Zionist Federation Yehezkiel Jacob condemned anti-Israel demonstrations held in India, in which an effigy of Moshe Dayan was burned, and thanked the individuals who had cabled their support to Premier Golda Meir.

Jewish communities in other countries in Asia were also free to express solidarity with Israel. In Bangkok where 250 Jews are living (of whom only twenty are local residents, the others being temporary Israeli or American residents), and in Japan, where there are approximately 1,000 Jews, prayer services were held and funds raised for Israel. The tiny Jewish community in Singapore, numbering some 400 Jews, outdid the rest. Here the Jews are not only free to express their sympathy with Israel, but many of them are well off financially. In the month of October the community raised a sum which, compared with other communities in the world, was rather large. They also contributed transistor radios and other articles for Israeli soldiers.

To sum up: Jews in most countries of the region were afraid when the Yom Kippur War began because (1) they feared the attitude of governments and the Muslim populations toward Jews and Israelis; (2) they were tiny and unorganized communities; and (3) they had no source of reliable information on the situation at the fronts. These small communities were concerned for their own lives and for their relations living in Israel.

The Jews in Arab countries were fortunate in being spared from harm during the present war. The reason for this is that the Arabs felt that they had been successful, and there were no feelings of frustration or failure, and at least for the present, no need for revenge. However, the threat to the 50,000 Jews living in Arab countries will be greatly increased if there is a renewal of hostilities. They are generally accused of being Zionists, regardless of the fact that they have no connection with Zionism, and have been made to suffer because they are Jews. Their position went from bad to worse with the growth of the Zionist movement and the establishment of the State of Israel. Only their departure can guarantee their safety.

Document of Albert Memmi

Professor Memmi, born in Tunis, now teaching sociology at the Sorbonne, addressed these remarks to Libyan President Qaddafi at a colloquium in Paris, arranged by four European newspapers on November 23, 1973.*

Mr. President,

Let me confine myself to asking you a few questions from a viewpoint which probably no one else here can adopt.

I am a Jewish writer, born in a country with an Arab majority, who speaks Arabic, who left that country only at the end of his adolescence, and who still has strong ties with the people who live there and with their culture.

At the same time, I very early started to understand,

*As reprinted by Israel Academic Committee for Middle East.

approve and support the national revival of the Arab peoples, served it with my pen, and sometimes worked for it physically. I say this so as to show that I am one of the people here, and perhaps in the whole world, who understands you best; which also lends particular weight to my questions and, I suggest, entitles me to hope for your special attention.

Disappearance of Israel

Is it correct that you have stated that you do not propose discussing the importance of territories to be given back, or of borders to be adjusted, or even of a settlement for the Arabs of Palestine, but rather to resume the war and continue it until Israel has entirely disappeared?

If that is the case, how can you so radically dispose of the Jewish liberation movement and the State which is its outcome, while you yourself are one of the exponents of the Arab national movement? Why should only the Jews not be entitled to what, after your religious conviction, you hold most sacred, to a national existence?

Is it correct that you have declared that once the Jews from Europe have been sent back there, only Jews born in Arab countries will be allowed to continue to live in them?

Do you seriously believe that the Jews from Germany or Poland, or rather the few of them that have survived, can go and live again where their parents, wives, husbands and children were burned in the gas ovens?

And what would you do about the children of those Jews who were since born in Israel and who by now account for 25 per cent of its population?

Or do you believe that the Jews who were born in Arab countries can go back to live in countries where they had been robbed, massacred and from which they had been expelled? Particularly since you propose to reinstate the Islamic law totally, to the extent, I am told, of cutting off thieves' right hands and sending the women back to the harem or to polygamous promiscuity. That, of course, is entirely your concern. Supposing that the Moslems would agree to it, do you believe that one could go back to live under such laws when one is not a Moslem?

Arab Myth

Is it correct that you have stated that the Jews have always lived at peace in the Arab countries; and that you have nothing against the Jews, but only against the Zionists?

Can you really believe in the myth that is being hawked around for the benefit of the Western world, about the idyllic life of the Jews in the Arab countries?

As late as 1912, any Jew daring to leave a Jewish quarter in Morocco had to take off his shoes, as if it were a sacrilege for him to touch the sacred Moroccan soil. In the same Morocco, in 1907, there was a great massacre of Jews in Casablanca, complete with rape, the carrying off of women to the mountains, the burning down of hundreds of houses and shops, and so on. In 1912, there was another great massacre in Fez, and in 1948 in Oudja and other towns. In Algeria, there was the massacre of Constantine of 1934, with 24 killed and dozens upon dozens seriously wounded. In Egypt, the massacre of 1948—this time with the refinement of hundreds of bombs. In Aden, in 1946, the local authorities declared that Jews were not entitled to live like human beings. A few months later, 82 were killed and 76 wounded, with two-thirds of the shops looted and burned. In Iraq, between the 2nd and the 3rd of June 1941, 600 were killed, 1000 seriously wounded, 600 shops looted, women raped and 1000 houses burned. To keep to your own country, there were the massacres at Tripoli on November 5, 1945 and those of Zanzour, Zaouia, Foussabat, Ziltayin and elsewhere on November 6 and 7, with girls and women raped in the sight of their families, pregnant women having their bellies slit open and foetuses dragged out, children beaten to death with iron bars. In 1967, a hundred were murdered in spite of the protection of King Idriss. All this may be found in the newspapers of those days, including the *New York Times* and the local Arab press, and in the works of serious historians like Smith, Fattal, Gardst, Brunschwig, Van Bery, Vajda and others.

We always get what may have been the mistake of Deir Yassin thrown in our faces. Good Heavens! We have suffered a hundred, a thousand Deir Yassins! And not only in Russia, in

Germany or in Poland, but actually in Arab lands, with the world never caring.

But why do I need references and historical records? My own grandfather and father always remembered being afraid of being beaten over the head by any Arab who happened to come by. I myself, as a child, used to play in the lanes of an Arab village—like you, Mr. President, I suppose. Do you remember what you thought of the little Jews and how you treated them? I remember only too well, unfortunately!

And don't tell me, please, that all that is due to Zionism. That is another myth.

With the exception of two or three periods, and a great deal of nonsense has been said about them, this idyllic life never existed. What is more, the Jews were not only at the mercy of the populace, they had a status which in a way justified such slavery. That status is a matter of record: ever since the days of the Abassids, it has been part of the Charter of Omar that, to put it briefly, the Jew is at best protected like a dog that is part of the chattels. But let him but raise his head or behave like a human being, and he must be beaten to within an inch of his life, to remind him of his condition.

We have, among other records, an unimpeachable witness to this: Père de Foucauld, who could not be suspected of loving Jews unduly, wanted to travel incognito among Arabs and decided to disguise himself, of all things, as a Jew. I suggest you read the long story of all the humiliations and threats this provisional Jew had to suffer.

The truth is that we have lived in the Arab countries in fear and humiliation. I shall not recite another litany—that of the massacres before Zionism. I can let you have the lists, if you want to know. The truth is that those young Jews from the Arab countries were Zionists before Auschwitz. The State of Israel is not the result of Auschwitz, but of the entire Jewish condition, including that in the Arab countries.

Jews and a State of Their Own

Is it correct that you have said that if the Jews absolutely wanted a state, all they needed to do was to establish it in Europe or America?

Need I tell you, who are so concerned for the values of your people, that one cannot establish a state just anywhere or with just any values?

Why should we Jews in countries with an Arab majority go and establish a state in Europe—or at the North Pole, for that matter—when we were born on the shores of the Mediterranean, to which we are attached, as you understand far better than anyone else?

Why should this soil, which you call Arab because you are in the majority on it, not belong partly to us? To us, whose ancestors were Berbers who converted to Judaism and who in many cases were here before yours? Is it enough to be born an Arab to be entitled to everything, and to be born a Jew to be entitled to nothing, except be doomed to remain second-class citizens to all eternity and be humiliated and killed off at set times? If you really wanted to prevent our settling down together in the little corner of the world which we have called Israel in order to renew our bond with an ancient tradition, why did you pursue and expel us wherever your writ runs? I am told that in this whole business you are mainly motivated by the fate of the Arabs of Palestine. If that is the case, how do you reconcile that rumor with your constant claim that the Arab nation is one? The Arabs of Palestine are admittedly experiencing a tragedy, no less than we; but at the negotiation table one will have to bear in mind that there are no more of them than of us, and that in many cases they are newcomers, just as we. When all is said and done, the disaster of the Arabs of Palestine amounts to their having been displaced for some fifty kilometers within the same, enormous nation. Is that so serious? How much more serious is our case: we Jews from Arab countries have been displaced for thousands of kilometers, after having also lost everything—and we Jews from Arab countries are a million and three hundred thousand by now, or half of the population of Israel; add the 25 per cent of children of Western Jews, and you have 75 per cent of the native-born population. In short, if one wants to make this ridiculous account, the Jews are at home in Israel to at least the same extent as the Arabs. But Israel, I say it again, is the outcome of the entire Jewish condition, and therefore also of Auschwitz; and the German, Polish and Russian Jews are also at home. And no one has the right to deny us the possibility of ingathering our refugees, those of yesterday and, alas, those of tomorrow.

Oil Blackmail

We are also being told that you have come to France to buy yet more arms and to stress the oil blackmail. If so, would it not be disastrous to make the conflict break out again just as many Arab countries are finally moving in the direction of a settlement that would put an end to our mutual suffering? You know the saying that a bad settlement is better than a good court case. Is it not time that we reached a settlement amongst us, even if it is only a moderately good one?

Mr. President, your language, a language of the heart, a language of determination born out of a recovered dignity, is one I understand very well; the better, because it is that of our youth, yours and ours.

Don't you think that you underestimate the determination of the Jews, not only of the Israelis but of those of the entire world? It is not their motor trips on Sunday or the gadgets made of oil compounds that the new generation of Jews are defending; they know that their physical and cultural existence is at stake.

When two determinations so strong—strong because they are based on sheer existence—confront each other, the result may be endless misery or great advantages. You have just discovered the oil weapon; tomorrow, the Jews will discover the appropriate answer. Don't you think that this is the point to stop this mutual suicide, which is perhaps applauded secretly by powerful interests?

Don't you think that we should both give up past quarrels, cruel as they may be, that we should make an effort to outgrow the myths we believe about each other?

Could we not at last combine the talents we have regained in order to build a world in which each of us will have his nation and his free state—this time not united by contradictory and destructive myths but by economic and cultural benefits?

I suggest, Mr. President, that you not only abandon the

purchase of new weapons, but that with the same generous impulse which inspires you, you become the sponsor of a great conference, in Tripoli or in Tel-Aviv or in a neutral country—Geneva, perhaps, though alas, hardly Paris—where not only Jews and Arabs, but naturally also Israelis and Palestinians, could meet as brothers. For such a dialogue, I, a Jew born among Arabs, am at your disposal.

View from Jerusalem: Perspectives

Arye L. Dulzin

In the weeks immediately following the Arab attack on the State of Israel, together with Pinchas Sapir and Haim Laskov, I toured Jewish communities in different parts of the world. Our mission was primarily to ask Jews living in these places to help Israel meet the extraordinary financial demands resulting from the sudden and overwhelming increase in military and civilian services.

We visited the United States and Canada, and in Europe met with Jewish leaders in London, Paris, Zurich, and Brussels; in the latter city we conferred with representatives from Jewish communities in Germany, Austria, Holland, Denmark, and Sweden. No matter whom we spoke with, the answer was always the same: *"Tell us what we can do!"*

I had become convinced in recent years that the Jewish people was going through a profound transformation in its self-awareness and in the relationship between the Diaspora and Israel. But in the aftermath of the Yom Kippur War I began to realize that it would be no exaggeration to speak in terms of a new age in our contemporary history. We have moved into a *Zionist* era, when almost the whole of the Jewish people the world over has become Zionist. Of course, there are numerous Jews who ignore their Jewishness and are assimilated. But of those Jews who declare and cherish their Jewish identity, the majority has absorbed—perhaps imperceptibly and subconsciously—the philosophy of Zionism, which implies the unity and the fate of the Jewish nation, wherever it may be.

Following the Six Day War many such Jews realized for the first time how attached emotionally they were to the State of Israel and their brothers, the Israelis. Since that time the attachment has grown deeper and the relationship crucial to the life and well-being of Jews who live outside of Israel. It was evident that the Jews who responded were not waiting for appeals to come to Israel's aid, but were acting out their deep-felt personal involvements and commitments to their Jewishness. Their attachment to Israel was by no means merely philanthropic; Israel was an inherent and essential part of their Jewishness. Again and again I was told during those fateful months by Jews in the United States and other Diaspora communities: "Without Israel my life will have no sense or meaning."

An experience which moved me deeply was my meeting with a gracious lady from the state of Texas, who rose at a gathering to announce that she was selling her jewels in order to be able to make a substantial contribution of her own to the emergency fund for Israel. She explained: "Until there is peace in Israel I shall not want to take pleasure in my jewels, and if peace comes to Israel, as I pray it shall soon, then I will be so happy I won't need jewels to give me pleasure."

We have experienced many astounding phenomena of emotional upsurge, political support, and financial assistance for Israel among Diaspora Jews. But the Yom Kippur War brought out not only new dimensions of aid, it inspired a radically novel quality of Jewishness and the deepest consciousness of the role of Israel in Jewish life. The sensitivity to everything connected with Israel is unprecedented. And the intensity of the expressions of support for Israel undoubtedly reflects a personal determination to view Israel and the future of Jewish existence as inextricably bound together.

Relevant to this point is the story of the man in his forties whose contribution to the Israel fund was so large that people who knew his circumstances were astounded. When asked why he was donating almost a third of his assets, he replied by recalling the time he had asked *his* father what he had done to help fellow Jews during the Holocaust. The father had no answer. And the young man explained that he wanted *his* conscience to be clear. If his children ever ask him what he did to help the Jewish people, he will answer, "I did everything I could."

I have no doubt that it was not the Yom Kippur War alone which caused such intensely personal reactions. We are participating in a continuing process which started in 1948 with the establishment of the State of Israel and was accelerated by its unequalled achievement in the *aliyah* and absorption of one and a half million immigrants and the revival of an independent and free Jewish national life. After the Six Day War this process was quickened, and it had its most amazing and spectacular expression in the Zionist revival and the urge for *aliyah* that sprang up among Jews in the Soviet Union. It is impressive to realize that in October 1973, the month of the worst fighting, 4,200 immigrants arrived in Israel from the Soviet Union, the largest number to arrive in any one month since the start of the exodus from Russia. In that same month, 1,400 other immigrants came from North and South America and Europe. I believe that as Israel continues to develop and resolve its problems in its special manner, immigration will grow and more and more Jews will find their way physically to the real land which until now has only been a historical vision to them.

Ever since the *haskalah,* that period of enlightenment which arose among Jews in Europe during the eighteenth and nineteenth centuries, there was an uninterrupted search for solutions for the contemporary Jewish predicament, ranging from total assimilation to a variety of religious expressions and political and economic philosophies. Such solutions receded as it became obvious that the only effective—and truly Jewish—solution to the problem of Jewish existence in the modern situation is the Zionist solution. This conviction was enhanced and deepened by the Yom Kippur War. That the Jewish response was so forceful and personal, especially among men and women in their twenties, thirties, and forties, many with no previous Zionist ties, is indicative of a growing and continuous development, which the war brought out into the open, deepening and broadening convictions and commitments. It is these young people who have so generously and whole-heartedly expressed their love for Israel whom we must bring closer to us, educate, and mobilize to work with us for the future of the Jewish people.

Zionism has come a long and often tortuous way from its inception, when it represented a social-political platform for a controversial minority, to our own days when it has become the all-pervasive view of life shared by most consciously-Jewish Jews.

In evaluating the present situation of Israel-Diaspora relations I am convinced that there can be no question about the profound meaning of recent trends. They unequivocally point to the essence of my thesis, that we have entered a *Zionist* age in contemporary Jewish history. The only cohesive element in Jewish life today is the widespread and growing conviction that the Jews exist as a united people and that their fate is indivisible from the future of Israel.

I should like to close with a very personal note. I was born in the city of Minsk in that part of Eastern Europe known as White Russia. When I was three years old my world was the close-knit Jewish community of Minsk. I know that I did not then know the name of the city of Moscow, or the name of the city of Leningrad, probably not even the name of the city of Minsk. But I *did* know the name of Jerusalem. Therein lies the crux of the situation: Jews in the free world have learned what their ancestors in the *shtetl* were born knowing; it is often hard to be a Jew, but it is always good to be a Jew. The Zionist dream of making it *always* good to be a Jew comes closer and closer, as the Jews of the world turn their hearts more and more to Jerusalem.

View from Jerusalem: Perspectives

Avraham Harman

What seems to emerge from the reports we have had from world Jewry in the aftermath of the Yom Kippur War is that the readiness to put Jewish power—and by this I mean spiritual and psychological, as well as material power—at our disposal is greater than it has ever been. The coming ten years are bound to be exceedingly trying for us, and I believe we should make the Jewish people aware of this. A number of extremely strong forces are working against us: the newly-found unity in action among the Arabs, the obviously improved Arab military prowess, and Israel's political isolation, exacerbated by the dependence of the industrialized nations on Arab oil.

To counteract this we have the power of the Jewish people, which can be put to use in several ways. I see no reason to doubt our strength and ability.

We must bear in mind that Israel was created for three purposes by the Jewish people. First: to provide themselves with the capacity for self-defense; to dispose of, once and for all times, the Warsaw Ghetto syndrome. A basic characteristic of the Warsaw Ghetto was that while there was Jewish victory and Jewish heroism, there was absolutely no possibility of being victorious. To extrapolate, it seems to me that there are two themes of heroism in Jewish history. One is the Samson theme, or the Masada theme—you pull the enemy down with you, or you die to the last man, resisting aggression. The other is the Maccabean theme, or the David and Goliath theme, the victory of the few against the many. The Warsaw Ghetto symbolizes the Masada theme. The people of the Ghetto had absolutely no chance of escaping. With no alternative to dying, they chose a heroic death. Israel is not the Warsaw Ghetto in that sense. The State of Israel is an attempt to demonstrate the viability of the Maccabean theme, that a small people has the right to live, can equip itself, and has a fighting chance to survive, to resist aggression. This is what the Israeli soldier proved in the Yom Kippur War.

In answer to the often-heard argument that we get our equipment from the United States, I reply that the other side also gets its equipment from an outside power. Had it not been for the Arab equipment from the Soviet Union, our chance for victory would have been much greater. Although we are very heavily dependent on outside resources of war materiel, it is important to point out that it is not anything like the extent to which the Arab military machine is almost totally dependent on external support. For example, a decisive weapon in the naval war was a weapon of our own production and invention, the Gabriel. And at least two of the missile boats using this weapon were built in Israel. We are proving that Israel has the ability, even in this area where it is almost impossible to be totally independent, to diminish progressively the area of dependence. and that is an image of Israel that Jews must be made to see.

I think certain historical facts can be used to strengthen this image of Israel for the coming period (because we do not know what the future is going to bring). Thirty-five years ago, in 1938, two events symbolized the defenselessness of the Jewish people: Kristallnacht, the public initiation of Hitler's "final solution," and the Evian Conference, where Jews were abandoned by the world on the most vital, elemental, human needs. Compare that with 1973, when the State of Israel successfully defended itself against an unexpected and brutal attack and, had it not been for the imposition of the cease-fire, would have gone further in curbing Arab military aggression.

The second purpose for Israel's creation was to provide an "open door" for oppressed Jews, wherever they may be. And the fact that immigration continued to Israel during the Yom Kippur War proves that we are defending the open door of the Jewish people. Immigration during the month of October 1973 rose to 5,000, or perhaps more. Obviously Jews are making the decision that they as people and as Jews have a better fighting chance in *this* Israel than in the country they want to get out of. It is an unorganized *aliyah.* Nobody can organize the *aliyah* of Russian Jews. There are no *shlichim* from the Jewish Agency in Russia. But Soviet Jews did get exit visas and came out during the war month. And they want to continue to come out. It is important for us to know this. First of all, because it's a demonstration that Israel is a Jewish need. And second, because that is what we are defending—a crucial life-line for the Jewish people.

The question is not whether the Jewish people can remain alive without the State of Israel. The Jewish people should not even ask this question. The Jewish people is duty bound to examine its total capacity to reinforce Jewish life everywhere, and first and foremost on the central front of Jewish existence, the State of Israel. If the centrality of Israel is approached from this point of view, then it is unequivocal. When there is a campaign on a global scale to defend the existence of the Jewish people, which has a central front, then all our power and resources must be directed to that front.

The third purpose of the State of Israel is the continuity of Jewish civilization. My own conviction—and it is backed up by public opinion polls conducted by Elihu Katz and A.L. Gutman during the war—is that, despite the nature of the Arab attack, we did not lose our sense of values. This is a country in which, by and large, most people do not hate Arabs. The Arab population on the West Bank, in the Gaza Strip, in Israel, was not harassed. I am not saying that Israelis are angels. But there has been nothing on this subject in the press because nothing has happened. I mention that as an indication of the fact that we have retained our values, Jewish values, and therefore we have kept ourselves ready for peace making.

These are the three purposes for which we have established Israel and these are the purposes I think we must bear in mind constantly. Now to get back to the image of Israel. There is no question at all that Arab propaganda since the Six Day War has changed. One sees indications of it in many ways. Arabs have abandoned talk about destroying Israel and are stressing the question of occupied territory. They have succeeded in covering up the fact that what they did on October 6 was an act of aggression and a breach of the

1967 cease-fire resolution of the Security Council. As you know, they were not condemned for it; in many circles they were even seen to be justified.

I think that our propaganda, I use that word unabashedly, has got to respond to this new Arab approach, be much more sophisticated, and has to touch on the basic issues the Arabs raise in order to befuddle the problem. What was the origin of the 1967 war? Who was responsible for it? Can the Arabs be allowed to get away with their two-stage theory: first, return the occupied territory, then the Palestine problem will be solved? And who is the representative of the Palestine people? Arafat. What is Arafat's concept of the future of Israel? The answer is, he has no concept of a Middle East which includes the existence of the State of Israel.

The basic fact, which we take for granted, is that we are a people, a nation, and we therefore have the right of self-determination and self-government. Obviously we have a State of Israel which expresses our national personality in political form. All these are concepts which Arab propaganda has been trying to subvert. One thing that is absolutely unknown in the outside world is the composition of our population. We are thought of, and represented by Arabs as being European interlopers in the Middle East, which we are not. Even European Jews here are not European. We are not settlers, nor colonialists. We are Jews. This is our homeland.

In the United States, for example, they know absolutely nothing about Jews from Arab countries, except when there is publicity in the media about "Ashkenazi oppression" of oriental Jews. I think this is a very serious matter that requires attention. I think we have to stop choosing Israeli representatives on the basis of facility in English language and must send people abroad who speak English with an obvious accent, or who speak Arabic and who can relate from personal experience what it means to be a Jew in so-called democratic Arab societies, the ones Arafat wants to send us back to.

What many people do not know is that ninety per cent of the Jewish population of Beersheba, for example, consists of Jews from Morocco, Iraq, and other Arab countries. And that of all the Jewish children in Israel through the age of fourteen, seventy per cent are the children of immigrants from oriental communities. These facts are just not known—not even in highly sophisticated policy-making circles. It's certainly not known by the general public. And I think that what we must do is admit frankly that our own propaganda is to blame for past images. I do not think we should go to the other extreme and present ourselves as a pitiful, miserable underdog who needs his hand outstretched in order to continue to live. There is an enormous life force in this country and we proved it in this war. We do not have to go around bragging about it, or blowing our trumpets as we did after the '67 war. But we need to present the picture of Israel as it is. I think we in Israel have to be much more aware of who we are and what difficulties we face to be absolutely clear about it ourselves. Images of Israel are created in many ways. They are made in our propaganda, they are made in public speeches of our leaders, in what is written in our press, in the kind of programs we arrange for tourists, and everything else.

Basically, one of the shocks that we have to relate to, both internally and in terms of our image abroad, is that we thought of ourselves on the eve on Yom Kippur as being a normal society. If you analyze the nature of the political platforms that were being drawn up by the parties before Yom Kippur, you will find that the issues were housing, wages, inflation. The assumption was that our external political situation was normal and that we could afford to occupy ourselves exclusively with the questions of a normal society, which takes its existence and its security for granted. What had happened was that the abnormal aspects of our "normalcy" had come to be taken for granted. If somebody said that we had to pull in our belts because of defense, people would simply shrug it off as an annoyance. Even military service, the annual military call-up, was taken for granted. This had become part of the normality. The abnormal aspect of our situation was that we were facing an unsolved problem of ominous military significance. Tourists came and saw an image of Israel as a country, economically vigorous with much building going on, rising standards of living, and so on, and all this was true. It is also true that there was much they could not see.

The big test I think we face, in the coming period, in

relation to the basic theme of the Jews of Israel and the Jews of the world, is how we are going to behave in a totally new phase in our history, a period which will last at least a decade, as I see it, when we shall have to be a highly self-disciplined people in every respect. The quality of all relations, personal and group, must be re-examined. We can not achieve national objectives during this period if materialist motivation is allowed to get out of hand as it was before the war. We must think about an entirely new way of life

What strengthens my conviction on this point is the dramatic evidence of thousands of American Jews who volunteered or wished to volunteer their services during the war. Many were in touch with me personally. These were students, high-level professionals, affluent business people, and a host of others in *all* strata of the community, who responded in the classic *halutz* mode: whatever Israel needs I am prepared to do. Such volunteers constitute a special kind of *oleh*, an idealist who wants to become part of what he sees as an idealistic society. It is our business to re-make Israel into that kind of society.

This ultimately is linked to the question of *aliyah*. During the past six years we have confused two different factors: on the one hand, the motives for *aliyah*, and on the other, the services provided for the immigrant. Every immigrant requires special attention because of the fact of his having taken the step of coming to Israel. But there are others in Israel who require special attention—veteran immigrants or their children, who for one reason or another, require special treatment. The problem in the past has been approached from the point of view of the need to promote *aliyah*. There is no need to promote *aliyah*. What is necessary is to give the immigrant the services he requires to enable him to integrate quickly. The decision to come to Israel is a personal one which comes from internal motivation. I believe that one of the conclusions to be drawn, about what has happened in the Yom Kippur War and its aftermath here in Israel and in the Jewish world, is that a *halutz* movement needs to be created consisting of small groups in a manner similar to the classic period of Zionism. Just as we do not want to be ashamed of the word "Zionist," we should not be ashamed of the term *halutz*.

This means *aliyah* with no strings attached, *aliyah* in order to live just like every Israeli and to struggle with one's personal fate—because this is the central front of the Jewish people in the battle for its very existence.

View from Jerusalem: Comment

Moshe Rivlin

I was born in Jerusalem and, when I was four, the 1929 riots broke out. From then on, there were riots and wars every few years. Nevertheless, when my contemporaries—not to mention previous generations—wanted to characterize an epoch, they did not refer to "the period of the 1929 riots" or "the period of the 1936 riots." They spoke of them as periods of immigration—the First Aliyah, the Second Aliyah, the Third Aliyah, the Fourth Aliyah—because that was what counted. Since the establishment of the State it has been wars by which periods are designated—the War of Independence, the Sinai War, the Six Day War, the Yom Kippur War—although many great events have occurred during these periods which are not war-connected.

The State of Israel was not created to make war. And its history is not the story of a succession of wars, even if these have been forced upon us. The State of Israel was created in order to build a home for the Jewish people. And I think we have to ask ourselves whether—despite the wars—we are fulfilling our objectives or not. We should say, "This happened during the period of the Yemenite immigration," or "the Polish immigration"—and not identify events according to wars. I think this is important from an educational point of view and it is important from a Zionist point of view—to put the State of Israel in its proper perspective.

After the fighting, when I was in England and America, I said to the Jews I met—I'll tell you a story that symbolized for me the mood of the Yom Kippur War. It was on the third day of the war—one of the very worst days we experienced, both in the North and the South. Up to the Yom Kippur War we in the Jewish Agency had been preoccupied with the Schoenau Affair and, on the very eve of Yom Kippur, a Jewish Agency

278

representative had met with the Austrian Minister of the Interior to find some solution and the representative was due back on Sunday morning to report to us. The war broke out and he could not get back. His report arrived on Monday morning on a plane bringing immigrants.

We had a session of the Jewish Agency Executive and a few minutes before ten, I received a telephone call saying, "The Prime Minister wants to know what's in the report." I replied that I would send it to her in Tel Aviv. "No," I was told, "the Prime Minister wants to report to the Cabinet meeting, so tell me what it says." Shortly after 1 P.M. I was informed that the government had discussed the report. It was only later that day that I discovered how serious the war situation had been, but I also learned that the government had found time to discuss how Jews could continue to immigrate to Israel from the Soviet Union. Indeed, not a day of the war passed without the arrival of a plane bringing Russian immigrants. This means that at a time when planes could not be gotten for the most vital needs, they were never lacking to bring immigrants to Israel. This for me symbolized the Yom Kippur War.

The struggle of Soviet Jews for *aliyah* has had its impact on most age groups and sectors of the Jewish people, who see two goals in it: the liberation of human beings and securing the right of people to immigrate to their national home. This struggle unites all the elements of the Jewish people—the Jews living in the Soviet Union who fought for their right to leave; Jews in the other countries of the Diaspora who aroused public opinion on behalf of their brethren; and the State of Israel which absorbed them. In this light, the younger generation has learned to see the Jewish condition not as a problem belonging to past history but as an immediate problem, that of three million Jews living in the Soviet Union whose difficult situation requires immediate solution. Young people in Baltimore or in Cleveland do not have a solution to this condition, but they are aware that there is such a thing as a Jewish people and that the three million Jews in the Soviet Union are part of this people. In addition, they are aware that the State of Israel exists and can provide a haven, a solution to the aspiration of the Jews of the Soviet Union.

A new generation has now emerged which has become involved in Israel-oriented activities through fund raising. However, this must not be misconstrued. These young people did not conceive of these activities as only providing financial aid, but through fund-raising activities on behalf of Israel they found a way of expressing their identification with the State and the Jewish people.

One of the most noteworthy factors during the Yom Kippur War was the decisive role played by the younger generation in all that took place. It must be understood that it was not only the shock of the Yom Kippur War which had its effect, but also the work which had been done between the Six Day and Yom Kippur Wars to raise the consciousness of the young leadership. A generation has grown up which has gone to visit the Warsaw Ghetto and the concentration camp at Bergen Belsen, has become aware of the plight of Soviet Jewry, and has changed its attitudes towards its own Jewishness. Thus a striking aspect of the assistance given during the Yom Kippur War was that campaigns were headed by young people with youthful temperament, with the faith of young people, with enthusiasm for the pragmatic, an enthusiasm which inspired others.

Particularly outstanding during the Yom Kippur War was the Jewish community of Great Britain, which achieved results over and above any expectations in the field of fund raising, directed primarily by young people. During the days of the war and even two weeks after the cease-fire, the offices of the Israel Appeal in Great Britain looked like a war operations headquarters. In a room normally occupied by one person, ten people were working. They began at 6 A.M. and ceased only at two the next morning. The majority were volunteers: those who went out to solicit contributions, women who made out receipts, and the accountants who, after a day's work, made the entries into the Appeal's books.

Expressions of self-denial for the State of Israel were manifold. In Australia a group of young Jews had registered for a new housing project. When war broke out they cancelled their registration and donated the monies they had saved for this project to Israel. Young people gave up a new car or a new apartment and gave to the Appeal instead.

It seems to me that all this compels us to think in the deepest terms about our responsibilities, especially *aliyah*. In order to evolve a process of *aliyah*, planning and preparation are required. This is not a decision that a person can make from one day to the next. Even after the Six Day War it took at least a year for a change to come about.

A number of plans for encouraging *aliyah* have been made. We intend to help in the development of a movement of volunteers for a period of one to two years' service, in the hope that many of these people will remain in Israel. Jewish centers and communities, which a short while ago were reluctant to be involved in volunteer or *aliyah* projects, are prepared to do so now. For example, B'nai B'rith is prepared to assist in *aliyah*. Also, the Board of Governors of the National Jewish Welfare Board held its convention in Israel; and at this meeting it became apparent that they would stress the idea of voluntary work in Israel among members of their communities. It is still early to tell whether such efforts will bear fruit, but it is quite clear that Diaspora Jewish leadership is now prepared to assist in promoting *aliyah*.

Will we know how to exploit possibilities which have opened up before us? It seems, at least in this instance, the gap between the generations has not had a negative effect on future possibilities. The contrary holds true—the activities of the young leaders are beginning to have their impact. This leadership is free from the anxieties and inhibitions of its elders. It has discovered something new and is facing it squarely, not in apprehension. It must be remembered that the young Diaspora Jew lives in a society which is open to him both for its economic possibilities and educational opportunities. Thus, the approach of the young person to Israel is positive, deriving from internal motivation and not from the negation of a situation or from an attempt to escape. Consequently, I am certain that Israel must invest concentrated efforts to increase Jewish education and awareness among these young leaders. This leads to the vital need to relate our Israeli young leaders with their counterparts in the Diaspora communities.

Oral Documentation: Introduction

Geoffrey Wigoder

The excerpts that follow are not meant to give a systematic coverage of reactions to the Yom Kippur War, but rather to add elements of immediacy to the subject matter in other sections of the volume. Some are interviews about areas where written documentation was sparse and the object was to supplement, not duplicate. Some have been included as illustrative of a particular event or mood, others because of their own intrinsic interest, and still others because they add information and personal evaluations.

Certain aspects of world Jewish reaction emerged with particular vividness from a particular country, but this does not mean that such phenomena were confined to that country. Thus, the story of the volunteer movement emerged most clearly from interviews recorded in the United States, although, of course, the volunteer movement was worldwide. Similarly, reactions of children are taken from interviews in the United States and reactions about women came from an interview in Europe. These must be seen only as examples of universal reactions.

Interviews with emigrants from the Soviet Union and Rumania relate personal stories and impressions of Jews who have come to Israel since the war. It was not possible to obtain interviews inside Russia or Eastern Europe, nor was it possible to interview people concerning events inside Moslem lands.

From the point of view of the Institute of Contemporary Jewry's Oral History Division, this project has certain pioneering aspects. Ideally these excerpts should be seen within their total context and anyone who wishes to do so can consult the Division at the Hebrew University of Jerusalem.*

*The transcript in microfilm is obtainable from the Microfilming Corporation of America, Glen Rock, New Jersey.

In general, oral history is conducted within a historical perspective and the interviewee is questioned about events going back many years. This project (like a similarly limited one conducted immediately after the Six Day War) is "instant" history. It lacks the considered hindsight of historical research, but allows for freshness and accuracy. There are flashes of spontaneity that will not be recaptured later; for example, the interviews with the St. Louis school children conducted by Bernard Lipnick or that of a discussion with Ezra Shapiro during his mission in South Africa.

The authentic emotions here recaptured represent not only individual reactions but in a unique way reflect a major event in Jewish history. They form a microcosm of the identification of Jews the world over with the State of Israel.

Oral Documentation: United States

Charlotte Jacobson

Chairman of the World Zionist Organization-American Section. Participant at the meeting of President Katzir with the World Zionist Organization's Executive, December 1973.

It seemed as though pulled by a magnet, everyone converged on 515 Park Avenue—the office of the American Section of the World Zionist Organization. Jews felt the need to be together to share every crumb of news.

And then the deluge started. Telephone calls came all hours of the day and night and we had to arrange to have the switchboard manned twenty-four hours a day. We received offers of help for every kind of volunteer service. This included not only those who wanted to fight or those who wanted to help the kibbutzim and factories, but also offers from policemen and firemen who felt their special talents would be essential to keep these services functioning. One policeman said, "I can prevent traffic jams in Tel Aviv." I had to explain to him that with so many cars and trucks pressed into service, there was little chance of traffic jams. He found this hard to accept.

The medical profession was fantastic. Doctors were bitter in their disappointment when their offers of help were not needed. Several doctors who had previously spent their sabbatical time working in Israel called me at home to plead with me to get them space on El Al, as they just had to get to Israel to be at the side of their Israeli friends and colleagues. Blood bank centers informed us of thousands of people who wanted to send their blood to Israel.

On the fourth day, a woman walked into the office and said, "I want to pay the debt my son owes to the World Zionist Organization." One could not tell from her opening remark

285

the heart-rending story that was to follow. She told me her son had gone on *aliyah* a year ago and had taken a loan for his plane fare. She was notified that he was killed in action and her first thought was to repay this loan. She said in simple terms, "I know this is what he would want me to do."

Another conversation was with a young man who volunteered " to do anything." He was too young to help in the 1967 war and felt he had to be part of the activity in Israel or else his life would be meaningless.

There was a telephone call from a man who knew where ships were available for sale. "Did the Israel Navy need them?" he asked. Another offer was to round up private planes.

But I guess the most moving experience of all was to observe the people walking in the streets with transistor radios to their ears in order to hear every bulletin. Their sense of anguish was in their eyes. People wanted to talk about only one thing—the war.

Israelis are known for their patriotism but the sense of compulsion to return home to be at the side of comrades and friends was demonstrated by their insistence that the W.Z.O. help them return to Israel, even though they were not called back. Some of them came back every day until they got a place on the plane. I spoke to several of them after they returned to the United States. They described to me with great emotion the reception they got from their fighting units when they turned up at the front. How can one evaluate such loyalty?

For the last few years, on *Simchat Torah,* the Jewish community has held a large Solidarity Parade on behalf of Soviet Jewry. This holiday was selected to coordinate with the demonstrations held by Soviet Jewish youth outside the large synagogue in Moscow on this special holiday. The New York demonstration is usually a project of all the Jewish youth movements to convey a message of unity from American Jewish youth to Russian Jewish youth.

This year, because of the Yom Kippur War, the Solidarity Parade took on an added dimension—solidarity with Israel. The crowd stretched from the United Nations Plaza to as far as one could see. The police told me it was one of the largest demonstrations that ever assembled in New

York. I was one of the speakers and we found it difficult to control our emotions at the solid mass of Jews who only wanted to chant *Am Yisrael Chai.* Women came with their baby carriages because they could not bear to be absent from such a demonstration.

Youth groups and Hebrew school classes asked for the names of soldiers with whom they could correspond. These young people asked me wistfully if I didn't agree that such letters would be welcomed and appreciated.

Everyone knew this was a war of self-defense. We felt we were on the battlefront, even though we were not facing the fire. We knew Jewish destiny was at stake.

Edith Kepes

Attending Anesthesiologist at Montefiore Hospital Medical Center, New York City; Associate Professor, Anesthesiology, Albert Einstein Medical College. Interviewed in New York by Geoffrey Wigoder, February 1974.

On Monday, which was the third day of the war, when I got to my hospital, I called up the Chief of Surgery and asked him whether a team was going to be formed, and whether we would be going to Israel. He said that he had just come from the Chairman's meeting, and the Director of the Hospital would allow anybody who wished to go if he could be spared, and encouraged all of us to do so. And he put down my name as one of the volunteers who was willing to go.

Q. How was it organized here?

A. The Chief of Orthopedic Surgery, Ed Lieberman, was in daily telephone contact with Hadassah. He has worked there every year. And by the end of the week, they asked for orthopedic surgeons, plastic surgeons and anesthesiologists. So it was my specialty that got me to Israel. Sunday morning Mrs. Matzkin called my home and expressed need for three top anesthesiologists. I was able to recommend one other. We arrived at Hadassah Hospital in Jerusalem the next day and got down to work the following morning at 8 o'clock. We worked on two shifts—12 hours each—from 8 to 8.

There are nine operating rooms, and they were working twenty-four hours a day, as long as the war was on. In the mornings we took care of those wounded who had already had their emergency treatment on arrival because no war wound is ever closed immediately, even if it's a very minor wound. Because of the battle conditions, the wounds are badly infected, and unless they are treated for four or five days openly with anti-biotics and fluids and the rest, they do not heal properly. Every single wounded soldier has to have two operations—first, cleaning the wound, and then closing it. This is called a "delayed primary closure." In the morning we did all these delayed primary closures, and we got through around 2-3 o'clock. By that time, the helicopter or ambulance arrived with the fresh wounded from the day's battle, and then we started again around 4 P.M. and worked right through the night. After the cease-fire the day became a shorter one.

Q. How did the soldiers react to you being a volunteer from abroad? Did they realize this?

A. First, they were very impressed and every soldier spoke English. I do not speak any Hebrew. I introduced myself and told them I did not speak Hebrew and that I'm a volunteer from New York. They thanked me, and I thanked them for saving Israel, and I was very impressed how brave they were—not a single complaint, not a whimper. I found the whole experience a very trying one emotionally. Really I was not prepared to see these young, healthy boys mutilated and wounded. I've been in medicine many, many years, and in an operating room all my adult life, but this was really very special.

Q. Were there other volunteers in Hadassah?

A. Yes, there were people from the United States; then from France, three very nice young doctors who were in the last year of training, and they used their vacation to come over to Israel and to volunteer.

Q. Did you meet any other volunteers who came or were elsewhere in the country?

A. Well, one of the most interesting persons I spoke to was Dr. Marav. He's a resident in training at Montefiore Hospital in Cardiac Surgery. He has been here with his family from Israel for some years, and he immediately went back. And he was stationed in Sinai. I spoke to him and his report was very interesting; the efficiency with which the medical profession was prepared for war was really impressive. He told us that of the 2,000 soldiers who reached that hospital alive, only four did not make it out. They arrived at Hadassah with the most fantastic lifesaving operations down there, and he told us that once, when he ran out of some test tubes, he called up the Chief Surgeon at Montefiore Hospital to say that he needed some test tubes, and in twenty hours they had been sent from New York to Sinai.

Q. Were there any volunteers among the nurses?

A. Yes. There was a Scotch girl who came over, she was not Jewish, and then there was another from New Jersey who shared the apartment in Hadassah with us. She left her four children and husband and came over—an operating nurse.

Q. Since your return, has there been any attempt to get the volunteers to meet together?

A. No, not really. But I have been invited to speak about my experiences—by Hadassah groups, and the American Medical Association has asked me to speak.

Since I've been back in New York, people have been asking me "How were you able to get there?" And when I left, all my family said was, "I envy you." It wasn't, "Take care of yourself, don't get killed." But it was an attitude of "I envy you that you can do something."

B'nai Amoona Congregation: High School Youth
St. Louis, Mo.

These excerpts are from a group interview conducted by Rabbi Bernard Lipnick, in February 1974, with members of his high school classes. The students spent summers at Meshek Nir Galim, near Ashdod; they lived with families, to whom they now refer as their Israeli families.

Rabbi Lipnick: What were your immediate feelings on hearing about the Yom Kippur War?

Rona Wieselman: We heard about it when we came to Shul on Yom Kippur, and we really didn't know what was going on. But when we got home and turned on the TV, we found out what was happening, and I was just so worried I couldn't believe what was happening, and I started crying. At school we tried to collect money. And I wanted to call my Israeli family that I had stayed with in the summer and I did; and it really helped me. I was just so worried about everything. And I hadn't gotten any letters from anybody in a long time, and I've just been—I don't know.

Q. You say you collected money at your public high school?

A. Yes. We have a Hebrew Club and we had a bake sale and we collected about $500. And we sold buttons and bumper stickers and all sorts of things.

Q. Did only Jews participate in this effort?

A. No. Lots of people bought things. Some people came in and said that Christians care too—I don't remember what religion they were—but something like that.

Steve Kurtz: At first we thought the war would be over very quick like in '67 and that Israel would come out all right. But things didn't start going that way. And after being in Israel a summer, all of us had an attachment to the State itself and none of us could imagine that the places that we had been at last summer wouldn't be there anymore. And to even think of the destruction of the State kind of made us sick. So we held a bike-a-thon and we collected about $300.

Q. What is a bike-a-thon?

A. Well, kids take a predetermined route they're going to ride so many miles and have people sponsor them by the mile. And so for as many miles they go they get paid so much money.

Barbie Kiem: I don't have anything specific that I can point out and say, well, I did this and I did that. But it's all still so clear in my mind. I can remember, you know, every little incident that happened because it left such an impression on me when I found out about the war. Like, I remember where I was standing and who I was with and who told me there was a little skirmish in Israel. And then I remember going home and on the way home we were listening to the radio and it kept getting bigger and bigger. And then late Tuesday, I stayed after school, and my mother picked me up and we were listening to the radio and we both started crying, 'cause it really was getting bad. So I decided to call Israel 'cause I was afraid that someone in my Israeli family was killed. And I decided that it was better for me to feel afraid than for them to be afraid by themselves. So I called anyway and they were very, very happy and cried, and it did a lot of good, I think. And they just told me, like they reassured me, and they felt so confident that everything was going to be all right and it was almost as if they were ignoring the fact that something could happen to the State of Israel, 'cause they felt so strong.

Miriam Klotzer: When I first heard about it I was really surprised, but I didn't realize what it really meant. I thought, well, okay, maybe there's a small attack or something, and it would be over with. And then they said, okay a few days. And it got to be longer and longer and it was really tough—it really got me worried and everything. And the girl I had stayed with in Israel likes to write so I got a lot of letters. And she'd like to doodle—she'd doodle a soldier at the edge of a cliff, like he was about to fall, and he says, "Who's going to push me?" And one time she wrote, "Shalom," and then she put "When?" I really felt like I was there and I wanted to be there so bad. We just kept watching and we kept waiting. It really upset me a lot and I couldn't believe it was happening, and I couldn't believe that they had started it—and it was just that all the letters I got were so positive they'd win. They just thought it would be a lot quicker than it was.

Betty Sonnenwirth: I remember on Yom Kippur when we were sitting in Shul and Rabbi Lipnick made some announcement about some attack in Israel at first I laughed because every day you hear "Oh, Sadat says he's going to wage war" and this and that, and I really didn't believe it at all. But as the day went on, there were more announcements and I started to realize that it was really happening. I think that, as it was Yom Kippur, it was one of the first times that I really remember praying in my life because I think people pray a lot more when there's a crisis in the family or when things are happening. Towards the end of the day I started thinking: Is this really happening? And my mind started wandering back to Israel. I hadn't been there in more than a year, but the feeling that you have for it is not something that you forget. And standing there praying and thinking about it I remembered being in Nir Galim and being in the synagogue there. I think that for the first week especially, I was more scared than anything . . . and I started writing letters. I would write letters every day and I got a lot of letters.

Q. How many people do you write to, Betty, in Israel?

A. Now I write to my family.

W. Your family meaning your family from Nir Galim or your real family?

A. My family from Nir Galim. And I write to I guess about four or five friends there.

Q. So there are about five or maybe six people or groups of people with whom you maintain correspondence in Israel?

A. Also my cousins—

Q. You do have blood cousins in Israel?

A. Yes.

A. Where do they live?

Betty: All over. Of course we were worried for everyone. And in Nir Galim we do have a lot of cousins there, so we were worried about them. I just got really jumpy and I couldn't really concentrate at school because you know all my friends would come up to me and say, "What's going on in Israel?" And I would just snap at them. And I'd say, 'Oh, what do you know about it?'' And I would get really upset with them and we'd have debates in all my classes about the war and it got to the point where I just thought only one thing about it and I sort of forgot that there were two sides.

Q. What do you mean?

A. Well, when we would have Arab-Israel debates in my classes I would just say Israel's one hundred per cent right no matter what happens. Everything Israel does is fine.

Q. Were there some who opposed that point of view and said that Israel was wrong?

A. There were a lot who held that point of view—a lot of my good friends.

Q. Jewish friends or Christian friends?

A. Both. I think it was mainly that they felt that the Arabs, especially the Palestinians, were not being given a fair time; that they deserved a homeland, and so on; and I found out how many people in my school and kids that I've grown up with, especially non-Jewish kids, really didn't understand what Israel was at all, or even that it existed. And I never realized it before. So I found myself constantly walking around my school explaining to people who would come up to me and say, "What is this Israel business? I don't understand it." And I would talk to them about it.

We were really scared about our cousins. One of our cousins got killed in the war. I had only met his parents, but it really touched me so deeply because of the whole story about his family. His father had left Germany in the '30s and walked to Israel, through Europe, and this was his oldest son. And I just thought, well, here's just me, Betty Sonnenwirth in the middle of St. Louis and I know so many people there and I have my own contacts—and to think that this must be happening to so many families in Israel. Everyone has just so many tragedies already in their family and it started to seem to me that I can't believe that this is happening to so many people. I think as it went on and we found out about more and more people and we heard about friends in Nir Galim who had relatives who were killed or hurt, the whole thing became so real.

Frank Yawitz: When I first heard about it, I just thought it was some kind of joke, I mean that's what I said. But as Yom Kippur wore on, I realized that this was really happening and it was a serious sort of attack and the Israelis had really been caught off guard. It made me first think, or course, of the people in Nir Galim who I knew, and I worried a lot. The next day I made a tape to send and I mailed that. But I also talked to some friends of mine who aren't Jewish and they didn't know anything about it. And it seemed, like Betty said, they didn't care at all about it. They said "Oh, so it's another war, so it's no big deal." But to me it was an emotional thing, it was something that had me thinking about it all the time. And I guess the one thing that made it most real to me was when I heard about the brother of a friend of mine from Nir Galim who was killed. I also saw that Israel was isolated among all the other countries. You'd read about what the United Nations would say and how they didn't have any cease-fire until Israel was finally starting to win. You see that Israel has only us to depend on, us Jews here. And I felt helpless, 'cause I wanted to do something but all I could do was give money so I did some of that and I tried to help with that thing at school. I wanted to telephone for a long time and so did a lot of other people in our group. And so we decided to call together. We really didn't get a whole lot of information out of the conversation. But it was just so great to be able to talk to them and know that they're ok. It was weird. We were all running around handing the phone to each other. We spoke for fifteen minutes and we all paid for it—and my Mom paid for the wrong number we got first.

Sherut La'am

Special Civilian Volunteeer Program under the auspices of the American Zionist Youth Foundation. Extracts from a group interview with Haim Ganel, Executive Director of the American Zionist Youth Foundation; Cathy Gay, Director of Long Term Programs in Israel; Sandy Rogner and Shraga Milstein. Interview by Geoffrey Wigoder in New York, February 1974.

Haim Ganel: Our general feeling is that the majority of the volunteers were those who had been to Israel before, for longer or shorter periods. But surprisingly enough, there were quite a number of people who had never been to Israel. During the orientation given prior to a departure, someone mentioned the word *aliyah,* and a boy sitting next to me asked, "What is *aliyah?*"

Cathy Gay: Part of our organized effort included a screening procedure, which is what we put into operation this time. It meant that here, and in delegated offices around the United States, an applicant had to fill out an application, had to have a complete medical form, and had to be interviewed first by a staff member and then a qualified psychologist, psychiatrist, or social worker. All of this material was then compiled in a file and sent to New York where it was screened, and each applicant was then considered individually as to whether or not he would be accepted or rejected.

Also, people called us who had absolutely no relationship to the work which we were doing. They called here to donate blood; they called here if they wanted advice; they called us—an organization geared toward youth—if they were 80 years old; they called here if they were 12 years old. We had phones set up everywhere. We had people who volunteered their services to work here as well as in offices throughout the United States—just to man phones, do mailings, all this kind of thing—there was continual motion and commotion.

Shraga Milstein: During the period of the war itself where the response, as has been explained, was very favorable, we had assistance from Jewish Federations and Jewish Community Centers, social workers, rabbis, parents— who raised, to my surprise, very little objection to children leaving while the war was on and during the period immediately after. But after the cease-dire, an entirely different atmosphere was created. It tapered off and decreased to an extent where I would say the situation became entirely different in terms of people being ready to go and so on.

Sandy Rogner: I think credit should be given on some level to a number of universities. When the program became established—and it was obvious that kids were going to Israel, kids would come to their universities and say, "First of all, I want to have a leave of absence; and secondly, is it possible to get any credit for the time period I'm spending in Israel?" And there were quite a few universities throughout the country who did give credit for participation on the program. Not as many as we'd like to think, but there were some—in the Chicago area alone there are eight different such schools.

One other thing deserves stressing. Besides the volunteers that went to Israel, there were so many people that just could not go to Israel, for all sorts of reasons—because of other commitments etc.—and we had thousands of people, who helped in various ways. There were high school students who came out at 8 A.M. the Sunday morning after the war and began to distribute flyers all over; and there were people who gave up their own jobs for days, and even weeks, to work here for no pay. And all the interviewers—the psychologists and social workers who were interviewing these kids day in and day out—were volunteering their time.

We had strange incidents. There was the phone call made to a student who had volunteered to notify him of his flight to Israel. The father picked up the phone, pretended he was the boy, and said, "I'm really sorry, I wanted to go, but I found out I just can't make it." And then, at the same time, just as we were ready to hang up, the boy picked up the phone on another extension and said "Wait, wait, I'm coming, I'm coming."

And there were cases to the contrary. I had one telephone call from a mother on the second or third day of the war when things looked really bad, just begging that we take her 16-year old son. She said, "Listen, I have to find a way for him to go. He wants to go. I want him to go. He has to go. But he's only 16—so please do something."

Q. Did you send him?

A. No, we didn't. But speaking about Jewish parents, generally it was the Jewish fathers who were against, and the Jewish mothers who were not.

Cathy Gay: The preliminary orientation sessions were great. With each flight that left, we had an orientation that same day at a hotel or motel near the airport. This started at nine o'clock in the morning and as the flight usually left not earlier than three in the afternoon, and very often late at night, we could have an all-day session. We spent the time trying to inform the kids as to what exactly was going to be happening to them. And to say that it was a place where emotions ran the gamut, would probably be to minimize. Parents came, and some kids got cold feet the last minute; and some of them, I think, ended up quite the contrary, being very inspired, and called their friends and told them to get on the next plane.

Oral Documentation: Canada

Alan Rose

Associate Executive Director, Canadian Jewish Congress.
Interviewed by Perry Cohen in Montreal, February 1974.

I think this war touched the very deepest emotions of all Jewish people in Canada. It touched the recent immigrants, it touched the survivors, it touched the Sephardim, it touched the establishment, which is very considerable, it touched the rich, it touched the poor, it touched the assimilated, it touched the intermarried, it even touched the converted. I know of people who had converted but came back, identified themselves, and offered any kind of help.

As far as the organized community is concerned, we now have the Canada-Israel Committee (CIC), composed of the Canadian Zionist Federation and the Canadian Jewish Congress. During the war, on October 11, the B'nai B'rith joined us. Therefore, we have virtually complete coverage of Canadian Jewry, because these three organizations represent the totality of the affiliated Jewish community.

Religious groups, from the left of the Reform movement to the right of the Orthodox movement, save for some very esoteric Orthodox groups like the followers of the Satmarer Rebbe, all supported our work with zeal. Indeed, one of the focal points of mobilization in support of Israel was the synagogues.

The Jewish leadership, through the CIC, provided the possibility for Jews to express fervent solidarity with Israel. This was done with mass public meetings, so that Jews could come out onto the streets or into halls in an organized and responsible way, or march to demonstrate publicly for Israel. Such events took place from coast to coast and whole communities turned out. In Winnipeg forty per cent of the community turned out in sub-zero weather for public demonstrations in support of Israel. These were not just centrally organized demonstrations. There were demonstrations in the synagogues and in the Y's and in the community councils—so that everybody had an opportunity to identify.

In the universities we had an interesting situation. Until four years ago Jews played a very important role on the campus, calling for meetings of one kind or another, whether it was Vietnam, or human rights, or support for anti-American movements, or support for progressive causes in Canada, or support for the Quebec separatists. Over the past four years it has been impossible to get anyone to a meeting. The campuses are dead—it is a phenomenon of 1971–1974. But what happened now was that the events of October touched a great number of Jews who formerly had sympathies with the left or were not involved with Zionist activities at all. I would say that most Jewish students really were not interested in Israel as an aspect of their own Jewishness. But we did get a huge student reaction to the Yom Kippur War. What concerns me is whether we will be able to sustain this interest and arouse a sense of affinity for Jewish peoplehood.

Canadian Christian reaction to the Middle East crisis is a very complex issue. One must distinguish the Catholics from the Protestants. The Catholics have been very circumspect; they haven't said very much generally, and that is because they are part and parcel of a Church which has a global policy on Israel and the Middle East.

As for the Protestants, Canada has the same problem as the United States, namely, the most progressive elements of the Protestant denominations, which were friendly towards Israel prior to 1967, now tend to be anti-Israel because they have joined the crusade of the Third World. "Israel is in the imperialist camp. Israel is the handmaiden of the United States. Israel is a capitalist society. Israel represses the Arabs." Therefore our problem has been particularly with the Protestants in Canada.

Among the Protestants, the largest community is the United Church, and its leadership until very recently has been notoriously anti-Israel. The Canadian Jewish Congress participates in an interfaith group with the Canadian Council of Churches, the central body of Protestant churches in Canada.

This group issued two very wishy-washy statements because they have pro-Arab affiliates (for instance, the Greek Orthodox Church and certain Eastern rites). Their statement irritated both Jews and Arabs. While the situation appears to be improving, there are still active anti-Israel groups within the Protestant denominations—not within the Anglicans, but within the United Church and similar groups.

Irrespective of that, a number of Christian theologians of great distinction in Toronto and elsewhere issued a statement of their own, a Christian statement of concern for Israel which received very wide support. (See Appendix III, p. 356.) This distinguished group of theologians did not speak on behalf of the Church but spoke as individual Christians, and that I think caused some embarrassment to the Canadian Council of Churches.

I think that the Yom Kippur War will have its effect for a long time on Jewish life in the Canadian community. It is sad that we have to have wars to do it, but I think the sense of solidarity that has come about since the Yom Kippur War has been profound and will last.

Thomas Mauskopf

Viennese-born student, presently in Joint Honours Program in Art History and German Literature at McGill University, Canada.

Q. When the war broke out in October where were you and what type of personal reaction did you have when you first heard the news?

A. My father was here on a visit from Vienna and I was at the Young Israel Synagogue during the Yom Kippur services. The Rabbi announced that the war broke out in Israel. At first people thought it won't be a long war. And they weren't really frightened. The next day, however, when we read in the newspapers that the Arabs crossed the Suez and the Golan Heights, which were the former borders, we really got scared. My first reaction was to go to Israel. I have two cousins who are fighting in the army; one is in the regular army and the other is a paratrooper. I was in Israel five times and I lived there for a while. My roommate, a *Lubavitcher* from Brooklyn, also wanted to go to Israel. We went to the Israel Consulate but were told to wait until Israel said it needed people. We decided to wait and meanwhile started talking about school, about how we could get out of school without losing too much and how we could get out of our apartment lease. The third day of the war we again went to the Consulate and they said again they did not need anybody. Then we went to the Jewish Agency on Greene Avenue and they told us that they need people. Now we didn't know what to do. We read that in New York there were people arranging flights to Israel and that they needed people. Then, on the fourth day, our Israeli friends got letters stating that they had to come home. We then knew it was serious since they were calling the Israeli students back to Israel. I called my parents in Vienna and asked them if I could go. They told me no, they were afraid, I should wait, I shouldn't risk a year, it wasn't so bad, and how can I help, etc., etc. So we waited until the war was over. The brother of my best friend, a paratrooper, was killed in a battle on the other side of the Suez Canal. My friend went to Israel to look after things and my roommate also went to Israel on the first day of the cease-fire. We tried to get money to go to Israel. We both had no money. We went to the Jewish Agency to try and get help but they said they could only help us if we signed for a whole year. But, to sign for a year means losing a year of University, which is pretty bad because it's hard to pick up again.

Q. Why did you want to go to Israel?

A. First of all, I thought the situation was pretty bad and I thought they would need everybody to help in the fighting. It was a very emotional reaction because I knew my fighting would not help them very much. Then, there were economic reasons. When the war was over the situation was really bad in Israel economically. They needed workers. We didn't know how long the soldiers would have to stay in the army and how long the situation would remain as it is. I called one of my friends in Israel who lives on a kibbutz and he said they needed people desperately to pick the fruit and nobody was there to do it because all the kids were in the army.

Q. But what draws you, personally, to Israel?

A. I was born in Austria but I feel my country is Israel. I would like to live there later. I have no patriotic feelings towards Austria but I do feel that Israel is the mother country of every Jew. I feel that every Jew has an obligation to help Israel when she is in need and I think everybody knows that as long as Israel exists the Jews will have somewhere to go and have security. What happened during the Second World War and the Nazi Period will never happen again because Israel will take care of her own, and Israel is the only place where Jews can feel secure their whole life. This is why I feel we all have to help Israel to continue to exist. I do not think that money is enough.

Q. While you were here did you or your friends do anything special in terms of what you can do here to participate in the struggle and to help?

A. As soon as I found out that I couldn't go to Israel, I tried to find out what I could do here. I think it was the fourth day of the war that we here at McGill Hillel decided we had to do something. There was an ad in the newspaper put in by Arab students announcing a demonstration for the Palestinians and the Arab side and against the Israel aggression. We *had* to tell the students at McGill that the war was a result of Arab aggression and that Israel is not imperialist. So we organized a demonstration in front of the student union at McGill with Myer Bick, National Executive Director of the Canada-Israel Committee, as speaker and although we had hoped for more people to attend it wasn't bad because quite a few people got involved. Then there was a group called *Tsdakah,* organized by Robert Wise the Social Leader of Vanier Hillel, which worked on fund raising for Israel. They held a rally in front of the Y.M.H.A. which was pretty good. There were about three thousand people, and a substantial sum was raised. Then we went to the Shar Hashomayim Synagogue. On the evening before there was a mass rally at the Queen Elizabeth Hotel. I fhen wrote a letter to WUJS (World Union of Jewish Students) to organize international demonstrations to take place throughout Europe on the same day, but by the time I got an answer the war was over.

Q. Would you say that prior to the war you agreed with

Israeli policies in relation to the Arab countries?

A. I believe the biggest problem is the Palestinian problem. If this question is settled, there will be a way to get peace. I know it's not Israel's fault. Arabs created the problem but accused Israel of doing it. I do think that Israel did not really try to settle the problem. I know if they start to talk directly with the Palestinians it will be a big step closer to peace.

Q. Do you think Israel explains its policies properly and effectively to the public?

A. I have the personal feeling that Israel tries to explain why they have to keep the Golan Heights or Sharm el Sheikh, and why there is a Palestinian problem. The Israelis say that they want to talk to the Palestinians and to the Arab countries but they do not want to talk through other people. On one thing I do not agree with Israel—its propaganda. The Arabs, with the help of the Russians, have very good propaganda now, especially in the socialist countries in Europe, such as Sweden, Germany and Austria. I think the youngsters there sympathize with the Arabs, because they have very effective propaganda. What about the Jews from the Arab countries, such as Egypt, Syria? Nobody talks about them even though they are in the same situation as the Palestinians. Just read the *McGill Daily* and you'll find hundreds of letters on the poor Palestinians, and no answers. I am sure if people wrote about it, they would print it.

Q. Why do you think Jewish students don't write to the *Daily?* Is it that they don't care? Is it that they are apathetic? Or, is it that they don't have the information?

A. They don't agree. I know they don't like it and I have heard many people say, "I'm going to write a letter." Some people wrote. We had a working circle here and we tried to write articles and letters and propaganda but it fell apart. I think it's a kind of apathy and a kind of laziness, too.

Q. How did the war affect you personally?

A. It made me think that I had to do more for Israel. I will finish my studies, then go over and try to work there.

Q. What about your contemporaries? Do you think this has influenced them the same way?

A. Probably after the war it did. But you know time goes by and people get into the same thing again—school and tests, etc.—and they forget about it. While the threat is there they realize how much Israel needs them and how much they need Israel but then they get back to everyday life and forget about it.

Oral Documentation: Latin America

Yaakov Tsur

World Chairman of the Keren Kayemet Le-Yisrael (Jewish National Fund). Excerpts from a written statement and oral interview with Haim Avni, January 1974.

On Thursday, October 4, I was requested by the Israel Foreign Ministry to lead the official Israeli delegation to the inauguration ceremony of President Juan Perón which was to take place on October 11 in Buenos Aires. I was requested to undertake this mission because I served as Israel's first Ambassador to Argentina during the years 1949–1953 and during this period I developed friendly relations with Perón. I renewed this friendship when I visited him in exile in Madrid in August 1973. I had a long talk with him shortly before he left for Buenos Aires where he was elected to the Presidency.

Immediately on arrival in the Argentinian capital, it became clear to me that reports on the Middle East situation reaching that country were extremely sparse and completely one-sided. Representatives of all the TV and radio stations, and of the leading newspapers met me upon arrival at the airport and the information I was able to give them was in fact the first reliable account of events from the Israeli side to reach them. Jerusalem had issued only short restricted official bulletins and the newspapers and the other communication media based their detailed reports on information sent by the large telegraphic agencies from Cairo, Damascus and especially from Beirut. The public was given a picture of a resounding Arab victory. Despite this, I found that my Jewish friends were in an optimistic mood and there appeared to be far less concern among the Jewish community than during the Six Day War in 1967. From the onset of this war, the Jews believed that this time too, as was the case six years ago, Israel had not revealed the extent of her victories in order to stave off the

304

intervention of the great powers. The Jewish community placed no faith in the reports coming in from the Arab capitals, even when they were correct (for example, they did not take as serious the Syrian announcement of the capture of the outpost on Mount Hermon), since they had become accustomed to the boasting of the Arabs.

Once the reports of heavy battles on the Golan Heights and in Sinai were confirmed, there was general concern and also personal anxiety. Many families in Buenos Aires have children in Israel and many of the men took part in the fighting. Fathers and mothers were worried about their sons' welfare. Telephone contact with Israel was most difficult and often people had to wait twenty-four hours for a telephone call. Anyone who knew a high official in the post office tried to use his influence to get through as quickly as possible. In several homes, families spent anxious hours sitting by the telephone waiting for a call to their sons. And when the reports of the first victims came in (the first notices to inform two families of their loss were received at the Embassy on the fifth day of the war and the families were notified personally by the Ambassador) the community began to realize the seriousness of the situation.

Among the Jewish youth there were large numbers of Peronist supporters. Moreover, following the rise of the New Left, the Jewish leftists at the universities took a more violent anti-Israel stand and accused it of persecuting the Arabs, of oppressing the Palestinians. Even certain elements among the Zionist youth groups (Hashomer Hatzair and Habonim) were attracted to these ideologies and publicly expressed criticism of Israeli government policy. A few weeks prior to the war, left-wing Zionist young people organized disturbances at a large mass rally held to mark Israel's 25th anniversary.

With the outbreak of the war, their attitude underwent a radical change. This was caused by the fact that many envisaged the State of Israel as being in great danger. Large numbers of young people expressed their identification with Israel. Many of them realized that the Zionists were not oppressors nor were the Arabs oppressed. The sudden attack by the Arabs shocked the youth, just as it shocked the adults.

Members of the youth federations and university students who had not previously supported the Zionist youth movement participated in pro-Israel activities. Their main complaint was against local Zionist leaders who, they claimed, had not succeeded in leading local Jewry towards significant acts of solidarity with Israel. The leadership was also accused of preaching *aliyah* while failing to set a personal example.

The large newspapers printed advertisements expressing solidarity with Israel; these were signed by artists, writers and leading professors at the universities. There were no expressions of anti-Semitism or provocation against Israel, except for one most interesting case. On the day of President Perón's inauguration, leaflets were thrown into the crowd bearing the imprint of an extreme leftist wing of the Peronists called "Montoñeros." The leaflet was extremely strong in its wording and contained an attack against Israel and charges against the Jews of Argentina written in an anti-Semitic style. The leaflet upset the Jewish community, but a few days later an issue of the Montoñeros' official newspaper carried an item entitled "Provocation," denying that the leaflet had been published by their organization. Later it was learned that this leaflet had been a forgery, and was in fact published by the Arab League's Buenos Aires office using the name of a Peronist group to create the impression that the ruling party was anti-Jewish and against the State of Israel. Acts of this nature had occurred on previous occasions.

During the period I spent in Buenos Aires there was a feeling that Israel's information services had not fulfilled their function. Even the Embassy received only limited reports and these were couched in very vague terms. The organizational weakness of the local Zionist organization was also apparent. An emergency council was set up with representatives of all the Jewish organizations in Buenos Aires, but this institution proved to be unwieldy and was unable to control the situation effectively. The individual Jew turned out to be more effective than the Jewish leadership.

José Yehuda Moskovits

President of *She'erit Hapleta* (Holocaust Survivors) Organization in Argentina. Interviewed by Moshe Nes-El in
Jerusalem, December 1973.

About 9:00 P.M. after Yom Kippur services, representatives of all institutions got together to discuss what we could
do the next day on behalf of Israel. There were people from all
organizations—they came to the DAIA building without
having to be notified.

Q. Ashkenazim and Sephardim?

A. Certainly, the Sephardim participated at all levels.

Q. And the Bundists and the Communists?

A. The Bundists did not participate as an organized
group but I saw Bundists participating in the demonstrations
on behalf of Israel. They did not participate as such in that
Saturday night meeting. On the other hand, the Communist
group corresponding to Maki in Israel, who had broken away
from the ICUF, took part in that meeting and in all subsequent
activities.

Q. What was on the agenda at that meeting?

A. It was entirely devoted to what action should be
taken. It was not a normal evening and we acted upon our own
initiative. It was decided to hold a big demonstration the next
day; we discussed an emergency appeal; and we spoke about
public influence on press, radio and television. The atmosphere was tense—but this was because of the war and not
because of any inner dissension. We got news via Arab radio
stations and these were not encouraging. There was little
discussion and the decisions were unanimous. The first
decision was to rally everyone for the demonstration on the
next day and to make great effort that this should be a success.
The different organizations undertook to rally their members
and immediately after this general meeting, the individual
organizations held their own meetings, beginning after
midnight. My group—the *She'erit Hapleta*—met until 4 A.M.
and everyone made up a list of 100–200 members, whom we
called in the morning. The demonstration itself was held in

the afternoon in the Libertad synagogue and, apart from the adults, there were over 10,000 youngsters and all this without any publicity in the press (because it was too late to get it in) or on the radio. It was like an Israeli call-up!

Q. Were there activities among the non-Jews?

A. DAIA worked among the non-Jews to get them to sign declarations for publication in the press and during the first days it was not easy. Some of us were given special assignments. I was asked to speak with one of the leading deputies. He received me very sympathetically—"My dear Moskovits" and all that sort of thing. But all the sympathy and interest was of no use when it came to asking him to sign. Then it was the line of his party that determined his actions. We came to a sort of compromise—that he could write a letter to our *She'erit Hapleta* organization and mention the Holocaust (he was once in Warsaw after the war) and would somehow mention Israel's fight in a meaningful way. It arrived after the cease-fire. Meanwhile, DAIA had been in touch with both the Peronists and the Radicalists. The Radicalists put out some sort of a statement calling for direct negotiations without the Powers and speaking against the war. It could not be called a completely pro-Israel document. But we survivors of the Holocaust placed a big notice in the papers and this moved priests, politicians and journalists. Several hundred non-Jews came forward to sign pro-Israel declarations. I must stress that their initial hesitation was not caused by any anti-Israel feeling, but they were wary of identification.

Haim Finkelstein

Head of the Jewish Agency Education and Culture Department. Interviewed about visit to Paraguay by Moshe Nes-El in Jerusalem, December 1973.

The main identification maintained by Jews in Latin America, especially in small communities, is with Israel. Without Israel, they have no spiritual strength. Even tiny remote communities devoid of all basic cultural activities—either religious or secular—are sustained by the recognition that they have Israel and that they are inseparably linked to the State. They feel themselves as belonging to the State and to the Jewish people—even though for various reasons they cannot come to Israel. They see themselves as the "home front" of the State of Israel. So it is understandable that whatever happens in Israel is close to their hearts. It is not the physical distance but the spiritual feeling that is relevant.

I visited various countries in South America. One of the smallest communities was in Paraguay. There I went to the Jewish school, and when I was there they were holding a memorial meeting for Israel's soldiers who had fallen in the war. All the pupils, including the non-Jews, attended. Ninety-five per cent of the pupils are Jewish. Most of the teachers are not Jewish. The pupils spoke, some in Hebrew, some in Spanish, and expressed their feelings so movingly that I felt tears upon my cheeks as the pupils at this assembly read the letters they had written to soldiers at the front in Israel or to other children in Israel or to members of their family in Israel. Many of them have relatives in Israel, and this family connection is more important than any ideology.

This gathering of children and the way they expressed themselves affected me deeply. In the entire school there are three Jewish teachers—the director and his wife (who come from Israel) and another teacher (who comes from Argentina). These teachers succeeded in developing a feeling of identification with Israel among all the pupils.

Oral Documentation:
South Africa and Australia

Ezra Shapiro

World Chairman of Keren Hayesod—United Israel Appeal.
He visited South Africa during the Yom Kippur War.
Interviewed in Jerusalem by Moshe Nes-El, November
1973.

The reaction of the South African Jewish community
was total and all-embracing. There were people who
abandoned their work for days and weeks to carry on the work
of the *Magbit* (Israel Campaign), many even slept in the Keren
Hayesod offices. The bookkeeping operation was a formidable
task and some forty accountants gave up days and nights to do
this job. There was an absolutely universal response on the
part of the Jewish community.

I was asked if I would address the parents of a group of
high school children, who at the time were in Israel. They
have a fine all-day high school in Johannesburg, the King
David School, and at that time the school had about one
hundred and fifty pupils studying in Jerusalem. The parents of
these children were concerned about their safety. Some of
them had urged their children to come home. All of the
children in Jerusalem answered, "We're not coming home—-
we're staying here in Jerusalem." The parents wanted to hear
from me about the situation, and wanted advice as to what
they should do. I told them that our policy was not to
determine the matter collectively, but where any parents
wanted their children home and the children agreed to go, we
would help them reach their respective destinations. I spoke
very frankly about the situation at this very somber, tense
meeting. I stated that in Jerusalem we felt secure; nevertheless, there was some element of danger. One could
never know whether Jordan would enter the war, and then of
course the situation in Jerusalem might be more serious. When

I finished, I invited any parent who wanted help to bring his child home, to say so; not a single one of them asked to do so. There was a great deal of emotion and many tears welled up in the eyes of these parents; this was only natural, but the reaction was positive and unanimous.

The significance of our coming from Israel to Jews in the Diaspora, during this period, was to serve as the medium whereby one could transmit what was happening in the country, while, at the same time, they could transmit to the *yishuv*, through us, their unbelievably strong, universal sense of identification with what was going on in Israel. Identification is really a weak description of this manifestation. It was really the transmission of a sense of oneness, rather than a matter of partnership, since partnerships can be terminated at will, very readily. There was the feeling that if anything happened in Israel they would be affected and that their own lives were at stake. This desire to be so involved in what was happening in Israel and this feeling of total solidarity was felt in nearly every country, in varying degrees; but I felt it to the fullest in South Africa.

John Levi

Rabbi, Temple Beth Israel of Melbourne, Australia; member of Executive of the Victorian Jewish Board of Deputies. Interviewed by Geoffrey Wigoder in Jerusalem, January 1974.

In 1973, we had a new government in Australia—a Labor government, which means a Social Democratic government. The Prime Minister, Gough Whitlam, is a very competent and intelligent man, with great ambitions to make Australia a force in the Third World. His approach to the Middle East crisis was completely new. He did not support Israel, as all Australian governments have done to date. Whitlam decided that Australia had to be neutral, "evenhanded." His government appointed an ambassador to Saudi Arabia after the Yom Kippur War and a number of very disturbing trends have emerged. Government officials have started to refuse visas to Israeli generals and others who wished to come to the community for fund-raising purposes. They have delayed visas for Israelis coming to participate in cultural events. They have suspended negotiations going on for reciprocal landing rights between El Al and the Australian International Airlines, Qantas. And there have been a number of disappointing things as, for example, when the leaders of the Australian Jewish community, the Board of Deputies, wanted to interview Mr. Whitlam, he put them off repeatedly; and finally when he saw them it was an unsatisfactory interview. In other words, for the first time in its history the Australian Jewish community faces a government that is not sympathetic. It's been unpleasant.

Q. But Mr. Whitlam is only one man in the party. What about the rest of the party?

A. No. He is the dominating force. Without him, the party wouldn't have come to power. He was able to present the Labor Party as a progressive, educated force, in a middle-class constituency. And he's an outstanding lawyer. Without his presence the Labor Party would not have been elected by middle-class Australians.

Q. What are the traditional Jewish voting patterns in Australia?

A. Traditionally, as everywhere else, Jews have tended to vote more left than their economic status would warrant. I'm quite sure that the Australian Jewish community in the last election voted largely for Mr. Whitlam. And there were pictures in the *Jewish News* of Whitlam speaking to Golda Meir and smiling, and so forth. The past president of the Executive Council of Australian Jewry spoke out very vigorously and predicted that Whitlam was going to be anti-Israel, but since he is very much a right-winger people just discounted what he said. So what happened came as a shock to those in the community. And it wasn't just the general Jewish population that was surprised. It was the leaders as well. Australian Jewry is divided into two groups—Sydney and Melbourne. The Sydney group had no traditional Labor Party supporters. And so it took a while for the trend to make an impression upon the leaders of Australian Jewry.

Q. How did the community react in its assistance for Israel?

A. Quite differently from the Six Day War. I think a lot of people did some choosing. In the Six Day War it was sort of valiant to be supporting Israel and everybody did, anyway. In the Yom Kippur War, Jews had to choose and they suddenly found themselves out of step with the government and with many other people. It was a different kind of reaction.

In my congregation, I even noticed it within the generations. I got the list of all members and we·went through it for donations. Then we had a meeting of our teenagers—a kind of mini-appeal—and I know that a lot of young people gave more money than their parents! Some of the parents, very assimilated and not particularly pro-Israel, gave token sums of money, and were outstripped by their 17-and 18-years olds who would not have known how much, or how little, money their parents had given. We raised $5,000–$6,000 from the kids; we thought we'd raise about $1,000. So it has been a traumatic time for us.

Q. Were there any other reactions among the youth? Was there a large number of volunteers who wished to come to Israel?

A. Yes, but not as many as in the Six Day War. Then of course there had been weeks of preparation for what happened, and when it did happen, the Zionist headquarters was jammed with volunteers, Jewish and non-Jewish.

Of course, the Yom Kippur War for us wasn't on Yom Kippur. We got the news the day after Yom Kippur. For us, the trauma of it having happened in synagogue on Yom Kippur didn't exist. And then there was the delay of the news and so on. Some people knew about it the day after Yom Kippur, but nobody really knew how big it was until Monday.

Q. It was almost a Sukkot war for you.

A. It practically was.

Isidore Magit

President of the Federal Keren Hayesod of Australia.
Interviewed by Joel S. Fishman in Jerusalem, January
1974.

The community was petrified by the fear that Israel was
not ready. Probably this fear brought some positive reactions
in the sense that there was an outpouring of communal
emotions, not so much in the form of public meetings of
support, but in urging the leadership into action to assist
Israel as quickly as possible. There was a great fear that Israel
would suffer tremendous losses and would lose much more
territories than it finally did. It was a general fear for the fate of
Israel and its people.

Q. Would you tell us about news sources?

A. Australia had very good news coverage, particularly
during the war. Generally, there's not very much written about
Israel unless something happens of international consequence. However, during the war, the coverage was coming
through America, through England, but mainly from Cairo.
The news from Tel Aviv was much more sketchy and scanty.
The Jews in Australia developed the knack of listening every
hour to the radio, as Israelis do, and I don't think there was a
Jewish family which did not listen every hour on the hour to
the news—and the bulletins usually started off with the news
about the war in the Middle East.

Q. I'm interested to know about the Jews and the wider
Jewish community in Australia.

A: I think that the pattern of reaction throughout
Australia was the same, whether it was in Melbourne, Sydney
or in smaller Jewish communities. The reaction of Jews was
outstanding in the sense of its explosive patriotism and
affiliation. It was not only the Zionist Jews. It was the Jewish
youth in general who stormed the communal centers—both in
Melbourne and Sydney—and many of them offered their
services to go to Israel. Most of them were ready to drop their
jobs for whatever time was required. We had more United
Israel Appeal meetings for Jewish youth than ever before, and

we had hundreds and hundreds of young people coming whom we have never seen or heard of before.

Q: How is the relationship between the generations?

A: Well, like anywhere else, there is a gap. We also have had our share of dissent as far as even Israel is concerned. In all universities, there are groups of Communist-oriented Jews, and there are even some extremists who participate in what is known to be an al-Fatah movement within the university. This is numerically insignificant, although it is very vociferous. But this was completely subdued during the period of the war. Their voices were completely unheard— even the left-oriented, Communist-sympathetic, Arab-sympathetic Jews came and offered their services to Israel when the fate of Israel, as they felt at that moment, was at stake.

Q: Did you have the experience this time as in 1967 that Jews "were known to come out of the wordwork"?

A: Not only did we have the same experience—we had much greater experience this time and the impact was very much greater. Whilst normally only 53 per cent of the Jewish population participate in the United Israel Appeal, in 1967 we had 71 per cent participation. In the October war, we reached 94 per cent of the known Jewish population, which is an absolutely unheard-of figure. We have reached the maximum that we can hope for.

Oral Documentation: Western Europe

Alex Friedman

Former Chairman, Jewish Youth Organization of Austria.
Interviewed in Vienna (in German), December, 1973.

The attitude of the Austrian Jewish community was a special one, when compared to other Jewish communities in the world. During the Yom Kippur War we were still in a state of shock caused by the previous week's Schoenau affair, when Austrian premier Kreisky yielded to the demand of Arab terrorists to close down the transit camp for Jews leaving the U.S.S.R. This meant that we now suffered from the consequences of two shocks, the first caused by the attitude of the Austrian government toward Israel and the Jews, and the second by the realization that Israel's victory in the Middle East was not to be achieved easily.

Q: One of the highlights of the reaction to the Yom Kippur War was the declaration of support for Israel signed by prominent Austrians. This caused some particularly sharp reactions on the part of the Arabs. How do you explain this? Did the personalities of the Austria-Israel society who signed this declaration carry so great a political and official weight, or was this simply a general Arab reaction to any public pro-Israel statement?

A: I believe that the reaction of the Arabs in this case was particularly sharp because the personalities who signed this declaration were very well known, including presidents of the National Council, Trade Union officials, as well as personalities prominent in Austria's cultural and political life. Naturally this upset the Arabs. Evidently they did not expect this attitude, particularly as they had already threatened to use the oil weapon.

Q: Would you consider this pro-Israel reaction of political personalities as a consciously intended counterweight to the anti-Israel Schoenau stand? Or, do you believe that this stems from personal pro-Israel emotions?

A. One must remember that the Schoenau decision was not unanimously accepted by many leading figures. At least at first, the decision concerning Schoenau was made by the Chancellor and by him alone; others, eventually, followed suit, especially as public opinion turned out to be anti-Israel. The fact that well-known personalities signed the pro-Israel declaration is nothing new as these people had previously taken a pro-Israel stand. I would say that their attitude toward Israel has not changed. I do not believe that a counterweight to the Schoenau Affair had been consciously planned—it simply worked out that way.

So far as official Austrian policy is concerned, I believe it is dictated almost exclusively by the interests of the state, whatever the attitude of public opinion, leading personalities, or the mass media may be. I believe that one should probably expect that future actions will be decisively influenced by Bruno Kreisky's opinions, as well as by the Trade Unions and industrial leadership.

Q. How did Christians in general react to the Mideast conflict? In particular, what was the reaction of the Catholic Church, by far the most important church in Austria?

A. Officially the Catholic Church did not take any stand, except for the expression of humanitarian views, e.g. one should put an end to all this bloodshed, etc. As in 1967, the Catholic Church did not express any opinion. There were no open anti-Semitic manifestations. Anti-Semitism found expression in a typically Austrian way, that is, through remarks by the man in the street. The Schoenau affair brought anti-Semitic prejudices to the surface. It has to be stated that the Church has little influence on Austrian anti-Semitism except perhaps in rural regions, which are, however, so far as the Jews are concerned, of no special importance, as the Jews live in the big cities, mainly in Vienna.

Q. The majority of the Austrian students has been said to be probably pro-Israel. How do you explain this attitude?

A. I believe that the majority of the pro-Israel students should be evaluated in the same way as the philo-Semites in Austria. They have not, for the most part, adopted pro-Israel positions out of any positive motivations. Many students are pro-Israel, simply because they do not like the Arabs—in other words: another form of racism. Yet others again are pro-Israel,

318 THE YOM KIPPUR WAR *Israel and the Jewish People*

because they are philo-Semitic, as for them this is one and the same thing. There is no doubt that the place which the Israeli question and the Mideast conflict has occupied in the mass media during the past years has played an important role. The coverage by the mass media was predominantly pro-Israel and this has undoubtedly influenced the students, as well as the rest of the population. The students and the rest of the Austrians have adopted the same attitude as the mass media, even if the attitude of the students was somewhat more critical, most likely because of their higher intellectual level.

Q. Would you say that the Jewish reaction was similar to that of the Six Day War or have other elements emerged?

A. The fear of re-emerging anti-Semitism—which was felt quite distinctly during the Schoenau affair—had, undoubtedly, a definite bearing on the attitude of the Jews during this war. The fact that the Jews realized how isolated they were in the midst of a non-Jewish world played an important part as far as the intensity of their link with Israel was concerned. Add to this, the fact that for the first time in a long period, one felt that Israel was in real danger, that Israel was the only real ally of the Jews in the world, and that inversely the Jews were Israel's only ally—all these considerations played a considerable and possibly a decisive role.

Raya Jaglom

President, WIZO (Women's International Zionist Organization). Interviewed in Jerusalem by Devorah Sussman, November 1973.

Some of our members really thought that it was the end. We had an outpouring of letters, of cables, of telephones. One telephone call which moved me more than anything else during the Yom Kippur War came from Hong Kong, where I had organized a group in May when I visited there. At the time I asked how many Jews there were, and they told me two hundred. I said I would like to talk to the women, and that's how the group came into being. On the second day of the Yom Kippur War, I received a phone call from Hong Kong. They

said, "We want to do something for you. Can we send you blood?" I said, "We give our own."

Their whole outpouring of sympathy was for Israel, their dedication to and solidarity with Israel was unbelievable. Whether from New Zealand, or Europe, or South America, the women who called, were really fearful about Israel's fate. It's good for us to know we have such an army of women behind us.

Q. You were in Switzerland and France. Did you notice differences?

A. Yes. Jewish communities get very assimilated to their surroundings and to the ways of life of their countries. So obviously the Swiss Jewish community is very Swiss-minded. And the French Jewish community is very French-minded.

In Switzerland during the Yom Kippur War they raised an enormous amount of money, I think three times more than during the Six Day War. My women colleagues in Switzerland told me that the sympathy was somewhat less this time in the non-Jewish community. Some non-Jewish Swiss donated funds, but the sympathy in the street was not as great as in 1967. For one thing, Europe felt the shortage of oil. Cars could not be used on Sunday in Switzerland and the heating was lowered in all housing. Maybe they are really tired of hearing about Israel and its problems. After all, non-Jews don't react exactly the same way as Jews. Of course there are some who are still very much with us, like those in the Swiss-Israel Association. But in the street the picture is not the same as it used to be.

Let us make another comparison. Years ago when WIZO had its campaign to sell oranges in the street for a Swiss-sponsored agricultural school in Israel, Nachlat Yehuda, the mayor of Zurich sold oranges in the street for WIZO. Today, that can't happen. There are some shops in Geneva which informed my colleagues they would not sell oranges for Israel anymore. Why? Because of pressure from the Arabs in Geneva and Lausanne.

In France, WIZO is the best organized Zionist movement. I felt and saw what it means to have 20,000 strong WIZO members when I attended a meeting there. They did a marvelous job of inviting the presidents of non-Jewish organizations in Paris, such as Le Bureau de l'Europe, a platform for conferences on all subjects concerning Europe, and the non-Jewish mothers' organization in France. There were important professional women present and they wanted to hear about Israel, about the war, and about the women's work during the war. As an outcome of this meeting, they decided on their own initiative to hold a public meeting for a non-Jewish audience to explain Israel's position in the Middle East. One of the non-Jewish women said to me, "Please don't consider us ex-friends. We, the French people, are friends of Israel. It is the government which has a different attitude." To hear this said in public was reassuring indeed.

Abraham Soetendorp

Rabbi of Amsterdam Reform Community. Interviewed in
Amsterdam, November 1973, by Rabbi Jacob Soetendorp.

The small Jewish community of Holland reacted to the news of Yom Kippur as one person. Before the outbreak of the war, two events had been planned: an emergency demonstration against the closing of Schoenau Castle and a teach-in to protest the situation of the Jews in Russia. Both had been set for October 7th, and in order to make the maximum impact on government circles, I had contacted representatives of the various political parties, who had agreed to appear on that Sunday to protest the closure of Schoenau.

When Jewish leaders met on Yom Kippur night to consider the demonstration for the next day, we decided to inform the political leaders that we would understand if they withdrew their support, because we knew the meeting would be one expressing solidarity with Israel in its hour of need. But these men, who represented all the political parties in Holland, decided to join us in protest against the aggression of the Arab countries and I feel this may have had an effect on the attitude expressed by the Dutch government the next day. Fifteen hundred members of the Jewish community rallied to one meeting on Sunday and were unanimous in voicing a feeling of brotherhood with Israel and in backing Israel policy. At that time, there were no critical voices. A second gathering attended by the Minister of Defense drew a crowd of five thousand.

I tried to contact members of church groups, with whom I had been in touch in the past, to get a pro-Israel statement from them. No group would make an official statement, although many individuals expressed support of Israel. After two weeks we suddenly heard that the churches were going to announce general support of both sides. All church groups, Protestant and Catholic, would be asked to support all victims of the war—Arab and Israeli soldiers. I felt that two weeks after the outbreak of the war the first official reaction from the Church should be more pro-Israel. I was not against giving help to the victims—every victim has to be helped. But this action expressed a kind of neutrality.

The rabbis of Holland then sent a letter to the church groups articulating their horror and shock at the fact that churches had not spoken out against aggression. We condemned them for not castigating the aggressor nations. We could not understand why the Church, always promoting movements toward peaceful understanding, had failed to speak out against massive, calculated aggression, and instead, by its silence almost implied that it condoned such acts. We said that past statements about the relationship between Judaism and Christianity no longer seemed very plausible Finally, we condemned an attitude of neutrality in such a situation.

Individual Protestant leaders replied with expressions of solidarity, admitting that they had not done enough to make their true sentiment public, that Judaism and Israel could not be separated. And finally, the Protestant churches issued a formal statement of strong solidarity with Jews and Israel.

The Catholics, on the other hand, never announced support for Israel, but spoke favorably about the fight of the Palestinians. I tried repeatedly to reach an outstanding Catholic leader; his assistant answered that he was trying his best to get any statement from him. Eventually the assistant called one night at half past twelve to tell me, somewhat ashamed, that he hadn't been able to get a positive reaction. This made us wonder about the meaning of Catholic "neutrality."

Oral Documentation: View from Jerusalem

Mordecai Bar-On

Member, Jewish Agency Executive; Head, World Zionist Organization's Youth and Pioneering Department. Interviewed by Aharon Kedar in Jerusalem, February 1974.

Rather than describe my experiences with youth groups in different countries, I prefer to suggest a typology of Jewish youth and their reactions to the war.

First of all, there are those young people who were already committed before the Yom Kippur War. When I say "committed," I mean committed to their Jewishness because I do not think that in the Diaspora there are many who are committed to Israel except by way of their Jewish commitment—just as there are very few devoted to their Jewishness who are not thereby devoted to Israel. A person who is committed may be critical of Israel and may differ on certain issues, but he essentially sees Israel as an integral aspect of the panorama of his Jewishness. All those whose Jewish ties were strong before October, became even more dedicated to their ethnic loyalties as a result of the war. The shock and the tension deepened their identification.

The second group is the uncommitted—and these are the overwhelming majority. Although it is difficult to be statistically accurate, I would say that this group includes at least seventy-five per cent, and in the United States perhaps eighty-five per cent, of youth over the age of 16. In the October war, the uncommitted remained uncommitted; they did not move any further away, but they did not move closer. The affair did not touch them. In fact, from some aspects it could be said that this war gave them further reason to ignore their Jewishness. The war was a stereotype, with many casualties, with little advantages or victories to anyone, finishing in a sort of draw. Israel ended up in a state of confusion and is still licking its wounds, with internal dissension, and all the vibrations emanating from Israel are complex and frustrated.

322

All this diminishes any potential toward commitment that might have existed.

A third grouping consists of those actively opposed to the State of Israel. They are not many in number and we tend to exaggerate the phenomenon. But just as there is a minority committed to Israel, so there is a small minority opposed to Israel. These young people are highly vocal and belong to anti-Israel groups, whose significance we exaggerate because they annoy us. But Jewish youth can be found among the Trotskyists and the Maoists and similar sects, whose universalist outlook includes a hatred of Israel. And this war reinforced their animosity.

There is a fourth group—probably the smallest, consisting of young Jews committed to Jewishness but alienated from Israel. Many of them pursue Jewish studies intensively, learn Yiddish, are keenly concerned with the Holocaust, are fascinated by East European culture. Some of them teach Hebrew or are engaged in other aspects of Jewish education. This Diaspora-centricity expresses itself in various forms. Some of them seem to agree with Simon Dubnow that there have to be various Jewish centers. Then, there are Bundists for whom the Jewish center in Israel is a negative phenomenon and only impedes Jewish survival. There are others who accept the idea of Israel as the center but demand increased importance and autonomy for the Diaspora.

Following the war some of these viewpoints gained public attention. One of them—which for Israelis is shocking—is the thought that Israel might not survive for long and may be just a passing episode. Believers of this theory claim that Jewish history is one of migration, of flight from a region of oppression to a haven of safety. And they see Israel as concentrating all the Jews in one danger area, which is a major center of anti-Semitism. A further argument is that Israel's constant involvement in wars detracts from its potentiality as a spiritual center. What happens in Israel is not relevant to Diaspora survival, and therefore it is essential to protect the other alternative—Diaspora Jewry—which, according to some, is the *authentic* Judaism. Others claim that Israel's economic demands lead to a lack of funds for essential activities in the Diaspora, especially in the field of Jewish education.

This last attitude, developed largely in opposition to the enthusiasm of the Jewish establishment for Israel following the Six Day War, has been heightened by recent events. These groups are numerically small but they present us with a serious ideological challenge.

Avraham Schenker

Member of the World Zionist Organization Executive and Head of its Organization and Information Department. Interviewed in Jerusalem by Aharon Kedar, February 1974.

The Jewish Agency Organization and Information Department was in contact with communities in over thirty countries. Our first task was to feed their hunger for news and information, to keep them in the picture, to encourage them, and to assist the fund-raising activities. They were happy to get what we sent them—but they all wanted more. They wanted to know what was happening *inside* Israel—not only on the war fronts. They wanted to know about the relations between the soldiers and the home front. They wanted to know what was happening to the economy. In response, we increased and broadened the information services we were sending out daily through telex and cable. It is significant that information activity was particularly intensified in those countries where official policy was not sympathetic to Israel, such as France and Australia.

One basic fact that has affected communal attitudes is the extent of immigration to Israel since the Six Day War. About 80,000–90,000 immigrants have come from Western countries—about half of them from the U.S.—and this increased the personal interest among Western Jewry in what was happening in Israel. So many of them had a member of the family here, a neighbor, a friend, an old schoolmate. We felt this personal concern in our contacts, alongside the more abstract concern for the State of Israel, and this reaction emanated from every community with which we were in touch.

An interesting development during the Yom Kippur War was that many communities began to issue daily bulletins themselves, based on the material received from us. These were circulated in non-Jewish as well as Jewish circles. For example, on October 7, in Caracas in Venezuela—a city with about 12,000 Jews—it was announced that a meeting would be held every evening at 7 P.M. under the auspices of the Zionist Federation to impart the latest news from Israel. Without any special publicity for this service, 1,200–1,300 Jews gathered every evening to hear the news and receive instructions as to what they should do the next day on behalf of Israel. Twice a day they issued bulletins for the press and distributed them to the Jewish leadership, and to groups of Jewish students who had organized themselves to convey this information to television and radio stations, etc. One of the lessons we derived from our experience in the war is the importance of sending out "raw" information material to be adapted in each country according to its own setting and requirements. We also saw the need for long-range information planning, with greater coordination both inside Israel and abroad, with the Zionist Organization serving as the initiator.

We have a special problem in the large countries where there are scattered and often small communities—in contrast to the small countries where the Jews are often concentrated in the capital cities. In France, for example, there are Jews in over a hundred localities. Even in Australia, with its 70,000 Jews, we had to reach over twenty communities. In Sweden, the 15,000 Jews are in sixty places—ranging from half a dozen families to the large concentration in Stockholm, which was in touch with all the smaller communities throughout the war. They realized that Jews in isolated towns were hardly going to influence the course of events. But they felt it was essential to maintain this connection for the sake of their Jewish identity and identification with Israel.

As an example of what happened in countries with small communities, it is instructive to look at Scandinavia—for instance, Finland. Numerically, it is weak, but there is a communal structure and even a Jewish school. During the war, the Jews of Finland were helped by the Jews of Sweden. The latter sent two of its members to Finland and together with the local Jews organized a rally in the Community Center where Finnish Jewry expressed its support for Israel. In

Norway, where there are only 800 Jews, they also held a rally in their synagogue. The Jews of Finland and Norway realized that they were not going to be able to influence the policies of their governments—so they concentrated on fund raising and systematically organized a campaign that would reach every Jew in the country. This happened in small communities throughout the world. The Zionist Federations played a key role, often in conjunction with other organizations, such as the B'nai B'rith or women's organizations. Indeed in many instances it was felt that donors had reached their maximum contributions and the way to increase the total was to increase the number of participants in the Appeal. To this end, efforts were made to contact and enroll every known Jew. It is noteworthy that students came to the fore in fund-raising efforts for the first time during Yom Kippur—another example of the importance of fund raising on a popular level as an educational instrument to give expression for one's identification with Israel.

Daniel Singer

American day-school student describes his Bar Mitzvah in Jerusalem on Sukkot.

About a year and a half ago when my family was discussing what we should do for my Bar Mitzvah, we thought that we would have a big party in Miami. Then we got the idea to celebrate it in Israel. We had good reasons. My grandparents who live in Jerusalem and my grandparents from Miami wanted the family to be together in Israel. I had already been there and had enjoyed myself very much, and the whole event would mean more to me. Besides, my Bar Mitzvah came out on the first day of Sukkot, which is one of the *shalosh regalim,* and even though there is no Temple today, it seemed like a great idea to "go up" to Jerusalem.

I believe my Jewish education had a lot to do with my decision to have the Bar Mitzvah in Israel. After going to the Hebrew Academy of Greater Miami for eight years, I can read and write Hebrew pretty well, and I know the meaning and history of biblical places.

As the Bar Mitzvah date drew closer the excitement got greater. By Rosh Hashonah we really were excited. Then on Yom Kippur, as I walked into our synagogue, someone told me that war had broken out. I didn't believe it. Then I saw my aunt, and she said that Israel had been attacked by Egypt and Syria. I was stunned and still couldn't believe it, but during the break in the services we went home and listened to the radio.

Everyone was worried about my grandparents, aunt and uncle, cousins and friends, who were in Israel. We were afraid we wouldn't be able to go. We tried to call Israel but couldn't get through. All that night we prayed for the good of Israel. On Sunday we confirmed our tickets for Monday's flight. Finally Monday came and we all went to the airport, even though my parents' friends said not to go because of the danger. But we were not afraid for ourselves.

Once on the plane (which left after a long delay) they served what you could call a morning-dinner. And then I fell asleep. The plane was jam-packed with Israelis going back as reservists. There was a reporter on the plane and she asked if I was afraid and I answered, "Only about reading my *haftarah* right!"

The flight seemed slow because we were so excited and anxious. When the Israeli shore came into view the people on the plane started cheering, and before we landed they sang *heveinu shalom aleichem.*

As we got off the plane, everything was real dark because of the blackout. On the ride to Jerusalem in the darkest dark, our driver Yitzhak was racing with an Arab taxi. My mother didn't like that at all. But once we got to Jerusalem we all felt better and a bit more relaxed.

The next day we walked through Jerusalem and went to the *kotel.* We went to see the rabbi at the Center for Conservative Judaism, where my Bar Mitzvah was going to be, and then we went to visit Rabbi Alexander Gross, the principal of my day school who is on a sabbatical in Israel.

I also visited Dr. Schindler, the director of the center, to ask if I could do some volunteer work after the Bar Mitzvah. He said he would let me know if anything came up. (After Sukkot

he called to say that some young people were going to collect
garbage around the new part of Jerusalem, and that I could
come and help. My father and uncle are both doctors but they
could not get any volunteer work to do. I collected garbage.)

When the Bar Mitzvah day came, we got up and dressed and
went to Shul. They called me to the Torah, and I chanted the
prayers and my *haftarah*. Rabbi Peli delivered a very beautiful
sermon. He said that in times of stress Jews read books of
affirmation and hope, and that the Book of Daniel is such a
book—and my name is Daniel. He also said that it was good
that we came at this time to share our *simcha* with them. Then
we had a reception in the gardens and *sukkah* behind the Shul.
The food was great.

It is a funny coincidence that my *haftarah* tells how the day
will come when Jerusalem and its people will be safe—and
that very day Israel pushed the Egyptians back to the other
side of the Suez Canal. I thought it was a miracle.

New *Olim* from Eastern Europe

Brief selections from testimonies of five *olim* who arrived
in Israel during the fighting or shortly afterwards.
Interviewed in Hebrew and Yiddish by Dov Levin, in
Rumanian by Maya Kriegel, at Absorption Centers,
January–February, 1974.

Professor of Mathematics from the Caucasus

When the war broke out I was in Moscow with
permission to leave Russia. We left Moscow on October 7. I
heard the news in the evening from the BBC and learned that
there was fighting. I was not particularly moved. I thought the
Arabs must be fools—and that if they chose such a day to
begin a war, the Jews would give it to them where it would
hurt.

Q. Were you in the synagogue that day?

A. Yes, but nobody in the synagogue knew yet what
had happened. There was other news. In particular about
Kreisky in Vienna. I was afraid we would not be able to cross

the border at Brest. Even when I learned about the war, my prime worry was whether we would be allowed to cross the border. There were others to worry about the war, and I trusted them. I was sure they were ready. My concern was what would happen at Brest. I did not realize that the war was so serious. There were plenty of problems at Brest with customs officials and train conductors. It was terrible. But we got through. Even after we arrived in Vienna, I did not realize what was happening. The only people we had a chance to speak to were Jewish Agency officials and they told us it would be fine. It was only after we had been in Israel for a few days that we understood the real situation.

Rumanian *Oleh*

I really felt that I was useless in Rumania and that my place was in Israel. Perhaps there were some doubts as well—or not so much doubts as a bit of fear. After all, I hadn't been in Israel before. Yet despite this fear, I had the wish to be in the center of things.

Q. Had you considered the fact that Israel is so small and that it had been attacked by much larger Arab countries? Had you considered the danger that Israel would cease to exist?

A. No, never. I had absolute trust in the Israeli soldier, I knew about his heroism and how well he fights, and I was acquainted with the strategy of the Israeli commanders who brought about the victory of 1967. My trust was total.

Q. During the days you were waiting, you met Jews in Bucharest. Did you hear of Jews who postponed their *aliyah* because of the war?

A. No. On the contrary, I happen to know that some Jews went to the customs to arrange for their departure in the midst of the war.

Q. Taking into account the psychology of Rumanian Jewry, do you think Jews will still want to emigrate? What influence will the war have?

A. Here we must make clear distinctions. There are several categories of Rumanian Jews. Some take the path of assimilation and do everything to hide the fact that they are

Jews. On the other hand, there are Jews on whom the war will have no effect and they will continue to come on *aliyah*. The situation mobilized the Jewish youth. After all, the situation of our country (Israel) was very difficult, and patriotic sentiments came to the fore.

Q. What about anti-Semitism in Rumania today?

A. Anti-Semitism in Rumania does exist and therefore the Jews in Rumania—just as Jews everywhere in the world—have only one fatherland, and since this fatherland has been created we now have the possibility to return to it. It doesn't matter whether anti-Semitism is stronger or weaker. In either case the Jew has only one solution and one duty, to return to his country. For those who are young the situation in Israel offers great chances. I said to myself that so many good years of my life had been devoted to a country which was only my adopted fatherland, now my experience and my labor will be useful to my real fatherland.

Q. What was the opinion of Jews holding responsible jobs but not thinking of coming to Israel regarding the war?

A. To tell the truth, I didn't mix with them very much. The Jews who don't want to make *aliyah* avoid me and I avoid them. Once I had decided to make *aliyah*, I avoided having any contacts with them. At any rate, there are only a few of them and even those who remain are on the way to being demoted or thrown out. Here in Israel things are different. Here one can see the capacity of a new people, a revitalized people, that fights when its existence is threatened.

Young Engineer from Kiev

I was in my home in Kiev a little after midday on Yom Kippur when a Russian neighbor, who knew we were awaiting our permit to go to Israel, came in to tell me that war had broken out and that it had been started by Israel. They had begun to talk about it over the radio. That evening I was visited by an American tourist, a very religious man, and I and other young people from Kiev were very disturbed. "What are you disturbed about?" the American asked. "You shouldn't worry at all. Everything will be O.K. and our enemies will surely get their deserts."

Q. Was there a time when you realized that the situation in Israel was dangerous?

A. Well first of all, we did not believe any news from the Soviet radio. We thought they were lying. But when we began to hear disturbing reports from the British and U.S. radio, we realized they were true. It was difficult for us when we learnt that the Egyptians had crossed the Suez Canal—and it was especially difficult when we learnt that Jews who had been holding out in the fortifications had been ordered to surrender and go into captivity. We wept and thought that the position must really be very bad. My wife has strong nerves but when she heard this, she too was crying. The Russians kept on repeating this story over the radio. They also announced that some of our planes had fallen and that Israeli soldiers in the area—some of them wounded—were saying that they did not care if our planes fell. They wanted to show that our soldiers were indifferent to the war.

Q. What was the reaction of your Russian and Ukrainian neighbors?

A. My acquaintances and the man on the street were delighted. "That's what the Jews deserve and that's what they're getting." They never accepted a Jewish state which could hit the Arabs hard. "Jews are always cowards"—that's what I heard on the street. But after a couple of weeks, I thought that if the war lasted another week it would be like the Vietnam War for the Russians—they lost interest in it. They no longer cared one way or the other.

Q. When did your mood improve?

A. When we first learnt that Israel soldiers had crossed the Suez Canal. At first they spoke of a small group and we thought they were in a very serious situation. We did not realize at first the importance of this breakthrough. But when the BBC and U.S. radio began to talk about it all the time—and we believe these broadcasts—we knew it was significant.

Q. Did you know anything about world Jewish support for Israel?

A. We knew nothing of that. We were told that, like in the Six Day War, the Americans were fighting alongside the Israelis. The Russians certainly thought that not only Jews were fighting and that U.S. pilots in particular were supporting Israel.

In the middle of the war, I received my permit to leave. My parents are still living in Russia. My mother is very ill and I could not bring her to Israel because she has been bedridden for three years and cannot travel in the train. When we got our permits, we went and told my parents. And although it was the middle of the war, their advice was, "Leave—right away." There was no question in the mind of any Jew that Israel would be victorious. A lot of Jews received permits at that time and they were all anxious to get out. To my knowledge, only three families in all of Kiev were deterred from leaving because of the war—and they were only a tiny percentage of the total.

Q. When you crossed the frontier, did the Russians make any comment?

A. No. That was interesting. On the journey, we were sitting next to some Russian officers who were en route to the Middle East—perhaps to Syria, perhaps to Egypt. They knew where we were going—but this did not bother them. It has become usual. They even permitted themselves to talk with us—on neutral topics.

Artist from Vilna

I lived in Vilna with my family. On Yom Kippur I was in the Choral Synagogue, the only one left in Vilna, and about 2 or 3 P.M. people who had heard the news of the outbreak of the war on the BBC came and told us.

Q. Was there any discussion as to who had started the war?

A. Well, on Soviet television that night, they said that the Jews had attacked. The day after Yom Kippur, many Jews went to enquire about getting permits to leave for Israel—they wanted to show that they were not worried about the war and were not frightened to travel to Israel. For example, an acquaintance of mine—a former army officer who had already made several applications and had always been turned down, went demonstratively on that Sunday to complain that he had not been permitted to leave.

Q. In general, what was known about the war in Israel?

A. Chiefly, what we were told on the Soviet radio and the press, but some listened to the BBC—this was one of the foreign stations we could pick up—and they also listened to stations in Germany broadcasting in Russian. Of course, the war was the main subject of conversation wherever Jews gathered. Everyone related what information he had been able to pick up. Those who knew French listened to the French radio. One person stayed up all night trying to pick up foreign stations. On one occasion somebody told me that by chance he had picked up transmission from Israel.

Q. What was the general opinion among the Jews?

A. That Israel had made a mistake and had not been prepared when the war started—and perhaps that the Israelis had become inebriated with the victories of the Six Day War and had lulled themselves into believing that the Arabs would not attack.

Q. How did the Jews react to the news?

A. On *Simchat Torah,* many of the youth, wearing small yarmulkes, participated in the traditional gathering. It is interesting that the first song they sang as they were going around was "It is good to die for our land." But, of course, there was a great deal of worry because everyone had relatives and friends in Israel and we imagined that they were participating in the war.

Q. How did the non-Jewish Lithuanians react?

A. They hate the Russians so much that they sided with Israel. They felt that, despite everything, Israel would come to terms with the Arabs.

Engineer from Minsk

I first heard the news at 3:30 P.M. in my hometown, Minsk. A Jewish acquaintance of mine who has a kiosk told me that he had just heard over the radio that Israel had attacked the Arabs.

Q. Was he upset?

A. Not at all. He said that the Jews of Israel would give them a mighty blow. Then at 7 P.M. I saw and heard the news for myself on radio and television. On TV they showed people being called up in Tel Aviv. We saw empty streets with young people driving cars and delivering call-up notices to homes.

Q. Was there a time when you felt concerned about the situation in Israel?

A. I felt very concerned—not from any fear we might lose but because of the casualties. The Russian radio and press gave out news very regularly—at first we heard bulletins every half hour, later every hour. They reported that Egyptians had begun to counterattack, that they had crossed the Bar-Lev line and were advancing through Sinai on Israel. I did not feel that the war would last long—I was sure of that. I knew that the Egyptians and Syrians would not be victorious and that ninety per cent of what they told us in the press and over the air was lies and could be discounted. When I read carefully the Tass dispatch on Sunday morning, I grasped the situation. It was obvious that if one side attacks, the other is not going to counterattack immediately and therefore it must have been the Egyptians who attacked first.

Q. Among the Jews were there some who were concerned or even hysterical?

A. There was no hysteria, but all were uneasy and worried about Israel—all the Jews, without exception, those who were in official positions and those who were not in official positions. They were all complaining and asking, "Why haven't we hit them back hard?" They all expected that a day or two after the cease-fire, we would mop up the western side of the Canal and destroy the Third Army. They were amazed, therefore, when Kissinger and Brezhnev decided to stop the war—they had not expected that.

Q. Had you previously been preparing to emigrate?

A. Yes, I had put in my application but had not yet received my permit—this came later.

Q. Did you contemplate putting off your departure for a few weeks?

A. The Ovir officials hoped I would change my mind about leaving—there was one family in Minsk which changed its mind after the war broke out. He was a barber, or housepainter, and he returned the documents he had received.

Q. But the authorities did not tell you directly that you should not travel?

A. No, they described the situation in their propaganda and said that Tel Aviv was being bombed and the Arabs had already reached the walls of Jerusalem and Tel Aviv. They did this throughout the war as they wanted to deter Jews from emigrating.

Q. And what happened when you left?

A. The conductors and railroad workers made fun of us and said, "Why are you going to Israel? You are being fools and you will still change your minds."

Reflections on an Agenda for the Future

Moshe Davis

In seeking to interpret the nature and meaning of world Jewish reaction to the unended Yom Kippur War, we recognize that the tide of history may alter present conclusions. Nevertheless, we should not postpone the development of working hypotheses drawn from the lessons of the war; such hypotheses would be directed to future thought and planning in the broadest areas of world Jewish interaction. Not only in this volume, but in articles and essays in various languages, substantive documentation and interpretation of the Yom Kippur War as historic event, and in relation to contemporary existence, are available. Indeed, in the war's aftermath, certain salient features continue to pervade world Jewry's response as a whole. In that sense, the Yom Kippur War may be both summation and beginning.

We open our discussion with a reference to external forces which act upon the Jewish group in different societies, because Jewish experience—certainly in our times—cannot be comprehended through internal behavior alone. Jewish communities today are an integral part of the contemporary scene, a component of world history. Consequently, their motivations and strivings can best be understood in terms of their environing cultures and by their ties to world Jewry and its center, Eretz Yisrael.

Israel as Seismograph of Contemporary Civilization

The Jews are not an insular people. This is not the first time that history has placed them on the frontier of humanity's search for world order. The State of Israel was born following the century's second world war, when the entire world was struggling to rebuild itself, and this young nation serves as both a reality and symbol of that struggle. The reality is

337

Israel's stubborn will to live—stubbornness being defined as stiff-neckedness or consecration, depending on one's perspective. Israel's role in the Middle East as a bridgehead between Occident and Orient, antiquity and modernity, spiritual conviction and technological progress is a symbol of the world's quest to rebuild itself.

The commitment to that role has been deflected by the inner growth problems of a fledgling state confronted by tumultuous factors of world Jewish history, by the geo-political and economic interests of world powers, and by the unremitting assaults of neighboring countries on its security and statehood. Despite all this, long-range goals have not been abandoned and, as was demonstrated in the Yom Kippur War, Israel is determined to stand fast, refusing to be another Czechoslovakia sacrificed to the Russian master plan.

Paradoxically, Israel's isolation by the industrialized oil-hungry nations has bound the Jewish people even more firmly—not only in relation to the brotherhood of Jews, but as involved citizens in the countries of the free world. In a paper on "The Middle East Conflict in Perspective," Eugene W. Rostow, distinguished American scholar and statesman, unequivocally expresses the position that:

> All would be mortally threatened by Soviet control of the space and resources of the great arc which extends from Morocco to Iran. There is no conflict between our feelings as Jews and our duty as American citizens. The national interests of Israel and of the United States in this prolonged conflict are parallel and compatible, and they are of nearly equal consequence.[1]

Other voices too have spoken, each in his own way—Hans Morgenthau in the United States, Hans Habe in France, Günter Grass in Germany—and have been heard in many other parts of the world.[2] When the *New York Times* declared in an editorial on Solzhenitszyn's expulsion that

1. Delivered before National Executive Council, American Jewish Committee, October 28, 1973.
2. See statement of National Committee on American Foreign Policy, Prof. Hans J. Morgenthau, Chairman, *New York Times*, April 10, 1974; Hans Habe, *Proud Zion*, Indianapolis and New York, 1974; Günter Grass, "Reflections after a Year of Good Will with a Bad End." *Süddeutsche Zeitung*, Munich, December 1973.

"Russia despite the revolution has changed little since Czar Nicholas I—except perhaps for the worse," the issue was no longer Israel's survival but rather Russia's tyranny over "life and the living."[3]

Governments, it has been said, do not react to ideas, but they do understand events. The Yom Kippur War, the oil weapon, and the subsequent failure of nerve in the Western democracies raise perilous questions about the future.[4] But those whose memory of the past generation has not failed them, ask with Professor Chaim Perelman, as activist in the Belgian Resistance movement during the Nazi period, the precise question he put to his comrade survivors: "After Israel, who is next?"

Renascent Anti-Semitism

It is a cruel fact of contemporary history that the lesson of the Holocaust has not yet been learned. In that cataclysm, Jewish history and world history converged. For a brief while it seemed that a movement of enlightenment about Jews and Judaism would prevail, but within a few years, anti-Jewish and anti-Judaic manifestations assumed a variety of new and old-new forms. The sterotype of the two-headed hydra so deeply ingrained in Western culture, returned in fresh guise: anti-Semitism as anti-Zionism or anti-Israelism. The Arab world fomented a more palatable version of Jew-hatred through public, sometimes innocent-seeming, communications channels. Compounded by expedient economic alliances and political policies in Europe and Africa, the fever of the new anti-Semitism masking as anti-Zionism began to rise. The old Arab adage that "the enemy of my enemy is my friend" was enacted by Arabs and their allies before the Yom Kippur War. Since then Arab manipulations have succeeded in subverting even countries once thought to be Israel's friends.[5]

3. "Dead Souls," February 13, 1974; Cf. Earl Callem, "Moscow: Notes on a Scientific Conference," *Atlantic*, May, 1974, pp. 16–25.
4. Cf. Fritz Stern, "The End of the Postwar Era," *Commentary*, April 1974, pp. 27–35.
5. Cf. Arnold Foster and Benjamin R. Epstein, *The New Anti-Semitism*, New York, 1974. Especially, chapter I, pp. 1–18.

How words and ideas can be distorted when organized hatred spews them out is illustrated by disparate examples in Western countries. On December 3, 1973, a BBC broadcaster said that one reason for Holland's pro-Israel policy was that Jews *control* (italics M.D.) the trade of Amsterdam. The following night a pseudo-joke was told: Japan was free to follow a pro-Israel policy because it had no Jewish problem. Such media innuendos and mis-information are signals of what easily may be coordinated trans-national planning. In the United States that "line" is the "Zionist Connection," posed as detrimental to the economic welfare of the United States and fostering resentment in the American population. Advocates of the "line" issue a dire warning: "Such resentments could engender perceived—if not actual—anti-Semitism, a development that would be tragic for all America."[6]

In Latin America, where anti-Semitism is often violent and the perpetrators of blood libels and criminal acts against Jews and their institutions are freer to move about, the Holocaust-Zionist-Israel syndrome has become more pronounced. In the streets of Buenos Aires there are posters that read: "Zionists to the crematorium." And on the European continent, a recent American Jewish Committee report states that new movements such as anti-Zionist committees and an anti-Zionist documentation center have been formed. The language of these groups is ominously clear: Jews are "blood relatives of the Israeli pillagers." And the method is Hitlerian: one Italian organization has prepared an alphabetical list including names of the synagogue, the rabbi, the president of the Jewish community, and the names of each Jewish man, woman and child in the city.[7]

Are these echoes—or new voices—of an ancient design? Jewish sensibility has learned to cope with the chameleon of anti-Semitism as it changes colors and forms, and to fortify itself against this affliction of civilization. Intuitive response was exemplified on October 16, in the wake of the Yom Kippur War, as the Jews of Rome gathered to

6. Jack Forsyth, "Arab Oil and the 'Zionist Connection'," *The Link* (published by Americans for Middle East Understanding), January/February, 1974.
7. *JTA Daily News Bulletin*, February 19, 1974.

commemorate the thirtieth anniversary of the Nazi raid on the old ghetto. In 1943 the ransom for two thousand Jews was set at fifty kilograms of gold; in 1973 twice the ransom sum was raised. Thus commemoration became an act of dedication to the people of Israel.

One does not have to explain what the heart feels. The impulse toward a Holocaust and Arab onslaught are moving toward a fearful union.

Christian Concern

Contemporary Israel as "triple cord"—the theological idea of Israel, the People, and the State—has called for a fundamental re-examination within the Christian Church of doctrine and past relationships. While being aware of the difficulties facing the Christian world in this effort, we must recognize that even the best intentions have not yet succeeded in creating reformulation. And insofar as basic relationships with the State of Israel are concerned, very little significant forward movement has taken place. During the Six Day War, the Christian quandary, except in limited circles, resulted in a silent Church. Later, many Christians felt a need to sympathize with Israel. Thus, while the response of Christian churchmen to the Yom Kippur War is difficult to measure, it was undoubtedly more positive than in the earlier crisis.

We do know that from many quarters and in various countries—Sweden, Holland, South Africa, Canada and the United States—supportive response was immediate and forceful. Christians joined Jewish community leaders in addressing public rallies for Israel and on behalf of Israeli prisoners of war. In the United States, the *Christians Concerned for Israel Newsletter* (CCI) called for strong moral and political support. This issue, which went to 9,000 Christian clergy and lay officials, required a rapid second printing. According to Franklin Littell, President of CCI, the Christian response was "conspicuously better than the neutralism of 1967."

An evocative "Statement of Christian Concern About the Middle East," reflecting the deep roots of the theological conflict within the Church, and now being cited by different religious groups, was issued in Toronto, Canada, on October

17, 1973. Signed by an august group of Catholics and Protestants, its observations call for elimination of the "mythology" which portrays the Arab-Israel conflict as an Arab struggle for liberation from Zionist imperialism and oppression. "In a military conflict in which the apparent object is not merely the recovery of occupied territory, but the destruction of the Jewish political community, and, if Arab rhetoric is to be taken literally, to 'drive the Zionists into the sea,' Christians must, in our view, stand with Israel, and stand without equivocation."[8]

Statements of this kind, while representing merely a "still small voice" in contemporary Christian circles, may yet evoke a new spirit of understanding in the Christian world accompanied by an acceptance of the Jews as a world people and of Judaism as a continuing tradition. However, as Robert T. Handy, Professor of Church History at Union Theological Seminary in New York, writes:

> The views of many North American Christians—probably the majority—seem to oscillate between a sympathetic interest in the State of Israel and certain negative feelings that come in part out of the memories of the period of "Christendom" in Western civilization. Others, deeply concerned with the refugee problem and the situation of Christian churches in the Middle East, hope for the development of a bi-national state or a division of the territory."[9]

The problem remains. Most Christians have not thought through the issues relating to Israel from their theological and biblical perspectives. The hope—and the task—is to continue to work with responsive church leaders in this direction.

9. Letter to the writer. For a review of important Christian statements on the Yom Kippur War (including those of the Vatican, World Council of Churches, Anglican Archbishop in Jerusalem—the Most Rev. George Appleton) and covering Britain, France, Germany, the United States, Canada, and Israel, see *Christian Attitudes on Jews and Judaism*, Institute of Jewish Affairs (IJA), C. C. Aronfeld (ed.), December 19, 1973, pp. 1–9. A survey stressing long-range implications for Christian-Jewish relations is *Christian Responses to the Yom Kippur War* by Judith Hershcopf Banki, American Jewish Committee, New York, 1974.

8. See full text in Appendix III, pp. 356–358.

The Awakening

Keeping these global factors in mind, we turn to the more specific Jewish response. While the thrust of reaction varied in major Jewish settlements, many Jews remaining apart and indifferent, the thoughts and actions of individual Jews ought not to be confused with Jewish communality. In the time perspective of Judaism's tradition of mutual responsibility, world Jewish solidarity with the State of Israel reached a new level of intensity. Not only the young State was under attack, but *Am Yisrael,* the entire Jewish people.

The most striking indicator of this correlation was the spontaneous support throughout the Diaspora of Israel's inviolability. In 1967, when Arab forces mounted their *jihad* against Israel, world Jewry cried: *Lo Od Shoah*—Never Another Holocaust! On Yom Kippur, when the Egyptians and Syrians unleashed Soviet missiles, the Jewish voice was heard around the world: *Am Yisrael Hai*—the Jewish People lives!

Why did Jewish emotion respond with commitment, responsibility and sacrifice on multiple levels of personal and communal consciousness? Was it the isolation of Israel? Or the renewed fear of a Holocaust? Or the feeling that if Israel were diminished, the Jewish future was blighted? Or the intuition that, without Israel, the very roots of Jewish group life would be torn up?

It was all of these elements and more. First, the conscious and subconscious trauma of the Holocaust which prompted the feeling that Auschwitz could be repeated at any time—under different circumstances—unless Jews arose to repel the threat. Secondly, there was an understanding of Jewish brotherhood, transcending differences of countries of origin and bridging the gulfs between Israel and the Diaspora. Thirdly, there was the perception of Israel's meaning for each Jew and the terrifying glimpse of the possibility of a world without Israel. Jews abroad ceased to think of Israelis in terms of "you" but rather as "we." Ultimately, for the Jews of the world, Israel was no longer a state of mind, but a state of being with a powerful and continuing hold on the psyche of Jews as individuals and Jews as a people.

If, as underlined by several authors in this volume, the

effect of October 1973 can be conceived as an intensification
of Jewish consciousness, we are challenged to transform this
heightened feeling into constructive action and to avoid the
recessions of the past. While the solidarity of world Jewry
with Israel has been proved once again, crisis solidarity does
not constitute enduring identification.

Moreover, in evaluating the war's aftermath we dare not
defer examination of the questions which have come to the
fore—in Israel as well as in the Diaspora. (I do not include
among these questions the apocalyptic, conscious and
subconscious, thoughts which rise in some minds during the
wars of Israel.) Nor can we ignore the ambivalence in response
between crisis and after-crisis: on the one hand, the rush to
assuage Israel's pain; and on the other, resistance to Israel as
the vital force of the Jewish future everywhere.

Basic questions require basic answers. Revolutionary
changes have altered the world Jewish condition, and the
present historical situation outstrips national boundaries.
Neither the fiction of Diaspora-centrism nor the ideology of
Israel-centrism can serve as the basis for world Jewish
interdependence. A world view has always been the source of
our faith and destiny. The terms "Israel" and "Diaspora" are
not dichotomous. Together *Eretz Yisrael* and the Diaspora
constitute one entity. To counterpose Israel to the Diaspora is
a false presentation of historic reality. Israel is *within* the
Jewish People, and not separate from it. To use the Hebrew
idiom, the *yishuv* in *Eretz Yisrael* is not *k'lal Yisrael;* nor can
one conceive of *k'lal Yisrael* without *Eretz Yisrael.*

The Image

One of the serious pitfalls confronting analysis of
current events is the tendency to telescope one's time
perspective. Caught in the acceleration of change, decades
become years, and years become days. Inevitably this leads to
confusion between symptoms and substance, between drift
and historical process. Too often immediate light is deflected
light.

Appearing throughout the volume are continual references to Israel's supposed military posture of invincibility; a
description which, correctly or incorrectly, has become

common parlance, and which compresses the history of Israel into the years '67–'73. Is this stance, or the so-called "Masada complex," what modern Jewish history is all about? Was this the Zionist response to world history? Where are the cadences of "auto-emancipation," "spiritual center," "self-defense," "redemption through labor," "house of refuge," "ingathering"? Why, if one insists on a military connotation, is not *Zahal* seen as it is—"a people's army" invoking memories of the Maccabees?

Indeed, where is the Zionist ideal: the literal rebirth of a people, land and language—the kibbutz as experiment in social planning—Holocaust survivors regenerated into creative life—the revitalization of the intellectual and spiritual vigor of a people—the Land of the ultimate Return where the Covenant people is to establish a fellowship for the benefit of all humanity?

And if one only looks at the past twenty-five years, is not the more apposite portrait that of Israel as a *family?* Which other nation has a Law of Return proclaiming the ancestral right of every Jew to come to his home? Where else has there been published and distributed to every single citizen in the land a *Yizkor*—a Remembrance Book including the names of the Fallen and the Missing, so that every household will be consecrated by their eternal memory? And even the so-called "protest" movements. Are they composed of the marginal, the disaffected, the alienated of society? They are the people themselves, those who fought, and those who are still on active duty. They are the people who went out, together, to face death. And they are the people who wish to struggle together for peace. Are they not also to be included in the composite image? And will not this image of *Aheinu Kol Beit Yisrael* —our brothers, the entire House of Israel—inspire the world Jewish family, the *mishpachah,* in its personal commitment to the members of the family dwelling in the Land of Israel?

Life's power transcends the contemporary. It seems to be within the nature of social and spiritual transformations that their deeper meaning eludes even those through whose sacrifice and effort the new order comes into existence. All the more reason then to try to capture Israel's essence in a new self-image, rooted in Jewish historic consciousness, one which recognizes the multi-faceted aspects of modern Jewish experience, and one which immediately explains that the State of Israel is in every sense the creation of the entire Jewish people of all generations, living the reality of *Aheinu Kol Beit Yisrael.*

Considerations for an Agenda

In his introduction, President Katzir has distilled the essence of the Seminar's conclusion that world Jewry must rise to "a new plateau of Jewish cooperation, culturally, economically, scientifically. . . ." Prerequisite to such programmatic action is a conceptual framework based on reorientation to the facts of Jewish existence and founded on the choice of contemporary Jews to build simultaneously the singular State of Israel and multi-dimensional communal structures in the Diaspora. What is required is a contemporary formulation of the historic *Am Yisrael* ideology—an ideology which, on the one hand, eschews viewing the nuclear part of the Jewish people in Israel as the whole dependent on and involved in world Jewry, but not responsible to it or for it; and on the other, an ideology which establishes a theoretical framework for Israel's creative interaction with world Jewish communities, and their interpenetration in religious, cultural, and educational spheres.

Unified theories are created neither by "a call" nor by conferences. But continuing collective thinking can clarify basic postulates and develop the mood and the need for individual or team inventiveness. It can also re-order priorities, combining forces in arduous search for common goals. Towards such an evolving ideology we need, as expressed above, to restore the historical image of the concept of Israel representing at once the essentials of its idea, growth, and actual state. We also need guidelines for a re-evaluation of world Jewish interrelationships, among the communities and with Israel. As indicated not only by the volume of writings on the subject but by public grass-roots discussion in Israel and throughout the Diaspora, these imperatives seem to be uppermost concerns following the Yom Kippur War.

By way of introduction for an ongoing discussion of an

image-ideology of "The Entire House of Israel" within the State and binding the world of Jews, I suggest the following considerations based on my reading of contemporary Jewish existence in a changing world order.

1) World Jewish planning should take into account the choice of the majority of Jews to live outside Israel, and build their homes and their Jewish group life in open societies of expanding freedom.

2) Israel has a creative role to play in the development of a continuing Diaspora; and world Jewish communities share responsibility for the shaping of the *Jewish* future in Israel.

3) In many countries of the contemporary Diaspora the Jewish religion, in its theological and institutional components, is the accepted legitimate differentiation between Jews and other citizens. Nevertheless, the spectrum of Jewish identity includes secular, cultural, political, communal, and individual elements. In the creative interplay between Israel and world Jewish communities, Israel can help intensify the Jewish identity of all elements which seek brotherhood with the Jewish community by opening avenues of identification for marginal Jews.

4) Raising a generation literate in Judaism is a mutual responsibility of the Diaspora communities and the State of Israel. The best instrument for this purpose is intensive Jewish education with stress on the Hebrew language. Consequently, the highest priority must be accorded to educational and cultural programs on all levels in the Diaspora with the active cooperation of Israeli and Zionist agencies.

5) Jewish communities should emphasize their collective role in the future of Israel by fulfilling *mitzvat yishuv Eretz Yisrael*. This *mitzvah*—the encouraging and sponsoring of *aliyah*—is an historic function of Diaspora communities. In our time, world Jewish communities together with Israel should accept the responsibility for initiating and implementing *aliyah*.

Jewish history is global history—in space and in time. This book, composed during a period of anguish, records and interprets a moment of that history, a moment which will endure in Jewish consciousness.

Jewish Organizations and Institutions

(appearing in this volume)

Agudah (Agudath Israel)
American Israel Public Affairs Committee
American Council for Judaism
American Jewish Archives (AJA)
American Jewish Committee (AJC)
American Jewish Congress
American Red Magen David for Israel *(Magen David Adom)*
American Sephardi Federation
American Zionist Federation
American Zionist Youth Foundation (AZYF)
Anti-Defamation League of B'nai B'rith
Appel Unifie Juif de France (AUJF)

B'nai B'rith
B'nai B'rith Hillel Foundations
Board of Deputies of British Jews
Bombay Zionist Federation

Canada-Israel Committee (CIC)
Canadian Friends of Soviet Jewry
Canadian Jewish Congress (CJC)
Canadian Zionist Federation
Central Conference of American Rabbis (CCAR)
Centre Communautaire Laïc Juif (CCLJ)
Collectif de la Jeunesse Juive
Comité Central Israelita del Uruguay (Jewish Central Committee)
Comité d'Action pour Israël (Belgium)
Confederación Juvenil Judeo Argentina
Conference of Presidents of Major American Jewish Organizations
Conseil Représentatif des Institutions Juives de France (CRIF)
Consistoire Central de France
Council of Jewish Federations and Welfare Funds (CJFWF)

Delegación de Asociaciones Israelitas Argentinas (DAIA)

European Council of Jewish Community Services
Executive Council of Australian Jewry

Federación Sionista del Argentina
Federal United Israel Appeal (of Australia)
Federation of Jewish Philanthropies (of New York)
Fonds Social Juif Unifié

Habonim
Hadassah, The Women's Zionist Organization of America
Hashomer Hatzair
Hebrew Union College—Jewish Institute of Religion (HUC—JIR)

Hebrew University of Jerusalem
Histadruth Campaign

Israel Bonds—Development Corporation for Israel
Israel United Appeal (of Union of South Africa) (IUA)

Jewish Theological Seminary of America
Jewish War Veterans of the U.S.A.
Joint Israel Appeal (of Great Britain)

Kehilla (of Argentina)
Keren Hayesod
Keren Kayemet Le-Yisrael (Jewish National Fund)

Labor Zionist Alliance (U.S.A.)

Maccabi World Union of Jewish Sports Associations
Mizrachi

National Federation of Temple Brotherhoods
National Federation of Temple Sisterhoods
National Jewish Community Relations Advisory Council (NJCRAC)
National Jewish Welfare Board
North American Jewish Students Appeal
North American Jewish Students Network (Network)

Rabbinical Assembly of America (RA)

She'erit Hapleta (Holocaust Survivors) Organization
Sherut La'am
South African Federation of Jewish Students
South African Zionist Federation
State of Israel Bond Organization

Union of American Hebrew Congregations (UAHC)
Union des Juifs Progressistes de Belgique
Unione democratica amici d'Israele (UDAI)
United Jewish Appeal (UJA)
United Synagogue of America

Victorian Jewish Board of Deputies of Australia
Victoria Union of Jewish Students

Women's International Zionist Organization (WIZO)
World Jewish Congress (WJC)
World Union for Progressive Judaism
World Union of Jewish Students (WUJS)
World Zionist Organization (WZO)

Yeshiva University
Yiddisher Cultur Farband (of Argentina) (ICUF)

Zionist Federation of the United Kingdom

Appendix I

Statement by a Group of Professors

The Hebrew University, Jerusalem
9th October 1973

For the fifth time since its creation, Israel is engaged in battle with the neighbouring Arab world. It is a battle which is uneven in two respects. In the first place, if Israel wins, the Arab world will endure; if the Arabs win, Israel will cease to exist. Secondly, there is no equivalence in the forces engaged. Syria and Egypt have drawn on enormous forces, both of manpower and materiel. Sixteen other Arab countries have expressed their solidarity with them, and a number have already sent units of their Armed Forces to join in the battle. Israel faces this situation as a small people fighting on its own. Nearly all of our students, and most of our colleagues are today in uniform.

We, the undersigned, have always used our right as free men to express our views on our country's policies, both external and internal, and some of us have disagreed with some of these policies in the past.

Today, it is clear to all of us beyond any shadow of doubt, that Egypt and Syria prepared this attack over a long period, and deliberately chose to launch it on the Day of Atonement, the most sacred day in the Jewish calendar.

It is equally clear to us that, though aware of the Egyptian and Syrian plans, the Government of Israel chose to abstain from a pre-emptive strike, and rather to do all it could to avert the danger by a diplomatic effort. The real issue today, as it was in 1967 is the determination by Egypt and Syria to destroy Israel.

We are deeply convinced that the road to meaningful negotiations for a peaceful outcome has always been open to the Arab states. Had that road been taken by the Arab states, the response of our people and our Government would have been such as to ensure that every conceivable step to bringing these negotiations to a mutually acceptable and positive conclusion would have been made.

The Egyptian and Syrian attack against us on the Day of Atonement has led us to the painful conclusion that the policy of the present Governments of the Arab states, is to go to any length in order to destroy the existence of Israel.

There can be no peace in the Middle East unless the right of our people to independence and continued existence in Israel is fully recognised by our neighbours.

There can be no peace until the Arab states change their policy, and understand that the future of the Middle East must take the form of peaceful co-existence between them and Israel.

The cause of organising a peaceful world is based on the right of all peoples to free existence and harmonious national self-expression and self-government. These rights cannot be denied to Israel and its people.

For this reason, we feel that it is the duty of free men throughout the world who cherish the cause of peace and see it as a pre-condition for humanity's survival and development, to insist on the overriding duty of the Arab states to recognise Israel's right to exist in peace and to demonstrate that by agreeing immediately to meet the representatives of Israel for discussion and negotiation.

The Arab doctrine of prior agreement by Israel to withdraw from territory, is illogical and unacceptable. Every one of us is wholly convinced that our very existence today and, that we have been able, at considerable cost in lives, to withstand the Egyptian and Syrian assault and turn it back are due to the fact that this doctrine was rejected by us. The way in which the Egyptian and Syrian attack was prepared and launched, must convince the world that this rejection was thoroughly justified.

The argument has been heard that having suffered military defeat in the past, the Arabs cannot be expected to negotiate with Israel without a "gesture" from Israel. The "gesture" demanded has been that Israel should place the Arabs unconditionally, and before any agreement or commitment on their part, in a situation where, as experience shows, it would be made easier for them to attack Israel.

We cannot agree that this is morally acceptable or practically feasible. Nor should the world agree. For the fifth time since 1948, we have seen our country besieged and attacked, our friends and relatives killed. We have been the targets of terror on a world-wide scale; yet today, when every one of us has members of his family, students and colleagues at the Front, we say that we remain ready for a peace process with our Arab neighbours.

A peace process must mean mutual recognition, with peaceful co-existence as its goal, achieved by free negotiation. In the circumstances which have arisen, the secure nature of the agreed boundaries is, more than ever, seen to be imperative. The nature of the territorial settlement will only emerge as a function of mutual trust.

We address ourselves to our colleagues, to students and to men of good-will all over the world, in the hope that they will use their influence to the utmost to bring home to the Arab countries the demand of the world that the language of hate and vilification, and the dialogue of war must be replaced by the dialogue of peaceful co-existence.

Professor Shlomo Avineri
Professor Joseph Ben-David
Professor Ernst David Bergmann
Professor Aryeh Dvoretzky
Professor Samuel Eisenstadt
Professor Saul Friedlander
Professor Natan Goldblum
Professor Jack Gross
Professor Yehoshafat Harkabi
Mr. Avraham Harman
Professor Alex Keynan

Professor Don Patinkin
Professor Joshua Prawer
Professor Michael Rabin
Professor Nathan Rotenstreich
Professor Gershom Scholem
Professor Moshe Shilo
Professor Gabriel Stein
Professor Jacob Talmon
Professor Ephraim Urbach
Professor David W. Weiss

Concluding portion from *The Mideast War: A Reply*

New York Review of Books
November 29, 1973

[In the November 15 *issue of the* New York Review *appeared a statement on the Middle East war signed by twenty-one members of the Hebrew University in Jerusalem. The following reply has been received from Professor Daniel Amit of the Racah Institute of Physics of the Hebrew University. It is in the form of an open letter to Professor Jacob Talmon, one of the signers of the statement.*]

Following the official Israeli line, your letter brings up as principles of paramount importance the recognition of Israel and direct talks. If we were considering the most desirable forms of conducting international relations, these principles would be accorded a prominent role. However, within the immediate situation they provide little more than an instrument, albeit an efficient one, toward creating favorable public opinion; their meaning is questionable. For quite a few years Arab foreign policy has related to Israel as Israel. In both the Jarring document and in Resolution 242 of the Security Council specific mention is made of sovereign states signing agreements with each other and of respecting each other's boundaries. In their favorable response to these documents the Arab states show that their refusal to recognize Israel is not one of basic principle. Possibly one cannot conclude from these responses that they represent the real intentions of the Arabs. But your own letter concludes that their intentions are the opposite.

I will not be telling you anything new if I mention that official recognition has special significance in the eyes of the Arab states for historical reasons; and that if we can trust their words, recognition will be the result of an overall agreement in our region. The same applies to the issue of direct talks. These two topics, which Westerners generally find difficult to understand, have acquired deep symbolic significance in the consciousness of the two sides in conflict. Take for example the Palestinian problem. Can one doubt that the problem of the Palestinian people represents one of the most complex and painful elements of the conflict? Yet Israel does not recognize the existence of the Palestinian people and she is not willing to negotiate with them. In my opinion this is a direct result of the fact that recognition of their national aspirations, and serious efforts to satisfy them, would have traumatic effects on Israeli society. Official Arab recognition of Israel and entering into direct talks with her will have similar effects in Arab societies.

To conclude, I must add that the above comments are not directed to those who see themselves within the propaganda machine that apparently is inevitable in times of war. Rather, I ask whether you do not believe with me that it is possible to justify the existence of the State of Israel, and to provide the moral strength with which to defend her, by applying honest historical standards and careful reasoning. Don't you believe that only a discussion of this kind will reveal, if and when they appear, the paths leading to peace?

Let us recall the painful words of George Orwell in his summary of his desperate attempt to reveal to the world just a few of the real facts concerning the Spanish civil war: "I saw, in fact, history, written not by what happened but by what should have happened according to a certain 'party line.'"

Even in this difficult hour there must be someone who will tell this nation and its friends that the key to ending the war is political and not military. That today, no less than at any other time, what is needed is (1) an Israeli declaration of readiness to replace the cease-fire lines of greater Israel with borders based on the lines of June 4, 1967, and (2) recognition of the existence of the Palestinian nation, and a readiness to enter into negotiations with her to settle the outstanding problems between the two nations. Within the framework of an agreement it must be ensured that there is provision for demilitarized zones that will give Israel security and will inhibit aggression. And now, more than at any other time, we must be sensitive to the fact that it is dangerous to continue analyzing the developments in the region according to prior estimates of the balance of power. There are now clear signs of possible escalation in which the local balance of power will become irrelevant and in which the Arab-Israeli wars will be no more than a confrontation and testing ground for the armaments of the USA and the USSR, with all the attendant dangers this poses to the very existence of Israel.

Daniel Amit

Hebrew University, Jerusalem

Appendix II

Canadian Professors for Peace in the Middle East

Towards a Just and Lasting Peace

War has again convulsed the Middle East. Amid the rhetoric, the de-humanizing statistics, and the fear of Big Power involvement, there is the numbing feeling that this 4th war in 25 years may not be the last.

We believe that real peace will only come to the Middle East when certain fundamental principles—obscured by the avalanche of words and events—are recognized and reaffirmed.

1. The territorial integrity and political independence of all states in the Middle East must be respected. The refusal of the Arab states to recognize the legitimate existence of the State of Israel for over 25 years is a standing violation of the U.N. charter and a constant threat to the peace. The legitimacy of Israel is non-negotiable; its right to live within peaceful and secure boundaries must be openly and unequivocally recognized by her Arab neighbours.
2. The surprise Yom Kippur attack by Syrian and Egyptian forces—and the massing of the Arab and Communist world against Israel since that attack—should not be seen as a "limited aggression" only. Again and again Arab leaders have told their own people that the recovery of lands lost in 1967 would represent only the first stage in their struggle against the existence of the Jewish state. To stand silent in the face of such aggression is to licence it and to encourage its repetition; to require Israel to withdraw from the occupied territories in consequence of this latest Arab aggression—and in the absence of a negotiated peace—is to reward it.
3. The parties to the conflict must be the parties to the peace. An enduring peace can only be achieved when the combatants sit down together and negotiate a peace treaty. We believe that all contentious questions—agreed borders, refugee compensation and settlement, Jerusalem and the Holy Places—can be resolved in a negotiated treaty leading to a just and lasting peace for the Middle East and the World.

We call upon the Canadian people to support these principles and make their views known to the Canadian government; we call upon the Canadian government to use its good offices and take such initiatives as are necessary to implement these principles.

Appendix III

Statement of Canadian Christian Clergymen

We, the undersigned, a group of Christians in Toronto, moved by the tragic war now raging in the Middle East, wish to express our concern for the victims of this conflict, and wish, in particular, to share some Christian reflections both with the larger Christian community and with the community-at-large. The following observations are made with a deep sense of Christian contribution for the many past 'silences' of the churches at those critical moments when the christian conscience has been tested and found wanting. We believe that another crisis of conscience has arrived, and that, on no account, must another silence be condoned.

The Arab-Israeli struggle has for years been coloured by a mythology which continues to obscure the political and human dimensions of the collision of two peoples in the Middle East. This is the mythology of a Zionism consistently represented by anti-Zionists as a racist, imperialistic Nazi-type creed imposed upon the Middle East to dispossess and oppress non-Jews, and to establish presumably a "Jewish Empire". Many Christians, unfamiliar with Zionist ideas, having been more or less persuaded of the basic truth of this mythology, tend as a result to interpret present-day events in its light. Thus, the current war is regarded as a war of liberation designed to remove the Zionist yoke in the name of humanity and justice. Such Christians are frequently disbelieving if informed that (a) Zionism is not a dirty word, like Nazism, but a complex phenomenon with its roots in both Jewish tradition and modern Jewish experience; (b) modern Zionism was born as the stepchild of western gentile anti-semitism, the anti-semitism of the Christian churches and a Christian culture, and was therefore an early liberation movement incorporating the response of disillusioned European Jews to the hostility of a Christian-Gentile world which refused to accept their presence; (c) the rhetoric of anti-Zionism is as old as the Zionist movement itself (that masterpiece of modern anti-semitism, *The Protocols of the Elders of Zion*, was published about the time of the first Zionist Congress in 1897), and every important anti-semite of this century has made repeated use of this rhetoric, from Henry Ford to Adolf Hitler to current Russian propaganda. One example illustrates this trend. In *Mein Kampf*, Hitler attacked (Zionist) Jews for seeking to build a Jewish empire in the Middle East as "a central organization for their international world swindle. . . ." Incidentally, the *Protocols* are presently in widespread circulation in the Arab-Islamic world, and definitely a factor in the Middle Eastern struggle.

To understand the issues fairly, this mythology must be stripped away. When it is gone, one sees the tragic encounter of two peoples, each with legitimate claims and aspirations, over the same territory. Christians are involved on both sides of this encounter. They are involved on the Arab side, because modern Arab nationalism owes some of its roots to the Christian missionary presence since the last century. They are involved on the Jewish side, because Jewish nationalism is the stepchild of Christian prejudice, and because Israel, by its very existence, is both a reminder and a rebuke to Christians for their role in the Jewish plight in the twentieth century, with its holocaust and its murdered children. Israel, to Jews, is more than another nation; it is a resurrection symbol following the near extinction of the Jewish people within living memory. For this reason, we believe, Christians must affirm Israel as the visible and tangible manifestation of both Jewish survival and Jewish security. For the possibility of a second Auschwitz is something which no Christian should view with equanimity and any semblance of moral neutrality. Indeed, as matters now stand, the option of remaining neutral in an apparent life-and-death struggle does not exist. To affirm Israel is not to pretend that Israel, as a nation-state, stands above the moral criteria derived from the canons of international justice and the conscience of rational man which apply to other nations. Clearly, no nation-state is innocent or can be innocent, since power, especially military power, is always subject to misuse, and nation-states by definition are vast impersonal concentrations of power. Once the Jewish state was born, it took upon itself the moral ambiguity of a world replete with power struggles, and the moral dilemmas which are always entailed in the possession of power. Israel can be criticized as any other nation can be criticized, but it is profoundly wrong to oppose Israel because of its Jewish foundations, and to seek to dismantle its Jewish character, as the anti-Zionists invariably desire. In a military conflict in which the apparent object is not merely the recovery of occupied territory, but the destruction of the Jewish political community, and, if Arab rhetoric is to be taken literally, to "drive the Zionists into the sea", Christians must, in our view, stand with Israel, and stand without equivocation.

The plight of the Palestinian refugees is a cause which has stirred much Christian sympathy, and which has become the focal point for the convergence of liberal sentiment (Christian and non-Christian) and the ideology of the Third World with its Marxist analysis. Israel has been identified by both groups as the oppressor, the Palestinian Arabs as the oppressed. This plight, in our view, is the other side of the tragic encounter between the aspirations of two peoples: tragic because injustice in one form or another is seemingly unavoidable. Christians are involved on this side of the conflict as well. In our opinion, however, the present attack of the Arab nations against Israel cannot be justified in these terms, because the former have themselves repeatedly revealed no small measure of indifference to the refugees during recent years. Moreover, in much Christian opinion, the refugees have unwittingly emerged as a comfort for a troubled conscience, which, preferring not to dwell on Christian guilt with regard to the Jews, dwells instead on Jewish guilt with regard to the Arabs. Nor are the churches in a position of moral objectivity whereby they can successfully play a mediatorial role between the Jewish and Arab worlds, balancing the claims and counter-claims of the two warring communities. We have long since disqualified ourselves for any such task, and should not adopt an attitude of moral superiority in a situation which exposes too many of our own failings.

Father Edward A. Synan, President, Pontifical Institute of Mediaeval Studies; Father Gregory Baum, Professor, St. Michael's College, University of Toronto; Sister Mary Jo Leddy, Teaching Assistant, P.h.D. (cand.), University of Toronto; Father John M. Kelly, President, St. Michael's College; John C. Meagher, Director, Institute of Christian Thought, St. Michael's College; Reverend Herbert Richardson, Professor, St. Michael's College; Father Arthur Gibson, Chairman, Department of Religious Studies, St. Michael's College; Alan T. Davies, Assistant Professor, Victoria College, University of Toronto; William O. Fennell, Principal, Emmanuel College, Victoria University; David E. Demson, Associate Professor, Emmanuel College, Victoria University; Donald R. Keating, Teaching Assistant, York University; B. Robert Bater, Minister, Eglinton United Church; Sister Donna Purdy, Executive Director, Canadian Committee on Social Ministry; and Dr. G. S. French, President, Victoria University, Toronto.

Appendix IV

Universitarios Uruguayos ante el Conflicto en el Medio Oriente

Montevideo, Octubre de 1973.

En nuestra condición de universitarios y ciudadanos uruguayos sentimos la necesidad de hacer conocer nuestra opinión con respecto al conflicto en el Medio Oriente.

1) Consideramos fundamental reiterar la convicción de que el Estado de Israel tiene el incuestionable derecho de existir y desarrollarse en paz.

2) Las diferencias que enfrentan a las partes involucradas en la crisis del Medio Oriente podrán encontrar solución constructiva si las mismas dialogan en un clima de confianza mutua y con la intención de superar definitivamente las diferencias que las separan.

3) La paz entre Israel y los países árabes abrirá el cauce para una cooperación fecunda para el mejoramiento de las condiciones de vida de sus pueblos.

Appendix V

Comité de Solidarité Française avec Israël

La Voix de la France

Signez tous ce manifeste

Pour la quatrième fois en 25 ans, l' **Etat d'Israël doit faire face** à l'agression pour préserver son existence nationale. La responsabilité de la guerre incombe entièrement à l'Egypte et à la Syrie, selon l'aveu même du Ministre égyptien des Affaires Etrangères.

En attaquant par surprise Israël, un jour de recueillement national et religieux, l'agresseur a apporté la preuve que la présence d'Israël dans les territoires contestés constituait pour l'Etat hébreu, la meilleure garantie de sécurité ce qu'ignore la déclaration du Ministre français des Affaires Etrangères.

Les intérêts à long terme de la France exigent qu'elle mène au Proche-Orient **une politique d'équilibre et de conciliation** et non pas qu'elle s utienne sans discrimination ni nuance les thèses arabes.

Israël a le droit de vivre en paix à l'intérieur de frontières sûres et reconnues. Aucun calcul à court terme ne saurait prévaloir contre cet impératif de la morale internationale, et nul ne peut ignorer qu'Israël est aujourd'hui menacé ouvertement de destruction totale alors qu'il ne proclame aucune intention analogue envers aucun de ses voisins.

Nous souhaitons que ceux-ci comprennent que seules des négociations directes et sans préalable entre les belligérants pourront aboutir á une paix véritable fondée sur la coexistence et la coopération de tous les peuples de la région.

General de BENOUVILLE
député de Paris,
Président du groupe d'amitié France-Israël
á l'Assemblée Nationale

Diomede CATROUX
ancien Ministre
Président de l'Association
France-Israël

Pierre GIRAUD
sénateur de Paris,
Président du groupe d'amitié
France-Israël au Sénat

Andre MONTEIL
ancien Ministre
Président de l'Alliance
France-Israël

Appendix VI
Manifestazione per la Pace e l'Amicizia tra i Popoli

25 anni d'indipendenza israeliana
25 anni di costituzione italiana

Questa Manifestazione

Sotto una tenda delle Nazioni Unite, soldati israeliani e soldati egiziani si sono, finalmente, stretti la mano dopo i terribili giorni della guerra che, ancora una volta, ha sconvolto la regione medioorientale.

Ora comincia il difficile cammino verso, la pace senza la quale non è possibile la collaborazione tra i popoli del Medio Oriente. In venticinque anni di indipendenza il popolo israeliano ha mostrato al mondo quale contributo di pionierismo agricolo, di tecnica industriale, di elevazione culturale esso è in grado di apportare alla vita di tutta la regione.

Venticinque anni di democrazia israeliana coincidono con i venticinque anni di democrazia italiana fondata sulla Costituzione Repubblicana del 1948. I due anniversari segnano tappe di sviluppo civile esemplare e legano simbolicamente i due popoli, che nel secolo scorso hanno lottato per il loro Risorgimento in nome del diritto nazionale nella libertà e nella pace.

Al tavolo della pace tutto può essere salvato: con la violenza e la sopraffazione tutto può essere perduto. Questo è il significato dell'amicizia italoisraeliana a venticinque anni dall'inizio della vita libera e democratica dei due popoli di antica civiltà mediterranea.

Gli amici dell'UDAI, mentre dichiarano tutta la loro solidarietà per le azioni di pace e di ricostruzione, esprimono il loro apprezzamento per le iniziative diplomatiche ed umanitarie del governo e dei partiti democratici italiani ed invitano i militanti della democrazia, gli uomini della Resistenza, della politica, dei sindacati ad unirsi in un fronte solidale che favorisca rapide e giuste trattative di pace nell'interesse comune dei popoli arabi ed israeliano ed in quello superiore di tutti i popoli del mondo.

Appendix VII
Témoignage de solidarité de groupes chrétiens de Belgique avec Israël, pour la paix

Service de Documentation
Pour les Relations Entre Chrétiens et Juifs
Soeurs de Sion; Rue Félix Delhasse, 2 - 1060 Bruxelles

19 novembre 1973

En ce moment où la paix se cherche au Moyen Orient, des chrétiens de différentes églises désirent témoigner de leur solidarité avec le peuple juif et avec Israël dans sa recherche d'un accord équitable.

Notre intervention ne constitue ni une déclaration théologique, ni un manifeste politique ; elle s'inscrit davantage dans un effort de compréhension cordiale vis-à-vis de frères en difficultés.

1. Nous ne pouvons oublier nos racines communes avec le peuple juif, berceau de notre enfance spirituelle, communauté de l'élection dans l'unique Alliance accomplie en Jésus-Christ, d'où le christianisme et l'Islam tirent leur origine. Les dons de Dieu sont sans repentance. Le salut a pris le chemin d'Israël car « le salut vient des juifs » comme le dit Jésus dans son dialogue avec la samaritaine (Jn 4,22). Une foi commune nous lie de manière spéciale avec le peuple de la Bible, et c'est à partir de ce lien que nous nous efforçons de vivre notre solidarité avec toutes les nations, afin que s'accomplissent les espérances de paix des prophètes et le vœu d'unité exprimé par Jésus-Christ « afin que tous soient un » (Jn 17,22).

2. En ce moment crucial pour Israël comme pour les peuples arabes, et plus largement pour l'humanité, un choix s'impose aux chrétiens : celui de la paix, d'une paix véritable où chacun soit effectivement reconnu dans ses aspirations légitimes et dans sa particularité inaliénable. Il ne s'agit donc pas de refuser le droit d'exister à l'Etat d'Israël pour faire place aux Palestiniens, pas plus que de contester aux Palestiniens le droit à l'existence, car rejeter ou opprimer l'autre n'apporte pas de solution équitable au conflit. Mais notre choix délibéré pour la paix doit passer par une communion profonde avec le peuple juif dans sa relation concrète avec l'Etat d'Israël. Si le christianisme en ce moment avait peur de témoigner de sa relation avec le peuple d'Israël, il perdrait le droit de rappeler à celui-ci la responsabilité commune d'Israël et de l'Eglise envers les Palestiniens.

3. La majorité des Juifs du monde entier se sent unie à l'Etat d'Israël dont le nom n'est pas un hasard. Il exprime en effet l'espoir porté par la prière du peuple juif pendant tant de siècles de voir enfin se réaliser la promesse de Dieu rassemblant dans l'unité ses enfants dispersés. Cela ne signifie pas qu'on ratifie sans critique la politique de cet Etat. Cela signifie tout d'abord que les blessures qu'il subit sont ressenties comme les blessures de tout le peuple juif, que les morts d'Israël sont ses morts, que lorsqu'Israël est touché, tout le peuple juif est en deuil.

4. Un proverbe juif dit : « No console pas ton ami lorsque son mort se trouve encore devant lui ». Ceci veut dire qu'il ne s'agit pas de parler beaucoup lorsqu'on se trouve devant une souffrance, mais que la seule expression de solidarité est la présence. En témoignant maintenant de notre solidarité, nous voulons agir comme des amis et des membres de la famille en deuil. C'est au moment où le deuil des morts d'Israël et l'angoisse pour le sort des frères est le plus grand, que nous voulons être présents auprès de nos frères juifs ici même.

5. Israël ne mérite la haine de personne, mais pour faire la vérité nous voulons discerner les vraies responsabilités. Israël ne peut oublier l'attitude d'hostilité dont il a été victime en Europe occidentale et en Russie tout au long d'une histoire de plus de 15 siècles. Réduits à toute extrémité, les Juifs n'ont plus eu d'autre issue que de fonder un Etat indépendant. La prédication antijuive de l'Eglise durant des siècles et la propagande areligieuse ont contribué à cet état de choses. Au moment où l'Etat d'Israël a été proclamé en 1948, après le sommet dramatique des persécutions juives, ce ne sont ni la Russie, ni l'Occident qui ont payé la note, mais les Palestiniens. A présent encore, Israël, comme les Palestiniens risque d'être le jouet des grandes puissances mondiales et de leurs intérêts financiers et commerciaux.

6. Aussi prenons-nous conscience, comme chrétiens, de notre part de responsabilité et reconnaissons-nous que l'Occident est réellement impliqué dans ce conflit et cette recherche de paix. Les restrictions que nous pourrons subir ne sont qu'une minime contribution en règlement de notre dette à l'égard de nos frères juifs et arabes. Nous agirions avec un cynisme cruel si nous nous désolidarisions d'Israël à cause du compte qui nous est présenté actuellement et laissions celui-ci en subir seul les dommages. Par ailleurs ne pas discerner l'ambiguïté d'une politique d'intimidation et de pression, pourvu que nos intérêts et notre profit soient saufs, serait agir avec une désinvolture aussi coupable. Nous nous inscrivons donc contre toute déclaration politique qui condamnerait sans appel et nous invitons nos frères chrétiens è manifester leur solidarité avec Israël, y compris par un geste concret au point de vue financier.

LES COMMISSIONS CATHOLIQUE ET PROTESTANTE POUR LES RELATIONS ENTRE CHRÉTIENS ET JUIFS EN BELGIQUE
DE KONTAKTGROEPEN VOOR DE JOODS-CHRISTELIJKE BETREKKINGEN TE ANTWERPEN
DE CHRISTELIJKE STUDIEGROEPEN VAN HET JODENDOM TE BRUSSEL
LA COMMUNAUTÉ DES SOEURS DE SION DE BRUXELLES